Welcome to

The Official Guide to the GRE® revised General Test

The book you're holding is a one-of-a-kind resource: the only GRE guide created by the ETS team that produces the actual exam. This book is uniquely suited to help you do your best on this challenging test.

Here's what you'll find inside:

- **Official information on the GRE revised General Test.** Get the facts about the revised test format you'll encounter starting in August 2011—straight from ETS.

- **ETS's own test-taking strategies.** Learn valuable hints and tips that can help you get your best score.

- **Authentic GRE questions in the revised test format.** Practice with real test questions created by the test-makers.

- **Real full-length GRE practice test.** Sharpen your skills with an actual test in the revised format.

- ***POWERPREP* II software on CD-ROM:** Experience an actual computer-based GRE revised General Test.

About ETS

At nonprofit ETS, we advance quality and equity in education for people worldwide by creating assessments based on rigorous research. ETS serves individuals, educational institutions, and government agencies by providing customized solutions for teacher certification, English language learning, and elementary, secondary, and post-secondary education, as well as conducting education research, analysis, and policy studies. Founded in 1947, ETS develops, administers, and scores more than 50 million tests annually — including the TOEFL® and TOEIC® tests, the GRE® tests and *The Praxis Series*™ assessments—in more than 180 countries, at over 9,000 locations worldwide. For more information, visit **www.ets.org**

IMPORTANT

ETS makes available free test preparation materials for individuals planning to take a GRE test. *POWERPREP* II software is available for individuals planning to take the computer-based GRE revised General Test, and the *Practice Book for the Paper-based GRE revised General Test* is available for individuals planning to take the paper-based test. The information about how to prepare for the revised General Test, test-taking strategies, question strategies, etc., that is included in the free test preparation is also included in this *Guide*. The *Guide* also provides you with additional sets of practice questions and an additional full-length practice test with explanatory materials.

For more information about the GRE revised General Test, free GRE test preparation materials, and other GRE products and services, please visit the GRE website at

www.ets.org/gre

Inquiries concerning the practice test questions in this book should be sent to the GRE testing program at

GRETestQuestionInquiries@ets.org

The OFFICIAL GUIDE to the

GRE®

revised General Test

**INSIDE LOOK AT THE TEST CHANGES
EFFECTIVE AUGUST 1, 2011**

New York | Chicago | San Francisco | Lisbon | London | Madrid | Mexico City
Milan | New Delhi | San Juan | Seoul | Singapore | Sydney | Toronto

Copyright © 2010 by Educational Testing Service. All rights reserved. Except as permitted under the United States Copyright Act of 1976, no part of this publication may be reproduced or distributed in any form or by any means, or stored in a data base or retrieval system, without the prior written permission of the publisher.

Printed in the United States of America.

1 2 3 4 5 6 7 8 9 10 11 12 13 14 15   QDB/QDB   1 9 8 7 6 5 4 3 2 1 0

ISBN: P/N 978-0-07-170049-8 of set
          978-0-07-170052-8
MHID: P/N 0-07-170049-8 of set
          0-07-170052-8

ETS, the ETS logo, LISTENING. LEARNING. LEADING., E-RATER, GRADUATE RECORD EXAMINATIONS, GRE, POWERPREP, TOEFL, and TOEIC are registered trademarks of Educational Testing Service (ETS) in the United States and other countries, and are used under license. THE PRAXIS SERIES is a trademark of ETS.

Sponsoring Editor: Charles Wall
Production Supervisor: Tama Harris McPhatter
Interior Designer: Jane Tenenbaum
Typesetters: Jane Tenenbaum and Chris Cott

Library of Congress Cataloging-in-Publication Data

GRE : the official guide to the revised general test / Educational Testing Service.
    p. cm.
  ISBN 978-0-07-170052-8 — ISBN 978-0-07-170049-8 (book for set) —
  ISBN 978-0-07-170053-5 (cd)
  1. Graduate Record Examinations — Study guides. I. Educational Testing Service.
  II. Title: Graduate Record Examinations.
  LB2367.4.G65 2010
  378.1'662--dc22
                                                          2010039564

Contents

1

Introducing the GRE® revised General Test   1

2

GRE® Analytical Writing   11

3

GRE® Verbal Reasoning   43

4

GRE® Verbal Reasoning Practice Questions

53

5

GRE® Quantitative Reasoning

107

6

GRE® Quantitative Reasoning Practice Questions

143

7 GRE® Math Review 207

8 Authentic GRE® Practice Test 303

How to Use This Book/CD Package

This book/CD package provides a large amount of important information about the GRE revised General Test, the kinds of questions it includes, and the knowledge and skills that it measures. The book and CD-ROM will help you:

- Familiarize yourself with the test format and the test question types
- Identify the test-taking skills you most need to focus on
- Review the math topics you need to know for the test
- Check your progress with Verbal Reasoning and Quantitative Reasoning practice questions
- Practice your test-taking skills using actual GRE tests

The following six-step program has been designed to help you make the best use of this book and CD-ROM.

STEP 1 Learn About the GRE revised General Test Format

Chapter 1 of this book provides official information about the structure of the GRE revised General Test. Read this chapter to learn about the different test sections, the number of questions in each section, and the section time limits. You'll also find valuable test-taking strategies from ETS and important information about how the test is scored.

STEP 2 Study the Different GRE Question Types

Chapters 2, 3, and 5 of this book describe the types of questions you'll encounter in the three sections of the GRE revised General Test. Chapter 2 describes the Analytical Writing section, which requires you to write essays in response to prompts that you will be given. Chapter 3 describes the Verbal Reasoning question types. Chapter 5 describes the Quantitative Reasoning question types. In each case, you will learn what the questions are designed to measure, and you will get tips for answering each question type. You will also see samples of each question type, with helpful explanations.

STEP 3 Practice Answering GRE Verbal and Quantitative Reasoning Questions

Chapters 4 and 6 offer sets of practice Verbal Reasoning and Quantitative Reasoning questions in the format of the GRE revised General Test. The question sets are arranged in order of increasing difficulty, from easy through medium to hard. Answer the questions in each set, then read through the explanations to see which test topics you found most challenging. Look for patterns. Did specific question formats give you trouble? When did you need to guess at the answer? Use your results to identify your weaknesses and to sharpen your test-taking skills.

STEP 4   Use the Test Preview Tool on the CD-ROM

The Test Preview Tool includes a sample of each of the question types formatted as they would be on the actual computer-based test. The Tool also contains the Help screens, the Review screen, the word-processing software for the Analytical Writing section, and the on-screen calculator, so that you can become familiar with all of the features of the computer-based GRE revised General Test.

STEP 5   Review GRE Math Topics

Chapter 7 provides a review of math topics tested in the GRE revised General Test Quantitative Reasoning sections. You do not necessarily need to tackle every topic in the review, or to work through the review in the order in which it is presented. Skip around if you like, but remember to focus on the topics that you know give you trouble. Each section of the review ends with practice problems that you can use to see how well you have mastered the material. If you get a problem wrong, go back into the review section and re-read the corresponding instructional text.

STEP 6   Take the Practice Tests

Once you have completed your review, get ready for the real exam by taking the authentic GRE Practice Tests in Chapter 8 of this book and on the CD-ROM. When you take each test, try to simulate actual testing conditions. If you are taking the test in Chapter 8, sit in a quiet space, time yourself, and work through as much of the test as time allows. If you are taking the test on the CD-ROM, each test section will be timed for you. You'll gain experience with the test format, and you'll learn to pace yourself so that you can earn your highest score in the time allowed.

Please Note: for users of the CD-ROM

If you need screen magnification or selectable colors to take the computer-based GRE revised General Test, you can download a special version of ZoomText software from the GRE website at **www.ets.org/gre/powerprep2**.

Introducing the GRE® revised General Test

What Are the Main Features of the Revised Test?

The GRE® revised General Test is composed of revised Analytical Writing, Verbal Reasoning, and Quantitative Reasoning measures. Each of the measures has been revised to better focus on skills that are necessary for success in graduate school.

- **The Analytical Writing measure** asks you to provide more focused responses to questions, to more accurately demonstrate your skill in directly responding to the task presented.

- **The Verbal Reasoning measure** places a greater emphasis on higher cognitive skills, as a truer, deeper assessment of your ability to understand what you read and how to apply your reasoning skills.

- **The Quantitative Reasoning measure** tests the same basic mathematical concepts, but includes more data analysis and more real-life scenarios, to better gauge your skills.

The revised General Test delivers a friendlier, more flexible test-taking experience. Now you will be able to edit or change your answers, and skip questions, all within a section, and more—giving you the freedom to use your own personal test-taking strategies. In addition, a calculator is available on the Quantitative Reasoning measure to reduce the emphasis on computation.

The GRE revised General Test is offered on computer throughout the year on a continuous basis in the United States, Canada, and other regions of the world. Paper-based administrations are offered in areas of the world where computer-based testing is not available.

For the most up-to-date information about the GRE revised General Test, visit the GRE website at **www.ets.org/gre.**

Structure of the Test

Computer-Based revised General Test

The computer-based GRE® revised General Test contains six sections:

- an Analytical Writing section with two tasks, which always comes first in the test
- two Verbal Reasoning sections
- two Quantitative Reasoning sections
- one unscored section, typically a Verbal Reasoning or Quantitative Reasoning section, that may appear at any point in the test

Questions in the unscored section are being tried out either for possible use in future tests or to ensure that scores on new editions of the test are comparable to scores on earlier editions.

An identified research section may be included in place of the unscored section. The research section will always appear at the end of the test. Questions in this section are included for the purpose of ETS research and will not count toward your score.

The Verbal Reasoning, Quantitative Reasoning, and unidentified/unscored sections may appear in any order; therefore, you should treat each section as if it counts toward your score.

The Verbal Reasoning and Quantitative Reasoning measures are section-level adaptive. The computer selects the second section of a measure based on your performance on the first.

The Verbal Reasoning and Quantitative Reasoning measures allow you to preview other questions within the specific section on which you're working, review questions you've already answered, and change your answers.

Typical Computer-Based revised General Test

Total testing time is 3 hours and 45 minutes, including the unscored section. The directions at the beginning of each Verbal Reasoning and Quantitative Reasoning section specify the total number of questions in the section and the time allowed for the section. For the Analytical Writing section, the timing for each task is shown when the task is presented.

Section	Number of Questions	Time
Analytical Writing (1 section)	2 separately timed writing tasks	30 min. per task
Verbal Reasoning (2 sections)	Approximately 20 questions per section	30 min. per section
Quantitative Reasoning (2 sections)	Approximately 20 questions per section	35 min. per section
Unscored*	Approximately 20 questions	30–35 min. per section
Research **	Varies	Varies

*An unidentified unscored section that does not count toward a score may be included and may appear in any order.

**An identified research section that is not scored may be included, and it will always be at the end of the test.

Paper-Based revised General Test

The paper-based GRE® revised General Test contains six sections:
- two Analytical Writing sections, which always come first and second in the test
- two Verbal Reasoning sections
- two Quantitative Reasoning sections.

Typical Paper-Based revised General Test

Total testing time is approximately 3 hours and 30 minutes. The directions at the beginning of each section specify the total number of questions in the section and the time allowed for the section.

Section	Number of Questions	Time
Analytical Writing (2 sections)	1 writing task per section	30 min. per section
Verbal Reasoning (2 sections)	Approximately 25 questions per section	35 min. per section
Quantitative Reasoning (2 sections)	Approximately 25 questions per section	40 min. per section

Unlike the previous paper-based GRE General Test and the GRE Subject Tests, which use separate answer sheets, the paper-based GRE revised General Test is self-contained: you will enter all responses for the Analytical Writing tasks and the Verbal Reasoning and Quantitative Reasoning sections in the test book itself. Also, you are allowed to use a basic hand-held calculator on the Quantitative Reasoning sections. The calculator will be provided to you at the test site; you may not use your own calculator. Information about using the calculator to help you answer questions appears in the free *Practice Book for the Paper-based GRE revised General Test*, which is available at **www.ets.org/gre/revised/prepare**.

Preparing for the Test

Preparation for the test will depend on the amount of time you have available and your personal preferences for how to prepare. At a minimum, before you take the GRE® revised General Test, you should know what to expect from the test, including the administrative procedures, types of questions and directions, approximate number of questions, and amount of time for each section.

The administrative procedures include registration and appointment scheduling, date, time, test center location, cost, score-reporting procedures, and availability of special testing arrangements. You can find out about the administrative procedures for the revised General Test in the *GRE® Information and Registration Bulletin*. Information is also available online at **www.ets.org/gre/revised/bulletinandforms**.

Before taking the revised General Test, it is important to become familiar with the content of each of the measures. In this publication, you'll find information specific to each measure of the test. You can use this information to understand the type of material on which you'll be tested and the question types within each measure.

It is also important to spend some time preparing for the Analytical Writing section by reviewing the skills measured, scoring guides and score level descriptions, sample topics, scored sample essay responses, and reader commentary.

Test-taking Strategies for the Computer-based Test

Analytical Writing Section

The Analytical Writing measure of the computer-based revised General Test uses an elementary word processor developed by ETS so that individuals familiar with a specific commercial word processing software do not have an advantage or disadvantage. This software contains the following functionality: insert text, delete text, cut and paste, and undo the previous action. Tools such as a spelling checker and grammar checker are not available in the ETS software, in large part to maintain fairness with those examinees who must handwrite their essays at paper-based administrations.

It is important to budget your time. Within the 30-minute time limit for each task, you'll need to allow sufficient time to think about the topic, plan a response, and compose your essay. Although GRE readers understand the time constraints under which you write and will consider your response a first draft, you will still want to produce the best possible example of your writing.

Save a few minutes at the end of each timed task to check for obvious errors. Although an occasional typographical, spelling, or grammatical error will not affect your score, severe or persistent errors will detract from the overall effectiveness of your writing and lower your score.

Verbal Reasoning and Quantitative Reasoning Sections

The questions in the Verbal Reasoning and Quantitative Reasoning measures have a variety of formats. Some require you to select a single answer choice; others require you to select one or more answer choices, and yet others require you to enter a numeric answer. Make sure when answering a question that you understand what response is required. An onscreen calculator will be provided at the test center for use during the Quantitative Reasoning sections.

When taking the computer-based GRE revised General Test, you are free to skip questions that you might have difficulty answering. The testing software has a "mark and review" feature that enables you to mark questions you would like to revisit during the time provided to work on that section. The testing software also lets you view a complete list of all the questions in the section on which you're working, indicates whether you've answered each question and identifies the questions you've marked for review. Additionally, you can review questions you've already answered and change your answers, provided you still have time remaining to work on that section.

A sample review screen appears at the top of the facing page. The review screen is intended to help you keep track of your progress on the test. Do not spend too much time on the review screen, as this will take away from the time allotted to read and answer the questions on the test.

Your Verbal Reasoning and Quantitative Reasoning scores will be determined by the number of questions you answer correctly. Nothing is subtracted from a score if you answer a question incorrectly. Therefore, to maximize your scores on the Verbal Reasoning and Quantitative Reasoning measures, it is best to answer every question.

Work as rapidly as you can without being careless. Since no question carries greater weight than any other, do not waste time pondering individual questions you find extremely difficult or unfamiliar.

You may want to go through each of the Verbal Reasoning and Quantitative Rea-

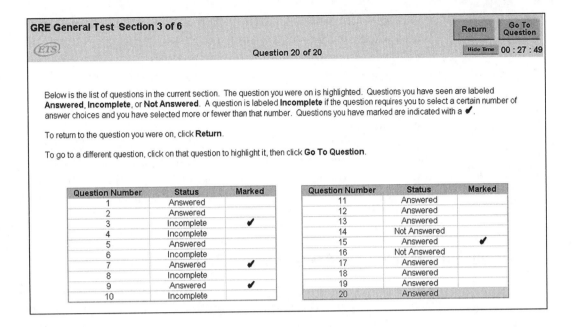

soning sections rapidly first, stopping only to answer questions you can answer with certainty. Then go back and answer the questions that require greater thought, concluding with the difficult questions if you have time.

During the actual administration of the revised General Test, you may work only on one section at a time and only for the time allowed. Once you have completed a section, you may not go back to it.

Scratch Paper

You will receive a supply of scratch paper before you begin the test. You can replenish your supply of scratch paper as necessary throughout the test by asking the test administrator.

Breaks

There is a 10-minute break following the third section and a one-minute break between the other test sections. You might want to replenish your supply of scratch paper during each scheduled break. Section timing will not stop if you take an unscheduled break, so you should proceed with your test without interruption once it begins.

Test-taking Strategies for the Paper-based Test

Analytical Writing Sections

In the paper-based revised General Test, the topics in the Analytical Writing measure will be presented in the test book, and you will handwrite your essay responses in the test book in the space provided.

It is important to budget your time. Within the 30-minute time limit for each section, you'll need to allow sufficient time to think about the topic, plan a response, and compose your essay. Although GRE readers understand the time constraints under which you write and will consider your response a first draft, you will still want to produce the best possible example of your writing.

Save a few minutes at the end of each timed section to check for obvious errors. Although an occasional spelling or grammatical error will not affect your score, severe and persistent errors will detract from the overall effectiveness of your writing and lower your score.

During the actual administration of the revised General Test, you may work only on the particular writing section the test center supervisor designates and only for the time allowed. You may *not* go back to an earlier section of the test after the supervisor announces, "Please stop work" for that section. The supervisor is authorized to dismiss you from the center for doing so.

Verbal Reasoning and Quantitative Reasoning Sections

The questions in the Verbal Reasoning and Quantitative Reasoning measures have a variety of formats. Some require you to select a single answer choice; others require you to select one or more answer choices, and yet others require you to enter a numeric answer. Make sure when answering a question that you understand what response is required. A calculator will be provided at the test center for use during the Quantitative Reasoning sections.

When taking a Verbal Reasoning or Quantitative Reasoning section, you are free, within that section, to skip questions that you might have difficulty answering and come back to them later during the time provided to work on that section. Also during that time you may change the answer to any question in that section by erasing it completely and filling in an alternative answer. Be careful not to leave any stray marks in the answer area, as they may be interpreted as incorrect responses. You can, however, safely make notes or perform calculations on other parts of the page. No additional scratch paper will be provided.

Your Verbal Reasoning and Quantitative Reasoning scores will be determined by the number of questions you answer correctly. Nothing is subtracted from a score if you answer a question incorrectly. Therefore, to maximize your scores on the Verbal Reasoning and Quantitative Reasoning measures, it is best to answer every question.

Work as rapidly as you can without being careless. Since no question carries greater weight than any other, do not waste time pondering individual questions you find extremely difficult or unfamiliar.

You may want to go through each of the Verbal Reasoning and Quantitative Reasoning sections rapidly first, stopping only to answer questions you can answer with certainty. Then go back and answer the questions that require greater thought, concluding with the difficult questions if you have time.

During the actual administration of the revised General Test, you may work only on the section the test center supervisor designates and only for the time allowed. You may *not* go back to an earlier section of the test after the supervisor announces, "Please stop work" for that section. The supervisor is authorized to dismiss you from the center for doing so. All answers must be recorded in the test book.

Breaks

There is a 10-minute break following the second Analytical Writing section.

Understanding GRE Scoring

Analytical Writing Measure

For the Analytical Writing measure, each essay receives a score from two readers using a six-point holistic scale. In holistic scoring, readers are trained to assign scores based on the overall quality of an essay in response to the assigned task. If the two scores differ by more than one point on the scale, the discrepancy is adjudicated by a third GRE® reader.

Otherwise, the two scores on each essay are averaged. The final scores on the two essays are then averaged and rounded up to the nearest half-point interval. A single score is reported for the Analytical Writing measure.

The primary emphasis in scoring the Analytical Writing section is on your critical thinking and analytical writing skills. Scoring guides for the Issue and Argument prompts are included in this publication, and they are available on the GRE website at **www.ets.org/gre/revised/scoreguides**.

In 2012, the GRE Program expects to implement *e-rater*® scoring technology in the scoring process for the computer-based Analytical Writing measure of the GRE® revised General Test. The *e-rater* scoring engine is a computerized natural language–processing program developed by ETS. After the *e-rater* program is implemented, information about it will be available on the GRE website at **www.ets.org/gre**.

Independent Intellectual Activity

During the scoring process for the revised General Test, your essay responses on the Analytical Writing section will be reviewed by ETS essay-similarity-detection software and by experienced essay readers. In light of the high value placed on independent intellectual activity within graduate schools and universities, ETS reserves the right to cancel test scores of any test taker when there is substantial evidence that an essay response includes, but is not limited to, any of the following:

- Text that is similar to that found in one or more other GRE essay responses

- Quoting or paraphrasing, without attribution, language that appears in published or unpublished sources

- Unacknowledged use of work that has been produced through collaboration with others without citation of the contribution of others

- Essays that are submitted as work of the examinee when the words have, in fact, been borrowed from elsewhere or prepared by another person

When one or more of the above circumstances occurs, your essay text, in ETS's professional judgment, does not reflect the independent, analytical writing skills that this test seeks to measure. Therefore, ETS must cancel the Analytical Writing score as invalid and cannot report the GRE General Test scores of which the Analytical Writing score is an indispensable part.

Test takers whose scores are canceled will forfeit their test fees and must pay to take the entire GRE General Test again at a future administration. No record of the score cancellations, or the reason for cancellation, will appear on their future score reports sent to colleges and universities.

Verbal Reasoning and Quantitative Reasoning Measures of the Computer-based Test

Your scores on the Verbal Reasoning and Quantitative Reasoning measures depend on your performance on the questions given.

The Verbal Reasoning and Quantitative Reasoning measures are section-level adaptive. This means the computer selects the second section of a measure based on your performance on the first. Within each section, all questions contribute equally to the final score. For each of the two measures, a raw score is computed. The raw score is the number of questions you answered correctly.

The raw score is then converted to a scaled score through a process known as equating. The equating process accounts for minor variations in difficulty from test to test as well as differences in difficulty among individuals' tests introduced by the section-level adaptation. Thus, a given scaled score reflects the same level of performance regardless of which section was administered and when the test was taken.

Verbal Reasoning and Quantitative Reasoning Measures of the Paper-based Test

Scoring of the Verbal Reasoning and Quantitative Reasoning measures is essentially a two-step process. First a raw score is computed for each measure. The raw score for each measure is the number of questions answered correctly in the two sections for that measure.

The Verbal Reasoning and Quantitative Reasoning raw scores are then converted to scaled scores through a process known as equating. The equating process accounts for minor variations in difficulty among the different test editions. Thus, a given scaled score for a particular measure reflects the same level of performance regardless of which edition of the test was taken.

Score Reporting

Three scores will be reported on the revised General Test:

- a Verbal Reasoning score reported on a new 130–170 score scale, in 1-point increments

- a Quantitative Reasoning score reported on a new 130–170 score scale, in 1-point increments

- an Analytical Writing score reported on a 0–6 score scale, in half-point increments

If you do not answer any questions at all for a measure (Verbal Reasoning, Quantitative Reasoning, or Analytical Writing), you receive a No Score (NS) for that measure.

Descriptions of the analytical writing abilities characteristic of particular score levels are available in this publication on page 41, and on the GRE website at **www.ets.org/gre/revised/scoreguides**.

Score Reporting Timeframes

Typically, scores on the computer-based GRE revised General Test are reported 10 to 15 days after the test date. However, due to the statistical processes that must take place after the revised test is introduced in August 2011, scores from tests taken from August through October 2011 will be reported beginning in November 2011. If you are applying to a graduate program, be sure to review the appropriate admissions deadlines and plan to take the test in time for your scores to reach the institution.

For specific information on score reporting dates for tests administered from August through October 2011, visit the GRE website at **www.ets.org/gre/scoreschedule**.

Scores from paper-based revised General Test administrations will be reported up to six weeks after the administration.

Score reporting is cumulative. Scores are reportable for five testing years following the testing year in which you test. All scores earned during this time will be reported to the institutions you designate.

2 GRE® Analytical Writing

Your goals for this chapter

- ❧ Recognize the two types of Analytical Writing tasks
- ❧ Study examples of each type of writing task
- ❧ Learn strategies for responding to the writing tasks
- ❧ Review actual student responses and ETS reader commentary

Overview of the Analytical Writing Measure

The Analytical Writing measure assesses your critical thinking and analytical writing skills. It assesses your ability to articulate and support complex ideas, construct and evaluate arguments, and sustain a focused and coherent discussion. It does not assess specific content knowledge.

The Analytical Writing measure consists of two separately timed analytical writing tasks:

- a 30-minute "Analyze an Issue" task

- a 30-minute "Analyze an Argument" task

The Issue task presents an opinion on an issue of broad interest followed by specific instructions on how to respond to that issue. You are required to evaluate the issue, considering its complexities, and develop an argument with reasons and examples to support your views.

The Argument task presents a different challenge from that of the Issue task: it requires you to evaluate a given argument according to specific instructions. You will need to consider the logical soundness of the argument rather than to agree or disagree with the position it presents.

The two tasks are complementary in that one requires you to construct your own argument by taking a position and providing evidence supporting your views on the issue, whereas the other requires you to evaluate someone else's argument by assessing its claims and evaluating the evidence it provides.

Preparing for the Analytical Writing Measure

Everyone — even the most practiced and confident of writers — should spend some time preparing for the Analytical Writing measure before arriving at the test center. It is important to review the skills measured and how the section is scored. It is also useful to review the scoring guides and score level descriptions, sample topics, scored sample essay responses, and reader commentary for each task.

The tasks in the Analytical Writing measure relate to a broad range of subjects — from the fine arts and humanities to the social and physical sciences — but no task requires specific content knowledge. In fact, each task has been field-tested to ensure that it possesses several important characteristics, including the following:

- GRE test takers, regardless of their field of study or special interests, understood the task and could easily respond to it.

- The task elicited the kinds of complex thinking and persuasive writing that university faculty consider important for success at the graduate level.

- The responses were varied in content and in the way the writers developed their ideas.

To help you prepare for the Analytical Writing measure, the GRE Program has published the entire pool of tasks from which your test tasks will be selected. You might find it helpful to review the Issue and Argument pools. You can view the published pools at **www.ets.org/gre/revised/awtopics**.

General Strategies

- **It is important to budget your time.** Within the 30-minute time limit for the Issue task, you will need to allow sufficient time to consider the issue and the specific instructions, plan a response, and compose your essay. Within the 30-minute time limit for the Argument task, you will need to allow sufficient time to consider the argument and the specific instructions, plan a response, and compose your essay. Although GRE readers understand the time constraints under which you write and will consider your response a first draft, you still want it to be the best possible example of your writing that you can produce under the testing conditions.

- **Save a few minutes at the end of each timed task to check for obvious errors.** Although an occasional spelling or grammatical error will not affect your score, severe and persistent errors will detract from the overall effectiveness of your writing and thus lower your score.

Analyze an Issue Task

Understanding the Issue Task

The Analyze an Issue task assesses your ability to think critically about a topic of general interest according to specific instructions and to clearly express your thoughts about it in writing. Each issue topic makes a claim that test takers can discuss from various perspectives and apply to many different situations or conditions. The issue statement is followed by specific instructions. Your task is to present a compelling case for your own position on the issue according to the specific instructions. Before beginning your written response, be sure to read the issue and instructions carefully and think about the issue from several points of view, considering the complexity of ideas associated with those views. Then, make notes about the position you want to develop and list the main reasons and examples that you could use to support that position.

It is important that you address the central issue according to the specific instructions. Each task is accompanied by one of the following sets of instructions.

- Write a response in which you discuss the extent to which you agree or disagree with the statement and explain your reasoning for the position you take. In developing and supporting your position, you should consider ways in which the statement might or might not hold true and explain how these considerations shape your position.

- Write a response in which you discuss the extent to which you agree or disagree with the recommendation and explain your reasoning for the position you take. In developing and supporting your position, describe specific circumstances in which adopting the recommendation would or would not be advantageous and explain how these examples shape your position.

- Write a response in which you discuss the extent to which you agree or disagree with the claim. In developing and supporting your position, be sure to address the most compelling reasons and/or examples that could be used to challenge your position.

- Write a response in which you discuss which view more closely aligns with your own position and explain your reasoning for the position you take. In developing and supporting your position, you should address both of the views presented.

- Write a response in which you discuss the extent to which you agree or disagree with the claim and the reason on which that claim is based.

- Write a response in which you discuss your views on the policy and explain your reasoning for the position you take. In developing and supporting your position, you should consider the possible consequences of implementing the policy and explain how these consequences shape your position.

The GRE readers scoring your response are not looking for a "right" answer — in fact, there is no correct position to take. Instead, the readers are evaluating the skill with which you address the specific instructions and articulate and develop an argument to support your evaluation of the issue.

Understanding the Context for Writing: Purpose and Audience

The Issue task is an exercise in critical thinking and persuasive writing. The purpose of this task is to determine how well you can develop a compelling argument supporting your own evaluation of an issue and to effectively communicate that argument in writing to an academic audience. Your audience consists of GRE readers who are carefully trained to apply the scoring criteria identified in the scoring guide for the Analyze an Issue task (see pages 37–38).

To get a clearer idea of how GRE readers apply the Issue scoring criteria to actual responses, you should review scored sample Issue essay responses and reader commentary. The sample responses, particularly at the 5 and 6 score levels, will show you a variety of successful strategies for organizing, developing, and communicating a persuasive argument. The reader commentary discusses specific aspects of evaluation and writing, such as the use of examples, development and support, organization, language fluency, and word choice. For each response, the reader commentary points out aspects that are particularly persuasive as well as any that detract from the overall effectiveness of the essay.

Preparing for the Issue Task

Because the Issue task is meant to assess the persuasive writing skills that you have developed throughout your education, it has been designed neither to require any particular course of study nor to advantage students with a particular type of training.

Many college textbooks on composition offer advice on persuasive writing and argumentation that you might find useful, but even this advice might be more technical and specialized than you need for the Issue task. You will not be expected to know specific critical thinking or writing terms or strategies; instead, you should be able to respond to the specific instructions and use reasons, evidence, and examples to support your position on an issue. Suppose, for instance, that an Issue topic asks you to consider a policy that would require government financial support for art museums and the implications of implementing the policy. If your position is that government should fund art museums, you might support your position by discussing the reasons art is important and explain that government funding would make access to museums available to everyone. On the other hand, if your position is that government should not support museums, you might point out that, given limited governmental funds, art museums are not as deserving of governmental funding as are other, more socially important, institutions, which would suffer if the policy were implemented. Or, if you are in favor of government funding for art museums only under certain conditions, you might focus on the artistic criteria, cultural concerns, or political conditions that you think should determine how — or whether — art museums receive government funds. It is not your position that matters so much as the critical thinking skills you display in developing your position.

An excellent way to prepare for the Issue task is to practice writing on some of the published topics. There is no "best" approach: some people prefer to start practicing without regard to the 30-minute time limit; others prefer to take a "timed test" first and practice within the time limit. No matter which approach you take when you practice the Issue task, you should review the task directions, then

● carefully read the claim and the specific instructions and make sure you understand them; if they seem unclear, discuss them with a friend or teacher

- think about the claim and instructions in relation to your own ideas and experiences, to events you have read about or observed, and to people you have known; this is the knowledge base from which you will develop compelling reasons and examples in your argument that reinforce, negate, or qualify the claim in some way

- decide what position on the issue you want to take and defend

- decide what compelling evidence (reasons and examples) you can use to support your position

Remember that this is a task in critical thinking and persuasive writing. The most successful responses will explore the complexity of the claim and instructions. As you prepare for the Issue task, you might find it helpful to ask yourself the following questions:

- What precisely is the central issue?

- What precisely are the instructions asking me to do?

- Do I agree with all or with any part of the claim? Why or why not?

- Does the claim make certain assumptions? If so, are they reasonable?

- Is the claim valid only under certain conditions? If so, what are they?

- Do I need to explain how I interpret certain terms or concepts used in the claim?

- If I take a certain position on the issue, what reasons support my position?

- What examples — either real or hypothetical — could I use to illustrate those reasons and advance my point of view? Which examples are most compelling?

Once you have decided on a position to defend, consider the perspective of others who might not agree with your position. Ask yourself:

- What reasons might someone use to refute or undermine my position?

- How should I acknowledge or defend against those views in my essay?

To plan your response, you might want to summarize your position and make brief notes about how you will support the position you're going to take. When you've done this, look over your notes and decide how you will organize your response. Then write a response developing your position on the issue. Even if you don't write a full response, you should find it helpful to practice with a few of the Issue topics and to sketch out your possible responses. After you have practiced with some of the topics, try writing responses to some of the topics within the 30-minute time limit so that you have a good idea of how to use your time in the actual test.

It would probably be helpful to get some feedback on your response from an instructor who teaches critical thinking or writing or to trade papers on the same topic with other students and discuss one another's responses in relation to the scoring guide. Try to determine how each paper meets or misses the criteria for each score point in the guide. Comparing your own response to the scoring guide will help you see how and where you might need to improve.

The Form of Your Response

You are free to organize and develop your response in any way that you think will effectively communicate your ideas about the issue and the instructions. Your response may, but need not, incorporate particular writing strategies learned in English composition or writing-intensive college courses. GRE readers will not be looking for a particular developmental strategy or mode of writing; in fact, when GRE readers are trained, they review hundreds of Issue responses that, although highly diverse in content and form, display similar levels of critical thinking and persuasive writing. Readers will see, for example, some Issue responses at the 6 score level that begin by briefly summarizing the writer's position on the issue and then explicitly announcing the main points to be argued. They will see others that lead into the writer's position by making a prediction, asking a series of questions, describing a scenario, or defining critical terms in the quotation. The readers know that a writer can earn a high score by giving multiple examples or by presenting a single, extended example. Look at the sample Issue responses, particularly at the 5 and 6 score levels, to see how other writers have successfully developed and organized their arguments.

You should use as many or as few paragraphs as you consider appropriate for your argument — for example, you will probably need to create a new paragraph whenever your discussion shifts to a new cluster of ideas. What matters is not the number of examples, the number of paragraphs, or the form your argument takes but, rather, the cogency of your ideas about the issue and the clarity and skill with which you communicate those ideas to academic readers.

Sample Issue Task

> As people rely more and more on technology to solve problems, the ability of humans to think for themselves will surely deteriorate.
>
> Discuss the extent to which you agree or disagree with the statement and explain your reasoning for the position you take. In developing and supporting your position, you should consider ways in which the statement might or might not hold true and explain how these considerations shape your position.

Strategies for This Topic

In this task, you are asked to discuss the extent to which you agree or disagree with the statement. Thus, responses may range from strong agreement or strong disagreement, to qualified agreement or qualified disagreement. You are also instructed to explain your reasoning and consider ways in which the statement might or might not hold true. A successful response need not comment on all or any one of the points listed below and may well discuss other reasons or examples not mentioned here in support of its position.

Although this topic is accessible to respondents of all levels of ability, for any response to receive a top score, it is particularly important that you remain focused on the task and provide clearly relevant examples and/or reasons to support the point of view you are expressing. Lower level responses may be long and full of examples of modern technology, but those examples may not be clearly related to a particular position. For example, a respondent who strongly disagrees with the statement may choose to use computer technology as proof that thinking ability is not deteriorating. The mere existence of computer technology, however, does not adequately prove this point (perhaps the ease of computer use inhibits our thinking ability). To receive a higher-level score, the respondent should explain in what ways computer technology may call for or require thinking ability.

This topic could elicit a wide variety of approaches, especially considering the different possible interpretations of the phrase "the ability of humans to think for themselves." Although most respondents may take it to mean problem solving, others, with equal effectiveness, could interpret it as emotional and social intelligence (i.e., the ability to communicate/connect with others). With any approach, it is possible to discuss examples such as calculators, word processing tools such as spell and grammar check, tax return software, Internet research, and a variety of other common household and business technologies.

You may agree with the prompt and argue that:

- reliance on technology leads to dependency; we come to rely on problem solving technologies to such a degree that when they fail, we are in worse shape than if we didn't have them in the first place

- everyday technologies such as calculators and cash registers have decreased our ability to perform simple calculations, a "use it or lose it" approach to thinking ability

Or you may take issue with the prompt and argue that technology facilitates and improves our thinking skills, arguing that:

- developing, implementing, and using technology requires problem solving

- technology frees us from mundane problem solving (e.g., calculations), and allows us to engage in more complex thinking

- technology provides access to information otherwise unavailable

- technology connects people at a distance and allows them to share ideas

- technology is dependent on the human ability to think and make choices (every implementation of and advance in technology is driven by human intelligence and decision making)

On the other hand, you could decide to explore the middle ground in the debate and point out that while technology may diminish some mental skill sets, it enables other (perhaps more important) types of thinking to thrive. Such a response might distinguish between complex problem solving and simple "data maintenance" (i.e., performing calculations and organizing information). Other approaches could include taking a historical, philosophical, or sociological stance, or, with equal effectiveness, using personal examples to illustrate a position. One could argue that the value or detriment of relying on technology is determined by the individual (or society) using it or that only those who develop technology (i.e., technical specialists) are maintaining their problem solving skills, while the rest of us are losing them.

Again, it is important for you to avoid overly general examples, or lists of examples without expansion. It is also essential to do more than paraphrase the prompt. Please keep in mind that what counts is the ability to clearly express a particular point of view in relation to the issue and specific task instructions and to support that position with relevant reasons and/or examples.

Essay Responses and Reader Commentary

Score 6 Response *

The statement linking technology negatively with free thinking plays on recent human experience over the past century. Surely there has been no time in history where the lived lives of people have changed more dramatically. A quick reflection on a typical day reveals how technology has revolutionized the world. Most people commute to work in an automobile that runs on an internal combustion engine. During the workday, chances are high that the employee will interact with a computer that processes information on silicon bridges that are .09 microns wide. Upon leaving home, family members will be reached through wireless networks that utilize satellites orbiting the earth. Each of these common occurences would have been inconceivable at the turn of the 19th century.

The statement attempts to bridge these dramatic changes to a reduction in the ability for humans to think for themselves. The assumption is that an increased reliance on technology negates the need for people to think creatively to solve previous quandaries. Looking back at the introduction, one could argue that without a car, computer, or mobile phone, the hypothetical worker would need to find alternate methods of transport, information processing, and communication. Technology short circuits this thinking by making the problems obsolete.

However, this reliance on technology does not necessarily preclude the creativity that marks the human species. The prior examples reveal that technology allows for convenience. The car, computer, and phone all release additional time for people to live more efficiently. This efficiency does not preclude the need for humans to think for themselves. In fact, technology frees humanity to not only tackle new problems, but may itself create new issues that did not exist without technology. For example, the proliferation of automobiles has introduced a need for fuel conservation on a global scale. With increasing energy demands from emerging markets, global warming becomes a concern inconceivable to the horse-and-buggy generation. Likewise dependence on oil has created nation-states that are not dependent on taxation, allowing ruling parties to oppress minority groups such as women. Solutions to these complex problems require the unfettered imaginations of maverick scientists and politicians.

In contrast to the statement, we can even see how technology frees the human imagination. Consider how the digital revolution and the advent of the internet has allowed for an unprecedented exchange of ideas. WebMD, a popular internet portal for medical information, permits patients to self research symptoms for a more informed doctor visit. This exercise opens pathways of thinking that were previously closed off to the medical layman. With increased interdisciplinary interactions, inspiration can arrive from the most surprising corners. Jeffrey Sachs, one of the architects of the UN Millenium Development Goals, based his ideas on emergency care triage techniques. The unlikely marriage of economics and medicine has healed tense, hyperinflation environments from South America to Eastern Europe.

This last example provides the most hope in how technology actually provides hope to the future of humanity. By increasing our reliance on technology, impossible goals can now be achieved. Consider how the late 20th century witnessed the complete elimination of smallpox. This disease had ravaged the human race since prehistorical days, and yet with the technology of vaccines, free thinking humans dared to imagine a

---

*All responses in this publication are reproduced exactly as written, including errors, misspellings, etc., if any.

world free of smallpox. Using technology, battle plans were drawn out, and smallpox was systematically targeted and eradicated.

Technology will always mark the human experience, from the discovery of fire to the implementation of nanotechnology. Given the history of the human race, there will be no limit to the number of problems, both new and old, for us to tackle. There is no need to retreat to a Luddite attitude to new things, but rather embrace a hopeful posture to the possibilities that technology provides for new avenues of human imagination.

Reader Commentary

The author of this essay stakes out a clear and insightful position on the issue and follows the specific instructions by discussing ways in which the statement might or might not hold true, using specific reasons and examples to support that position. The essay cogently argues that technology does not decrease our ability to think for ourselves. It merely provides "additional time for people to live more efficiently." In fact, the problems that have developed alongside the growth of technology (pollution, political unrest in oil producing nations) actually call for more creative thinking, not less. In further examples, the essay shows how technology allows for the linking of ideas that may never have been connected in the past (like medicine and economic models), pushing people to think in new ways. Examples are persuasive and fully developed; reasoning is logically sound and well-supported.

Ideas in the essay are connected logically, with effective transitions used both between paragraphs ("However," or "In contrast to the statement") and within paragraphs. Sentence structure is varied and complex, and the essay clearly demonstrates facility with the "conventions of standard written English (i.e., grammar, usage, and mechanics)" (see Issue Scoring Guide, pages 37–38), with only minor errors appearing. Thus, this essay meets all the requirements for receiving a top score, a 6.

Score 5 Response

Surely many of us have expressed the following sentiment, or some variation on it, during our daily commutes to work: "People are getting so stupid these days!" Surrounded as we are by striding and strident automatons with cell phones glued to their ears, PDA's gripped in their palms, and omniscient, omnipresent CNN gleaming in their eyeballs, it's tempting to believe that technology has isolated and infantilized us, essentially transforming us into dependent, conformist morons best equipped to sideswip one another in our SUV's.

Furthermore, hanging around with the younger, pre-commute generation, whom tech-savviness seems to have rendered lethal, is even less reassuring. With "Teen People" style trends shooting through the air from tiger-striped PDA to zebra-striped PDA, and with the latest starlet gossip zipping from juicy Blackberry to teeny, turbo-charged cell phone, technology seems to support young people's worst tendencies to follow the crowd. Indeed, they have seemingly evolved into intergalactic conformity police. After all, today's tech-aided teens are, courtesy of authentic, hands-on video games, literally trained to kill; courtesy of chat and instant text messaging, they have their own language; they even have tiny cameras to efficiently photodocument your fashion blunders! Is this adolescence, or paparazzi terrorist training camp?

With all this evidence, it's easy to believe that tech trends and the incorporation of technological wizardry into our everyday lives have served mostly to enforce conformity, promote dependence, heighten comsumerism and materialism, and generally create a culture that values self-absorption and personal entitlement over cooperation and collaboration. However, I argue that we are merely in the inchoate stages of learning to live with technology while still loving one another. After all, even given the examples provided earlier in this essay, it seems clear that technology hasn't impaired our thinking and problem-solving capacities. Certainly it has incapacitated our behavior and manners; certainly our values have taken a severe blow. However, we are inarguably more efficient in our badness these days. We're effective worker bees of ineffectiveness!

If technology has so increased our senses of self-efficacy that we can become veritable agents of the awful, virtual CEO's of selfishness, certainly it can be beneficial. Harnessed correctly, technology can improve our ability to think and act for ourselves. The first challenge is to figure out how to provide technology users with some direly-needed direction.

Reader Commentary

The language of this essay clearly illustrates both its strengths and weaknesses. The flowery and sometimes uncannily keen descriptions are often used to powerful effect, but at other times, this descriptive language results in errors in syntax. See, for example, the problems of parallelism in the second to last sentence of paragraph 2 ("After all, today's tech-aided teens . . . ").

There is consistent evidence of facility with syntax and complex vocabulary ("Surrounded as we are by striding and strident automatons with cell phones glued to their ears, PDA's gripped in their palms, and omniscient, omnipresent CNN gleaming in their eyeballs, it's tempting to believe . . . "). Such lucid prose, however, is often countered with an over-reliance upon abstractions and tangential reasoning (what does the fact that video games "literally train [teens] to kill" have to do with the use or deterioration of thinking abilities, for example?).

Because this essay takes a complex approach to the issue (arguing, in effect, that technology neither enhances nor reduces our ability to think for ourselves, but can be used to do one or the other depending on the user) and because the author makes use of "appropriate vocabulary and sentence variety" (see Issue Scoring Guide, pages 37–38), a score of 5 is appropriate.

Score 4 Response

In all actuality, I think it is more probable that our bodies will surely deteriorate long before our minds do in any significant amount. Who can't say that technology has made us lazier, but that's the key word, lazy, not stupid. The ever increasing amount of technology that we incorporate into our daily lives makes people think and learn every day, possibly more than ever before. Our abilities to think, learn, philosophize, etc. may even reach limits never dreamed of before by average people. Using technology to solve problems will continue to help us realize our potential as a human race.

If you think about it, using technology to solve more complicating problems gives humans a chance to expand their thinking and learning, opening up whole new worlds for many people. Many of these people are glad for the chance to expand their horizons by learning more, going to new places, and trying new things. If it wasn't for the invention of new technological devices, I wouldn't be sitting at this computer trying to philosophize about technology. It would be extremely hard for children in much poorer countries to learn and think for themselves with out the invention of the internet. Think what an impact the printing press, a technologically superior mackine at the time, had on the ability of the human race to learn and think.

Right now we are seeing a golden age of technology, using it all the time during our every day lives. When we get up there's instant coffee and the microwave and all these great things that help us get ready for our day. But we aren't allowing our minds to deteriorate by using them, we are only making things easier for ourselves and saving time for other important things in our days. Going off to school or work in our cars instead of a horse and buggy. Think of the brain power and genius that was used to come up with that single invention that has changed the way we move across this globe.

Using technology to solve our continually more complicated problems as a human race is definately a good thing. Our ability to think for ourselves isn't deteriorating, it's continuing to grow, moving on to higher though functions and more ingenious ideas. The ability to use what technology we have is an example

Reader Commentary

This essay meets all the criteria of a 4-level essay. The writer develops a clear position ("Using technology to solve problems will continue to help us realize our potential as a human race"). The position is then developed with relevant reasons ("using technology to solve more complicat[ed] problems gives humans a chance to expand their thinking and learning . . . " and "we are seeing a golden age of technology"). Point 1, "Using technology," is supported with the simple, but relevant notions that technology allows us access to information and abilities to which we would not normally have access. Similarly, point 2, "the golden age," is supported by the basic description of our technologically saturated social condition. Though the development and organization of the essay does suffer from an occasional misstep (see paragraph 3's abrupt progression from coffee pots to the benefits of technology to cars), the essay as a whole flows smoothly and logically from one idea to the next.

It is useful to compare this essay to the 3 level essay presented next. Though they both utilize some very superficial discussion and often fail to probe deeply into the issue, this writer does, however, take the analysis a step further. In paragraph 2, the distinction between this essay and the next one (the 3 level response) can most clearly be seen. To support the notion that advances in technology actually help increase thinking ability, the writer draws a clever parallel between the promise of modern, sophisticated technology (computer) and the equally substantial/pervasive technology of the past (printing press).

Like the analysis, the language in this essay clearly meets the requirements for a score of 4. The writer displays sufficient control of language and the conventions of standard written English. The preponderance of mistakes are of a cosmetic nature ("using technology to solve more complicating problems"). There is a sentence fragment ("Going off . . . ") along with a comma splice ("Our ability . . . isn't deteriorating, it's continuing to grow . . . ") in paragraph 4. These errors, though, are minor and do not interfere with the clarity of the ideas being presented.

Score 3 Response

> There is no current proof that advancing technology will deteriorate the ability of humans to think. On the contrary, advancements in technology had advanced our vast knowledge in many fields, opening opportunities for further understanding and achievement. For example, the problem of dibilitating illnesses and diseases such as alzheimer's disease is slowing being solved by the technological advancements in stem cell research. The future ability of growing new brain cells and the possibility to reverse the onset of alzheimer's is now becoming a reality. This shows our initiative as humans to better our health demonstrates greater ability of humans to think.
>
> One aspect where the ability of humans may initially be seen as an example of deteriorating minds is the use of internet and cell phones. In the past humans had to seek out information in many different enviroments and aspects of life. Now humans can sit in a chair and type anything into a computer and get an answer. Our reliance on this type of technology can be detrimental if not regulated and regularily substituted for other information sources such as human interactions and hands on learning. I think if humans understand that we should not have such a reliance on computer technology, that we as a species will advance further by utilizing the opportunity of computer technology as well as the other sources of information outside of a computer. Supplementing our knowledge with internet access is surely a way for technology to solve problems while continually advancing the human race.

Reader Commentary

This essay never moves beyond a superficial discussion of the issue. The writer attempts to develop two points: that advancements in technology have progressed our knowledge in many fields and that supplementing rather than relying on technology is "surely a way for technology to solve problems while continually advancing the human race." Each point, then, is developed with relevant but insufficient evidence. In discussing the ability of technology to advance knowledge in many fields (a broad subject rife with possible examples), the writer uses only one limited and very brief example from a specific field (medicine and stem-cell research).

Development of the second point is hindered by a lack of specificity and organization. The writer creates what might most be comparable to an outline. The writer cites a need for regulation/supplementation and warns of the detriment of over-reliance upon technology. However, the explanation of both the problem and the solution is vague and limited ("Our reliance . . . can be detrimental . . . If humans understand that we should not have such a reliance . . . we will advance further"). There is neither explanation of consequences nor clarification of what is meant by "supplementing." This second paragraph is a series of generalizations, which are loosely connected and lack a much needed grounding.

In the essay, there are some minor language errors and a few more serious flaws (e.g., "The future ability of growing new brain cells" or "One aspect where the ability of humans may initially be seen as an example of deteriorating minds..."). Despite the accumulation of such flaws, though, meaning is generally clear. This essay earns a score of 3, then, primarily for its limited development.

Score 2 Response

In recent centuries, humans have developed the technology very rapidly, and you may accept some merit of it, and you may see a distortion in society occured by it. To be lazy for human in some meaning is one of the fashion issues in thesedays. There are many symptoms and resons of it. However, I can not agree with the statement that the technology make humans to be reluctant to thinkng thoroughly.

Of course, you can see the phenomena of human laziness along with developed technology in some place. However, they would happen in specific condition, not general. What makes human to be laze of thinking is not merely technology, but the the tendency of human that they treat them as a magic stick and a black box. Not understanding the aims and theory of them couses the disapproval problems.

The most important thing to use the thechnology, regardless the new or old, is to comprehend the fundamental idea of them, and to adapt suit tech to tasks in need. Even if you recognize a method as a all-mighty and it is extremely over-spec to your needs, you can not see the result you want. In this procedure, humans have to consider as long as possible to acquire adequate functions. Therefore, humans can not escape from using their brain.

In addition, the technology as it is do not vain automatically, the is created by humans. Thus, the more developed tech and the more you want a convenient life, the more you think and emmit your creativity to breakthrough some banal method sarcastically.

Consequently, if you are not passive to the new tech, but offensive to it, you would not lose your ability to think deeply. Furthermore, you may improve the ability by adopting it.

Reader Commentary

The language of this essay is what most clearly links it to the score point of 2. Amidst sporadic moments of clarity, this essay is marred by serious errors in grammar, usage and mechanics that often interfere with meaning. It is unclear what the writer means when he/she states, "To be lazy for human in some meaning is one of the fashion issues in thesedays," or ". . . to adapt suit tech to tasks in need." Despite such severe flaws, the writer has made an obvious attempt to respond to the prompt ("I can not agree with the statement that the technology make humans to be reluctant to thinking thoroughly") as well as an unclear attempt to support such an assertion ("Not understanding the aims and theory of them [technology] couses the disapproval problems" and "The most important thing to use the thechnology . . . is to comprehend the fundamental idea of them"). Holistically, the essay displays a seriously flawed but not fundamentally deficient attempt to develop and support its claims.

(Note: In this SPECIFIC case, the analysis is tied directly to the language. As the language falters, so too does the analysis.)

Score 1 Response

> Humans have invented machines but they have forgot it and have started everything technically so clearly their thinking process is deterioating.

Reader Commentary

The essay is clearly on topic, as evidenced by the writer's usage of the more significant terms from the prompt: "technically" (technologically), "humans", "thinking" (think) and "deterioating" (deteriorate). Such usage is the only clear evidence of understanding. Meaning aside, the brevity of the essay (1 sentence) clearly indicates the writer's inability to develop a response that addresses the specific instructions given ("Discuss the extent to which you agree or disagree with the statement above and explain your reasoning for the position you take").

The language, too, is clearly 1-level, as the sentence fails to achieve coherence. The coherent phrases in this one-sentence response are those tied to the prompt: "Humans have invented machines" and "their thinking process is deterioating." Otherwise, the point being made is unclear.

Analyze an Argument Task

Understanding the Argument Task

The Analyze an Argument task assesses your ability to understand, analyze, and evaluate arguments according to specific instructions and to clearly convey your evaluation in writing. The task consists of a brief passage in which the author makes a case for some course of action or interpretation of events by presenting claims backed by reasons and evidence. Your task is to discuss the logical soundness of the author's case according to the specific instructions by critically examining the line of reasoning. This task requires you to read the argument and instructions very carefully. You might want to read them more than once and possibly make brief notes about points you want to develop more fully in your response. In reading the argument, you should pay special attention to

- what is offered as evidence, support, or proof
- what is explicitly stated, claimed, or concluded
- what is assumed or supposed, perhaps without justification or proof
- what is not stated, but necessarily follows from what is stated

In addition, you should consider the *structure* of the argument — the way in which these elements are linked together to form a *line of reasoning*; that is, you should recognize the separate, sometimes implicit steps in the thinking process and consider whether the movement from each one to the next is logically sound. In tracing this line, look for transition words and phrases that suggest that the author is attempting to make a logical connection (e.g., *however, thus, therefore, evidently, hence, in conclusion*).

An important part of performing well on the Argument task is remembering what you are *not* being asked to do. You are not being asked to discuss whether the statements in the argument are true or accurate. You are not being asked to agree or disagree with the position stated. You are not being asked to express your own views on the subject being discussed (as you were in the Issue task). Instead, you are being asked to evaluate the logical soundness of an argument of another writer according to specific instructions and, in doing so, to demonstrate the critical thinking, perceptive reading, and analytical writing skills that university faculty consider important for success in graduate school.

It is important that you address the argument according to the specific instructions. Each task is accompanied by one of the following sets of instructions.

- Write a response in which you discuss what specific evidence is needed to evaluate the argument and explain how the evidence would weaken or strengthen the argument.

- Write a response in which you examine the stated and/or unstated assumptions of the argument. Be sure to explain how the argument depends on these assumptions and what the implications are for the argument if the assumptions prove unwarranted.

- Write a response in which you discuss what questions would need to be answered in order to decide whether the recommendation and the argument on which it is based are reasonable. Be sure to explain how the answers to these questions would help to evaluate the recommendation.

- Write a response in which you discuss what questions would need to be answered in order to decide whether the advice and the argument on which it is based are reasonable. Be sure to explain how the answers to these questions would help to evaluate the advice.

- Write a response in which you discuss what questions would need to be answered in order to decide whether the recommendation is likely to have the predicted result. Be sure to explain how the answers to these questions would help to evaluate the recommendation.

- Write a response in which you discuss what questions would need to be answered in order to decide whether the prediction and the argument on which it is based are reasonable. Be sure to explain how the answers to these questions would help to evaluate the prediction.

- Write a response in which you discuss one or more alternative explanations that could rival the proposed explanation and explain how your explanation(s) can plausibly account for the facts presented in the argument.

- Write a response in which you discuss what questions would need to be addressed in order to decide whether the conclusion and the argument on which it is based are reasonable. Be sure to explain how the answers to the questions would help to evaluate the conclusion.

"Analyze an Argument" is primarily a critical thinking task requiring a written response. Consequently, the analytical skills displayed in your evaluation carry great weight in determining your score; however, the clarity with which you convey ideas is also important to your overall score.

Understanding the Context for Writing: Purpose and Audience

The purpose of the task is to see how well equipped you are to insightfully evaluate an argument written by someone else and to effectively communicate your evaluation in writing to an academic audience. Your audience consists of GRE readers carefully trained to apply the scoring criteria identified in the scoring guide for the Analyze an Argument task (see page 39–40).

To get a clearer idea of how GRE readers apply the Argument scoring criteria to actual essays, you should review scored sample Argument essay responses and reader commentary. The sample responses, particularly at the 5 and 6 score levels, will show you a variety of successful strategies for organizing and developing an insightful evaluation. The reader commentary discusses specific aspects of analytical writing, such as cogency of ideas, development and support, organization, syntactic variety, and facility with language. For each response, the reader commentary will point out aspects that are particularly effective and insightful as well as any that detract from the overall effectiveness of the responses.

Preparing for the Argument Task

Because the Argument task is meant to assess analytical writing and informal reasoning skills that you have developed throughout your education, it has been designed so as not to require any specific course of study or to advantage students with a particular type of training. Many college textbooks on rhetoric and composition have sections on informal logic and critical thinking that might prove helpful, but even these might be more detailed and technical than the task requires. You will not be expected to know methods of analysis or technical terms. For instance, in one topic an elementary school principal might conclude that the new playground equipment has improved student attendance because absentee rates have declined since it was installed. You will not need to see that the principal has committed the *post hoc, ergo propter hoc* fallacy; you will simply need to see that there are other possible explanations for the improved attendance, to offer some common-sense examples, and perhaps to suggest what would be necessary to verify the conclusion. For instance, absentee rates might have decreased because the climate was mild. This would have to be ruled out in order for the principal's conclusion to be valid.

Although you do not need to know special analytical techniques and terminology, you should be familiar with the directions for the Argument task and with certain key concepts, including the following:

- **alternative explanation**: a possible competing version of what might have caused the events in question; an alternative explanation undercuts or qualifies the original explanation because it too can account for the observed facts

- **analysis**: the process of breaking something (e.g., an argument) down into its component parts in order to understand how they work together to make up the whole

- **argument**: a claim or a set of claims with reasons and evidence offered as support; a line of reasoning meant to demonstrate the truth or falsehood of something

- **assumption**: a belief, often unstated or unexamined, that someone must hold in order to maintain a particular position; something that is taken for granted but that must be true in order for the *conclusion* to be true

- **conclusion**: the end point reached by a line of reasoning, valid if the reasoning is sound; the resulting assertion

- **counterexample**: an example, real or hypothetical, that refutes or disproves a statement in the *argument*

- **evaluation**: an assessment of the quality of evidence and reasons in an argument and of the overall merit of an *argument*

An excellent way to prepare for the Analyze an Argument task is to practice writing on some of the published Argument topics. There is no one way to practice that is best for everyone. Some prefer to start practicing without adhering to the 30-minute time limit. If you follow this approach, take all the time you need to evaluate the argument. No matter which approach you take, you should

- carefully read the argument and the specific instructions — you might want to read them over more than once

- identify as many of the argument's claims, conclusions, and underlying assumptions as possible and evaluate their quality

- think of as many alternative explanations and counterexamples as you can

- think of what specific additional evidence might weaken or lend support to the claims

- ask yourself what changes in the argument would make the reasoning more sound

Write down each of these thoughts as a brief note. When you've gone as far as you can with your evaluation, look over the notes and put them in a good order for discussion (perhaps by numbering them). Then write an evaluation according to the specific instructions by fully developing each point that is relevant to those instructions. Even if you choose not to write a full essay response, you should find it very helpful to practice evaluating a few of the arguments and sketching out your responses. When you become quicker and more confident, you should practice writing some Argument responses within the 30-minute time limit so that you will have a good sense of how to pace yourself in the actual test. For example, you will not want to discuss one point so exhaustively or to provide so many equivalent examples that you run out of time to make your other main points.

You might want to get feedback on your response(s) from a writing instructor, a philosophy teacher, or someone who emphasizes critical thinking in his or her course. It can also be very informative to trade papers on the same topic with fellow students and discuss one another's responses in terms of the scoring guide. Focus not so much on giving the "right scores" as on seeing how the papers meet or miss the performance standards for each score point and what you therefore need to do in order to improve.

How to Interpret Numbers, Percentages, and Statistics in Argument Topics

Some arguments contain numbers, percentages, or statistics that are offered as evidence in support of the argument's conclusion. For example, an argument might claim that a certain community event is less popular this year than it was last year because only 100 people attended this year in comparison with 150 last year, a 33 percent decline in attendance. It is important to remember that you are not being asked to do a mathematical task with the numbers, percentages, or statistics. Instead you should evaluate these as evidence intended to support the conclusion. In the example above, the conclusion is that a community event has become less popular. You should ask yourself: does the difference between 100 people and 150 people support that conclusion? Note that, in this case, there are other possible explanations; for example, the weather might have been much worse this year, this year's event might have been held at an inconvenient time, the cost of the event might have gone up this year, or there might have been another popular event this year at the same time. Each of these could explain the difference in attendance, and thus would weaken the conclusion that the event was "less popular." Similarly, percentages might support or weaken a conclusion depending on what actual numbers the percentages represent. Consider the claim that the drama club at a school deserves more funding because its membership has increased by 100 percent. This 100 percent increase could be significant if there had been 100 members and now there are 200 members, whereas the increase would be much less significant if there had been 5 members and now there are 10. Remember that any numbers, percentages, or statistics in Argument tasks are used only as evidence in support of a conclusion, and you should always consider whether they actually support the conclusion.

The Form of Your Response

You are free to organize and develop your response in any way that you think will effectively communicate your evaluation of the argument. Your response may, but need not, incorporate particular writing strategies learned in English composition or writing-intensive college courses. GRE readers will not be looking for a particular developmental strategy or mode of writing. In fact, when GRE readers are trained, they review hundreds of Argument responses that, although highly diverse in content and form, display similar levels of critical thinking and analytical writing. Readers will see, for example, some essays at the 6 score level that begin by briefly summarizing the argument and then explicitly stating and developing the main points of the evaluation. The readers know that a writer can earn a high score by developing several points in an evaluation or by identifying a central feature in the argument and developing that evaluation extensively. You might want to look at the sample Argument responses, particularly at the 5 and 6 score levels, to see how other writers have successfully developed and organized their responses.

You should make choices about format and organization that you think support and enhance the overall effectiveness of your evaluation. This means using as many or as few paragraphs as you consider appropriate for your response — for example, creating a new paragraph when your discussion shifts to a new point of evaluation. You might want to organize your evaluation around the structure of the argument itself, discussing the argument line by line. Or you might want to first point out a central problem and then move on to discuss related weaknesses in the argument's line of reasoning. Similarly, you might want to use examples if they help illustrate an important point in your evaluation or move your discussion forward (remember, however, that, in terms of your ability to perform the Argument task effectively, it is your critical thinking and analytical writing, not your ability to come up with examples, that is being assessed). What matters is not the form the response takes, but how insightfully you evaluate the argument and how articulately you communicate your evaluation to academic readers within the context of the task.

Sample Argument Task

> In surveys Mason City residents rank water sports (swimming, boating, and fishing) among their favorite recreational activities. The Mason River flowing through the city is rarely used for these pursuits, however, and the city park department devotes little of its budget to maintaining riverside recreational facilities. For years there have been complaints from residents about the quality of the river's water and the river's smell. In response, the state has recently announced plans to clean up Mason River. Use of the river for water sports is, therefore, sure to increase. The city government should for that reason devote more money in this year's budget to riverside recreational facilities.
>
> Write a response in which you examine the stated and/or unstated assumptions of the argument. Be sure to explain how the argument depends on the assumptions and what the implications are if the assumptions prove unwarranted.

Strategies for This Topic

This argument cites a survey to support the prediction that the use of the Mason River is sure to increase and thus recommends that the city government should devote more money in this year's budget to the riverside recreational facilities.

In developing your evaluation, you are asked to examine the argument's stated and/or unstated assumptions and discuss what the implications are if the assumptions prove unwarranted. A successful response, then, must discuss both the argument's assumptions AND the implications of these assumptions for the argument. A response that does not address these aspects of the task will not receive a score of 4 or higher, regardless of the quality of its other features.

Though responses may well raise other points not mentioned here and need not mention all of these points, some assumptions of the argument, and some ways in which the argument depends on those assumptions, include:

- The assumption that people who rank water sports "among their favorite recreational activities" are actually likely to participate in them. (It is possible that they just like to watch them.) This assumption underlies the claim that use of the river for water sports is sure to increase after the state cleans up the Mason River and that the city should for that reason devote more money to riverside recreational facilities.

- The assumption that what residents say in surveys can be taken at face value. (It is possible that survey results exaggerate the interest in water sports.) This assumption underlies the claim that use of the river for water sports is sure to increase after the state cleans up the Mason River and that the city should for that reason devote more money to riverside recreational facilities.

- The assumption that Mason City residents would actually want to do water sports in the Mason River. (As recreational activities, it is possible that water sports are regarded as pursuits for vacations and weekends away from the city.) This assumption underlies the claim that use of the river for water sports is sure to increase after the state cleans up the Mason River and that the city should for that reason devote more money to riverside recreational facilities.

- The assumption that the park department devoting little of its budget to maintaining riverside recreational facilities means that these facilities are inadequately maintained. This assumption underlies the claim that the city should devote more money in this year's budget to riverside recreational facilities. If current facilities are adequately maintained, then increased funding might not be needed even if recreational use of the river does increase.

- The assumption that the riverside recreational facilities are facilities designed for people who participate in water sports and not some other recreational pursuit. This assumption underlies the claim that the city should devote more money in this year's budget to riverside recreational facilities.

- The assumption that the dirtiness of the river is the cause of its being little used and that cleaning up the river will be sufficient to increase recreational use of the river. (Residents might have complained about the water quality and smell even if they had no desire to boat, swim, or fish in the river.) This assumption underlies the claim that the state's plan to clean up the river will result in increased use of the river for water sports.

- The assumption that the complaints about the river are numerous and significant. This assumption motivates the state's plan to clean up the river and underlies the claim that use of the river for water sports is sure to increase. (Perhaps the complaints are coming from a very small minority; in which case cleaning the river might be a misuse of state funds.)

- The assumption that the state's clean up will occur soon enough to require adjustments to this year's budget. This assumption underlies the claim that the city should devote more money in this year's budget to riverside recreational facilities.

● The assumption that the clean up, when it happens, will benefit those parts of the river accessible from the city's facilities. This assumption underlies the claim that the city should devote more money to riverside recreational facilities

● The assumption that the city government ought to devote more attention to maintaining a recreational facility if demand for that facility increases.

● The assumption that the city should finance the new project and not some other agency or group (public or private).

Should any of the above assumptions prove unwarranted, the implications are:

● That the logic of the argument falls apart/ is invalid/ is unsound.

● That the state and city are spending their funds unnecessarily.

Essay Responses and Reader Commentary

Score 6 Response *

> While it may be true that the Mason City government ought to devote more money to riverside recreational facilities, this author's argument does not make a cogent case for increased resources based on river use. It is easy to understand why city residents would want a cleaner river, but this argument is rife with holes and assumptions, and thus, not strong enough to lead to increased funding.
>
> Citing surveys of city residents, the author reports city resident's love of water sports. It is not clear, however, the scope and validity of that survey. For example, the survey could have asked residents if they prefer using the river for water sports or would like to see a hydroelectric dam built, which may have swayed residents toward river sports. The sample may not have been representative of city residents, asking only those residents who live upon the river. The survey may have been 10 pages long, with 2 questions dedicated to river sports. We just do not know. Unless the survey is fully representative, valid, and reliable, it can not be used to effectively back the author's argument.
>
> Additionally, the author implies that residents do not use the river for swimming, boating, and fishing, despite their professed interest, because the water is polluted and smelly. While a polluted, smelly river would likely cut down on river sports, a concrete connection between the resident's lack of river use and the river's current state is not effectively made. Though there have been complaints, we do not know if there have been numerous complaints from a wide range of people, or perhaps from one or two individuals who made numerous complaints. To strengthen his/her argument, the author would benefit from implementing a normed survey asking a wide range of residents why they do not currently use the river.
>
> Building upon the implication that residents do not use the river due to the quality of the river's water and the smell, the author suggests that a river clean up will result in increased river usage. If the river's water quality and smell result from problems which can be cleaned, this may be true. For example, if the decreased water quality and

---

*All responses in this publication are reproduced exactly as written, including errors, misspellings, etc., if any.

aroma is caused by pollution by factories along the river, this conceivably could be remedied. But if the quality and aroma results from the natural mineral deposits in the water or surrounding rock, this may not be true. There are some bodies of water which emit a strong smell of sulphur due to the geography of the area. This is not something likely to be afffected by a clean-up. Consequently, a river clean up may have no impact upon river usage. Regardless of whether the river's quality is able to be improved or not, the author does not effectively show a connection between water quality and river usage.

A clean, beautiful, safe river often adds to a city's property values, leads to increased tourism and revenue from those who come to take advantage of the river, and a better overall quality of life for residents. For these reasons, city government may decide to invest in improving riverside recreational facilities. However, this author's argument is not likely significantly persuade the city goverment to allocate increased funding.

Reader Commentary

This insightful response identifies important assumptions and thoroughly examines their implications. The proposal to spend more on riverside recreational facilities rests on a number of questionable assumptions, namely that:

- The survey provides a reliable basis for budget planning;
- The river's pollution and odor are the only reasons for its limited recreational use;
- Efforts to clean the water and remove the odor will be successful.

By showing that each assumption is highly suspect, this essay demonstrates the weakness of the entire argument. For example, paragraph 2 points out that the survey might not have used a representative sample, might have offered limited choices, and might have contained very few questions on water sports. Paragraph 3 examines the tenuous connection between complaints and limited use of the river for recreation. Complaints about water quality and odor may be coming from only a few people, and even if such complaints are numerous, other completely different factors may be much more significant in reducing river usage. Finally, paragraph 4 explains that certain geologic features may prevent effective river clean up. Details such as these provide compelling support.

In addition, careful organization insures that each new point builds upon the previous ones. Note, for example, the clear transitions at the beginning of paragraphs 3 and 4, as well as the logical sequence of sentences within paragraphs (specifically paragraph 4).

Although this essay does contain minor errors, it still conveys ideas fluently. Note the effective word choices (e.g., "rife with…assumptions" and "may have swayed residents"). In addition, sentences are not merely varied; they also display skillful embedding of subordinate elements. Note, for example, the sustained parallelism in the first sentence of the concluding paragraph.

Since this response offers a cogent examination of the argument and also conveys meaning skillfully, it earns a score of 6.

Score 5 Response

The author of this proposal to increase the budget for Mason City riverside recreational facilities offers an interesting argument but to move forward on the proposal would definitely require more information and thought. While the correlations stated are logical and probable, there may be hidden factors that prevent the City from diverting resources to this project.

For example, consider the survey rankings among Mason City residents. The thought is that such high regard for water sports will translate into usage. But, survey responses can hardly be used as indicators of actual behavior. Many surveys conducted after the winter holidays reveal people who list exercise and weight loss as a top priority. Yet every profession does not equal a new gym membership. Even the wording of the survey results remain ambiguous and vague. While water sports may be among the residents' favorite activities, this allows for many other favorites. What remains unknown is the priorities of the general public. Do they favor these water sports above a softball field or soccer field? Are they willing to sacrifice the municipal golf course for better riverside facilities? Indeed the survey hardly provides enough information to discern future use of improved facilities.

Closely linked to the surveys is the bold assumption that a cleaner river will result in increased usage. While it is not illogical to expect some increase, at what level will people begin to use the river? The answer to this question requires a survey to find out the reasons our residents use or do not use the river. Is river water quality the primary limiting factor to usage or the lack of docks and piers? Are people more interested in water sports than the recreational activities that they are already engaged in? These questions will help the city government forecast how much river usage will increase and to assign a proportional increase to the budget.

Likewise, the author is optimistic regarding the state promise to clean the river. We need to hear the source of the voices and consider any ulterior motives. Is this a campaign year and the plans a campaign promise from the state representative? What is the timeline for the clean-up effort? Will the state fully fund this project? We can imagine the misuse of funds in renovating the riverside facilities only to watch the new buildings fall into dilapidation while the state drags the river clean-up.

Last, the author does not consider where these additional funds will be diverted from. The current budget situation must be assessed to determine if this increase can be afforded. In a sense, the City may not be willing to draw money away from other key projects from road improvements to schools and education. The author naively assumes that the money can simply appear without forethought on where it will come from.

Examining all the various angles and factors involved with improving riverside recreational facilities, the argument does not justify increasing the budget. While the proposal does highlight a possibility, more information is required to warrant any action.

Reader Commentary

Each paragraph in the body of this perceptive essay identifies and examines an unstated assumption that is crucial to the argument. The major assumptions discussed are:

- That a survey can accurately predict behavior,
- That cleaning the river will, in itself, increase recreational usage,
- That state plans to clean the river will actually be realized,
- That Mason City can afford to spend more on riverside recreational facilities.

Support within each paragraph is both thoughtful and thorough. Paragraph 2, for example, points out vagueness in the wording of the survey: Even if water sports rank among the favorite recreational activities of Mason City residents, other sports may still be much more popular. Thus, if the first assumption proves unwarranted, the argument to fund riverside facilities — rather than soccer fields or golf courses — becomes much weaker. Paragraph 4 considers several reasons why river clean up plans may not be successful (the plans may be nothing more than campaign promises, or funding may not be adequate). Thus, the weakness of the third assumption undermines the argument that river recreation will increase and riverside improvements will be needed at all.

Instead of dismissing each assumption in isolation, this response places them in a logical order and considers their connections. Note the appropriate transitions between and within paragraphs, clarifying the links among the assumptions (e.g., "Closely linked to the surveys..." or "The answer to this question requires...").

Along with strong development, this response also displays facility with language. Minor errors in punctuation are present, but word choices are apt and sentences suitably varied in pattern and length. The response uses a number of rhetorical questions, but the implied answers are always clear enough to support the points being made.

Thus, the response satisfies all requirements for a score of 5, but its development is not thorough or compelling enough for a 6.

Score 4 Response

The problem with the arguement is the assumption that if the Mason River were cleaned up, that people would use it for water sports and recreation. This is not necessarily true, as people may rank water sports among their favorite recreational activities, but that does not mean that those same people have the financial ability, time or equipment to pursue those interests.

However, even if the writer of the arguement is correct in assuming that the Mason River will be used more by the city's residents, the arguement does not say why the recreational facilities need more money. If recreational facilities already exist along the Mason River, why should the city allot more money to fund them? If the recreational facilities already in existence will be used more in the coming years, then they will be making more money for themselves, eliminating the need for the city government to devote more money to them.

According to the arguement, the reason people are not using the Mason River for water sports is because of the smell and the quality of water, not because the recreational facilities are unacceptable.

If the city government alloted more money to the recreational facilities, then the budget is being cut from some other important city project. Also, if the assumptions proved unwarranted, and more people did not use the river for recreation, then much money has been wasted, not only the money for the recreational facilities, but also the money that was used to clean up the river to attract more people in the first place.

Reader Commentary

This competent response identifies some important unstated assumptions:

- That cleaning up the Mason River will lead to increased recreational use,
- That existing facilities along the river need more funding.

Paragraph 1 offers reasons why the first assumption is questionable (e.g. residents may not have the necessary time or money for water sports). Similarly, paragraphs 2 and 3 explain that riverside recreational facilities may already be adequate and may, in fact, produce additional income if usage increases. Thus, the response is adequately developed and satisfactorily organized to show how the argument depends on questionable assumptions.

This essay does not, however, rise to a score of 5 because it fails to consider several other unstated assumptions (e.g. that the survey is reliable or that the efforts to clean the river will be successful). Furthermore, the final paragraph makes some extraneous, unsupported assertions of its own. Mason City may actually have a budget surplus so that cuts to other projects will not be necessary, and cleaning the river may provide other real benefits even if it is not used more for water sports.

This response is generally free of errors in grammar and usage and displays sufficient control of language to support a score of 4.

Score 3 Response

Surveys are created to speak for the people; however, surveys do not always speak for the whole community. A survey completed by Mason City residents concluded that the residents enjoy water sports as a form of recreation. If that is so evident, why has the river not been used? The blame can not be soley be placed on the city park department. The city park department can only do as much as they observe. The real issue is not the residents use of the river, but their desire for a more pleasant smell and a more pleasant sight. If the city government cleans the river, it might take years for the smell to go away. If the budget is changed to accomodate the clean up of the Mason River, other problems will arise. The residents will then begin to complain about other issues in their city that will be ignored because of the great emphasis being placed on Mason River. If more money is taken out of the budget to clean the river an assumption can be made. This assumption is that the budget for another part of city maintenance or building will be tapped into to. In addition, to the budget being used to clean up Mason River, it will also be allocated in increasing riverside recreational faciliites. The government is trying to appease its residents, and one can warrant that the role of the government is to please the people. There are many assumptions being made; however, the government can not make the assumption that people want the river to be cleaned so that they can use it for recreational water activities. The government has to realize the long term effects that their decision will have on the monetary value of their budget.

Reader Commentary

Even though much of this essay is tangential, it offers some relevant examination of the argument's assumptions. The early sentences mention a questionable assumption (that the survey results are reliable) but do not explain how the survey might have been flawed. Then the response drifts to irrelevant matters — a defense of the city park department, a prediction of budget problems, and the problem of pleasing city residents. Some statements even introduce unwarranted assumptions that are not part of the original argument (e.g., "The residents will then begin to complain about other issues," and "This assumption is that the budget for another part of city maintenance or building will be tapped into."). Near the end, the response does correctly note that city government should not assume that residents want to use the river for recreation. Hence, the proposal to increase funding for riverside recreational facilities may not be justified.

In summary, the language in this response is reasonably clear, but its examination of unstated assumptions remains limited, and therefore the essay earns a score of 3.

Score 2 Response

> This statement looks like logical, but there are some wrong sentences in it which is not logical.
>
> First, this statement mentions raking water sports as their favorite recreational activities at the first sentence. However, it seems to have a ralation between the first sentence and the setence which mentions that increase the quality of the river's water and the river's smell. This is a wrong cause and result to solve the problem.
>
> Second, as a reponse to the complaints from residents, the state plan to clean up the river. As a result, the state expects that water sports will increase. When you look at two sentences, the result is not appropriate for the cause.
>
> Third, the last statement is the conclusion. However, even though residents rank water sports, the city government might devote the budget to another issue. This statement is also a wrong cause and result.
>
> In summary, the statement is not logical because there are some errors in it. The supporting setences are not strong enough to support this issue.

Reader Commentary

Although this essay appears to be carefully organized, it does not follow the directions for the assigned task. In his/her vague references to causal fallacies, the writer attempts logical analysis but never refers explicitly or implicitly to any unusual assumptions. Furthermore, several errors in grammar and sentence structure interfere with meaning (e.g., "This statement looks like logical, but there are some wrong sentences in it which is not logical.").

Because this response "does not follow the directions for the assigned task" (see the Argument Scoring Guide, pages 39–40) and contains errors in sentence structure and logical development, it earns a score of 2.

Score 1 Response

> The statement assumes that everyone in Mason City enjoys some sort of recreational activity, which may not be necessarily true. They statement also assumes that if the state cleans up the river, the use of the river for water sports will definitely increase.

Reader Commentary

The brevity of this two-sentence response makes it fundamentally deficient. Sentence one states an assumption that is actually not present in the argument, and sentence two correctly states an assumption but provides no discussion of its implications. Although the response may begin to address the assigned task, it offers no development. As such, it clearly "provides little evidence of the ability to develop an organized response (i.e., is disorganized and/or extremely brief)" (see Argument Scoring Guide, pages 39–40) and should earn a score of 1.

GRE Scoring Guide: Analyze an Issue

Score 6

In addressing the specific task directions, a 6 response presents a cogent, well-articulated analysis of the issue and conveys meaning skillfully.

A typical response in this category
- articulates a clear and insightful position on the issue in accordance with the assigned task
- develops the position fully with compelling reasons and/or persuasive examples
- sustains a well-focused, well-organized analysis, connecting ideas logically
- conveys ideas fluently and precisely, using effective vocabulary and sentence variety
- demonstrates superior facility with the conventions of standard written English (i.e., grammar, usage, and mechanics) but may have minor errors

Score 5

In addressing the specific task directions, a 5 response presents a generally thoughtful, well-developed analysis of the issue and conveys meaning clearly.

A typical response in this category
- presents a clear and well-considered position on the issue in accordance with the assigned task
- develops the position with logically sound reasons and/or well-chosen examples
- is focused and generally well organized, connecting ideas appropriately
- conveys ideas clearly and well, using appropriate vocabulary and sentence variety
- demonstrates facility with the conventions of standard written English but may have minor errors

Score 4

In addressing the specific task directions, a 4 response presents a competent analysis of the issue and conveys meaning with acceptable clarity.

A typical response in this category
- presents a clear position on the issue in accordance with the assigned task
- develops the position with relevant reasons and/or examples
- is adequately focused and organized
- demonstrates sufficient control of language to express ideas with acceptable clarity
- generally demonstrates control of the conventions of standard written English but may have some errors

Score 3

A 3 response demonstrates some competence in addressing the specific task directions, in analyzing the issue, and in conveying meaning but is obviously flawed.

A typical response in this category exhibits ONE OR MORE of the following characteristics:

- is vague or limited in addressing the specific task directions and/or in presenting or developing a position on the issue
- is weak in the use of relevant reasons or examples or relies largely on unsupported claims
- is limited in focus and/or organization
- has problems in language and sentence structure that result in a lack of clarity
- contains occasional major errors or frequent minor errors in grammar, usage, or mechanics that can interfere with meaning

Score 2

A 2 response largely disregards the specific task directions and/or demonstrates serious weaknesses in analytical writing.

A typical response in this category exhibits ONE OR MORE of the following characteristics:

- is unclear or seriously limited in addressing the specific task directions and/or in presenting or developing a position on the issue
- provides few, if any, relevant reasons or examples in support of its claims
- is poorly focused and/or poorly organized
- has serious problems in language and sentence structure that frequently interfere with meaning
- contains serious errors in grammar, usage, or mechanics that frequently obscure meaning

Score 1

A 1 response demonstrates fundamental deficiencies in analytical writing.

A typical response in this category exhibits ONE OR MORE of the following characteristics:

- provides little or no evidence of understanding the issue
- provides little evidence of the ability to develop an organized response (e.g., is disorganized and/or extremely brief)
- has severe problems in language and sentence structure that persistently interfere with meaning
- contains pervasive errors in grammar, usage, or mechanics that result in incoherence

Score 0

Off topic (i.e., provides no evidence of an attempt to respond to the assigned topic), is in a foreign language, merely copies the topic, consists of only keystroke characters, or is illegible or nonverbal.

GRE Scoring Guide: Analyze an Argument

Score 6

In addressing the specific task directions, a 6 response presents a cogent, well-articulated examination of the argument and conveys meaning skillfully.

A typical response in this category
- clearly identifies aspects of the argument relevant to the assigned task and examines them insightfully
- develops ideas cogently, organizes them logically, and connects them with clear transitions
- provides compelling and thorough support for its main points
- conveys ideas fluently and precisely, using effective vocabulary and sentence variety
- demonstrates superior facility with the conventions of standard written English (i.e., grammar, usage, and mechanics) but may have minor errors

Score 5

In addressing the specific task directions, a 5 response presents a generally thoughtful, well-developed examination of the argument and conveys meaning clearly.

A typical response in this category
- clearly identifies aspects of the argument relevant to the assigned task and examines them in a generally perceptive way
- develops ideas clearly, organizes them logically, and connects them with appropriate transitions
- offers generally thoughtful and thorough support for its main points
- conveys ideas clearly and well, using appropriate vocabulary and sentence variety
- demonstrates facility with the conventions of standard written English but may have minor errors

Score 4

In addressing the specific task directions, a 4 response presents a competent examination of the argument and conveys meaning with acceptable clarity.

A typical response in this category
- identifies and examines aspects of the argument relevant to the assigned task but may also discuss some extraneous points
- develops and organizes ideas satisfactorily but may not connect them with transitions
- supports its main points adequately but may be uneven in its support
- demonstrates sufficient control of language to convey ideas with acceptable clarity
- generally demonstrates control of the conventions of standard written English but may have some errors

Score 3

A 3 response demonstrates some competence in addressing the specific task directions, in examining the argument, and in conveying meaning but is obviously flawed.

A typical response in this category exhibits ONE OR MORE of the following characteristics:

- does not identify or examine most of the aspects of the argument relevant to the assigned task, although some relevant examination of the argument is present
- mainly discusses tangential or irrelevant matters, or reasons poorly
- is limited in the logical development and organization of ideas

- offers support of little relevance and value for its main points
- has problems in language and sentence structure that result in a lack of clarity
- contains occasional major errors or frequent minor errors in grammar, usage, or mechanics that can interfere with meaning

Score 2

A 2 response largely disregards the specific task directions and/or demonstrates serious weaknesses in analytical writing.

A typical response in this category exhibits ONE OR MORE of the following characteristics:

- does not present an examination based on logical analysis, but may instead present the writer's own views on the subject
- does not follow the directions for the assigned task
- does not develop ideas, or is poorly organized and illogical
- provides little, if any, relevant or reasonable support for its main points
- has serious problems in language and sentence structure that frequently interfere with meaning
- contains serious errors in grammar, usage, or mechanics that frequently obscure meaning

Score 1

A 1 response demonstrates fundamental deficiencies in analytical writing.

A typical response in this category exhibits ONE OR MORE of the following characteristics:

- provides little or no evidence of understanding the argument
- provides little evidence of the ability to develop an organized response (e.g., is disorganized and/or extremely brief)
- has severe problems in language and sentence structure that persistently interfere with meaning
- contains pervasive errors in grammar, usage, or mechanics that result in incoherence

Score 0

Off topic (i.e., provides no evidence of an attempt to respond to the assigned topic), is in a foreign language, merely copies the topic, consists of only keystroke characters, or is illegible, or nonverbal.

Score Level Descriptions

Although the GRE Analytical Writing measure contains two discrete analytical writing tasks, a single combined score is reported because it is more reliable than is a score for either task alone. The reported score, the average of the scores for the two tasks, ranges from 0 to 6, in half-point increments.

The statements below describe, for each score level, the overall quality of critical thinking and analytical writing demonstrated across both the Issue and Argument tasks. The Analytical Writing section is designed to assess both critical thinking skills and writing ability. Thus, many aspects of analytical writing, including reasoning skills, organization, and degree of control of the conventions of standard written English are taken into consideration in the determination of a final score. For a full description of how these criteria are used to assess essay responses, please refer to the scoring guides for the Issue and Argument tasks, which are available on the GRE website at **www.ets.org/gre/revised/scoreguides**.

Scores 6 and 5.5: Sustains insightful, in-depth analysis of complex ideas; develops and supports main points with logically compelling reasons and/or highly persuasive examples; is well focused and well organized; skillfully uses sentence variety and precise vocabulary to convey meaning effectively; demonstrates superior facility with sentence structure and language usage but may have minor errors that do not interfere with meaning.

Scores 5 and 4.5: Provides generally thoughtful analysis of complex ideas; develops and supports main points with logically sound reasons and/or well-chosen examples; is generally focused and well organized; uses sentence variety and vocabulary to convey meaning clearly; demonstrates good control of sentence structure and language usage but may have minor errors that do not interfere with meaning.

Scores 4 and 3.5: Provides competent analysis of ideas; develops and supports main points with relevant reasons and/or examples; is adequately organized; conveys meaning with reasonable clarity; demonstrates satisfactory control of sentence structure and language usage but may have some errors that affect clarity.

Scores 3 and 2.5: Displays some competence in analytical writing, although the writing is flawed in at least one of the following ways: limited analysis or development; weak organization; weak control of sentence structure or language usage, with errors that often result in vagueness or lack of clarity.

Scores 2 and 1.5: Displays serious weaknesses in analytical writing. The writing is seriously flawed in at least one of the following ways: serious lack of analysis or development; lack of organization; serious and frequent problems in sentence structure or language usage, with errors that obscure meaning.

Scores 1 and 0.5: Displays fundamental deficiencies in analytical writing. The writing is fundamentally flawed in at least one of the following ways: content that is extremely confusing or mostly irrelevant to the assigned tasks; little or no development; severe and pervasive errors that result in incoherence.

Score 0: The examinee's analytical writing skills cannot be evaluated because the responses do not address any part of the assigned tasks, are merely attempts to copy the assignments, are in a foreign language, or display only indecipherable text.

Score NS: The examinee produced no text whatsoever.

GRE®
Verbal Reasoning

Your goals for this chapter	❧ Learn the three types of GRE Verbal Reasoning questions ❧ Get tips for answering each question type ❧ Study examples of GRE Verbal Reasoning questions

Overview of the Verbal Reasoning Measure

The Verbal Reasoning measure assesses your ability to analyze and evaluate written material and synthesize information obtained from it, to analyze relationships among component parts of sentences, and to recognize relationships among words and concepts.

Verbal Reasoning questions appear in several formats, each of which is discussed in detail below. About half of the measure requires you to read passages and answer questions on those passages. The other half requires you to read, interpret, and complete existing sentences, groups of sentences, or paragraphs. Many, but not all, of the questions are standard multiple-choice questions, in which you are required to select a single correct answer; others ask you to select multiple correct answers, and still others ask you to select a sentence from the passage. The number of choices varies depending on the type of question.

Verbal Reasoning Question Types

The Verbal Reasoning measure contains three types of questions:

● Reading Comprehension
● Text Completion
● Sentence Equivalence

In this section you will study each of these question types one by one, and you'll learn valuable strategies for answering each type. Turn the page to begin.

Reading Comprehension Questions

Reading Comprehension questions are designed to test a wide range of abilities required to read and understand the kinds of prose commonly encountered in graduate school. Those abilities include

- understanding the meaning of individual words
- understanding the meaning of individual sentences
- understanding the meaning of paragraphs and larger bodies of text
- distinguishing between minor and major points
- summarizing a passage
- drawing conclusions from the information provided
- reasoning from incomplete data, inferring missing information
- understanding the structure of a text, how the parts relate to one another
- identifying the author's perspective
- identifying the author's assumptions
- analyzing a text and reaching conclusions about it
- identifying strengths and weaknesses
- developing and considering alternative explanations

As this list implies, reading and understanding a piece of text requires far more than a passive understanding of the words and sentences it contains—it requires active engagement with the text, asking questions, formulating and evaluating hypotheses, and reflecting on the relationship of the particular text to other texts and information.

Each Reading Comprehension question is based on a passage, which may range in length from one paragraph to several paragraphs. The test contains approximately ten passages; the majority of the passages in the test are one paragraph in length, and only one or two are several paragraphs long. Passages are drawn from the physical sciences, the biological sciences, the social sciences, the arts and humanities, and everyday topics, and are based on material found in books and periodicals, both academic and nonacademic.

Typically, about half of the questions on the test will be based on passages, and the number of questions based on a given passage can range from one to six. Questions can cover any of the topics listed above, from the meaning of a particular word to assessing evidence that might support or weaken points made in the passage. Many, but not all, of the questions are standard multiple-choice questions, in which you are required to select a single correct answer; others ask you to select multiple correct answers, and still others ask you to select a sentence from the passage. These question types are presented in more detail below, and you should make sure that you are familiar with the differences between them.

General Advice

Reading passages are drawn from many different disciplines and sources, so you may encounter material with which you are not familiar. Do not be discouraged when this happens; all the questions can be answered on the basis of the information provided in the passage, and you are not expected to rely on any outside knowledge. If, however, you encounter a passage that seems particularly hard or unfamiliar, you may want to save it for last.

- Read and analyze the passage carefully before trying to answer any of the questions and pay attention to clues that help you understand less explicit aspects of the passage.

  - Try to distinguish main ideas from supporting ideas or evidence.
  - Try to distinguish ideas that the author is advancing from those he or she is merely reporting.
  - Similarly, try to distinguish ideas that the author is strongly committed to from those he or she advances as hypothetical or speculative.
  - Try to identify the main transitions from one idea to the next.
  - Try to identify the relationship between different ideas. For example:

    —Are they contrasting? Are they consistent?
    —Does one support the other?
    —Does one spell another out in greater detail?
    —Is one an application of another to a particular circumstance?

- Read each question carefully and be certain that you understand exactly what is being asked.

- Answer each question on the basis of the information provided in the passage and do not rely on outside knowledge. Sometimes your own views or opinions may conflict with those presented in a passage; if this happens, take special care to work within the context provided by the passage. You should not expect to agree with everything you encounter in the reading passages.

Reading Comprehension Multiple-Choice Questions: Select One Answer Choice

Description

These are the traditional multiple-choice questions with five answer choices of which you must select one.

> ### Tips for Answering
>
> - **Read *all* the answer choices before making your selection,** even if you think you know what the answer is in advance.
> - **Don't be misled by answer choices that are only partially true or only partially answer the question.** The correct answer is the one that most accurately and most completely answers the question posed. Be careful also not to pick an answer choice simply because it is a true statement.
> - **Pay attention to context.** When the question asks about the meaning of a word in the passage, be sure that the answer choice you select correctly represents the way the word is being used in the passage. Many words have quite different meanings in different contexts.

Reading Comprehension Multiple-Choice Questions: Select One or More Answer Choices

Description

These provide three answer choices and ask you to select all that are correct; one, two, or all three of the answer choices may be correct. To gain credit for these questions, you must select all the correct answers, and only those; there is no credit for partially correct answers. These questions are marked with square boxes beside the answer choices, not circles or ovals.

Tips for Answering

- **Evaluate each answer choice separately on its own merits.** When evaluating one answer choice, do not take the others into account.
- **Make sure the answer choice you pick accurately and completely answers the question posed.** Be careful not to be misled by answer choices that are only partially true or only partially answer the question. Be careful also not to pick an answer choice simply because it is a true statement.
- **Do not be disturbed if you think all three answer choices are correct.** Questions of this type can have three correct answer choices.

Reading Comprehension Questions: Select-in-Passage

Description

The question asks you to click on the sentence in the passage that meets a certain description. To answer the question, choose one of the sentences and click on it; clicking anywhere on a sentence will highlight it. In longer passages, the question will usually apply to only one or two specified paragraphs, marked by an arrow (➡); clicking on a sentence elsewhere in the passage will not highlight it.

Note. Because this type of question requires the use of the computer, it does not appear in the paper-based General Test. Similar multiple-choice questions are used in its place.

Tips for Answering

- **Be careful to evaluate each of the relevant sentences in the passage separately before selecting your answer.** Do not evaluate any sentences that are outside the paragraphs under consideration.
- **Do not select a sentence if the description given in the question only partially applies.** A correct answer choice must accurately match the description in the question. Note, however, that the description need not be complete, that is, there may be aspects of the sentence that are not fully described in the question.

Sample Question Set

Reviving the practice of using elements of popular music in classical composition, an approach that had been in hibernation in the United States during the 1960s, composer Philip Glass (born 1937) embraced the ethos of popular music without imitating it. Glass based two symphonies on music by rock musicians David Bowie and Brian Eno, but the symphonies' sound is distinctively his. Popular elements do not appear out of place in Glass's classical music, which from its early days has shared certain harmonies and rhythms with rock music. Yet this use of popular elements has not made Glass a composer of popular music. His music is not a version of popular music packaged to attract classical listeners; it is high art for listeners steeped in rock rather than the classics.

line
5

10

Select only one answer choice.

1. The passage addresses which of the following issues related to Glass's use of popular elements in his classical compositions?

    Ⓐ How it is regarded by listeners who prefer rock to the classics

    Ⓑ How it has affected the commercial success of Glass's music

    Ⓒ Whether it has contributed to a revival of interest among other composers in using popular elements in their compositions

    Ⓓ Whether it has had a detrimental effect on Glass's reputation as a composer of classical music

    Ⓔ Whether it has caused certain of Glass's works to be derivative in quality

Consider each of the three choices separately and select all that apply.

2. The passage suggests that Glass's work displays which of the following qualities?

    A⃞ A return to the use of popular music in classical compositions

    B⃞ An attempt to elevate rock music to an artistic status more closely approximating that of classical music

    C⃞ A long-standing tendency to incorporate elements from two apparently disparate musical styles

3. Select the sentence that distinguishes two ways of integrating rock and classical music.

Explanation

The passage describes in general terms how Philip Glass uses popular music in his classical compositions and explores how Glass can do this without being imitative. Note that there are no opposing views discussed; the author is simply presenting his or her views.

Question 1: One of the important points that the passage makes is that when Glass uses popular elements in his music, the result is very much his own creation (it is "distinctively his"). In other words, the music is far from being derivative. Thus one issue that the passage addresses is the one referred to in answer **Choice E**—it answers it in the negative. The passage does not discuss the impact of Glass's use of popular elements on listeners, on the commercial success of his music, on other composers, nor on Glass's reputation, so none of Choices A through D is correct.

The correct answer is **Choice E.**

Question 2: To answer this question, it is important to assess each answer choice independently. Since the passage says that Glass revived the use of popular music in classical compositions, answer **Choice A** is clearly correct. On the other hand, the passage also denies that Glass composes popular music or packages it in a way to elevate its status, so answer Choice B is incorrect. Finally, since Glass's style has always mixed elements of rock with classical elements, **Choice C** is correct.

Thus the correct answer is **Choice A** and **Choice C.**

Question 3: Almost every sentence in the passage refers to incorporating rock music in classical compositions, but only the last sentence distinguishes two ways of doing so. It distinguishes between writing rock music in a way that will make it attractive to classical listeners and writing classical music that will be attractive to listeners familiar with rock.

Thus the correct answer is **the last sentence of the passage.**

Text Completion Questions

Description

As mentioned above, skilled readers do not simply absorb the information presented on the page; instead, they maintain a constant attitude of interpretation and evaluation, reasoning from what they have read so far to create a picture of the whole and revising that picture as they go. Text Completion questions test this ability by omitting crucial words from short passages and asking the test taker to use the remaining information in the passage as a basis for selecting words or short phrases to fill the blanks and create a coherent, meaningful whole.

Question Structure

- Passage composed of one to five sentences

- One to three blanks

- Three answer choices per blank (five answer choices in the case of a single blank)

- The answer choices for different blanks function independently; that is, selecting one answer choice for one blank does not affect what answer choices you can select for another blank

- Single correct answer, consisting of one choice for each blank; no credit for partially correct answers

Tips for Answering

Do not merely try to consider each possible combination of answers; doing so will take too long and is open to error. Instead, try to analyze the passage in the following way:

- **Read through the passage to get an overall sense of it.**
- **Identify words or phrases that seem particularly significant,** either because they emphasize the structure of the passage (words like *although* or *moreover*) or because they are central to understanding what the passage is about.
- **Think up your own words for the blanks.** Try to fill in the blanks with words or phrases that seem to you to fit and then see if similar words are offered among the answer choices.
- **Do not assume that the first blank is the one that should be filled first.** Perhaps one of the other blanks is easier to fill first. Select your choice for that blank, and then see whether you can complete another blank. If none of the choices for the other blank seem to make sense, go back and reconsider your first selection.
- **Double check your answers.** When you have made your selection for each blank, check to make sure that the passage is logically, grammatically, and stylistically coherent.

Sample Questions

> **For each blank select one entry from the corresponding column of choices. Fill all blanks in the way that best completes the text.**

1. It is refreshing to read a book about our planet by an author who does not allow facts to be (i)_____ by politics: well aware of the political disputes about the effects of human activities on climate and biodiversity, this author does not permit them to (ii)_____ his comprehensive description of what we know about our biosphere. He emphasizes the enormous gaps in our knowledge, the sparseness of our observations, and the (iii)_____, calling attention to the many aspects of planetary evolution that must be better understood before we can accurately diagnose the condition of our planet.

Blank (i)	Blank (ii)	Blank (iii)
(A) overshadowed	(D) enhance	(G) plausibility of our hypotheses
(B) invalidated	(E) obscure	(H) certainty of our entitlement
(C) illuminated	(F) underscore	(I) superficiality of our theories

Explanation

The overall tone of the passage is clearly complimentary. To understand what the author of the book is being complimented on, it is useful to focus on the second blank.

Here, we must determine what word would indicate something that the author is praised for not permitting. The only answer choice that fits the case is "obscure," since enhancing and underscoring are generally good things to do, not things one should refrain from doing. Choosing "obscure" clarifies the choice for the first blank; the only choice that fits well with "obscure" is "overshadowed." Notice that trying to fill blank (i) without filling blank (ii) first is very hard—each choice has at least some initial plausibility. Since the third blank requires a phrase that matches "enormous gaps" and "sparseness of our observations," the best choice is "superficiality of our theories."

Thus the correct answer is **overshadowed** (Choice A), **obscure** (Choice E), and **superficiality of our theories** (Choice I).

2. Vain and prone to violence, Caravaggio could not handle success: the more his (i)_____ as an artist increased, the more (ii)_____ his life became.

Blank (i)	Blank (ii)
Ⓐ temperance	Ⓓ tumultuous
Ⓑ notoriety	Ⓔ providential
Ⓒ eminence	Ⓕ dispassionate

Explanation

In this sentence, what follows the colon must explain or spell out what precedes it. So roughly what the second part must say is that as Caravaggio became more successful, his life got more out of control. When one looks for words to fill the blanks, it becomes clear that "tumultuous" is the best fit for blank (ii), since neither of the other choices suggests being out of control. And for blank (i), the best choice is "eminence," since to increase in eminence is a consequence of becoming more successful. It is true that Caravaggio might also increase in notoriety, but an increase in notoriety as an artist is not as clear a sign of success as an increase in eminence.

Thus the correct answer is **eminence** (Choice C) and **tumultuous** (Choice D).

3. In parts of the Arctic, the land grades into the landfast ice so _____ that you can walk off the coast and not know you are over the hidden sea.

Ⓐ permanently
Ⓑ imperceptibly
Ⓒ irregularly
Ⓓ precariously
Ⓔ relentlessly

Explanation

The word that fills the blank has to characterize how the land grades into the ice in a way that explains how you can walk off the coast and over the sea without knowing it. The word that does that is "imperceptibly"; if the land grades imperceptibly into the ice, you might well not know that you had left the land. Describing the shift from land to ice as permanent, irregular, precarious, or relentless would not help to explain how you would fail to know.

Thus the correct answer is **imperceptibly** (Choice B).

Sentence Equivalence Questions

Description

Like Text Completion questions, Sentence Equivalence questions test the ability to reach a conclusion about how a passage should be completed on the basis of partial information, but to a greater extent they focus on the meaning of the completed whole. Sentence Equivalence questions consist of a single sentence with just one blank, and they ask you to find two choices that both lead to a complete, coherent sentence and that produce sentences that mean the same thing.

Question Structure

- Consists of:
  - a single sentence
  - one blank
  - six answer choices

- Requires you to select two of the answer choices; no credit for partially correct answers.

These questions are marked with square boxes beside the answer choices, not circles or ovals.

Tips for Answering

Do not simply look among the answer choices for two words that mean the same thing. This can be misleading for two reasons. First, the answer choices may contain pairs of words that mean the same thing but do not fit coherently into the sentence, and thus do not constitute a correct answer. Second, the pair of words that do constitute the correct answer may not mean exactly the same thing, since all that matters is that the resultant sentences mean the same thing.

- **Read the sentence to get an overall sense of it.**
- **Identify words or phrases that seem particularly significant,** either because they emphasize the structure of the sentence (words like *although* or *moreover*) or because they are central to understanding what the sentence is about.
- **Think up your own words for the blanks.** Try to fill in the blank with a word that seems to you to fit and then see if two similar words are offered among the answer choices. If you find some word that is similar to what you are expecting but cannot find a second one, do not become fixated on your interpretation; instead, see whether there are other words among the answer choices that can be used to fill the blank coherently.
- **Double check your answers.** When you have selected your pair of answer choices for the blank, check to make sure that each one produces a sentence that is logically, grammatically, and stylistically coherent, and that the two sentences mean the same thing.

Sample Questions

> Select the two answer choices that, when used to complete the sentence, fit the meaning of the sentence as a whole and produce completed sentences that are alike in meaning.

1. Although it does contain some pioneering ideas, one would hardly characterize the work as _____.

   [A] orthodox
   [B] eccentric
   [C] original
   [D] trifling
   [E] conventional
   [F] innovative

Explanation

The word "Although" is a crucial signpost here. The work contains some pioneering ideas, but apparently it is not overall a pioneering work. Thus the two words that could fill the blank appropriately are "original" and "innovative." Note that "orthodox" and "conventional" are two words that are very similar in meaning, but neither one completes the sentence sensibly.

Thus the correct answer is **original** (Choice C) and **innovative** (Choice F).

2. It was her view that the country's problems had been _____ by foreign technocrats, so that to ask for such assistance again would be counterproductive.

   [A] ameliorated
   [B] ascertained
   [C] diagnosed
   [D] exacerbated
   [E] overlooked
   [F] worsened

Explanation

The sentence relates a piece of reasoning, as indicated by the presence of "so that": asking for the assistance of foreign technocrats would be counterproductive because of the effects such technocrats have had already. This means that the technocrats must have bad effects; that is, they must have "exacerbated" or "worsened" the country's problems.

Thus the correct answer is **exacerbated** (Choice D) and **worsened** (Choice F).

4 GRE® Verbal Reasoning Practice Questions

Your goals for this chapter

- ➤ Practice answering GRE Verbal Reasoning questions on your own
- ➤ Study answer explanations, particularly for questions you answered incorrectly

This chapter contains six sets of GRE Verbal Reasoning practice questions. Three of the practice sets consist of examples of the discrete question types, Text Completion and Sentence Equivalence; and the other three sets consist of Reading Comprehension questions. The sets are arranged in order of increasing difficulty. The first two are easy, the next two are medium, and the final two are hard.

Following the last set are Answer Keys for quick reference. Then, at the end of the chapter, you will find complete explanations for every question. Each explanation is presented with the corresponding question, so that you can easily see what was asked and what the various answer choices were.

Sharpen your GRE Verbal Reasoning skills by working your way through these question sets. Begin with the easy sets and then move on to the medium-difficulty and hard sets. Review the answer explanations carefully, paying particular attention to the explanations for questions that you answered incorrectly. Turn the page to begin.

SET 1. Discrete Questions: Easy

> For Questions 1 to 5, select one entry for each blank from the corresponding column of choices. Fill all blanks in the way that best completes the text.

1. Dominant interests often benefit most from _____ of governmental interference in business, since they are able to take care of themselves if left alone.

(A) intensification
(B) authorization
(C) centralization
(D) improvisation
(E) elimination

2. Kagan maintains that an infant's reactions to its first stressful experiences are part of a natural process of development, not harbingers of childhood unhappiness or _____ signs of adolescent anxiety.

(A) prophetic
(B) normal
(C) monotonous
(D) virtual
(E) typical

3. An investigation that is _____ can occasionally yield new facts, even notable ones, but typically the appearance of such facts is the result of a search in a definite direction.

(A) timely
(B) unguided
(C) consistent
(D) uncomplicated
(E) subjective

4. It is (i)_____ that so many portrait paintings hang in art museums, since the subject matter seems to dictate a status closer to pictures in the family photograph album than to high art. But perhaps it is the artistic skill with which the portraits are painted that (ii)_____ their presence in art museums.

Blank (i)	Blank (ii)
(A) surprising	(D) challenges
(B) understandable	(E) justifies
(C) irrelevant	(F) changes

5. In stark contrast to his later (i)_____, Simpson was largely (ii)_____ politics during his college years, despite the fact that the campus he attended was rife with political activity.

Blank (i)	Blank (ii)
(A) activism	(D) devoted to
(B) apathy	(E) indifferent to
(C) affability	(F) shaped by

For Questions 6 to 8, select the two answer choices that, when used to complete the sentence, fit the meaning of the sentence as a whole and produce completed sentences that are alike in meaning.

---

6. As my eyesight began to _____, I spent a lot of time writing about it — both poems and "eye journals" — describing what I saw as I looked out through damaged eyes.

    A deteriorate
    B sharpen
    C improve
    D decline
    E recover
    F adjust

7. The judge's standing in the legal community, though shaken by phony allegations of wrongdoing, emerged, at long last, _____ .

    A unqualified
    B undiminished
    C undecided
    D undamaged
    E unresolved
    F unprincipled

8. Modern agricultural practices have been extremely successful in increasing the productivity of major food crops, yet despite heavy use of pesticides, _____ losses to diseases and insect pests are sustained each year.

    A incongruous
    B reasonable
    C significant
    D considerable
    E equitable
    F fortuitous

SET 2. Reading Comprehension Questions: Easy

For each of Questions 1 to 9, select <u>one</u> answer choice unless otherwise instructed.

---

1. A person who agrees to serve as mediator between two warring factions at the request of both abandons by so agreeing the right to take sides later. To take sides at a later point would be to suggest that the earlier presumptive impartiality was a sham.

    The passage above emphasizes which of the following points about mediators?

    (A) They should try to form no opinions of their own about any issue that is related to the dispute.

    (B) They should not agree to serve unless they are committed to maintaining a stance of impartiality.

    (C) They should not agree to serve unless they are equally acceptable to all parties to a dispute.

    (D) They should feel free to take sides in the dispute right from the start, provided that they make their biases publicly known.

    (E) They should reserve the right to abandon their impartiality so as not to be open to the charge of having been deceitful.

Was Felix Mendelssohn (1809–1847) a great composer? On its face, the question seems absurd. One of the most gifted prodigies in the history of music, he produced his first masterpiece at sixteen. From then on, he was recognized as an artist of preternatural abilities, not only as a composer but also as a pianist and conductor. But Mendelssohn's enduring popularity has often been at odds — sometimes quite sharply — with his critical standing. Despite general acknowledgment of his genius, there has been a noticeable reluctance to rank him with, say, Schumann or Brahms. As Haggin put it, Mendelssohn, as a composer, was a "minor master . . . working on a small scale of emotion and texture."

2. Select a sentence in the passage whose function is to indicate the range of Mendelssohn's musical talents.

3. The passage suggests that anyone attempting to evaluate Mendelssohn's career must confront which of the following dichotomies?
    (A) The tension between Mendelssohn's career as a composer and his career as a pianist and conductor
    (B) The contrast between Mendelssohn's popularity and that of Schumann and Brahms
    (C) The discrepancy between Mendelssohn's popularity and his standing among critics
    (D) The inconsistency between Mendelssohn's reputation during his lifetime and his reputation since his death
    (E) The gap between Mendelssohn's prodigious musical beginnings and his decline in later years

4. It can be inferred that the "reluctance" mentioned in the passage is being ascribed to
    (A) most composers since Mendelssohn
    (B) Schumann and Brahms
    (C) the music-listening public
    (D) music critics generally
    (E) Haggin exclusively

5. The author mentions Schumann and Brahms primarily in order to
    (A) provide examples of composers who are often compared with Mendelssohn
    (B) identify certain composers who are more popular than Mendelssohn
    (C) identify composers whom Mendelssohn influenced
    (D) establish the milieu in which Mendelssohn worked
    (E) establish a standard of comparison for Mendelssohn as a composer

While most scholarship on women's employment in the United States recognizes that the Second World War (1939–1945) dramatically changed the role of women in the workforce, these studies also acknowledge that few women remained in manufacturing jobs once men returned from the war. But in agriculture, unlike other industries where women were viewed as temporary workers, women's employment did not end with the war. Instead, the expansion of agriculture and a steady decrease in the number of male farmworkers combined to cause the industry to hire more women in the postwar years. Consequently, the 1950s saw a growing number of women engaged in farm labor, even though rhetoric in the popular media called for the return of women to domestic life.

6. It can be inferred from the passage that the manufacturing and agricultural sectors in the United States following the Second World War differed in which of the following respects?

Ⓐ The rate of expansion in each sector

Ⓑ The percentage of employees in each sector who were men

Ⓒ The trend in the wages of men employed in each sector

Ⓓ The attitude of the popular media toward the employment of women in each sector

Ⓔ The extent to which women in each sector were satisfied with their jobs

7. Which of the following statements about women's employment in the United States during and after the Second World War is most clearly supported by the passage?

Ⓐ Most women who joined the workforce during the Second World War wanted to return to domestic life when the war ended.

Ⓑ The great majority of women who joined the workforce during the Second World War were employed in manufacturing jobs.

Ⓒ The end of the Second World War was followed by a large-scale transfer of women workers from manufacturing to agriculture.

Ⓓ The increase in women's employment that accompanied the Second World War was longer lasting in agriculture than it was in manufacturing.

Ⓔ The popular media were more forceful in calling for women to join the workforce during the Second World War than in calling for women to return to domestic life after the war.

Since the Hawaiian Islands have never been connected to other land masses, the great variety of plants in Hawaii must be a result of the long-distance dispersal of seeds, a process that requires both a method of transport and an equivalence between the ecology of the source area and that of the recipient area.

line

5   There is some dispute about the method of transport involved. Some biologists argue that ocean and air currents are responsible for the transport of plant seeds to Hawaii. Yet the results of flotation experiments and the low temperatures of air currents cast doubt on these hypotheses. More probable is bird transport, either externally, by accidental attachment of the seeds to feathers, or internally, by the swallowing of

10 fruit and subsequent excretion of the seeds. While it is likely that fewer varieties of plant seeds have reached Hawaii externally than internally, more varieties are known to be adapted to external than to internal transport.

8.   The author of the passage is primarily concerned with

   (A) discussing different approaches biologists have taken to testing theories about the distribution of plants in Hawaii

   (B) discussing different theories about the transport of plant seeds to Hawaii

   (C) discussing the extent to which air currents are responsible for the dispersal of plant seeds to Hawaii

   (D) resolving a dispute about the adaptability of plant seeds to bird transport

   (E) resolving a dispute about the ability of birds to carry plant seeds long distances

9.   The author mentions the results of flotation experiments on plant seeds (lines 7–8) most probably in order to

   (A) support the claim that the distribution of plants in Hawaii is the result of the long-distance dispersal of seeds

   (B) lend credibility to the thesis that air currents provide a method of transport for plant seeds to Hawaii

   (C) suggest that the long-distance dispersal of seeds is a process that requires long periods of time

   (D) challenge the claim that ocean currents are responsible for the transport of plant seeds to Hawaii

   (E) refute the claim that Hawaiian flora evolved independently from flora in other parts of the world

SET 3. Discrete Questions: Medium

> For Questions 1 to 5, select one entry for each blank from the corresponding column of choices. Fill all blanks in the way that best completes the text.

1. It comes as no surprise that societies have codes of behavior; the character of the codes, on the other hand, can often be _____ .

Ⓐ	predictable
Ⓑ	unexpected
Ⓒ	admirable
Ⓓ	explicit
Ⓔ	confusing

2. Like Béla Bartók, Ruth Crawford not only brought a composer's acumen to the notation of folk music, she also had a marked (i)_____ the task. This was clear in her agonizing over how far to try to represent the minute details of a performance in a written text, and this (ii)_____ makes her work a landmark in ethnomusicology.

Blank (i)		Blank (ii)	
Ⓐ	reverence for	Ⓓ	fastidiousness
Ⓑ	detachment from	Ⓔ	didacticism
Ⓒ	curiosity about	Ⓕ	iconoclasm

3. Political advertising may well be the most (i)_____ kind of advertising: political candidates are usually quite (ii)_____, yet their campaign advertisements often hide important differences behind smoke screens of smiles and empty slogans.

Blank (i)		Blank (ii)	
Ⓐ	polemical	Ⓓ	interchangeable
Ⓑ	effective	Ⓔ	dissimilar
Ⓒ	deceptive	Ⓕ	vocal

4. Richard M. Russell said 52 percent of the nation's growth since the Second World War had (i)_____ invention. He said, (ii)_____ research, the government's greatest role in assuring continuing innovation is promoting a strong, modern patent office. "Unless we can (iii)_____ original ideas, we will not have invention," Mr. Russell said. Speculating on the state of innovation over the next century, several inventors agreed that the future lay in giving children the tools to think creatively and the motivation to invent.

Blank (i)	Blank (ii)	Blank (iii)
(A) been at the expense of	(D) in addition to restricting	(G) evaluate
(B) no bearing on	(E) aside from supporting	(H) protect
(C) come through	(F) far from exaggerating	(I) disseminate

5. Statements presented as fact in a patent application are (i)_____ unless a good reason for doubt is found. The invention has only to be deemed "more likely than not" to work in order to receive initial approval. And, although thousands of patents are challenged in court for other reasons, no incentive exists for anyone to expend effort (ii)_____ the science of an erroneous patent. For this reason the endless stream of (iii)_____ devices will continue to yield occasional patents.

Blank (i)	Blank (ii)	Blank (iii)
(A) presumed verifiable	(D) corroborating	(G) novel
(B) carefully scrutinized	(E) advancing	(H) bogus
(C) considered capricious	(F) debunking	(I) obsolete

> **For Questions 6 to 8, select the <u>two</u> answer choices that, when used to complete the sentence, fit the meaning of the sentence as a whole <u>and</u> produce completed sentences that are alike in meaning.**

6. Ever a demanding reader of the fiction of others, the novelist Chase was likewise often the object of _____ analyses by his contemporaries.

   A   exacting
   B   copious
   C   respectful
   D   acerbic
   E   scathing
   F   meticulous

7. Her _____ should not be confused with miserliness; as long as I have known her, she has always been willing to assist those who are in need.

   A   stinginess
   B   diffidence
   C   frugality
   D   illiberality
   E   intolerance
   F   thrift

8. A misconception frequently held by novice writers is that sentence structure mirrors thought: the more convoluted the structure, the more _____ the ideas.

   A   complicated
   B   engaged
   C   essential
   D   fanciful
   E   inconsequential
   F   involved

SET 4. Reading Comprehension Questions: Medium

For each of Questions 1 to 9, select **one** answer choice unless otherwise instructed.

Questions 1 and 2 are based on the following reading passage.

I enjoyed *A Dream of Light & Shadow: Portraits of Latin American Women Writers* for the same reasons that, as a child, I avidly consumed women's biographies: the fascination with how the biographical details of another female's life are represented and interpreted.

line
5   *A Dream* offers a rich read, varied in both the lives and texts of the women portrayed, and the perspectives and styles of the sixteen essayists. Yet, as an adult, I have come to demand of any really "great" book a self-consciousness about the tenuous nature of representations of reality, a critical contextualization of florid detail, and a self-awareness of the role of ideology in our lives. In these critical senses, *A Dream* is

10 inadequate.

For the following question, consider each of the choices separately and select all that apply.

1. The author of the passage suggests that *A Dream* falls short in which of the following respects?

    [A] It does not appear to recognize that representations of reality can be unreliable.

    [B] It seems to focus on stylistic variety at the expense of accuracy of detail.

    [C] It offers a wealth of detail without sufficient critical examination of that detail.

2. Which of the following best describes the function of the second sentence ("*A Dream* . . . essayists") in the context of the passage as a whole?

    (A) To give examples of how *A Dream* presents fascinating portraits that display awareness of the tenuous nature of representations of reality

    (B) To elaborate on how *A Dream* fulfills the author's childhood criteria for a pleasurable book

    (C) To suggest that the author enjoyed *A Dream* for reasons more sophisticated than the reasons she enjoyed certain books as a child

    (D) To illustrate ways in which the author finds *A Dream* to be inadequate in certain critical senses

    (E) To imply that *A Dream* is too varied in focus to provide a proper contextualization of the biographical details it offers

3. During the day in Lake Constance, the zooplankton *D. hyalina* departs for the depths where food is scarce and the water cold. *D. galeata* remains near the warm surface where food is abundant. Even though *D. galeata* grows and reproduces much faster, its population is often outnumbered by *D. hyalina*.

Which of the following, if true, would help resolve the apparent paradox presented above?

(A) The number of species of zooplankton living at the bottom of the lake is twice that of species living at the surface.

(B) Predators of zooplankton, such as whitefish and perch, live and feed near the surface of the lake during the day.

(C) In order to make the most of scarce food resources, *D. hyalina* matures more slowly than *D. galeata*.

(D) *D. galeata* clusters under vegetation during the hottest part of the day to avoid the Sun's rays.

(E) *D. galeata* produces twice as many offspring per individual in any given period of time as does *D. hyalina*.

Questions 4 and 5 are based on the following reading passage.

Tocqueville, apparently, was wrong. Jacksonian America was not a fluid, egalitarian society where individual wealth and poverty were ephemeral conditions. At least so argues E. Pessen in his iconoclastic study of the very rich in the United States between 1825 and 1850.

Pessen does present a quantity of examples, together with some refreshingly intelligible statistics, to establish the existence of an inordinately wealthy class. Though active in commerce or the professions, most of the wealthy were not self-made but had inherited family fortunes. In no sense mercurial, these great fortunes survived the financial panics that destroyed lesser ones. Indeed, in several cities the wealthiest one percent constantly increased its share until by 1850 it owned half of the community's wealth. Although these observations are true, Pessen overestimates their importance by concluding from them that the undoubted progress toward inequality in the late eighteenth century continued in the Jacksonian period and that the United States was a class-ridden, plutocratic society even before industrialization.

4. According to the passage, Pessen indicates that all of the following were true of the very wealthy in the United States between 1825 and 1850 EXCEPT:

   Ⓐ They formed a distinct upper class.
   Ⓑ Many of them were able to increase their holdings.
   Ⓒ Some of them worked as professionals or in business.
   Ⓓ Most of them accumulated their own fortunes.
   Ⓔ Many of them retained their wealth in spite of financial upheavals.

5. Which of the following best states the author's main point?

   Ⓐ Pessen's study has overturned the previously established view of the social and economic structure of early-nineteenth-century America.
   Ⓑ Tocqueville's analysis of the United States in the Jacksonian era remains the definitive account of this period.
   Ⓒ Pessen's study is valuable primarily because it shows the continuity of the social system in the United States throughout the nineteenth century.
   Ⓓ The social patterns and political power of the extremely wealthy in the United States between 1825 and 1850 are well documented.
   Ⓔ Pessen challenges a view of the social and economic systems in the United States from 1825 to 1850, but he draws conclusions that are incorrect.

The evolution of intelligence among early large mammals of the grasslands was due in great measure to the interaction between two ecologically synchronized groups of these animals, the hunting carnivores and the herbivores that they hunted. The inter-
line action resulting from the differences between predator and prey led to a general
5 improvement in brain functions; however, certain components of intelligence were improved far more than others.

The kind of intelligence favored by the interplay of increasingly smarter catchers and increasingly keener escapers is defined by attention — that aspect of mind carrying consciousness forward from one moment to the next. It ranges from a passive, free-
10 floating awareness to a highly focused, active fixation. The range through these states is mediated by the arousal system, a network of tracts converging from sensory systems to integrating centers in the brain stem. From the more relaxed to the more vigorous levels, sensitivity to novelty is increased. The organism is more awake, more vigilant; this increased vigilance results in the apprehension of ever more subtle signals as the
15 organism becomes more sensitive to its surroundings. The processes of arousal and concentration give attention its direction. Arousal is at first general, with a flooding of impulses in the brain stem; then gradually the activation is channeled. Thus begins concentration, the holding of consistent images. One meaning of intelligence is the way in which these images and other alertly searched information are used in the context of
20 previous experience. Consciousness links past attention to the present and permits the integration of details with perceived ends and purposes.

The elements of intelligence and consciousness come together marvelously to produce different styles in predator and prey. Herbivores and carnivores develop different kinds of attention related to escaping or chasing. Although in both kinds of animal,
25 arousal stimulates the production of adrenaline and norepinephrine by the adrenal glands, the effect in herbivores is primarily fear, whereas in carnivores the effect is primarily aggression. For both, arousal attunes the animal to what is ahead. Perhaps it does not experience forethought as we know it, but the animal does experience something like it. The predator is searchingly aggressive, inner-directed, tuned by the
30 nervous system and the adrenal hormones, but aware in a sense closer to human consciousness than, say, a hungry lizard's instinctive snap at a passing beetle. Using past events as a framework, the large mammal predator is working out a relationship between movement and food, sensitive to possibilities in cold trails and distant sounds — and yesterday's unforgotten lessons. The herbivore prey is of a different mind. Its
35 mood of wariness rather than searching and its attitude of general expectancy instead of anticipating are silk-thin veils of tranquillity over an explosive endocrine system.

6. The author refers to a hungry lizard (line 31) primarily in order to
   Ⓐ demonstrate the similarity between the hunting methods of mammals and those of nonmammals
   Ⓑ broaden the application of the argument by including an insectivore as an example
   Ⓒ make a distinction between higher and lower levels of consciousness
   Ⓓ provide an additional illustration of the brutality characteristic of predators
   Ⓔ offer an objection to suggestions that all animals lack consciousness

7. It can be inferred from the passage that in animals less intelligent than the mammals discussed in the passage
    (A) past experience is less helpful in ensuring survival
    (B) attention is more highly focused
    (C) muscular coordination is less highly developed
    (D) there is less need for competition among species
    (E) environment is more important in establishing the proper ratio of prey to predator

8. According to the passage, improvement in brain function among early large mammals resulted primarily from which of the following?
    (A) Interplay of predator and prey
    (B) Persistence of free-floating awareness in animals of the grasslands
    (C) Gradual dominance of warm-blooded mammals over cold-blooded reptiles
    (D) Interaction of early large mammals with less intelligent species
    (E) Improvement of the capacity for memory among herbivores and carnivores

9. According to the passage, as the process of arousal in an organism continues, all of the following may occur EXCEPT
    (A) the production of adrenaline
    (B) the production of norepinephrine
    (C) a heightening of sensitivity to stimuli
    (D) an increase in selectivity with respect to stimuli
    (E) an expansion of the range of states mediated by the brain stem

SET 5. Discrete Questions: Hard

> **For Questions 1 to 6, select one entry for each blank from the corresponding column of choices. Fill all blanks in the way that best completes the text.**

1. For some time now, _____ has been presumed not to exist: the cynical conviction that everybody has an angle is considered wisdom.

Ⓐ rationality
Ⓑ flexibility
Ⓒ diffidence
Ⓓ disinterestedness
Ⓔ insincerity

2. Human nature and long distances have made exceeding the speed limit a (i)_____ in the state, so the legislators surprised no one when, acceding to public demand, they (ii)_____ increased penalties for speeding.

Blank (i)	Blank (ii)
Ⓐ controversial habit	Ⓓ endorsed
Ⓑ cherished tradition	Ⓔ considered
Ⓒ disquieting ritual	Ⓕ rejected

3. Serling's account of his employer's reckless decision making (i)_____ that company's image as (ii)_____ bureaucracy full of wary managers.

Blank (i)	Blank (ii)
Ⓐ belies	Ⓓ an injudicious
Ⓑ exposes	Ⓔ a disorganized
Ⓒ overshadows	Ⓕ a cautious

4. No other contemporary poet's work has such a well-earned reputation for (i)_____, and there are few whose moral vision is so imperiously unsparing. Of late, however, the almost belligerent demands of his severe and densely forbidding poetry have taken an improbable turn. This new collection is the poet's fourth book in six years — an ample output even for poets of sunny disposition, let alone for one of such (ii)_____ over the previous 50 years. Yet for all his newfound (iii)_____, his poetry is as thorny as ever.

Blank (i)	Blank (ii)	Blank (iii)
(A) patent accessibility	(D) penitential austerity	(G) taciturnity
(B) intrinsic frivolity	(E) intractable prolixity	(H) volubility
(C) near impenetrability	(F) impetuous prodigality	(I) pellucidity

5. Managers who think that strong environmental performance will (i)_____ their company's financial performance often (ii)_____ claims that systems designed to help them manage environmental concerns are valuable tools. By contrast, managers who perceive environmental performance to be (iii)_____ to financial success may view an environmental management system as extraneous. In either situation, and whatever their perceptions, it is a manager's commitment to achieving environmental improvement rather than the mere presence of a system that determines environmental performance.

Blank (i)	Blank (ii)	Blank (iii)
(A) eclipse	(D) uncritically accept	(G) complementary
(B) bolster	(E) appropriately acknowledge	(H) intrinsic
(C) degrade	(F) hotly dispute	(I) peripheral

6. Philosophy, unlike most other subjects, does not try to extend our knowledge by discovering new information about the world. Instead it tries to deepen our understanding through (i)_____ what is already closest to us — the experiences, thoughts, concepts, and activities that make up our lives but that ordinarily escape our notice precisely because they are so familiar. Philosophy begins by finding (ii)_____ the things that are (iii) _____.

Blank (i)	Blank (ii)	Blank (iii)
(A) attainment of	(D) essentially irrelevant	(G) most prosaic
(B) rumination on	(E) utterly mysterious	(H) somewhat hackneyed
(C) detachment from	(F) thoroughly commonplace	(I) refreshingly novel

For **Questions 7 to 9**, select the <u>two</u> answer choices that, when used to complete the sentence, fit the meaning of the sentence as a whole <u>and</u> produce completed sentences that are alike in meaning.

7. The government's implementation of a new code of ethics appeared intended to shore up the ruling party's standing with an increasingly _____ electorate at a time when the party is besieged by charges that it trades favors for campaign money.

   A| aloof
   B| placid
   C| restive
   D| skittish
   E| tranquil
   F| vociferous

8. Overlarge, uneven, and ultimately disappointing, the retrospective exhibition seems too much like special pleading for a forgotten painter of real but _____ talents.

   A| limited
   B| partial
   C| undiscovered
   D| circumscribed
   E| prosaic
   F| hidden

9. Newspapers report that the former executive has been trying to keep a low profile since his _____ exit from the company.

   A| celebrated
   B| mysterious
   C| long-awaited
   D| fortuitous
   E| indecorous
   F| unseemly

SET 6. Reading Comprehension Questions: Hard

For each of Questions 1 to 8, select <u>one</u> answer choice unless otherwise instructed.

1. In the United States between 1850 and 1880, the number of farmers continued to increase, but at a rate lower than that of the general population.

   Which of the following statements directly contradicts the information presented above?

   (A) The number of farmers in the general population increased slightly in the 30 years between 1850 and 1880.

   (B) The rate of growth of the United States labor force and the rate of growth of the general population rose simultaneously in the 30 years between 1850 and 1880.

   (C) The proportion of farmers in the United States labor force remained constant in the 30 years between 1850 and 1880.

   (D) The proportion of farmers in the United States labor force decreased from 64 percent in 1850 to 49 percent in 1880.

   (E) The proportion of farmers in the general population increased from 68 percent in 1850 to 72 percent in 1880.

2. A ten-year comparison between the United States and the Soviet Union in terms of crop yields per acre revealed that when only planted acreage is compared, Soviet yields were equal to 68 percent of United States yields. When total agricultural acreage (planted acreage plus fallow acreage) is compared, however, Soviet yield was 114 percent of United States yield.

   From the information above, which of the following can be most reliably inferred about United States and Soviet agriculture during the ten-year period?

   (A) A higher percentage of total agricultural acreage was fallow in the United States than in the Soviet Union.

   (B) The United States had more fallow acreage than planted acreage.

   (C) Fewer total acres of available agricultural land were fallow in the Soviet Union than in the United States.

   (D) The Soviet Union had more planted acreage than fallow acreage.

   (E) The Soviet Union produced a greater volume of crops than the United States produced.

For hot desert locations with access to seawater, a new greenhouse design generates freshwater and cool air. Oriented to the prevailing wind, the front wall of perforated cardboard, moistened and cooled by a trickle of seawater pumped in, cools and mois-
line   tens hot air blowing in. This cool, humidified air accelerates plant growth; little water
5   evaporates from leaves. Though greenhouses normally capture the heat of sunlight, a double-layered roof, the inner layer coated to reflect infrared light outward, allows visible sunlight in but traps solar heat between the two layers. This heated air, drawn down from the roof, then mixes with the greenhouse air as it reaches a second sea-water-moistened cardboard wall at the back of the greenhouse. There the air absorbs
10   more moisture, which then condenses on a metal wall cooled by seawater, and thus distilled water for irrigating the plants collects.

For the following question, consider each of the choices separately and select all that apply.

3.   It can be inferred that the process described in the passage makes use of which of the following?

   A   The tendency of hot air to rise

   B   The directional movement of wind

   C   The temperature differential between the sea and the desert

For the following question, consider each of the choices separately and select all that apply.

4.   It can be inferred that the greenhouse roof is designed to allow for which of the following?

   A   The avoidance of intense solar heat inside the greenhouse

   B   The entry of sunlight into the greenhouse to make the plants grow

   C   The mixture of heated air with greenhouse air to enhance the collection of moisture

Many critics of Emily Brontë's novel *Wuthering Heights* see its second part as a counterpoint that comments on, if it does not reverse, the first part, where a romantic reading receives more confirmation. Seeing the two parts as a whole is encouraged by the novel's sophisticated structure, revealed in its complex use of narrators and time shifts. Granted that the presence of these elements need not argue for an authorial awareness of novelistic construction comparable to that of Henry James, their presence does encourage attempts to unify the novel's heterogeneous parts. However, any interpretation that seeks to unify all of the novel's diverse elements is bound to be somewhat unconvincing. This is not because such an interpretation necessarily stiffens into a thesis (although rigidity in any interpretation of this or of any novel is always a danger), but because *Wuthering Heights* has recalcitrant elements of undeniable power that, ultimately, resist inclusion in an all-encompassing interpretation. In this respect, *Wuthering Heights* shares a feature of *Hamlet*.

5. According to the passage, which of the following is a true statement about the first and second parts of *Wuthering Heights*?
   - (A) The second part has received more attention from critics.
   - (B) The second part has little relation to the first part.
   - (C) The second part annuls the force of the first part.
   - (D) The second part provides less substantiation for a romantic reading.
   - (E) The second part is better because it is more realistic.

6. Which of the following inferences about Henry James's awareness of novelistic construction is best supported by the passage?
   - (A) James, more than any other novelist, was aware of the difficulties of novelistic construction.
   - (B) James was very aware of the details of novelistic construction.
   - (C) James's awareness of novelistic construction derived from his reading of Brontë.
   - (D) James's awareness of novelistic construction has led most commentators to see unity in his individual novels.
   - (E) James's awareness of novelistic construction precluded him from violating the unity of his novels.

7. The author of the passage would be most likely to agree that an interpretation of a novel should
   - (A) not try to unite heterogeneous elements in the novel
   - (B) not be inflexible in its treatment of the elements in the novel
   - (C) not argue that the complex use of narrators or of time shifts indicates a sophisticated structure
   - (D) concentrate on those recalcitrant elements of the novel that are outside the novel's main structure
   - (E) primarily consider those elements of novelistic construction of which the author of the novel was aware

For the following question, consider each of the choices separately and select all that apply.

8. The author of the passage suggests which of the following about *Hamlet*?

    A *Hamlet* has usually attracted critical interpretations that tend to stiffen into theses.

    B *Hamlet* has elements that are not amenable to an all-encompassing critical interpretation.

    C *Hamlet* is less open to an all-encompassing critical interpretation than is *Wuthering Heights*.

ANSWER KEYS

SET 1. Discrete Questions: Easy

1. **Choice E**: elimination
2. **Choice A**: prophetic
3. **Choice B**: unguided
4. **Choice A**: surprising; **Choice E**: justifies
5. **Choice A**: activism; **Choice E**: indifferent to
6. **Choice A**: deteriorate; AND **Choice D**: decline
7. **Choice B**: undiminished; AND **Choice D**: undamaged
8. **Choice C**: significant; AND **Choice D**: considerable

SET 2. Reading Comprehension Questions: Easy

1. **Choice B**: They should not agree to serve unless they are committed to maintaining a stance of impartiality.
2. **Sentence 4**: From then on, he was recognized as an artist of preternatural abilities, not only as a composer but also as a pianist and conductor.
3. **Choice C**: The discrepancy between Mendelssohn's popularity and his standing among critics
4. **Choice D**: music critics generally
5. **Choice E**: establish a standard of comparison for Mendelssohn as a composer
6. **Choice B**: The percentage of employees in each sector who were men
7. **Choice D**: The increase in women's employment that accompanied the Second World War was longer lasting in agriculture than it was in manufacturing.
8. **Choice B**: discussing different theories about the transport of plant seeds to Hawaii
9. **Choice D**: challenge the claim that ocean currents are responsible for the transport of plant seeds to Hawaii

SET 3. Discrete Questions: Medium

1. **Choice B**: unexpected
2. **Choice A**: reverence for; **Choice D**: fastidiousness
3. **Choice C**: deceptive; **Choice E**: dissimilar
4. **Choice C**: come through; **Choice E**: aside from supporting; **Choice H**: protect
5. **Choice A**: presumed verifiable; **Choice F**: debunking; **Choice H**: bogus
6. **Choice A**: exacting; AND **Choice F**: meticulous
7. **Choice C**: frugality; AND **Choice F**: thrift
8. **Choice A**: complicated; **Choice F**: involved

SET 4. Reading Comprehension Questions: Medium

1. **Choice A**: It does not appear to recognize that representations of reality can be unreliable; AND **Choice C**: It offers a wealth of detail without sufficient critical examination of that detail.
2. **Choice B**: To elaborate on how *A Dream* fulfills the author's childhood criteria for a pleasurable book
3. **Choice B**: Predators of zooplankton, such as whitefish and perch, live and feed near the surface of the lake during the day.
4. **Choice D**: Most of them accumulated their own fortunes.
5. **Choice E**: Pessen challenges a view of the social and economic systems in the United States from 1825 to 1850, but he draws conclusions that are incorrect.
6. **Choice C**: make a distinction between higher and lower levels of consciousness
7. **Choice A**: past experience is less helpful in ensuring survival
8. **Choice A**: Interplay of predator and prey
9. **Choice E**: an expansion of the range of states mediated by the brain stem

SET 5. Discrete Questions: Hard

1. **Choice D**: disinterestedness
2. **Choice B**: cherished tradition; **Choice F**: rejected
3. **Choice A**: belies; **Choice F**: a cautious
4. **Choice C**: near impenetrability; **Choice D**: penitential austerity; **Choice H**: volubility
5. **Choice B**: bolster; **Choice D**: uncritically accept; **Choice I**: peripheral
6. **Choice B**: rumination on; **Choice E**: utterly mysterious; **Choice G**: most prosaic
7. **Choice C**: restive; AND **Choice D**: skittish
8. **Choice A**: limited; AND **Choice D**: circumscribed
9. **Choice E**: indecorous; AND **Choice F**: unseemly

SET 6. Reading Comprehension Questions: Hard

1. **Choice E**: The proportion of farmers in the general population increased from 68 percent in 1850 to 72 percent in 1880.
2. **Choice A**: A higher percentage of total agricultural acreage was fallow in the United States than in the Soviet Union.
3. **Choice B**: The directional movement of wind; AND **Choice C**: The temperature differential between the sea and the desert.
4. **Choice A**: The avoidance of intense solar heat inside the greenhouse; AND **Choice B**: The entry of sunlight into the greenhouse to make the plants grow; AND **Choice C**: The mixture of heated air with greenhouse air to enhance the collection of moisture.
5. **Choice D**: The second part provides less substantiation for a romantic reading.
6. **Choice B**: James was very aware of the details of novelistic construction.
7. **Choice B**: not be inflexible in its treatment of the elements in the novel
8. **Choice B**: *Hamlet* has elements that are not amenable to an all-encompassing critical interpretation.

Answers and Explanations

SET 1. Discrete Questions: Easy

> **For Questions 1 to 5, select one entry for each blank from the corresponding column of choices. Fill all blanks in the way that best completes the text.**

1. Dominant interests often benefit most from _____ of governmental interference in business, since they are able to take care of themselves if left alone.

(A) intensification
(B) authorization
(C) centralization
(D) improvisation
(E) elimination

Explanation

The sentence explains why dominant interests often benefit from a certain condition. Since the explanation is that they are able to take care of themselves if left alone, it follows that the condition is one in which interference is absent. Thus the best answer is "elimination." None of the other answer choices suggests an absence of interference — indeed "intensification," "authorization," and "centralization" suggest quite the opposite.

Thus the correct answer is **elimination** (Choice E).

2. Kagan maintains that an infant's reactions to its first stressful experiences are part of a natural process of development, not harbingers of childhood unhappiness or _____ signs of adolescent anxiety.

(A) prophetic
(B) normal
(C) monotonous
(D) virtual
(E) typical

Explanation

The sentence contrasts the infant's reactions, part of a normal developmental process, with future unhappiness and anxiety. The missing word describes signs of adolescent anxiety as they relate to the infant. Choice A is correct: "prophetic" signs, like harbingers, foretell future occurrences, and for the infant, adolescent anxiety is a future occurrence. Since an infant cannot literally display signs of adolescent anxiety, "normal," "monotonous," and "typical" are all incorrect. And "virtual" is incorrect, because virtual signs are not real signs, and what Kagan is denying is that the infant's reactions are not real signs of later unhappiness.

Thus the correct answer is **prophetic** (Choice A).

3. An investigation that is _____ can occasionally yield new facts, even notable ones, but typically the appearance of such facts is the result of a search in a definite direction.

(A)	timely
(B)	unguided
(C)	consistent
(D)	uncomplicated
(E)	subjective

Explanation

As the words "can occasionally" and "but typically" indicate, the missing word describes an investigation that contrasts with a "search in a definite direction." Among the answer choices, only "unguided" provides a contrasting description; none of the other choices suggests an appropriate contrast.

Thus the correct answer is **unguided** (Choice B).

4. It is (i)_____ that so many portrait paintings hang in art museums, since the subject matter seems to dictate a status closer to pictures in the family photograph album than to high art. But perhaps it is the artistic skill with which the portraits are painted that (ii)_____ their presence in art museums.

Blank (i)	Blank (ii)
(A) surprising	(D) challenges
(B) understandable	(E) justifies
(C) irrelevant	(F) changes

Explanation

In the part following "since," the first sentence of the paragraph suggests that the subject matter of portraits might not seem to fit with the idea of "high art." So the suggestion is that the presence of portrait paintings in art museums is in that sense odd or unfitting. Of the choices available for Blank (i), "surprising" is the one that expresses this sense. The second sentence, in contrast to the first, offers a point in favor of portraits — "artistic skill." So the second sentence is offering a reason why portraits should be in art museums. Of the choices for Blank (ii), "justifies" is the one that completes that thought.

Thus the correct answer is **surprising** (Choice A) and **justifies** (Choice E).

5. In stark contrast to his later (i)_____, Simpson was largely (ii)_____ politics during his college years, despite the fact that the campus he attended was rife with political activity.

Blank (i)	Blank (ii)
(A) activism	(D) devoted to
(B) apathy	(E) indifferent to
(C) affability	(F) shaped by

Explanation

The sentence tells us that there is a contrast between the way Simpson related to politics in his college years and how he related to politics later in life. So the choices that complete the blanks must contrast with each other. The part of the sentence beginning with "despite" indicates that Simpson's relation to politics in his college years did not involve engagement in the political activity that was "rife." Of the choices for Blank (ii), only "indifferent to" conveys that nonengagement. And of the choices for Blank (i), only "activism" supplies the required contrast with "indifferent to."

Thus the correct answer is **activism** (Choice A) and **indifferent to** (Choice E).

For Questions 6 to 8, select the <u>two</u> answer choices that, when used to complete the sentence, fit the meaning of the sentence as a whole <u>and</u> produce completed sentences that are alike in meaning.

---

6. As my eyesight began to _____, I spent a lot of time writing about it — both poems and "eye journals" — describing what I saw as I looked out through damaged eyes.

    A deteriorate
    B sharpen
    C improve
    D decline
    E recover
    F adjust

Explanation

The author has "damaged" eyes, and any word that fills the blank must reflect that fact. The words that best do so are "deteriorate" and "decline" (Choices A and D), which generate sentences alike in meaning. "Sharpen" and "improve" produce sentences alike in meaning, but neither word makes sense when inserted into the blank. Though "adjust" makes some sense when inserted into the blank, no other option produces a sentence similar in meaning.

Thus the correct answer is **deteriorate** (Choice A) and **decline** (Choice D).

7. The judge's standing in the legal community, though shaken by phony allegations of wrongdoing, emerged, at long last, _____ .

    A unqualified
    B undiminished
    C undecided
    D undamaged
    E unresolved
    F unprincipled

Explanation

The use of the word "though" establishes a contrast between the blank, which requires a description of the judge's standing, and "phony allegations of wrongdoing." Thus the words that best complete the blank must indicate that the judge's reputation was not adversely affected by these allegations. The only words that do so are "undiminished" and "undamaged" (Choices B and D), which produce sentences alike in meaning. "Undecided" and "unresolved" also produce sentences alike in meaning, but neither word makes sense when inserted into the blank.

Thus the correct answer is **undiminished** (Choice B) and **undamaged** (Choice D).

8.   Modern agricultural practices have been extremely successful in increasing the productivity of major food crops, yet despite heavy use of pesticides, _____ losses to diseases and insect pests are sustained each year.

|A| incongruous
|B| reasonable
|C| significant
|D| considerable
|E| equitable
|F| fortuitous

Explanation

The word "despite" suggests the level of losses is somehow surprising given the heavy use of pesticides. The only words that describe an appropriate level of losses are "significant" and "considerable" (Choices C and D), which produce sentences alike in meaning. "Reasonable" and "equitable" also produce sentences alike in meaning, but neither word generates the contrast necessary for the sentence to make sense.

Thus the correct answer is **significant** (Choice C) and **considerable** (Choice D).

SET 2. Reading Comprehension Questions: Easy

For each of Questions 1 to 9, select <u>one</u> answer choice unless otherwise instructed.

1.   A person who agrees to serve as mediator between two warring factions at the request of both abandons by so agreeing the right to take sides later. To take sides at a later point would be to suggest that the earlier presumptive impartiality was a sham.

The passage above emphasizes which of the following points about mediators?

Ⓐ They should try to form no opinions of their own about any issue that is related to the dispute.

Ⓑ They should not agree to serve unless they are committed to maintaining a stance of impartiality.

Ⓒ They should not agree to serve unless they are equally acceptable to all parties to a dispute.

Ⓓ They should feel free to take sides in the dispute right from the start, provided that they make their biases publicly known.

Ⓔ They should reserve the right to abandon their impartiality so as not to be open to the charge of having been deceitful.

Explanation

By pointing out the consequences of abandoning impartiality, the paragraph points out the importance for mediators of maintaining impartiality at all times. This is the point made in **Choice B**, which is therefore the correct answer. Choice A is incorrect, because it goes further than anything asserted in the passage. The passage does not rule out the possibility that one can have an opinion about issues related to a dispute without taking sides in the actual dispute. Choice C is incorrect because it is a presupposition on which the passage is based rather than the point of the passage; that is, the fact that the mediator is acceptable to both parties is a given, since they both ask the mediator to serve. Choices D and E are both inconsistent with the main point of the passage, the importance of impartiality at all times, so both are incorrect.

Questions 2 to 5 are based on the following reading passage.

Was Felix Mendelssohn (1809–1847) a great composer? On its face, the question seems absurd. One of the most gifted prodigies in the history of music, he produced his first masterpiece at sixteen. From then on, he was recognized as an artist of preternatural abilities, not only as a composer but also as a pianist and conductor. But Mendelssohn's enduring popularity has often been at odds — sometimes quite sharply — with his critical standing. Despite general acknowledgment of his genius, there has been a noticeable reluctance to rank him with, say, Schumann or Brahms. As Haggin put it, Mendelssohn, as a composer, was a "minor master . . . working on a small scale of emotion and texture."

Description

The passage starts by outlining the popular view that Mendelssohn was a great composer and then points out that critics do not generally accord him that status.

2. Select a sentence in the passage whose function is to indicate the range of Mendelssohn's musical talents.

Explanation

This question asks which sentence in the passage serves to indicate the range of Mendelssohn's musical talents. The correct answer is the **fourth sentence** ("From then . . . conductor"), the only sentence in the passage that mentions Mendelssohn's achievements across three different realms: composing, piano performance, and conducting. All the other sentences can be eliminated because, while they consider the question of Mendelssohn's claim to greatness, they do not specifically discuss the broad range of his musical talents.

3.   The passage suggests that anyone attempting to evaluate Mendelssohn's career must confront which of the following dichotomies?

Ⓐ The tension between Mendelssohn's career as a composer and his career as a pianist and conductor

Ⓑ The contrast between Mendelssohn's popularity and that of Schumann and Brahms

Ⓒ The discrepancy between Mendelssohn's popularity and his standing among critics

Ⓓ The inconsistency between Mendelssohn's reputation during his lifetime and his reputation since his death

Ⓔ The gap between Mendelssohn's prodigious musical beginnings and his decline in later years

Explanation

The passage clearly presents the discrepancy between Mendelssohn's popularity and his critical standing as an interpretive problem. Therefore, **Choice C** is correct. The other answer choices are incorrect because the passage never indicates that there was any conflict among the different aspects of Mendelssohn's professional life; never discusses Schumann's and Brahms's popularity; does not discuss any differences between Mendelssohn's reputation during his lifetime and after his death; and makes no mention of a decline in Mendelssohn's later life.

4.   It can be inferred that the "reluctance" mentioned in the passage is being ascribed to

Ⓐ most composers since Mendelssohn

Ⓑ Schumann and Brahms

Ⓒ the music-listening public

Ⓓ music critics generally

Ⓔ Haggin exclusively

Explanation

Choice D is correct. The "reluctance" is mentioned in the context of a discussion about Mendelssohn's critical standing and thus is being ascribed to music critics generally. Choices A and B can be eliminated because the passage does not discuss any composers' views of Mendelssohn. Choice C is incorrect because the word "reluctance" is mentioned only after the passage turns from discussing the popular view of Mendelssohn to the critical view. Choice E is incorrect because the words "As Haggin put it" indicate that Haggin is only one example of critics who have this reluctance.

5.   The author mentions Schumann and Brahms primarily in order to

Ⓐ provide examples of composers who are often compared with Mendelssohn

Ⓑ identify certain composers who are more popular than Mendelssohn

Ⓒ identify composers whom Mendelssohn influenced

Ⓓ establish the milieu in which Mendelssohn worked

Ⓔ establish a standard of comparison for Mendelssohn as a composer

Explanation

Schumann and Brahms are mentioned as a way of explaining how critics rank Mendelssohn — that is, as less accomplished than some other composers who are widely acknowledged as major. Therefore, **Choice E** is correct. Choice A might look like a correct answer at first glance. However, careful consideration reveals that the point the author is making when Schumann and Brahms are mentioned is not the frequency of that comparison but the results of it. Therefore, Choice A can be eliminated. Choices B, C, and D are incorrect because the passage does not discuss Schumann's and Brahms's popularity, Mendelssohn's influence on other composers, or the milieu in which Mendelssohn worked.

Questions 6 and 7 are based on the following reading passage.

While most scholarship on women's employment in the United States recognizes that the Second World War (1939–1945) dramatically changed the role of women in the workforce, these studies also acknowledge that few women remained in manufacturing jobs once men returned from the war. But in agriculture, unlike other industries where women were viewed as temporary workers, women's employment did not end with the war. Instead, the expansion of agriculture and a steady decrease in the number of male farmworkers combined to cause the industry to hire more women in the postwar years. Consequently, the 1950s saw a growing number of women engaged in farm labor, even though rhetoric in the popular media called for the return of women to domestic life.

Description

The first sentence states that the Second World War led to significant changes in women's employment, but that these changes were largely reversed in manufacturing after the war. The second sentence discusses the fact that unlike in other industries, employment of women in agriculture was more permanent; the third provides more detail regarding the trend in agriculture and the reasons for it; and the fourth summarizes the consequences of the trend.

6. It can be inferred from the passage that the manufacturing and agricultural sectors in the United States following the Second World War differed in which of the following respects?

    (A) The rate of expansion in each sector
    (B) The percentage of employees in each sector who were men
    (C) The trend in the wages of men employed in each sector
    (D) The attitude of the popular media toward the employment of women in each sector
    (E) The extent to which women in each sector were satisfied with their jobs

Explanation

The correct choice for this question is **Choice B**. We are told that few women remained in the manufacturing sector once men returned from the war, while the number of women who worked in agriculture increased after the war as the number of men in agriculture decreased. It is therefore inferable that the percentage of employees working in manufacturing who were men increased while the percentage of employees working in agriculture who were men decreased. Choices A, C, and E are incorrect because the passage provides no information about rates of expansion, wage trends, or women's job satisfaction. Choice D is incorrect because the only mention of the popular media occurs in the final sentence, and no distinction is made between the sectors there.

7. Which of the following statements about women's employment in the United States during and after the Second World War is most clearly supported by the passage?

    Ⓐ Most women who joined the workforce during the Second World War wanted to return to domestic life when the war ended.

    Ⓑ The great majority of women who joined the workforce during the Second World War were employed in manufacturing jobs.

    Ⓒ The end of the Second World War was followed by a large-scale transfer of women workers from manufacturing to agriculture.

    Ⓓ The increase in women's employment that accompanied the Second World War was longer lasting in agriculture than it was in manufacturing.

    Ⓔ The popular media were more forceful in calling for women to join the workforce during the Second World War than in calling for women to return to domestic life after the war.

Explanation

The correct choice for this question is **Choice D**. We are told in the passage that women's employment in manufacturing fell quickly after men returned from the war. However, not only did women's employment in agriculture not decline after the end of the war, it actually increased. The other choices are incorrect because the passage provides no information about what women who joined the workforce wanted to do; about the distribution of women across industries; about what happened to women who left manufacturing; nor about media appeals for women to join the wartime workforce.

Questions 8 and 9 are based on the following reading passage.

Since the Hawaiian Islands have never been connected to other land masses, the great variety of plants in Hawaii must be a result of the long-distance dispersal of seeds, a process that requires both a method of transport and an equivalence between the ecol-
line ogy of the source area and that of the recipient area.
5   There is some dispute about the method of transport involved. Some biologists argue that ocean and air currents are responsible for the transport of plant seeds to Hawaii. Yet the results of flotation experiments and the low temperatures of air currents cast doubt on these hypotheses. More probable is bird transport, either externally, by accidental attachment of the seeds to feathers, or internally, by the swallowing of
10   fruit and subsequent excretion of the seeds. While it is likely that fewer varieties of plant seeds have reached Hawaii externally than internally, more varieties are known to be adapted to external than to internal transport.

Description

The passage raises the question of how seeds reached the Hawaiian Islands. It introduces one possible method — ocean and air currents — but refers to evidence that casts doubt on that method. It then introduces a second method — bird transport — and discusses two ways in which that might occur.

8. The author of the passage is primarily concerned with
    (A) discussing different approaches biologists have taken to testing theories about the distribution of plants in Hawaii
    (B) discussing different theories about the transport of plant seeds to Hawaii
    (C) discussing the extent to which air currents are responsible for the dispersal of plant seeds to Hawaii
    (D) resolving a dispute about the adaptability of plant seeds to bird transport
    (E) resolving a dispute about the ability of birds to carry plant seeds long distances

Explanation

Given the description of the passage above, it is clear that **Choice B** is correct: the passage focuses on "different theories about the transport of plant seeds to Hawaii." Choice A can be eliminated: while the passage does refer to flotation experiments, it does not elaborate on experimental methods. Choice C identifies an idea that is part of the passage's main concern, but since this is only one of the competing theories discussed in the passage, not the primary focus, Choice C is incorrect. Choices D and E are incorrect because the passage does not resolve any disputes.

9. The author mentions the results of flotation experiments on plant seeds (lines 7–8) most probably in order to
    (A) support the claim that the distribution of plants in Hawaii is the result of the long-distance dispersal of seeds
    (B) lend credibility to the thesis that air currents provide a method of transport for plant seeds to Hawaii
    (C) suggest that the long-distance dispersal of seeds is a process that requires long periods of time
    (D) challenge the claim that ocean currents are responsible for the transport of plant seeds to Hawaii
    (E) refute the claim that Hawaiian flora evolved independently from flora in other parts of the world

Explanation

This question asks why the author mentions flotation experiments. Flotation experiments are mentioned in the passage in order to show that some evidence casts doubt on the claim that ocean currents were the means by which seeds were transported to Hawaii. Thus, **Choice D** is correct. Choice A is incorrect since the claim that plant distribution in Hawaii is the result of long-distance dispersal of seeds is a given in the passage, not an idea that the author feels a need to substantiate. Choice B is eliminable since the flotation experiments are introduced at a point where the author is challenging, rather than lending credibility to, the air current hypothesis and because flotation experiments would more likely reflect on ocean currents than air currents. Choice C is eliminable since the passage does not address the length of time required for long-distance seed dispersal. Finally, Choice E is eliminable since it too describes an idea that is not discussed in the passage.

SET 3. Discrete Questions: Medium

> **For Questions 1 to 5, select one entry for each blank from the corresponding column of choices. Fill all blanks in the way that best completes the text.**

1. It comes as no surprise that societies have codes of behavior; the character of the codes, on the other hand, can often be _____ .

Ⓐ predictable
Ⓑ unexpected
Ⓒ admirable
Ⓓ explicit
Ⓔ confusing

Explanation

The words "on the other hand" indicate that while the existence of societal codes of behavior is no surprise, their character may be quite surprising. Thus the correct answer is Choice B, **unexpected**, which means the same as surprising. "Predictable" is the very opposite of surprising, and none of the other answer choices means "surprising."

Thus the correct answer is **unexpected** (Choice B).

2. Like Béla Bartók, Ruth Crawford not only brought a composer's acumen to the notation of folk music, she also had a marked (i)_____ the task. This was clear in her agonizing over how far to try to represent the minute details of a performance in a written text, and this (ii)_____ makes her work a landmark in ethnomusicology.

Blank (i)	Blank (ii)
Ⓐ reverence for	Ⓓ fastidiousness
Ⓑ detachment from	Ⓔ didacticism
Ⓒ curiosity about	Ⓕ iconoclasm

Explanation

In this example, both blanks can be filled by focusing on the statement that Crawford agonized over the details in her representations of folk music performances. The only choice for blank (ii) that matches this description is "fastidiousness"; neither "didacticism" nor "iconoclasm" reflects the notion of agonizing over details. Similarly, only "reverence for" fits in Blank (i), since neither "detachment from" nor "curiosity about" reflects the degree of care Crawford took.

Thus the correct answer is **reverence for** (Choice A) and **fastidiousness** (Choice D).

3. Political advertising may well be the most (i)_____ kind of advertising: political candidates are usually quite (ii)_____, yet their campaign advertisements often hide important differences behind smoke screens of smiles and empty slogans.

Blank (i)	Blank (ii)
Ⓐ polemical	Ⓓ interchangeable
Ⓑ effective	Ⓔ dissimilar
Ⓒ deceptive	Ⓕ vocal

Explanation

Looking at Blank (i), it is hard to select a correct answer, since all three answer choices fit the immediate context well. Looking to the second part of the sentence, however, we can see such expressions as "hide" and "smoke screens," both of which suggest that the correct answer for Blank (i) is "deceptive." Making that assumption, we can go on to see that the answer for Blank (ii) is "dissimilar," since what is deceptive about political advertisements is that they hide important differences. Reading the sentence again with "deceptive" and "dissimilar" in place confirms those choices.

Thus the correct answer is **deceptive** (Choice C) and **dissimilar** (Choice E).

4. Richard M. Russell said 52 percent of the nation's growth since the Second World War had (i)_____ invention. He said, (ii)_____ research, the government's greatest role in assuring continuing innovation is promoting a strong, modern patent office. "Unless we can (iii)_____ original ideas, we will not have invention," Mr. Russell said. Speculating on the state of innovation over the next century, several inventors agreed that the future lay in giving children the tools to think creatively and the motivation to invent.

Blank (i)	Blank (ii)	Blank (iii)
Ⓐ been at the expense of	Ⓓ in addition to restricting	Ⓖ evaluate
Ⓑ no bearing on	Ⓔ aside from supporting	Ⓗ protect
Ⓒ come through	Ⓕ far from exaggerating	Ⓘ disseminate

Explanation

A quick overview of the paragraph shows that its topic is the encouragement of invention and innovation. This implies that Blank (i) should be filled with "come through," which emphasizes the importance of invention; the other choices suggest that invention is irrelevant or somehow harmed by growth. Again, the only one of the choices for Blank (ii) that continues the theme of encouraging invention is "aside from supporting." Finally, the second sentence emphasizes the importance for innovation of a strong patent office, and this thought is reaffirmed in the following quotation from Mr. Russell, which requires "protect" in Blank (iii).

Thus the correct answer is **come through** (Choice C), **aside from supporting** (Choice E), and **protect** (Choice H).

5. Statements presented as fact in a patent application are (i)_____ unless a good reason for doubt is found. The invention has only to be deemed "more likely than not" to work in order to receive initial approval. And, although thousands of patents are challenged in court for other reasons, no incentive exists for anyone to expend effort (ii)_____ the science of an erroneous patent. For this reason the endless stream of (iii)_____ devices will continue to yield occasional patents.

Blank (i)	Blank (ii)	Blank (iii)
(A) presumed verifiable	(D) corroborating	(G) novel
(B) carefully scrutinized	(E) advancing	(H) bogus
(C) considered capricious	(F) debunking	(I) obsolete

Explanation

The paragraph appears to be explaining some odd or unexpected aspect of the patent process. The third sentence helps to clarify what this aspect is; it discusses challenges to patents. The only choice for Blank (ii) that is concerned with challenging a patent is "debunking," since "corroborating" and "advancing" suggest support instead. This in turn provides the answer for the third blank, since the preceding sentence does explain how "bogus" devices may nonetheless get a patent. And we can also now better understand the first sentence — it too must help explain how bogus devices get patents, which it can do only if the blank is filled with "presumed verifiable," suggesting that patent applications are taken at face value and not dismissed out of hand nor subjected to careful scrutiny.

Thus the correct answer is **presumed verifiable** (Choice A), **debunking** (Choice F), and **bogus** (Choice H).

> **For Questions 6 to 8, select the <u>two</u> answer choices that, when used to complete the sentence, fit the meaning of the sentence as a whole <u>and</u> produce completed sentences that are alike in meaning.**

---

6. Ever a demanding reader of the fiction of others, the novelist Chase was likewise often the object of _____ analyses by his contemporaries.

   [A] exacting
   [B] copious
   [C] respectful
   [D] acerbic
   [E] scathing
   [F] meticulous

Explanation

The use of the word "likewise" indicates that the analyses of Chase's work by contemporaries were like the readings he gave the fiction of others. Since he is described as a "demanding reader," the words that best fit the blank will be similar in meaning to "demanding." The words that meet this requirement are "exacting" (Choice A) and "meticulous" (Choice F), and they produce sentences that are alike in meaning. Although "acerbic analyses" means close to the same thing as "scathing analyses," both "acerbic" and "scathing" have meanings that are quite different from "demanding," so neither fits well in the blank.

Thus the correct answer is **exacting** (Choice A) and **meticulous** (Choice F).

7. Her _____ should not be confused with miserliness; as long as I have known her, she has always been willing to assist those who are in need.

   A stinginess
   B diffidence
   C frugality
   D illiberality
   E intolerance
   F thrift

Explanation

The sentence explains that the person spoken of is not miserly, since she is quite prepared to be generous. So for the sentence to make sense, the word filling the blank has to be something that is consistent with generosity and yet might, by those without a full understanding of her behavior, be mistaken for miserliness. The words "frugality" and "thrift" fulfill this requirement and yield two sentences that are alike in meaning, so that pair forms the correct answer. Neither "stinginess" nor "illiberality" makes sense in the sentence, since they are synonymous with "miserliness" and inconsistent with generosity. Other choices, such as "diffidence," might perhaps make a sensible sentence if placed in the blank but do not form part of the correct answer since they have no companion word that would make a sentence of similar meaning.

Thus the correct answer is **frugality** (Choice C) and **thrift** (Choice F).

8. A misconception frequently held by novice writers is that sentence structure mirrors thought: the more convoluted the structure, the more _____ the ideas.

   A complicated
   B engaged
   C essential
   D fanciful
   E inconsequential
   F involved

Explanation

Because the second half of the sentence illustrates the idea that "structure mirrors thought," any word that fills the blank must be similar in meaning to "convoluted." The two words that are similar to "convoluted" are "complicated" and "involved" (Choices A and F), which produce sentences alike in meaning. "Fanciful," while somewhat similar in meaning to "convoluted," is not as similar to either "complicated" or "involved" as those words are to each other. The other answer choices are not similar in meaning to "convoluted," and thus do not produce coherent sentences.

Thus the correct answer is **complicated** (Choice A) and **involved** (Choice F).

SET 4. Reading Comprehension Questions: Medium

> For each of Questions 1 to 9, select <u>one</u> answer choice unless otherwise instructed.

Questions 1 and 2 are based on the following reading passage.

I enjoyed *A Dream of Light & Shadow: Portraits of Latin American Women Writers* for the same reasons that, as a child, I avidly consumed women's biographies: the fascination with how the biographical details of another female's life are represented and interpreted.

A Dream offers a rich read, varied in both the lives and texts of the women portrayed, and the perspectives and styles of the sixteen essayists. Yet, as an adult, I have come to demand of any really "great" book a self-consciousness about the tenuous nature of representations of reality, a critical contextualization of florid detail, and a self-awareness of the role of ideology in our lives. In these critical senses, *A Dream* is inadequate.

line

5

10

Description

The passage follows the following structure: the first sentence discusses a collection of biographical sketches and what the author found particularly appealing about similar works as a child; the second sentence describes several positive aspects of this particular collection and how it satisfies the author's early interests; the third sentence describes a demanding set of criteria that the author now applies when assessing such work; and in the fourth sentence the author says the collection being discussed does not meet those criteria.

For the following question, consider each of the choices separately and select all that apply.

1. The author of the passage suggests that *A Dream* falls short in which of the following respects?
   - [A] It does not appear to recognize that representations of reality can be unreliable.
   - [B] It seems to focus on stylistic variety at the expense of accuracy of detail.
   - [C] It offers a wealth of detail without sufficient critical examination of that detail.

Explanation

Choices A and C are correct. We know from the final sentence that the collection falls short of several criteria established by the author.

Choice A is correct: the book does not demonstrate sufficient awareness of the "tenuous nature of representations of reality."

Choice B is incorrect: there is no mention in the passage of any concern on the part of the author about the accuracy of detail.

Choice C is correct: the book does not offer an adequate "critical contextualization of florid detail."

2. Which of the following best describes the function of the second sentence ("*A Dream . . . essayists*") in the context of the passage as a whole?

     Ⓐ To give examples of how *A Dream* presents fascinating portraits that display awareness of the tenuous nature of representations of reality

     Ⓑ To elaborate on how *A Dream* fulfills the author's childhood criteria for a pleasurable book

     Ⓒ To suggest that the author enjoyed *A Dream* for reasons more sophisticated than the reasons she enjoyed certain books as a child

     Ⓓ To illustrate ways in which the author finds *A Dream* to be inadequate in certain critical senses

     Ⓔ To imply that *A Dream* is too varied in focus to provide a proper contextualization of the biographical details it offers

Explanation

This question asks about the function of the second sentence. The correct choice is **Choice B**. As discussed in the description of the passage, that sentence describes what is appealing about the collection in the context of the author's childhood tastes. Choice A is incorrect both because the sentence does not provide examples and because the collection does not display an awareness of the tenuous nature of representations of reality. Choice C is not correct: although one might suspect that the author's enjoyment of collections as an adult would be on a more sophisticated level than when she was young, there is no discussion or even suggestion of that in the passage. Choice D is incorrect because the sentence describes the virtues of the collection. The aspects of the collection that the author finds inadequate are not addressed until later. Choice E is incorrect because, according to the passage, the fact that the collection is varied makes it a "rich" read. There is no suggestion that the variety hinders proper contextualization.

3. During the day in Lake Constance, the zooplankton *D. hyalina* departs for the depths where food is scarce and the water cold. *D. galeata* remains near the warm surface where food is abundant. Even though *D. galeata* grows and reproduces much faster, its population is often outnumbered by *D. hyalina*.

    Which of the following, if true, would help resolve the apparent paradox presented above?

     Ⓐ The number of species of zooplankton living at the bottom of the lake is twice that of species living at the surface.

     Ⓑ Predators of zooplankton, such as whitefish and perch, live and feed near the surface of the lake during the day.

     Ⓒ In order to make the most of scarce food resources, *D. hyalina* matures more slowly than *D. galeata*.

     Ⓓ *D. galeata* clusters under vegetation during the hottest part of the day to avoid the Sun's rays.

     Ⓔ *D. galeata* produces twice as many offspring per individual in any given period of time as does *D. hyalina*.

Description

The paragraph presents an apparent paradox: the zooplankton that spends the day in less hospitable conditions often outnumbers the one that stays in more hospitable conditions.

Explanation

The presence of predators of zooplankton feeding near the surface during the day would suggest that *D. galeata* is consumed at a higher rate than *D. hyalina*: this would explain why *D. hyalina* is often more numerous, so **Choice B** is correct. Choices C and E are incorrect because although they help to explain why the two zooplankton reproduce at different rates, they do not help to resolve the apparent paradox. Choices A and D are incorrect because nothing is said in the paragraph to show the relevance of the presence of other species of zooplankton, nor of the habit of clustering under vegetation, to the relative population size of the two species.

Questions 4 and 5 are based on the following reading passage.

Tocqueville, apparently, was wrong. Jacksonian America was not a fluid, egalitarian society where individual wealth and poverty were ephemeral conditions. At least so argues E. Pessen in his iconoclastic study of the very rich in the United States between
line 1825 and 1850.
5   Pessen does present a quantity of examples, together with some refreshingly intelligible statistics, to establish the existence of an inordinately wealthy class. Though active in commerce or the professions, most of the wealthy were not self-made but had inherited family fortunes. In no sense mercurial, these great fortunes survived the financial panics that destroyed lesser ones. Indeed, in several cities the wealthiest one
10   percent constantly increased its share until by 1850 it owned half of the community's wealth. Although these observations are true, Pessen overestimates their importance by concluding from them that the undoubted progress toward inequality in the late eighteenth century continued in the Jacksonian period and that the United States was a class-ridden, plutocratic society even before industrialization.

Description

The passage describes Pessen's argument that Jacksonian America was not fluid and egalitarian but class-ridden and plutocratic, and criticizes it for leaping to an unjustified conclusion.

4.   According to the passage, Pessen indicates that all of the following were true of the very wealthy in the United States between 1825 and 1850 EXCEPT:

    Ⓐ They formed a distinct upper class.
    Ⓑ Many of them were able to increase their holdings.
    Ⓒ Some of them worked as professionals or in business.
    Ⓓ Most of them accumulated their own fortunes.
    Ⓔ Many of them retained their wealth in spite of financial upheavals.

Explanation

For this question, you are to identify the one statement that CANNOT be correctly attributed to Pessen. Therefore, you must first determine which of the statements given can be attributed to Pessen. According to the passage, Pessen maintains all of the following: there was a class of "inordinately wealthy" Americans (Choice A); in some places that class "constantly increased its share" (Choice B); its members were "active in commerce or the professions" (Choice C); and "these great fortunes survived the financial panics that destroyed lesser ones" (Choice E). However, Pessen also maintains, in contradiction to Choice D, that "most of the wealthy were not self-made but had inherited family fortunes." Therefore, **Choice D** is correct.

5. Which of the following best states the author's main point?

(A) Pessen's study has overturned the previously established view of the social and economic structure of early-nineteenth-century America.

(B) Tocqueville's analysis of the United States in the Jacksonian era remains the definitive account of this period.

(C) Pessen's study is valuable primarily because it shows the continuity of the social system in the United States throughout the nineteenth century.

(D) The social patterns and political power of the extremely wealthy in the United States between 1825 and 1850 are well documented.

(E) Pessen challenges a view of the social and economic systems in the United States from 1825 to 1850, but he draws conclusions that are incorrect.

Explanation

It is important to realize that although most of the passage is devoted to describing Pessen's study, the author's main point is to criticize the conclusion Pessen draws. Choices A, C, and D omit any reference to the author's critical evaluation of Pessen's study, and hence are not statements of the author's main point. Choice B is also incorrect. Because Pessen criticizes Tocqueville and the author criticizes Pessen, it might seem that the author's main point is to defend Tocqueville's analysis. However, the passage does not indicate that Tocqueville's analysis is definitive. **Choice E is correct.** According to the first paragraph, Pessen challenges Tocqueville's view, but according to the second paragraph, Pessen's conclusions are incorrect.

Questions 6 to 9 are based on the following reading passage.

The evolution of intelligence among early large mammals of the grasslands was due in great measure to the interaction between two ecologically synchronized groups of these animals, the hunting carnivores and the herbivores that they hunted. The inter-
line action resulting from the differences between predator and prey led to a general
5   improvement in brain functions; however, certain components of intelligence were improved far more than others.

The kind of intelligence favored by the interplay of increasingly smarter catchers and increasingly keener escapers is defined by attention — that aspect of mind carrying consciousness forward from one moment to the next. It ranges from a passive, free-
10   floating awareness to a highly focused, active fixation. The range through these states is mediated by the arousal system, a network of tracts converging from sensory systems to integrating centers in the brain stem. From the more relaxed to the more vigorous levels, sensitivity to novelty is increased. The organism is more awake, more vigilant; this increased vigilance results in the apprehension of ever more subtle signals as the
15   organism becomes more sensitive to its surroundings. The processes of arousal and concentration give attention its direction. Arousal is at first general, with a flooding of impulses in the brain stem; then gradually the activation is channeled. Thus begins concentration, the holding of consistent images. One meaning of intelligence is the way in which these images and other alertly searched information are used in the context of
20   previous experience. Consciousness links past attention to the present and permits the integration of details with perceived ends and purposes.

The elements of intelligence and consciousness come together marvelously to produce different styles in predator and prey. Herbivores and carnivores develop different kinds of attention related to escaping or chasing. Although in both kinds of animal,
25   arousal stimulates the production of adrenaline and norepinephrine by the adrenal

glands, the effect in herbivores is primarily fear, whereas in carnivores the effect is primarily aggression. For both, arousal attunes the animal to what is ahead. Perhaps it does not experience forethought as we know it, but the animal does experience some-
line thing like it. The predator is searchingly aggressive, inner-directed, tuned by the
30 nervous system and the adrenal hormones, but aware in a sense closer to human consciousness than, say, a hungry lizard's instinctive snap at a passing beetle. Using past events as a framework, the large mammal predator is working out a relationship between movement and food, sensitive to possibilities in cold trails and distant sounds — and yesterday's unforgotten lessons. The herbivore prey is of a different mind. Its
35 mood of wariness rather than searching and its attitude of general expectancy instead of anticipating are silk-thin veils of tranquillity over an explosive endocrine system.

Description

The passage describes improvements in certain components of intelligence among early large mammals of the grasslands. The second paragraph focuses on attention as a primary area of improvement, and the third paragraph outlines how attention differs in predator and prey species.

6.   The author refers to a hungry lizard (line 31) primarily in order to

(A) demonstrate the similarity between the hunting methods of mammals and those of nonmammals

(B) broaden the application of the argument by including an insectivore as an example

(C) make a distinction between higher and lower levels of consciousness

(D) provide an additional illustration of the brutality characteristic of predators

(E) offer an objection to suggestions that all animals lack consciousness

Explanation

Choice C is correct. The "hungry lizard's instinctive snap" is contrasted with the mammal's higher level of awareness. Choices A and B are incorrect. The example of the hungry lizard provides a contrast; it does not demonstrate a similarity or extend the author's argument. Choices D and E are incorrect. Brutality is not mentioned in the passage as a characteristic of predators, and there is no suggestion that all animals lack consciousness.

7.   It can be inferred from the passage that in animals less intelligent than the mammals discussed in the passage

(A) past experience is less helpful in ensuring survival

(B) attention is more highly focused

(C) muscular coordination is less highly developed

(D) there is less need for competition among species

(E) environment is more important in establishing the proper ratio of prey to predator

Explanation

Choice A is correct. In lines 18–20, the author defines intelligence in terms of an animal's use of past experience. In the context of the entire passage, it can be inferred that more intelligent animals, such as the grassland mammals discussed, are better able to use past experience to help them survive than less intelligent animals are. Choice B is incorrect. The second paragraph of the passage indicates that attention is more highly focused in animals of greater, rather than less, intelligence. Choices C, D, and E are incorrect. The author does not discuss muscular coordination as an element in intelligence, gives no indication that in less intelligent species there is less need for competition, and does not discuss how a proper ratio of prey to predator is established.

8. According to the passage, improvement in brain function among early large mammals resulted primarily from which of the following?
    - (A) Interplay of predator and prey
    - (B) Persistence of free-floating awareness in animals of the grasslands
    - (C) Gradual dominance of warm-blooded mammals over cold-blooded reptiles
    - (D) Interaction of early large mammals with less intelligent species
    - (E) Improvement of the capacity for memory among herbivores and carnivores

Explanation

Choice A is correct. It directly paraphrases the statement in lines 3–5, which describes the author's view of the development of improved brain function in early mammals. Choice B is incorrect. It is likely that the persistence of "free-floating awareness" played a part in the animals' survival, but there is no indication in the passage that brain function improved because of it. Choices C and D are incorrect: the passage does not discuss the relationship between mammals and reptiles or the interaction between large mammals and less intelligent species. Choice E is incorrect. Improved capacity for memory is an improvement in brain function, rather than a reason for improved brain function.

9. According to the passage, as the process of arousal in an organism continues, all of the following may occur EXCEPT
    - (A) the production of adrenaline
    - (B) the production of norepinephrine
    - (C) a heightening of sensitivity to stimuli
    - (D) an increase in selectivity with respect to stimuli
    - (E) an expansion of the range of states mediated by the brain stem

Explanation

This question asks you what does NOT occur during arousal. To answer the question, you must first determine what does occur. According to the passage, arousal does stimulate the production of adrenaline and norepinephrine (lines 24–26); does increase sensitivity to stimuli (lines 12–13); and does increase concentration on specific stimuli (lines 16–18). Thus Choices A through D all describe consequences of arousal. Only **Choice E** is correct. There is no indication in the passage that the range of states mediated by the brain stem expands during arousal.

SET 5. Discrete Questions: Hard

> **For Questions 1 to 6, select one entry for each blank from the corresponding column of choices. Fill all blanks in the way that best completes the text.**

1. For some time now, _____ has been presumed not to exist: the cynical conviction that everybody has an angle is considered wisdom.

Ⓐ rationality
Ⓑ flexibility
Ⓒ diffidence
Ⓓ disinterestedness
Ⓔ insincerity

Explanation

The colon indicates that the second part of the sentence will explain the first part. The missing word will describe the opposite of the cynical conviction that "everybody has an angle," that is, that each person is concerned primarily with his or her own interests. Since "disinterestedness" means lack of self-interest, Choice D is correct. None of the other answer choices means something that is contrasted with or opposed to being primarily concerned with one's own interests.

   Thus the correct answer is **disinterestedness** (Choice D).

2. Human nature and long distances have made exceeding the speed limit a (i)_____ in the state, so the legislators surprised no one when, acceding to public demand, they (ii)_____ increased penalties for speeding.

Blank (i)	Blank (ii)
Ⓐ controversial habit	Ⓓ endorsed
Ⓑ cherished tradition	Ⓔ considered
Ⓒ disquieting ritual	Ⓕ rejected

Explanation

The reference to human nature and long distances suggest that it is rather routine for drivers to exceed the speed limit in this state. "Cherished tradition" best fits this context for Blank (i), since there is nothing in the sentence to suggest that speeding here is "controversial" or "disquieting." In Blank (ii) we need to consider what the legislature would do that would surprise no one with regard to increased penalties for speeding. Given what we have learned so far, "rejected" is the best answer; it would be surprising if the legislature "endorsed" or even "considered" increased penalties for speeding.

   Thus the correct answer is **cherished tradition** (Choice B) and **rejected** (Choice F).

3. Serling's account of his employer's reckless decision making (i)_____ that company's image as (ii)_____ bureaucracy full of wary managers.

Blank (i)	Blank (ii)
(A) belies	(D) an injudicious
(B) exposes	(E) a disorganized
(C) overshadows	(F) a cautious

Explanation

The correct answer for Blank (i) must support, or at least be consistent with, the contrast between Serling's account, which emphasizes the recklessness of the company's decision making, and the company's image, that of a bureaucracy full of wary managers. For Blank (i), "belies" is the best choice since Serling's account would certainly belie or contradict the company's image. "Exposes" makes little sense since the image presumably is already out in the open, and there is nothing in the sentence that suggests Serling's account "overshadows" the company's image. As for Blank (ii), "a cautious" is the most logical choice. Neither "an injudicious" nor "a disorganized" makes sense in Blank (ii) as they both go against the notion of wariness.

Thus the correct answer is **belies** (Choice A) and **a cautious** (Choice F).

4. No other contemporary poet's work has such a well-earned reputation for (i)_____, and there are few whose moral vision is so imperiously unsparing. Of late, however, the almost belligerent demands of his severe and densely forbidding poetry have taken an improbable turn. This new collection is the poet's fourth book in six years — an ample output even for poets of sunny disposition, let alone for one of such (ii)_____ over the previous 50 years. Yet for all his newfound (iii)_____, his poetry is as thorny as ever.

Blank (i)	Blank (ii)	Blank (iii)
(A) patent accessibility	(D) penitential austerity	(G) taciturnity
(B) intrinsic frivolity	(E) intractable prolixity	(H) volubility
(C) near impenetrability	(F) impetuous prodigality	(I) pellucidity

Explanation

Since the author of the paragraph has described the poet's reputation as "well-earned," the correct completion for Blank (i) must be something that is consistent with what the rest of the passage says about the poet's work. Only "near impenetrability" fulfills this requirement, since the next sentence tells us that the poet's work is "severe" and "densely forbidding," which rule out both accessibility and frivolity. The Blank (ii) completion must contrast with "ample output," and of the available options, only "penitential austerity" does so. Finally, the word in Blank (iii), since it is preceded by "newfound," must refer to the change that has occurred in the poet's work. The change the paragraph has described is an increase in output, so "volubility" is the correct choice.

Thus the correct answer is **near impenetrability** (Choice C), **penitential austerity** (Choice D), and **volubility** (Choice H).

5.   Managers who think that strong environmental performance will (i)_____ their company's financial performance often (ii)_____ claims that systems designed to help them manage environmental concerns are valuable tools. By contrast, managers who perceive environmental performance to be (iii)_____ to financial success may view an environmental management system as extraneous. In either situation, and whatever their perceptions, it is a manager's commitment to achieving environmental improvement rather than the mere presence of a system that determines environmental performance.

Blank (i)	Blank (ii)	Blank (iii)
Ⓐ eclipse	Ⓓ uncritically accept	Ⓖ complementary
Ⓑ bolster	Ⓔ appropriately acknowledge	Ⓗ intrinsic
Ⓒ degrade	Ⓕ hotly dispute	Ⓘ peripheral

Explanation

The first two sentences introduce two contrasting sets of managers. The managers identified in the second sentence view systems designed to help manage environmental concerns as "extraneous," suggesting that they would view environmental performance to be "peripheral" (Choice I) to financial performance. The other options for Blank (iii) — "complementary" and "intrinsic" — are not consistent with the idea that environmental management systems are extraneous. With Blank (iii) filled in, we can go back to Blanks (i) and (ii) with greater confidence: "bolster" works best in Blank (i), since the two sets of managers have contrasting views. Blank (ii) is not straightforward — clearly these managers would not "hotly dispute" this claim, but "appropriately acknowledge" is less easily ruled out. "Uncritically accept" makes sense and is confirmed when we look at the final sentence in which the author warns that, in either situation, "the mere presence of a system" is not enough to achieve environmental improvement. In fact, a system is not even necessary. Thus the author of the paragraph does not regard the systems as particularly valuable, ruling out "appropriately acknowledge."

Thus the correct answer is **bolster** (Choice B), **uncritically accept** (Choice D), and **peripheral** (Choice I).

6. Philosophy, unlike most other subjects, does not try to extend our knowledge by discovering new information about the world. Instead it tries to deepen our understanding through (i)_____ what is already closest to us — the experiences, thoughts, concepts, and activities that make up our lives but that ordinarily escape our notice precisely because they are so familiar. Philosophy begins by finding (ii)_____ the things that are (iii) _____.

Blank (i)	Blank (ii)	Blank (iii)
Ⓐ attainment of	Ⓓ essentially irrelevant	Ⓖ most prosaic
Ⓑ rumination on	Ⓔ utterly mysterious	Ⓗ somewhat hackneyed
Ⓒ detachment from	Ⓕ thoroughly commonplace	Ⓘ refreshingly novel

Explanation

The first two sentences present a contrast between extending our knowledge by discovering "new information about the world" — which we are told philosophy does not do — and extending knowledge through some activity involving "things that are closest to us." The first blank asks us to identify that activity, and although "attainment" makes little sense in context, both "rumination on" and "detachment from" have some appeal. However, the clear implication that philosophy attends to things that ordinarily escape our notice eliminates "detachment from" as a correct answer. Blank (ii) requires something that suggests the importance of familiar things as subjects of philosophical rumination, and "utterly mysterious" does just that. "Essentially irrelevant" and "thoroughly commonplace" do not fit logically since they suggest that these "familiar" things are unimportant. Similarly, Blank (iii) needs to be consistent with the description of those things as familiar and close. "Most prosaic" fits that idea while "refreshingly novel" goes in the other direction. "Somewhat hackneyed" has some plausibility but is too negative given the overall tone of the sentence; there is no indication that those things are in any way trite.

Thus the correct answer is **rumination on** (Choice B), **utterly mysterious** (Choice E), and **most prosaic** (Choice G).

For Questions 7 to 9, select the <u>two</u> answer choices that, when used to complete the sentence, fit the meaning of the sentence as a whole <u>and</u> produce completed sentences that are alike in meaning.

---

7. The government's implementation of a new code of ethics appeared intended to shore up the ruling party's standing with an increasingly _____ electorate at a time when the party is besieged by charges that it trades favors for campaign money.
   - A aloof
   - B placid
   - C restive
   - D skittish
   - E tranquil
   - F vociferous

Explanation

The words filling the blank must be consistent with the idea that the ruling party needs to "shore up" its standing with the electorate. In their own way, Choices A, C, D, and F are consistent with that idea, but only two of these when taken together — "restive" and "skittish" — produce sentences that are alike in meaning. "Aloof" fits the blank reasonably well, but there is no other word offered that is nearly alike in meaning. The same holds for "vociferous." "Placid" and "tranquil" are similar in meaning but do not fit the context of the sentence.

Thus the correct answer is **restive** (Choice C) and **skittish** (Choice D).

8. Overlarge, uneven, and ultimately disappointing, the retrospective exhibition seems too much like special pleading for a forgotten painter of real but _____ talents.

    [A] limited
    [B] partial
    [C] undiscovered
    [D] circumscribed
    [E] prosaic
    [F] hidden

Explanation

The sentence is explaining why the exhibition of the painter's work was unsatisfactory, and since it says that the painter's talents were real, the word in the blank has to indicate why those talents were not, in the opinion of the author of the sentence, good enough. The words "limited" and "circumscribed" do so and also produce sentences that are alike in meaning, so this pair forms the correct answer. Although "undiscovered" and "hidden" are similar in meaning, they do not make sense in the context of the sentence, since they do not indicate why the painter's talents were not adequate. Other choices, such as "partial" and "prosaic" might make sense in context, but none of the other choices that meets that criterion also has a companion choice that would produce another sentence alike in meaning.

Thus the correct answer is **limited** (Choice A) and **circumscribed** (Choice D).

9. Newspapers report that the former executive has been trying to keep a low profile since his _____ exit from the company.

    [A] celebrated
    [B] mysterious
    [C] long-awaited
    [D] fortuitous
    [D] indecorous
    [F] unseemly

Explanation

The sentence needs to be completed with a word that suggests a reason for the executive to wish to keep a low profile. The words "indecorous" and "unseemly" both suggest such a reason, and the sentences completed with those two choices are alike in meaning. Therefore, that pair forms the correct answer. Although one might get a sensible sentence by filling the blank with another choice, such as "long-awaited," none of the other choices that meets that criterion also has a companion choice that would produce another sentence alike in meaning.

Thus the correct answer is **indecorous** (Choice E) and **unseemly** (Choice F).

SET 6. Reading Comprehension Questions: Hard

For each of Questions 1 to 8, select <u>one</u> answer choice unless otherwise instructed.

1. In the United States between 1850 and 1880, the number of farmers continued to increase, but at a rate lower than that of the general population.

    Which of the following statements directly contradicts the information presented above?

    Ⓐ The number of farmers in the general population increased slightly in the 30 years between 1850 and 1880.

    Ⓑ The rate of growth of the United States labor force and the rate of growth of the general population rose simultaneously in the 30 years between 1850 and 1880.

    Ⓒ The proportion of farmers in the United States labor force remained constant in the 30 years between 1850 and 1880.

    Ⓓ The proportion of farmers in the United States labor force decreased from 64 percent in 1850 to 49 percent in 1880.

    Ⓔ The proportion of farmers in the general population increased from 68 percent in 1850 to 72 percent in 1880.

Explanation

The given sentence indicates that the proportion of farmers in the general population decreased from 1850 to 1880. **Choice E** says exactly the opposite — that this proportion increased — and therefore it contradicts the passage and is the correct response. Choice A is incorrect because it agrees with the given sentence, and Choices B, C, and D are all incorrect because they refer to the labor force, about which the given sentence says nothing.

2. A ten-year comparison between the United States and the Soviet Union in terms of crop yields per acre revealed that when only planted acreage is compared, Soviet yields were equal to 68 percent of United States yields. When total agricultural acreage (planted acreage plus fallow acreage) is compared, however, Soviet yield was 114 percent of United States yield.

From the information above, which of the following can be most reliably inferred about United States and Soviet agriculture during the ten-year period?

Ⓐ A higher percentage of total agricultural acreage was fallow in the United States than in the Soviet Union.

Ⓑ The United States had more fallow acreage than planted acreage.

Ⓒ Fewer total acres of available agricultural land were fallow in the Soviet Union than in the United States.

Ⓓ The Soviet Union had more planted acreage than fallow acreage.

Ⓔ The Soviet Union produced a greater volume of crops than the United States produced.

Explanation

If crop yield per planted acre was less in the Soviet Union than it was in the United States, yet crop yield per total (planted plus fallow) agricultural acreage was greater in the Soviet Union than it was in the United States, the percentage of the total acreage that was left fallow must have been lower in the Soviet Union than in the United States. Therefore, **Choice A** is the correct answer. Since the information provided in the paragraph is given in terms of yield per acre, no conclusion can be drawn about actual acreage, so Choices B, C, and D are all incorrect. Similarly, it is impossible to determine the total volume of crops produced in the Soviet Union, so Choice E is incorrect.

Questions 3 and 4 are based on the following reading passage.

For hot desert locations with access to seawater, a new greenhouse design generates freshwater and cool air. Oriented to the prevailing wind, the front wall of perforated cardboard, moistened and cooled by a trickle of seawater pumped in, cools and moistens hot air blowing in. This cool, humidified air accelerates plant growth; little water
line evaporates from leaves. Though greenhouses normally capture the heat of sunlight,
5 a double-layered roof, the inner layer coated to reflect infrared light outward, allows visible sunlight in but traps solar heat between the two layers. This heated air, drawn down from the roof, then mixes with the greenhouse air as it reaches a second seawater-moistened cardboard wall at the back of the greenhouse. There the air absorbs more moisture, which then condenses on a metal wall cooled by seawater, and thus
10 distilled water for irrigating the plants collects.

Description

The passage describes a greenhouse design and the process by which the design generates freshwater and cool air in a desert environment lacking in these things.

For the following question, consider each of the choices separately and select all that apply.

3.   It can be inferred that the process described in the passage makes use of which of the following?

   [A] The tendency of hot air to rise
   [B] The directional movement of wind
   [C] The temperature differential between the sea and the desert

Explanation

Choices B and C are correct. This question asks the reader which of the three phenomena listed in the answer choices is used in the process described in the passage.

Choice A is incorrect: the passage does not indicate that the tendency of hot air to rise is used in the process, and in fact says that heated air is drawn down, not up, as part of the greenhouse design.

Choice B is correct: the second sentence describes the orientation of a perforated cardboard wall toward the prevailing wind so that hot air blows in and is moistened.

Choice C is correct: the passage describes the use of seawater to cool hot desert air and to provide moisture that is absorbed by heated air and then condensed on a seawater-cooled surface for the purpose of irrigating the plants.

For the following question, consider each of the choices separately and select all that apply.

4.   It can be inferred that the greenhouse roof is designed to allow for which of the following?

   [A] The avoidance of intense solar heat inside the greenhouse
   [B] The entry of sunlight into the greenhouse to make the plants grow
   [C] The mixture of heated air with greenhouse air to enhance the collection of moisture

Explanation

All three choices are correct. This question asks the reader which of the three effects listed in the answer choices are intended as part of the design of the greenhouse roof.

Choice A is correct: the purpose of the double-layered roof is to trap solar heat before it gets inside the greenhouse proper.

Choice B is correct: the coating on the inner layer of the roof allows visible sunlight into the greenhouse.

Choice C is correct: the last two sentences of the passage describe how heated air from the roof is drawn down to mix with greenhouse air, resulting in the collection of distilled water for irrigation purposes.

Many critics of Emily Brontë's novel *Wuthering Heights* see its second part as a counterpoint that comments on, if it does not reverse, the first part, where a romantic reading receives more confirmation. Seeing the two parts as a whole is encouraged by the novel's sophisticated structure, revealed in its complex use of narrators and time shifts.
Granted that the presence of these elements need not argue for an authorial awareness of novelistic construction comparable to that of Henry James, their presence does encourage attempts to unify the novel's heterogeneous parts. However, any interpretation that seeks to unify all of the novel's diverse elements is bound to be somewhat unconvincing. This is not because such an interpretation necessarily stiffens into a thesis (although rigidity in any interpretation of this or of any novel is always a danger), but because *Wuthering Heights* has recalcitrant elements of undeniable power that, ultimately, resist inclusion in an all-encompassing interpretation. In this respect, *Wuthering Heights* shares a feature of *Hamlet*.

line
5

10

Description

The passage discusses a critical view concerning the unity of structure of *Wuthering Heights*, then, following the use of "However," expresses a reservation about that view.

5. According to the passage, which of the following is a true statement about the first and second parts of *Wuthering Heights*?

(A) The second part has received more attention from critics.
(B) The second part has little relation to the first part.
(C) The second part annuls the force of the first part.
(D) The second part provides less substantiation for a romantic reading.
(E) The second part is better because it is more realistic.

Explanation

This question requires the reader to identify which of the given relationships between the novel's first and second parts is one that is described in the passage. According to the first sentence, the first part of the novel tends to confirm the "romantic" reading more strongly than the second. Therefore, **Choice D** is correct. Nothing in the passage suggests that critics have paid more attention to the second part, that the two parts have little relation, or that the second part is better. Therefore, Choices A, B, and E are incorrect. Choice C is a more extreme statement than any found in the passage, and therefore it is incorrect.

6. Which of the following inferences about Henry James's awareness of novelistic construction is best supported by the passage?

(A) James, more than any other novelist, was aware of the difficulties of novelistic construction.
(B) James was very aware of the details of novelistic construction.
(C) James's awareness of novelistic construction derived from his reading of Brontë.
(D) James's awareness of novelistic construction has led most commentators to see unity in his individual novels.
(E) James's awareness of novelistic construction precluded him from violating the unity of his novels.

Explanation

This question focuses on the passage's mention of Henry James and asks what can be inferred from it. The third sentence implies that James represents a very high degree of authorial awareness of novelistic construction and that no such claim is necessarily being made for Brontë. Thus, **Choice B** is the correct answer. Choice A is incorrect, since the passage does not imply that there are particular difficulties that James understood uniquely among novelists. Choice C is incorrect because the passage does not state or imply that James read Brontë. The passage also does not say anything about commentators' opinions of the unity of James's works; therefore Choice D is incorrect. Choice E is incorrect because the passage itself offers no information about the unity of James's novels.

7. The author of the passage would be most likely to agree that an interpretation of a novel should

  (A) not try to unite heterogeneous elements in the novel

  (B) not be inflexible in its treatment of the elements in the novel

  (C) not argue that the complex use of narrators or of time shifts indicates a sophisticated structure

  (D) concentrate on those recalcitrant elements of the novel that are outside the novel's main structure

  (E) primarily consider those elements of novelistic construction of which the author of the novel was aware

Explanation

This question requires the reader to determine what can be inferred from the passage about its author's view of the interpretation of novels. Choice A may seem attractive because in the passage the author says that *Wuthering Heights* has heterogeneous elements that resist inclusion in a unifying interpretive scheme. Choice A is incorrect, however, because the author does not indicate that the unification of different elements is to be avoided in interpretation generally. By contrast, the author's parenthetical statement about rigidity does present a general warning against inflexibility of interpretation, and it is this that supports **Choice B** as the correct answer. Choice C is incorrect, as the author actually suggests the contrary of this view in the second sentence of the passage. Although the author mentions recalcitrant elements of *Wuthering Heights*, there is no suggestion by the author that such elements deserve a special focus in interpretation. Therefore Choice D is incorrect. The author of the passage does not indicate which elements, if any, of novelistic construction are most worthy of consideration. Therefore Choice E is incorrect.

For the following question, consider each of the choices separately and select all that apply.

8. The author of the passage suggests which of the following about *Hamlet*?

    A *Hamlet* has usually attracted critical interpretations that tend to stiffen into theses.

    B *Hamlet* has elements that are not amenable to an all-encompassing critical interpretation.

    C *Hamlet* is less open to an all-encompassing critical interpretation than is *Wuthering Heights*.

Explanation

Choice B is correct. This question asks the reader which of the three statements about *Hamlet* listed in the answer choices are suggested by the author of the passage.

Choice A is incorrect: the passage does not provide information about the characteristics of the usual critical interpretations of *Hamlet*.

Choice B is correct: *Hamlet* is mentioned only in the final sentence of the passage, which refers to "this respect" in which *Hamlet* and *Wuthering Heights* are similar. The previous sentence reveals the point of similarity referred to: *Wuthering Heights* has elements that resist inclusion in an all-encompassing interpretive framework.

Choice C is incorrect: the passage mentions only a feature shared between *Hamlet* and *Wuthering Heights*. It does not suggest anything about a difference in their openness to a particular critical interpretation.

5 GRE® Quantitative Reasoning

Overview of the Quantitative Reasoning Measure

The Quantitative Reasoning measure of the GRE revised General Test assesses your:

- basic mathematical skills
- understanding of elementary mathematical concepts
- ability to reason quantitatively and to model and solve problems with quantitative methods

Some of the questions in the measure are posed in real-life settings, while others are posed in purely mathematical settings. The skills, concepts, and abilities are tested in the four content areas below.

Arithmetic topics include properties and types of integers, such as divisibility, factorization, prime numbers, remainders, and odd and even integers; arithmetic operations, exponents, and radicals; and concepts such as estimation, percent, ratio, rate, absolute value, the number line, decimal representation, and sequences of numbers.

Algebra topics include operations with exponents; factoring and simplifying algebraic expressions; relations, functions, equations, and inequalities; solving linear and quadratic equations and inequalities; solving simultaneous equations and inequalities; setting up equations to solve word problems; and coordinate geometry, including graphs of functions, equations, and inequalities, intercepts, and slopes of lines.

Geometry topics include parallel and perpendicular lines, circles, triangles—including isosceles, equilateral, and 30°-60°-90° triangles—quadrilaterals, other polygons, congruent and similar figures, three-dimensional figures, area, perimeter, volume, the Pythagorean theorem, and angle measurement in degrees. The ability to construct proofs is not tested.

Data analysis topics include basic descriptive statistics, such as mean, median, mode, range, standard deviation, interquartile range, quartiles, and percentiles; interpretation of data in tables and graphs, such as line graphs, bar graphs, circle graphs, boxplots, scatterplots, and frequency distributions; elementary probability, such as probabilities of compound events and independent events; random variables and probability distributions, including normal distributions; and counting methods, such as combinations, permutations, and Venn diagrams. These topics are typically taught in high school algebra courses or introductory statistics courses. Inferential statistics is not tested.

The content in these areas includes high school mathematics and statistics at a level that is generally no higher than a second course in algebra; it does not include trigonometry, calculus, or other higher-level mathematics. The publication *Math Review for the GRE revised General Test*, which is available at **www.ets.org/gre/revised/ prepare**, provides detailed information about the content of the Quantitative Reasoning measure. The *Math Review* is Chapter 7 in this book.

The mathematical symbols, terminology, and conventions used in the Quantitative Reasoning measure are those that are standard at the high school level. For example, the positive direction of a number line is to the right, distances are nonnegative, and prime numbers are greater than 1. Whenever nonstandard notation is used in a question, it is explicitly introduced in the question.

In addition to conventions, there are some assumptions about numbers and geometric figures that are used in the Quantitative Reasoning measure. Two of these assumptions are (i) all numbers used are real numbers and (ii) geometric figures are not necessarily drawn to scale. More about conventions and assumptions appears in the publication *Mathematical Conventions for the GRE revised General Test*, which is available at **www.ets.org/gre/revised/prepare** and at the end of this chapter.

Quantitative Reasoning Question Types

The Quantitative Reasoning measure has four types of questions:

- Quantitative Comparison questions
- Multiple-choice questions—Select One Answer Choice
- Multiple-choice questions—Select One or More Answer Choices
- Numeric Entry questions

Each question appears either independently as a discrete question or as part of a set of questions called a Data Interpretation set. All of the questions in a Data Interpretation set are based on the same data presented in tables, graphs, or other displays of data.

In the computer-based test, you are allowed to use a basic calculator—provided on-screen—on the Quantitative Reasoning measure. Information about using the calculator appears later in this chapter. For those taking the paper-based test, calculators will be provided at the test center for use during the test. Information about using the calculator to help you answer questions appears in the free *Practice Book for the Paper-based GRE revised General Test*, which is available at **www.ets.org/gre/ revised/prepare**.

Quantitative Comparison Questions

Description

Questions of this type ask you to compare two quantities—Quantity A and Quantity B—and then determine which of the following statements describes the comparison.

- Quantity A is greater.
- Quantity B is greater.
- The two quantities are equal.
- The relationship cannot be determined from the information given.

Tips for Answering

- **Become familiar with the answer choices.** Quantitative Comparison questions always have the same answer choices, so get to know them, especially the last answer choice, "The relationship cannot be determined from the information given." Never select this last choice if it is clear that the values of the two quantities can be determined by computation. Also, if you determine that one quantity is greater than the other, make sure you carefully select the corresponding choice so as not to reverse the first two choices.

- **Avoid unnecessary computations.** Don't waste time performing needless computations in order to compare the two quantities. Simplify, transform, or estimate one or both of the given quantities only as much as is necessary to compare them.

- **Remember that geometric figures are not necessarily drawn to scale.** If any aspect of a given geometric figure is not fully determined, try to redraw the figure, keeping those aspects that are completely determined by the given information fixed but changing the aspects of the figure that are not determined. Examine the results. What variations are possible in the relative lengths of line segments or measures of angles?

- **Plug in numbers.** If one or both of the quantities are algebraic expressions, you can substitute easy numbers for the variables and compare the resulting quantities in your analysis. Consider all kinds of appropriate numbers before you give an answer: e.g., zero, positive and negative numbers, small and large numbers, fractions and decimals. If you see that Quantity A is greater than Quantity B in one case and Quantity B is greater than Quantity A in another case, choose "The relationship cannot be determined from the information given."

- **Simplify the comparison.** If both quantities are algebraic or arithmetic expressions and you cannot easily see a relationship between them, you can try to simplify the comparison. Try a step-by-step simplification that is similar to the steps involved when you solve the equation $5 = 4x + 3$ for x, or similar to the steps involved when you determine that the inequality $\dfrac{3y + 2}{5} < y$ is equivalent to the simpler inequality $1 < y$. Begin by setting up a comparison involving the two quantities, as follows:

$$\text{Quantity A } \boxed{?} \text{ Quantity B}$$

where $\boxed{?}$ is a "placeholder" that could represent the relationship *greater than* ($>$), *less than* ($<$), or *equal to* ($=$) or could represent the fact that the relationship cannot be determined from the information given. Then try to simplify the comparison, step by step, until you can determine a relationship between simplified quantities. For example, you may conclude after the last step that $\boxed{?}$ represents equal to ($=$). Based on this conclusion, you may be able to compare Quantities A and B. To understand this strategy more fully, see sample questions 6 to 9.

Sample Questions

Compare Quantity A and Quantity B, using additional information centered above the two quantities if such information is given, and select one of the following four answer choices:

Ⓐ   **Quantity A is greater.**
Ⓑ   **Quantity B is greater.**
Ⓒ   **The two quantities are equal.**
Ⓓ   **The relationship cannot be determined from the information given.**

A symbol that appears more than once in a question has the same meaning throughout the question.

	Quantity A	Quantity B
1.	(2)(6)	2 + 6

Ⓐ   Quantity A is greater.

Ⓑ   Quantity B is greater.

Ⓒ   The two quantities are equal.

Ⓓ   The relationship cannot be determined from the information given.

Explanation

Since 12 is greater than 8, Quantity A is greater than Quantity B. **Thus, the correct answer is Choice A, Quantity A is greater.**

Lionel is younger than Maria.

	Quantity A	Quantity B
2.	Twice Lionel's age	Maria's age

Ⓐ   Quantity A is greater.

Ⓑ   Quantity B is greater.

Ⓒ   The two quantities are equal.

Ⓓ   The relationship cannot be determined from the information given.

Explanation

If Lionel's age is 6 years and Maria's age is 10 years, then Quantity A is greater, but if Lionel's age is 4 years and Maria's age is 10 years, then Quantity B is greater. Thus, the relationship cannot be determined.

   The correct answer is Choice D, the relationship cannot be determined from the information given.

Quantity A	Quantity B
3. 54% of 360	150

Ⓐ Quantity A is greater.

Ⓑ Quantity B is greater.

Ⓒ The two quantities are equal.

Ⓓ The relationship cannot be determined from the information given.

Explanation

Without doing the exact computation, you can see that 54 percent of 360 is greater than $\frac{1}{2}$ of 360, which is 180, and 180 is greater than Quantity B, 150.

Thus, the correct answer is Choice A, Quantity A is greater.

Figure 1

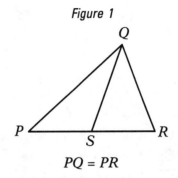

$PQ = PR$

Quantity A	Quantity B
4. *PS*	*SR*

Ⓐ Quantity A is greater.

Ⓑ Quantity B is greater.

Ⓒ The two quantities are equal.

Ⓓ The relationship cannot be determined from the information given.

Explanation

From Figure 1, you know that *PQR* is a triangle and that point *S* is between points *P* and *R*, so $PS < PR$ and $SR < PR$. You are also given that $PQ = PR$. However, this information is not sufficient to compare *PS* and *SR*. Furthermore, because the figure is not necessarily drawn to scale, you cannot determine the relative sizes of *PS* and *SR* visually from the figure, though they may appear to be equal. The position of *S* can vary alongside *PR* anywhere between *P* and *R*. Following are two possible variations of Figure 1, each of which is drawn to be consistent with the information $PQ = PR$.

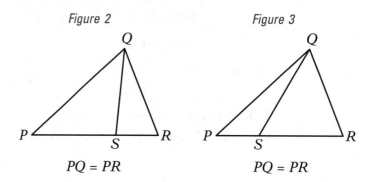

Figure 2 *Figure 3*

$PQ = PR$ $PQ = PR$

Note that Quantity A is greater in Figure 2 and Quantity B is greater in Figure 3.
Thus, the correct answer is Choice D, the relationship cannot be determined from the information given.

$$y = 2x^2 + 7x - 3$$

Quantity A	Quantity B
x	y

5.

Ⓐ Quantity A is greater.

Ⓑ Quantity B is greater.

Ⓒ The two quantities are equal.

Ⓓ The relationship cannot be determined from the information given.

Explanation

If $x = 0$, then $y = 2(0^2) + 7(0) - 3 = -3$, so in this case, $x > y$; but if $x = 1$, then $y = 2(1^2) + 7(1) - 3 = 6$, so in that case, $y > x$.

Thus, the correct answer is Choice D, the relationship cannot be determined from the information given.

Note that plugging numbers into expressions *may not* be conclusive. It *is* conclusive, however, if you get different results after plugging in different numbers: the conclusion is that the relationship cannot be determined from the information given. It is also conclusive if there are only a small number of possible numbers to plug in and all of them yield the same result, say, that Quantity B is greater.

Now suppose that there are an infinite number of possible numbers to plug in. If you plug many of them in and each time the result is, for example, that Quantity A is greater, you still cannot conclude that Quantity A is greater for every possible number that could be plugged in. Further analysis would be necessary and should focus on whether Quantity A is greater for all possible numbers or whether there are numbers for which Quantity A is not greater.

The following sample questions focus on simplifying the comparison.

$$y > 4$$

	Quantity A	Quantity B
6.	$\dfrac{3y + 2}{5}$	y

   Ⓐ   Quantity A is greater.

   Ⓑ   Quantity B is greater.

   Ⓒ   The two quantities are equal.

   Ⓓ   The relationship cannot be determined from the information given.

Explanation

Set up the initial comparison:

$$\frac{3y + 2}{5} \;\boxed{?}\; y$$

Then simplify:

Step 1: Multiply both sides by 5 to get

$$3y + 2 \;\boxed{?}\; 5y$$

Step 2: Subtract $3y$ from both sides to get

$$2 \;\boxed{?}\; 2y$$

Step 3: Divide both sides by 2 to get

$$1 \;\boxed{?}\; y$$

The comparison is now simplified as much as possible. In order to compare 1 and y, note that you are given the information $y > 4$ (above Quantities A and B). It follows from $y > 4$ that $y > 1$, or $1 < y$, so that in the comparison $1 \;\boxed{?}\; y$, the placeholder $\boxed{?}$ represents *less than* ($<$): $1 < y$.

    However, the problem asks for a comparison between Quantity A and Quantity B, not a comparison between 1 and y. To go from the comparison between 1 and y to a comparison between Quantities A and B, start with the last comparison, $1 < y$, and carefully consider each simplification step in reverse order to determine what each comparison implies about the preceding comparison, all the way back to the comparison between Quantities A and B if possible. Since step 3 was "*divide* both sides by 2," *multiplying* both sides of the comparison $1 < y$ by 2 implies the preceding comparison $2 < 2y$, thus reversing step 3. Each simplification step can be reversed as follows:

- Reverse step 3: *multiply* both sides by 2.
- Reverse step 2: *add* 3y to both sides.
- Reverse step 1: *divide* both sides by 5.

    When each step is reversed, the relationship remains *less than* ($<$), so Quantity A is less than Quantity B.

    Thus, the correct answer is Choice B, Quantity B is greater.

While some simplification steps like subtracting 3 from both sides or dividing both sides by 10 are always reversible, it is important to note that some steps, like squaring both sides, may not be reversible.

Also, note that when you simplify an *inequality*, the steps of multiplying or dividing both sides by a negative number change the direction of the inequality; for example, if $x < y$, then $-x > -y$. So the relationship in the final, simplified inequality may be the *opposite* of the relationship between Quantities A and B. This is another reason to consider the impact of each step carefully.

	Quantity A	Quantity B
7.	$\dfrac{2^{30} - 2^{29}}{2}$	2^{28}

Ⓐ Quantity A is greater.

Ⓑ Quantity B is greater.

Ⓒ The two quantities are equal.

Ⓓ The relationship cannot be determined from the information given.

Explanation

Set up the initial comparison:

$$\frac{2^{30} - 2^{29}}{2} \boxed{?} 2^{28}$$

Then simplify:

Step 1: Multiply both sides by 2 to get

$$2^{30} - 2^{29} \boxed{?} 2^{29}$$

Step 2: Add 2^{29} to both sides to get

$$2^{30} \boxed{?} 2^{29} + 2^{29}$$

Step 3: Simplify the right-hand side using the fact that $(2)(2^{29}) = 2^{30}$ to get

$$2^{30} \boxed{?} 2^{30}$$

The resulting relationship is *equal to* (=). In reverse order, each simplification step implies *equal to* in the preceding comparison. So Quantities A and B are also equal.

Thus, the correct answer is Choice C, the two quantities are equal.

Quantity A	Quantity B

8. $x^2 + 1$ 2$x - 1$

Ⓐ Quantity A is greater.

Ⓑ Quantity B is greater.

Ⓒ The two quantities are equal.

Ⓓ The relationship cannot be determined from the information given.

Explanation

Set up the initial comparison:

$$x^2 + 1 \boxed{?} 2x - 1$$

Then simplify by noting that the quadratic polynomial $x^2 - 2x + 1$ can be factored:

Step 1: Subtract $2x$ from both sides to get

$$x^2 - 2x + 1 \boxed{?} -1$$

Step 2: Factor the left-hand side to get

$$(x - 1)^2 \boxed{?} -1$$

The left-hand side of the comparison is the square of a number. Since the square of a number is always greater than or equal to 0, and 0 is greater than −1, the simplified comparison is the inequality $(x - 1)^2 > -1$ and the resulting relationship is *greater than* (>). In reverse order, each simplification step implies the inequality *greater than* (>) in the preceding comparison. Therefore, Quantity A is greater than Quantity B.

The correct answer is Choice A, Quantity A is greater.

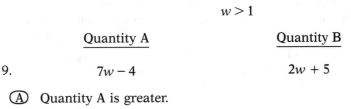

$$w > 1$$

Quantity A	Quantity B

9. $7w - 4$ $2w + 5$

Ⓐ Quantity A is greater.

Ⓑ Quantity B is greater.

Ⓒ The two quantities are equal.

Ⓓ The relationship cannot be determined from the information given.

Explanation

Set up the initial comparison:

$$7w - 4 \;\boxed{?}\; 2w + 5$$

Then simplify:

Step 1: Subtract $2w$ from both sides and add 4 to both sides to get

$$5w \;\boxed{?}\; 9$$

Step 2: Divide both sides by 5 to get

$$w \;\boxed{?}\; \frac{9}{5}$$

The comparison cannot be simplified any further. Although you are given that $w > 1$, you still don't know how w compares to $\frac{9}{5}$, or 1.8. For example, if $w = 1.5$, then $w < 1.8$, but if $w = 2$, then $w > 1.8$. In other words, the relationship between w and $\frac{9}{5}$ cannot be determined. Note that each of these simplification steps is reversible, so in reverse order, each simplification step implies that the *relationship cannot be determined* in the preceding comparison. Thus, the relationship between Quantities A and B cannot be determined.

The correct answer is Choice D, the relationship cannot be determined from the information given.

The strategy of simplifying the comparison works most efficiently when you note that a simplification step is reversible while actually taking the step. Here are some common steps that are always reversible:

- Adding any number or expression to both sides of a comparison
- Subtracting any number or expression from both sides
- Multiplying both sides by any nonzero number or expression
- Dividing both sides by any nonzero number or expression

Remember that if the relationship is an inequality, multiplying or dividing both sides by any *negative* number or expression will yield the opposite inequality. Be aware that some common operations like squaring both sides are generally not reversible and may require further analysis using other information given in the question in order to justify reversing such steps.

Multiple-choice Questions—Select One Answer Choice

Description

These questions are multiple-choice questions that ask you to select only one answer choice from a list of five choices.

> *Tips for Answering*
> - **Use the fact that the answer is there.** If your answer is not one of the five answer choices given, you should assume that your answer is incorrect and do the following:
>   - Reread the question carefully—you may have missed an important detail or misinterpreted some information.
>   - Check your computations—you may have made a mistake, such as mis-keying a number on the calculator.
>   - Reevaluate your solution method—you may have a flaw in your reasoning.
> - **Examine the answer choices.** In some questions you are asked explicitly which of the choices has a certain property. You may have to consider each choice separately, or you may be able to see a relationship between the choices that will help you find the answer more quickly. In other questions, it may be helpful to work backward from the choices, say, by substituting the choices in an equation or inequality to see which one works. However, be careful, as that method may take more time than using reasoning.
> - **For questions that require approximations, scan the answer choices to see how close an approximation is needed.** In other questions, too, it may be helpful to scan the choices briefly before solving the problem to get a better sense of what the question is asking. If computations are involved in the solution, it may be necessary to carry out all computations exactly and round only your final answer in order to get the required degree of accuracy. In other questions, you may find that estimation is sufficient and will help you avoid spending time on long computations.

Sample Questions

> **Select a single answer choice.**

   1.   If $5x + 32 = 4 - 2x$, what is the value of x ?

      Ⓐ -4

      Ⓑ -3

      Ⓒ 4

      Ⓓ 7

      Ⓔ 12

Explanation

Solving the equation for x, you get $7x = -28$, and so $x = -4$. The correct answer is Choice A, -4.

2. Which of the following numbers is farthest from the number 1 on the number line?

    Ⓐ −10

    Ⓑ −5

    Ⓒ   0

    Ⓓ   5

    Ⓔ 10

Explanation

Circling each of the answer choices in a sketch of the number line (Figure 4) shows that of the given numbers, −10 is the greatest distance from 1.

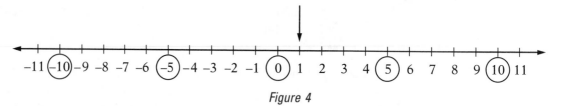

Figure 4

    Another way to answer the question is to remember that the distance between two numbers on the number line is equal to the absolute value of the difference of the two numbers. For example, the distance between −10 and 1 is $|-10-1| = 11$, and the distance between 10 and 1 is $|10-1| = |9| = 9$. **The correct answer is Choice A, −10.**

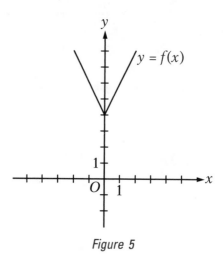

Figure 5

3. The figure above shows the graph of a function f, defined by $f(x) = |2x| + 4$ for all numbers x. For which of the following functions g defined for all numbers x does the graph of g intersect the graph of f?

    Ⓐ $g(x) = x-2$

    Ⓑ $g(x) = x + 3$

    Ⓒ $g(x) = 2x - 2$

    Ⓓ $g(x) = 2x + 3$

    Ⓔ $g(x) = 3x - 2$

Explanation

You can see that all five choices are linear functions whose graphs are lines with various slopes and y-intercepts. The graph of Choice A is a line with slope 1 and y-intercept -2, shown in Figure 6.

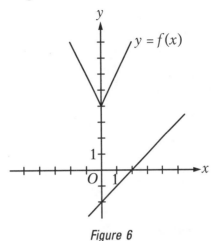

Figure 6

It is clear that this line will not intersect the graph of f to the left of the y-axis. To the right of the y-axis, the graph of f is a line with slope 2, which is greater than slope 1. Consequently, as the value of x increases, the value of y increases faster for f than for g, and therefore the graphs do not intersect to the right of the y-axis. Choice B is similarly ruled out. Note that if the y-intercept of either of the lines in Choices A and B were greater than or equal to 4 instead of less than 4, they would intersect the graph of f.

Choices C and D are lines with slope 2 and y-intercepts less than 4. Hence, they are parallel to the graph of f (to the right of the y-axis) and therefore will not intersect it. Any line with a slope greater than 2 and a y-intercept less than 4, like the line in Choice E, will intersect the graph of f (to the right of the y-axis).

The correct answer is Choice E, $g(x) = 3x - 2$.

4. A car got 33 miles per gallon using gasoline that cost \$2.95 per gallon. What was the approximate cost, in dollars, of the gasoline used in driving the car 350 miles?

   (A) \$10
   (B) \$20
   (C) \$30
   (D) \$40
   (E) \$50

Explanation

Scanning the answer choices indicates that you can do at least some estimation and still answer confidently. The car used $\frac{350}{33}$ gallons of gasoline, so the cost was $\left(\frac{350}{33}\right)(2.95)$ dollars. You can estimate the product $\left(\frac{350}{33}\right)(2.95)$ by estimating $\frac{350}{33}$ a little low, 10, and estimating 2.95 a little high, 3, to get approximately $(10)(3) = 30$ dollars. You can also use the calculator to compute a more exact answer and then round the answer to the nearest 10 dollars, as suggested by the answer choices. The calculator yields the decimal 31.287..., which rounds to 30 dollars.

Thus, the correct answer is Choice C, $30.

5. A certain jar contains 60 jelly beans—22 white, 18 green, 11 yellow, 5 red, and 4 purple. If a jelly bean is to be chosen at random, what is the probability that the jelly bean will be neither red nor purple?

   (A) 0.09
   (B) 0.15
   (C) 0.54
   (D) 0.85
   (E) 0.91

Explanation

Since there are 5 red and 4 purple jelly beans in the jar, there are 51 that are neither red nor purple, and the probability of selecting one of these is $\frac{51}{60}$. Since all of the answer choices are decimals, you must convert the fraction to its decimal equivalent, 0.85.

Thus, the correct answer is Choice D, 0.85.

Multiple-choice Questions—Select One or More Answer Choices

Description

These questions are multiple-choice questions that ask you to select one or more answer choices from a list of choices. A question may or may not specify the number of choices to select. These questions are marked with square boxes beside the answer choices, not circles or ovals.

> ### Tips for Answering
> - Note whether you are asked to indicate a specific number of answer choices or all choices that apply. In the latter case, be sure to consider all of the choices, determine which ones are correct, and select all of those and only those choices. Note that there may be only one correct choice.
> - In some questions that involve inequalities that limit the possible values of the answer choices, it may be efficient to determine the least and/or the greatest possible value. Knowing the least and/or greatest possible value may enable you to quickly determine all of the choices that are correct.
> - Avoid lengthy calculations by recognizing and continuing numerical patterns.

Sample Questions

Select one or more answer choices according to the specific question directions.

If the question does not specify how many answer choices to select, select all that apply.

- The correct answer may be just one of the choices or may be as many as all of the choices, depending on the question.
- No credit is given unless you select all of the correct choices and no others.

If the question specifies how many answer choices to select, select exactly that number of choices.

1. Which <u>two</u> of the following numbers have a product that is greater than 60 ?

   - [A]   −9
   - [B]   −7
   - [C]   6
   - [D]   8

Explanation

For this type of question, it is often possible to exclude some pairs of answer choices. In this question, the product must be positive, so the only possible products are either $(-7)(-9) = 63$ or $(6)(8) = 48$.

The correct answer consists of Choices A (−9) and B (−7).

2. Which of the following integers are multiples of both 2 and 3 ?

   Indicate <u>all</u> such integers.

   - [A]   8
   - [B]   9
   - [C]   12
   - [D]   18
   - [E]   21
   - [F]   36

Explanation

You can first identify the multiples of 2, which are 8, 12, 18, and 36, and then among the multiples of 2 identify the multiples of 3, which are 12, 18, and 36. Alternatively, if you realize that every number that is a multiple of 2 and 3 is also a multiple of 6, you can check which choices are multiples of 6.

The correct answer consists of Choices C (12), D (18), and F (36).

3. Each employee of a certain company is in either Department X or Department Y, and there are more than twice as many employees in Department X as in Department Y. The average (arithmetic mean) salary is $25,000 for the employees in Department X and is $35,000 for the employees in Department Y. Which of the following amounts could be the average salary for all of the employees in the company?

Indicate <u>all</u> such amounts.

- A $26,000
- B $28,000
- C $29,000
- D $30,000
- E $31,000
- F $32,000
- G $34,000

Explanation

One strategy for answering this kind of question is to find the least and/or greatest possible value. Clearly the average salary is between $25,000 and $35,000, and all of the answer choices are in this interval. Since you are told that there are more employees with the lower average salary, the average salary of all employees must be less than the average of $25,000 and $35,000, which is $30,000. If there were exactly twice as many employees in Department X as in Department Y, then the average salary for all employees would be, to the nearest dollar, the following weighted mean,

$$\frac{(2)(25,000) + (1)(35,000)}{2 + 1} \approx 28,333 \text{ dollars}$$

where the weight for $25,000 is 2 and the weight for $35,000 is 1. Since there are *more* than twice as many employees in Department X as in Department Y, the actual average salary must be even closer to $25,000 because the weight for $25,000 is greater than 2. This means that $28,333 is the greatest possible average. Among the choices given, the possible values of the average are therefore $26,000 and $28,000.

Thus, the correct answer consists of Choices A ($26,000) and B ($28,000).

Intuitively, you might expect that any amount between $25,000 and $28,333 is a possible value of the average salary. To see that $26,000 is possible, in the weighted mean above, use the respective weights 9 and 1 instead of 2 and 1. To see that $28,000 is possible, use the respective weights 7 and 3.

4. Which of the following could be the units digit of 57^n, where n is a positive integer?

    Indicate <u>all</u> such digits.

A	0
B	1
C	2
D	3
E	4
F	5
G	6
H	7
I	8
J	9

Explanation

The units digit of 57^n is the same as the units digit of 7^n for all positive integers n. To see why this is true for $n = 2$, compute 57^2 by hand and observe how its units digit results from the units digit of 7^2. Because this is true for every positive integer n, you need to consider only powers of 7. Beginning with $n = 1$ and proceeding consecutively, the units digits of 7, 7^2, 7^3, 7^4, and 7^5 are 7, 9, 3, 1, and 7, respectively. In this sequence, the first digit, 7, appears again, and the pattern of four digits, 7, 9, 3, 1, repeats without end. Hence, these four digits are the only possible units digits of 7^n and therefore of 57^n.

The correct answer consists of Choices B (1), D (3), H (7), and J (9).

Numeric Entry Questions

Description

Questions of this type ask you either to enter your answer as an integer or a decimal in a single answer box or to enter it as a fraction in two separate boxes—one for the numerator and one for the denominator. In the computer-based test, use the computer mouse and keyboard to enter your answer.

Tips for Answering

- **Make sure you answer the question that is asked.** Since there are no answer choices to guide you, read the question carefully and make sure you provide the type of answer required. Sometimes there will be labels before or after the answer box to indicate the appropriate type of answer. Pay special attention to units such as feet or miles, to orders of magnitude such as millions or billions, and to percents as compared with decimals.
- **If you are asked to round your answer, make sure you round to the required degree of accuracy.** For example, if an answer of 46.7 is to be rounded to the nearest integer, you need to enter the number 47. If your solution strategy involves intermediate computations, you should carry out all computations exactly and round only your final answer in order to get the required degree of accuracy. If no rounding instructions are given, enter the exact answer.

- Examine your answer to see if it is reasonable with respect to the information given. You may want to use estimation or another solution path to double-check your answer.

Sample Questions

Enter your answer as an integer or a decimal if there is a single answer box OR as a fraction if there are two separate boxes—one for the numerator and one for the denominator.

To enter an integer or a decimal, either type the number in the answer box using the keyboard or use the Transfer Display button on the calculator.

- First, click on the answer box—a cursor will appear in the box—and then type the number.
- To erase a number, use the Backspace key.
- For a negative sign, type a hyphen. For a decimal point, type a period.
- To remove a negative sign, type the hyphen again and it will disappear; the number will remain.
- The Transfer Display button on the calculator will transfer the calculator display to the answer box.
- Equivalent forms of the correct answer, such as 2.5 and 2.50, are all correct.
- Enter the exact answer unless the question asks you to round your answer.

To enter a fraction, type the numerator and the denominator in the respective boxes using the keyboard.

- For a negative sign, type a hyphen. A decimal point cannot be used in the fraction.
- The Transfer Display button on the calculator cannot be used for a fraction.
- Fractions do not need to be reduced to lowest terms, though you may need to reduce your fraction to fit in the boxes.

1. One pen costs $0.25 and one marker costs $0.35. At those prices, what is the total cost of 18 pens and 100 markers?

$ [ ]

Explanation

Multiplying $0.25 by 18 yields $4.50, which is the cost of the 18 pens; and multiplying $0.35 by 100 yields $35.00, which is the cost of the 100 markers. The total cost is therefore $4.50 + $35.00 = $39.50. Equivalent decimals, such as $39.5 or $39.500, are considered correct.

Thus, the correct answer is $39.50 (or equivalent).

Note that the dollar symbol is in front of the answer box, so the symbol $ does not need to be entered in the box. In fact, only numbers, a decimal point, and a negative sign can be entered in the answer box.

2. Rectangle *R* has length 30 and width 10, and square *S* has length 5. The perimeter of *S* is what fraction of the perimeter of *R* ?

Explanation

The perimeter of *R* is 30 + 10 + 30 + 10 = 80, and the perimeter of *S* is (4)(5) = 20. Therefore, the perimeter of *S* is $\frac{20}{80}$ of the perimeter of *R*. To enter the answer $\frac{20}{80}$, you should enter the numerator 20 in the top box and the denominator 80 in the bottom box. Because the fraction does not need to be reduced to lowest terms, any fraction that is equivalent to $\frac{20}{80}$ is also considered correct, as long as it fits in the boxes. For example, both of the fractions $\frac{2}{8}$ and $\frac{1}{4}$ are considered correct.

Thus, the correct answer is $\frac{20}{80}$ (or any equivalent fraction).

RESULTS OF A USED-CAR AUCTION

	Small Cars	Large Cars
Number of cars offered	32	23
Number of cars sold	16	20
Projected sales total for cars offered (in thousands)	$70	$150
Actual sales total (in thousands)	$41	$120

Figure 7

3. For the large cars sold at an auction that is summarized in the table above, what was the average sale price per car?

$ [   ]

Explanation

From Figure 7, you see that the number of large cars sold was 20 and the sales total for large cars was $120,000 (not $120). Thus the average sale price per car was $\frac{\$120,000}{20} = \$6,000$.

The correct answer is $6,000 (or equivalent).

(Note that the comma in 6,000 will appear automatically in the answer box in the computer-based test.)

4. A merchant made a profit of $5 on the sale of a sweater that cost the merchant $15. What is the profit expressed as a percent of the merchant's cost?

Give your answer to the <u>nearest whole percent</u>.

$$\boxed{}\ \%$$

Explanation

The percent profit is $\left(\dfrac{5}{15}\right)(100) = 33.333\ldots = 33.\overline{3}$ percent, which is 33%, to the nearest whole percent.

Thus, the correct answer is 33% (or equivalent).

If you use the calculator and the Transfer Display button, the number that will be transferred to the answer box is 33.333333, which is incorrect since it is not given to the nearest whole percent. You will need to adjust the number in the answer box by deleting all of the digits to the right of the decimal point (using the Backspace key).

Also, since you are asked to give the answer as a percent, the decimal equivalent of 33 percent, which is 0.33, is incorrect. The percent symbol next to the answer box indicates that the form of the answer must be a percent. Entering 0.33 in the box would give the erroneous answer 0.33%.

5. Working alone at its constant rate, machine A produces k car parts in 10 minutes. Working alone at its constant rate, machine B produces k car parts in 15 minutes. How many minutes does it take machines A and B, working simultaneously at their respective constant rates, to produce k car parts?

$$\boxed{}\ \text{minutes}$$

Explanation

Machine A produces $\dfrac{k}{10}$ parts per minute, and machine B produces $\dfrac{k}{15}$ parts per minute. So when the machines work simultaneously, the rate at which the parts are produced is the sum of these two rates, which is $\dfrac{k}{10} + \dfrac{k}{15} = k\left(\dfrac{1}{10} + \dfrac{1}{15}\right) = k\left(\dfrac{25}{150}\right) = \dfrac{k}{6}$ parts per minute. To compute the time required to produce k parts at this rate, divide the amount k by the rate $\dfrac{k}{6}$ to get $\dfrac{k}{\frac{k}{6}} = 6$.

Therefore, the correct answer is 6 minutes (or equivalent).

One way to check that the answer of 6 minutes is reasonable is to observe that if the slower rate of machine B were the same as machine A's faster rate of k parts in 10 minutes, then the two machines, working simultaneously, would take half the time, or 5 minutes, to produce the k parts. So the answer has to be *greater than 5 minutes*. Similarly, if the faster rate of machine A were the same as machine B's slower rate of k parts in 15 minutes, then the two machines, would take half the time, or 7.5 minutes, to produce the k parts. So the answer has to be *less than 7.5 minutes*. Thus, the answer of 6 minutes is reasonable compared to the lower estimate of 5 minutes and the upper estimate of 7.5 minutes.

Data Interpretation Sets

Description

Data Interpretation questions are grouped together and refer to the same table, graph, or other data presentation. These questions ask you to interpret or analyze the given data. The types of questions may be Multiple-choice (both types) or Numeric Entry.

Tips for Answering

- Scan the data presentation briefly to see what it is about, but do not spend time studying all of the information in detail. Focus on those aspects of the data that are necessary to answer the questions. Pay attention to the axes and scales of graphs; to the units of measurement or orders of magnitude (such as *billions*) that are given in the titles, labels, and legends; and to any notes that clarify the data.
- Bar graphs and circle graphs, as well as other graphical displays of data, are drawn to scale, so you can read or estimate data visually from such graphs. For example, you can use the relative sizes of bars or sectors to compare the quantities that they represent, but be aware of broken scales and of bars that do not start at 0.
- The questions are to be answered only on the basis of the data presented, everyday facts (such as the number of days in a year), and your knowledge of mathematics. Do not make use of specialized information you may recall from other sources about the particular context on which the questions are based unless the information can be derived from the data presented.

Sample Questions

Questions 1 to 3 are based on the following data.

ANNUAL PERCENT CHANGE IN DOLLAR AMOUNT OF SALES AT FIVE RETAIL STORES FROM 2006 TO 2008

Store	Percent Change from 2006 to 2007	Percent Change from 2007 to 2008
P	$+10$	-10
Q	-20	$+9$
R	$+5$	$+12$
S	-7	-15
T	$+17$	-8

Figure 8

1. If the dollar amount of sales at Store P was \$800,000 for 2006, what was the dollar amount of sales at that store for 2008 ?

    (A) \$727,200

    (B) \$792,000

    (C) \$800,000

    (D) \$880,000

    (E) \$968,000

Explanation

According to Figure 8, if the dollar amount of sales at Store P was $800,000 for 2006, then it was 10 percent greater for 2007, which is 110 percent of that amount, or $880,000. For 2008 the amount was 90 percent of $880,000, which is $792,000.

> **The correct answer is Choice B, $792,000.**

Note that an increase of 10 percent for one year and a decrease of 10 percent for the following year does not result in the same dollar amount as the original dollar amount because the base that is used in computing the percents is $800,000 for the first change but $880,000 for the second change.

2. At Store T, the dollar amount of sales for 2007 was what percent of the dollar amount of sales for 2008 ?

Give your answer to the <u>nearest 0.1 percent</u>.

$\boxed{}$ %

Explanation

If A is the dollar amount of sales at Store T for 2007, then 8 percent of A, or $0.08A$, is the amount of decrease from 2007 to 2008. Thus $A - 0.08A = 0.92A$ is the dollar amount for 2008. Therefore, the desired percent can be obtained by dividing A by $0.92A$, which equals $\dfrac{A}{0.92A} = \dfrac{1}{0.92} = 1.0869565\ldots$. Expressed as a percent and rounded to the nearest 0.1 percent, this number is 108.7%.

> **Thus, the correct answer is 108.7% (or equivalent).**

3. Which of the following statements must be true?

Indicate <u>all</u> such statements.

- [A] For 2008 the dollar amount of sales at Store R was greater than that at each of the other four stores.
- [B] The dollar amount of sales at Store S for 2008 was 22 percent less than that for 2006.
- [C] The dollar amount of sales at Store R for 2008 was more than 17 percent greater than that for 2006.

Explanation

For Choice A, since the only data given in Figure 8 are percent changes from year to year, there is no way to compare the actual dollar amount of sales at the stores for 2008 or for any other year. Even though Store R had the greatest percent increase from 2006 to 2008, its actual dollar amount of sales for 2008 may have been much smaller than that for any of the other four stores, and therefore Choice A is not necessarily true.

For Choice B, even though the sum of the two percent decreases would suggest a 22 percent decrease, the bases of the percents are different. If B is the dollar amount of sales at Store S for 2006, then the dollar amount for 2007 is 93 percent of B, or $0.93B$, and the dollar amount for 2008 is given by $(0.85)(0.93)B$, which is $0.7905B$. Note that this represents a percent decrease of $100 - 79.05 = 20.95$ percent, which is less than 22 percent, and so Choice B is not true.

For Choice C, if C is the dollar amount of sales at Store R for 2006, then the dollar amount for 2007 is given by $1.05C$ and the dollar amount for 2008 is given by $(1.12)(1.05)C$, which is $1.176C$. Note that this represents a 17.6 percent increase, which is greater than 17 percent, so Choice C must be true.

Therefore, the correct answer consists of only Choice C (The dollar amount of sales at Store R for 2008 was more than 17 percent greater than that for 2006).

Using the Calculator

Sometimes the computations you need to do in order to answer a question in the Quantitative Reasoning measure are somewhat tedious or time-consuming, like long division or square roots. For such computations, you can use the on-screen calculator provided in the computer-based test. The on-screen calculator is shown in Figure 9.

Figure 9

Although the calculator can shorten the time it takes to perform computations, keep in mind that the calculator provides results that supplement, but do not replace, your knowledge of mathematics. You must use your mathematical knowledge to determine whether the calculator's results are reasonable and how the results can be used to answer a question.

Here are some general guidelines for calculator use in the Quantitative Reasoning measure:

- Most of the questions don't require difficult computations, so don't use the calculator just because it's available.
- Use it for calculations that you know are tedious, such as long division, square roots, and addition, subtraction, or multiplication of numbers that have several digits.
- Avoid using it for simple computations that are quicker to do mentally, such as $10 - 490$, $(4)(70)$, $\frac{4,300}{10}$, $\sqrt{25}$, and 30^2.
- Avoid using it to introduce decimals if you are asked to give an answer as a fraction.
- Some questions can be answered more quickly by reasoning and estimating than by using the calculator.

- If you use the calculator, estimate the answer beforehand so that you can determine whether the calculator's answer is "in the ballpark." This may help you avoid key-entry errors.

The following guidelines are specific to the on-screen calculator in the computer-based test:

- When you use the computer mouse or the keyboard to operate the calculator, take care not to mis-key a number or operation.
- Note all of the calculator's buttons, including Transfer Display.
- The Transfer Display button can be used on Numeric Entry questions with a single answer box. This button will transfer the calculator display to the answer box. You should check that the transferred number has the correct form to answer the question. For example, if a question requires you to round your answer or convert your answer to a percent, make sure that you adjust the transferred number accordingly.
- Take note that the calculator respects order of operations, as explained below.

A mathematical convention called *order of operations* establishes which operations are performed before others in a mathematical expression that has more than one operation. The order is as follows: parentheses, exponentiation (including square roots), multiplications and divisions (from left to right), additions and subtractions (from left to right). With respect to order of operations, the value of the expression $1 + 2 \times 4$ is 9 because the expression is evaluated by first multiplying 2 and 4 and then by adding 1 to the result. This is how the on-screen calculator in the Quantitative Reasoning measure performs the operations. (Note that many basic calculators follow a different convention, whereby they perform multiple operations in the order that they are entered into the calculator. For such calculators, the result of entering $1 + 2 \times 4$ is 12. To get this result, the calculator adds 1 and 2, displays a result of 3, then multiplies 3 and 4, and displays a result of 12.)

- In addition to parentheses, the on-screen calculator has one memory location and three memory buttons that govern it: memory recall $\boxed{\text{MR}}$, memory clear $\boxed{\text{MC}}$, and memory sum $\boxed{\text{M+}}$. These buttons function as they normally do on most basic calculators.
- Some computations are not defined for real numbers; for example, division by zero or taking the square root of a negative number. If you enter $6 \boxed{\div} 0 \boxed{=}$, the word **Error** will be displayed. Similarly, if you enter $1 \boxed{\pm} \boxed{\sqrt{}}$, then **Error** will be displayed. To clear the display, you must press the clear button $\boxed{\text{C}}$.
- The calculator displays up to eight digits. If a computation results in a number larger than 99,999,999, then **Error** will be displayed. For example, the calculation $10,000,000 \boxed{\times} 10 \boxed{=}$ results in **Error**. The clear button $\boxed{\text{C}}$ must be used to clear the display.

Below are some examples of computations using the calculator.

1. Compute $4 + \dfrac{6.73}{2}$.

Explanation

Enter $4\;\boxed{+}\;6.73\;\boxed{\div}\;2\;\boxed{=}$ to get 7.365. Alternatively, enter $6.73\;\boxed{\div}\;2\;\boxed{=}$ to get 3.365, and then enter $\boxed{+}\;4\;\boxed{=}$ to get **7.365**.

2. Compute $-\dfrac{8.4 + 9.3}{70}$.

Explanation

Since division takes precedence over addition in the order of operations, you need to override that precedence in order to compute this fraction. Here are two ways to do that. You can use the parentheses for the addition in the numerator, entering $\boxed{(}\;8.4\;\boxed{+}\;9.3\;\boxed{)}\;\boxed{\div}\;70\;\boxed{=}\;\boxed{\pm}$ to get −0.2528571. Or you can use the equals sign after 9.3, entering $8.4\;\boxed{+}\;9.3\;\boxed{=}\;\boxed{\div}\;70\;\boxed{=}\;\boxed{\pm}$ to get the same result. In the second way, note that pressing the first $\boxed{=}$ is essential, because without it, $8.4\;\boxed{+}\;9.3\;\boxed{\div}\;70\;\boxed{=}\;\boxed{\pm}$ would erroneously compute $-\left(8.4 + \dfrac{9.3}{70}\right)$ instead.

Incidentally, the exact value of the expression $-\dfrac{8.4 + 9.3}{70}$ is the repeating decimal $-0.25\overline{285714}$, where the digits 285714 repeat without end, but the calculator rounds the decimal to **−0.2528571.**

3. Find the length, to the nearest 0.01, of the hypotenuse of a right triangle with legs of length 21 and 54; that is, use the Pythagorean theorem to calculate $\sqrt{21^2 + 54^2}$.

Explanation

Enter $21\;\boxed{\times}\;21\;\boxed{+}\;54\;\boxed{\times}\;54\;\boxed{=}\;\boxed{\sqrt{\,}}$ to get 57.939624. Again, pressing the $\boxed{=}$ before the $\boxed{\sqrt{\,}}$ is essential because $21\;\boxed{\times}\;21\;\boxed{+}\;54\;\boxed{\times}\;54\;\boxed{\sqrt{\,}}\;\boxed{=}$ would erroneously compute $21^2 + 54\sqrt{54}$. This is because the square root would take precedence over the multiplication in the order of operations. Note that parentheses could be used, as in $\boxed{(}\;21\;\boxed{\times}\;21\;\boxed{)}\;\boxed{+}\;\boxed{(}\;54\;\boxed{\times}\;54\;\boxed{)}\;\boxed{=}\;\boxed{\sqrt{\,}}$ but they are not necessary because the multiplications already take precedence over the addition. Incidentally, the exact answer is a nonterminating, nonrepeating decimal, or an irrational number, but the calculator rounds the decimal to 57.939624. Finally, note that the problem asks for the answer to the nearest 0.01, so the correct answer is **57.94**.

4. Compute $(-15)^3$.

Explanation

Enter $15\;\boxed{\pm}\;\boxed{\times}\;15\;\boxed{\pm}\;\boxed{\times}\;15\;\boxed{\pm}\;\boxed{=}$ to get **−3,375.**

5. Convert 6 miles per hour to feet per second.

Explanation

The solution to this problem uses the conversion factors 1 mile = 5,280 feet and 1 hour = 3,600 seconds as follows:

$$\left(\frac{6 \text{ miles}}{1 \text{ hour}}\right)\left(\frac{5,280 \text{ feet}}{1 \text{ mile}}\right)\left(\frac{1 \text{ hour}}{3,600 \text{ seconds}}\right) = ? \frac{\text{feet}}{\text{second}}$$

Enter 6 $\boxed{\times}$ 5280 $\boxed{\div}$ 3600 $\boxed{=}$ to get 8.8. Alternatively, enter 6 $\boxed{\times}$ 5280 $\boxed{=}$ to get the result 31,680, and then enter $\boxed{\div}$ 3600 $\boxed{=}$ to get **8.8 feet per second.**

6. At a fund-raising event, 43 participants donated $60 each, 21 participants donated $80 each, and 16 participants donated $100 each. What was the average (arithmetic mean) donation per participant, in dollars?

Explanation

The solution to this problem is to compute the weighted mean $\frac{(43)(60) + (21)(80) + (16)(100)}{43 + 21 + 16}$. You can use the memory buttons and parentheses for this computation, as follows:

Enter 43 $\boxed{\times}$ 60 $\boxed{=}$ $\boxed{M+}$ 21 $\boxed{\times}$ 80 $\boxed{=}$ $\boxed{M+}$ 16 $\boxed{\times}$ 100 $\boxed{=}$ $\boxed{M+}$ $\boxed{MR}$ $\boxed{\div}$ $\boxed{(}$ 43 $\boxed{+}$ 21 $\boxed{+}$ 16 $\boxed{)}$ $\boxed{=}$ to get 73.25, or **$73.25 per participant**.

When the $\boxed{M+}$ button is first used, the number in the calculator display is stored in memory and an **M** appears to the left of the display to show that the memory function is in use. Each subsequent use of the $\boxed{M+}$ button adds the number in the current display to the number stored in memory and replaces the number stored in memory by the sum. When the $\boxed{MR}$ button is pressed in the computation above, the current value in memory, 5,860, is displayed. To clear the memory, use the $\boxed{MC}$ button, and the **M** next to the display disappears.

Mathematics Conventions for the Quantitative Reasoning Measure of the GRE revised General Test

The mathematical symbols and terminology used in the Quantitative Reasoning measure of the test are conventional at the high school level, and most of these appear in the *Math Review* (Chapter 7). Whenever nonstandard or special notation or terminology is used in a test question, it is explicitly introduced in the question. However, there are some assumptions about numbers and geometric figures that are particular to the test. These assumptions appear in the test at the beginning of the Quantitative Reasoning sections, and they are elaborated below.

Also, some notation and terminology, while standard at the high school level in many countries, may be different from those used in other countries or from those used at higher or lower levels of mathematics. Such notation and terminology are clarified below. Because it is impossible to ascertain which notation and terminology should be clarified for an individual test taker, more material than necessary may be included.

Finally, there are some guidelines for how certain information given in test questions should be interpreted and used in the context of answering the questions—information such as certain words, phrases, quantities, mathematical expressions, and displays of data. These guidelines appear at the end.

Numbers and Quantities

- All numbers used in the test questions are real numbers. In particular, integers and both rational and irrational numbers are to be considered, but imaginary numbers are not. This is the main assumption regarding numbers. Also, all quantities are real numbers, although quantities may involve units of measurement.
- Numbers are expressed in base 10 unless otherwise noted, using the 10 digits 0 through 9 and a period to the right of the ones digit, or units digit, for the decimal point. Also, in numbers that are 1,000 or greater, commas are used to separate groups of three digits to the left of the decimal point.
- When a positive integer is described by the number of its digits, e.g., a two-digit integer, the digits that are counted include the ones digit and all the digits further to the left, where the left-most digit is not 0. For example, 5,000 is a four-digit integer, whereas 031 is not considered to be a three–digit integer.
- Some other conventions involving numbers: *one billion* means 1,000,000,000, or 10^9 (not 10^{12}, as in some countries); *one dozen* means 12; the Greek letter π represents the ratio of the circumference of a circle to its diameter and is approximately 3.14.
- When a positive number is to be rounded to a certain decimal place and the number is halfway between the two nearest possibilities, the number should be rounded to the greater possibility. For example, 23.5 rounded to the nearest integer is 24, and 123.985 rounded to the nearest 0.01 is 123.99. When the number to be rounded is negative, the number should be rounded to the lesser possibility. For example, −36.5 rounded to the nearest integer is −37.
- Repeating decimals are sometimes written with a bar over the digits that repeat, as in $\frac{25}{12} = 2.08\overline{3}$ and $\frac{1}{7} = 0.\overline{142857}$.
- If r, s, and t are integers and $rs = t$, then r and s are *factors*, or *divisors*, of t; also, t is a *multiple* of r (and of s) and t is *divisible* by r (and by s). The factors of an integer include positive and negative integers. For example, −7 is a factor of

35, 8 is a factor of −40, and the integer 4 has six factors: −4, −2, −1, 1, 2, and 4. The terms *factor*, *divisor*, and *divisible* are used only when r, s, and t are integers. However, the term *multiple* can be used with any real numbers s and t provided r is an integer. For example, 1.2 is a multiple of 0.4, and -2π is a multiple of π.

- The *least common multiple* of two nonzero integers a and b is the least positive integer that is a multiple of both a and b. The *greatest common divisor* (or *greatest common factor*) of a and b is the greatest positive integer that is a divisor of both a and b.

- When an integer n is divided by a nonzero integer d resulting in a quotient q with remainder r, then $n = qd + r$, where $0 \le r < |d|$. Furthermore, $r = 0$ if and only if n is a multiple of d. For example, when 20 is divided by 7, the quotient is 2 and the remainder is 6; when 21 is divided by 7, the quotient is 3 and the remainder is 0; and when −17 is divided by 7, the quotient is −3 and the remainder is 4.

- A *prime number* is an integer greater than 1 that has only two positive divisors: 1 and itself. The first five prime numbers are 2, 3, 5, 7, and 11. A *composite number* is an integer greater than 1 that is not a prime number. The first five composite numbers are 4, 6, 8, 9, and 10.

- Odd and even integers are not necessarily positive; for example, −7 is odd, and −18 and 0 are even.

- The integer 0 is neither positive nor negative.

Mathematical Expressions, Symbols, and Variables

- As is common in algebra, italic letters like x are used to denote numbers, constants, and variables. Letters are also used to label various objects, such as line ℓ, point P, function f, set S, list T, event E, random variable X, Brand X, City Y, and Company Z. The meaning of a letter is determined by the context.

- When numbers, constants, or variables are given, their possible values are all real numbers unless otherwise restricted. It is common to restrict the possible values in various ways. Here are some examples: n is a nonzero integer; $1 \le x < \pi$; and T is the tens digits of a two–digit positive integer, so T is an integer from 1 to 9.

- Standard mathematical symbols at the high school level are used. These include the arithmetic operations $+, -, \times$, and $\div$, though multiplication is usually denoted by juxtaposition, often with parentheses, e.g., $2y$ and $(3)(4.5)$; and division is usually denoted with a horizontal fraction bar, e.g., $\frac{w}{3}$. Sometimes mixed numbers, or mixed fractions, are used, like $4\frac{3}{8}$ and $-10\frac{1}{2}$. These two numbers are equal to $\frac{35}{8}$ and $-\frac{21}{2}$, respectively. Exponents are also used, e.g., $2^{10} = 1{,}024$, $10^{-2} = \frac{1}{100}$, and $x^0 = 1$ for all nonzero numbers x.

- Mathematical expressions are to be interpreted with respect to *order of operations*, which establishes which operations are performed before others in an expression. The order is as follows: parentheses; exponentiation; negation; multiplication and division (from left to right); addition and subtraction (from left to right). For example, the value of the expression $1 + 2 \times 4$ is 9, because the expression is evaluated by first multiplying 2 and 4 and then adding 1 to the result. Also, -3^2 means "the negative of '3 squared'" because exponentiation takes precedence over negation. Therefore, $-3^2 = -9$, but $(-3)^2 = 9$ because parentheses take precedence over exponentiation.

- Here are examples of other standard symbols with their meanings:

$x \leq y$ x is less than or equal to y

$x \neq y$ x and y are not equal

$x \approx y$ x and y are approximately equal

$|x|$ the absolute value of x

$\sqrt{x}$ the nonnegative square root of x, where $x \geq 0$

$-\sqrt{x}$ the nonpositive square root of x, where $x \geq 0$

$n!$ the product of all positive integers less than or equal to n, where n is any positive integer and, as a special definition, $0! = 1$.

$\ell \parallel m$ lines ℓ and m are parallel

$\ell \perp m$ lines ℓ and m are perpendicular

- Because all numbers are assumed to be real, some expressions are not defined. For example, for every number x, the expression $\frac{x}{0}$ is not defined; if $x < 0$, then $\sqrt{x}$ is not defined; and 0^0 is not defined.

- Sometimes special symbols or notation are introduced in a question. Here are two examples:

The operation $\diamond$ is defined for all integers r and s by $r \diamond s = \frac{rs}{1+r^2}$.

The operation $\sim$ is defined for all nonzero numbers x by $\sim x = -\frac{1}{x}$.

- Sometimes juxtaposition of letters does *not* denote multiplication, as in "consider a three–digit integer denoted by XYZ, where X, Y, and Z are digits." The meaning is taken from the context.

- Standard function notation is used in the test. For example, "the function g is defined for all $x \geq 0$ by $g(x) = 2x + \sqrt{x}$." If the domain of a function f is not given explicitly, it is assumed to be the set of all real numbers x for which $f(x)$ is a real number. If f and g are two functions, then the *composition* of g with f is denoted by $g(f(x))$.

Geometry

- In questions involving geometry, the conventions of plane (or Euclidean) geometry are followed, including the assumption that the sum of the measures of the interior angles of a triangle is 180 degrees.

- Lines are assumed to be "straight" lines that extend in both directions without end.

- Angle measures are in degrees and are assumed to be positive and less than or equal to 360 degrees.

- When a square, circle, polygon, or other closed geometric figure is described in words but not shown, the figure is assumed to enclose a convex region. It is also assumed that such a closed geometric figure is not just a single point or a line segment. For example, a quadrilateral **cannot** be any of the following:

Not closed   Not convex

- The phrase *area of a rectangle* means the area of the region enclosed by the rectangle. The same terminology applies to circles, triangles, and other closed figures.

- The *distance between a point and a line* is the length of the perpendicular line segment from the point to the line, which is the shortest distance between the point and the line. Similarly, the *distance between two parallel lines* is the distance between a point on one line and the other line.

- In a geometric context, the phrase *similar triangles* (or other figures) means that the figures have the same shape. See the Geometry section of the *Math Review* for further explanation of the terms *similar* and *congruent*.

Geometric Figures

- Geometric figures consist of points, lines, line segments, curves (such as circles), angles, and regions; also included are labels, and markings or shadings that identify these objects or their sizes. A point is indicated by a dot, a label, or the intersection of two or more lines or curves. All figures are assumed to lie in a plane unless otherwise indicated.

- If points A, B, and C do not lie on the same line, then line segments AB and BC form two angles with vertex B—one angle with measure less than 180° and the other with measure greater than 180°, as shown below. Unless otherwise indicated, angle ABC, also denoted by angle B, refers to the *smaller* of the two angles.

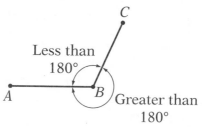

- The notation AB may mean the line segment with endpoints A and B, or it may mean the length of the line segment. The meaning can be determined from the usage.

- Geometric figures **are not necessarily** drawn to scale. That is, you should **not** assume that quantities such as lengths and angle measures are as they appear in a figure. However, you should assume that lines shown as straight are actually straight, and when curves are shown, you should assume they are not straight. Also, assume that points on a line or a curve are in the order shown, points shown to be on opposite sides of a line or curve are so oriented, and more generally, assume all geometric objects are in the relative positions shown. For questions with geometric figures, you should base your answers on geometric reasoning, not on estimating or comparing quantities by sight or by measurement.

- To illustrate some of these conventions, consider the geometric figure below.

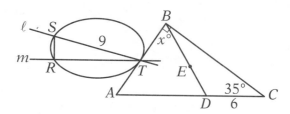

The following can be determined from the figure.

- ○ *ABD* and *DBC* are triangles, and points *R*, *S*, and *T* lie on the closed curve.
- ○ Points *A*, *D*, and *C* lie on a straight line, so *ABC* is a triangle with sides *AB*, *BC*, and *AC*.
- ○ Point *D* is a distinct point between points *A* and *C*.
- ○ Points *A* and *S* are on opposite sides of line *m*.
- ○ Point *E* is on *BD*.
- ○ *AD* < *AC*
- ○ *ST* = 9, *DC* = 6, and the measure of angle *C* is 35 degrees.
- ○ Angle *ABC* is a right angle, as indicated by the small square symbol at point *B*.
- ○ The measure of angle *ABD* is *x* degrees, and *x* < 90.
- ○ Line *ℓ* intersects the closed curve at points *S* and *T*, and the curve is tangent to *AB* at *T*.
- ○ The area of the region enclosed by the curve is greater than the area of triangle *RST*.

The following **cannot** be determined from the figure.

- ○ *AD* > *DC*
- ○ The measures of angles *BAD* and *BDA* are equal.
- ○ The measure of angle *DBC* is less than *x* degrees.
- ○ The area of triangle *ABD* is greater than the area of triangle *DBC*.
- ○ Angle *SRT* is a right angle.
- ○ Line *m* is parallel to line *AC*.

Coordinate Systems

- • Coordinate systems, such as *xy*-planes and number lines, **are** drawn to scale. Therefore, you can read, estimate, or compare quantities in such figures by sight or by measurement, including geometric figures that appear in coordinate systems.
- • The positive direction of a number line is to the right.
- • As in geometry, distances in a coordinate system are nonnegative.
- • The rectangular coordinate plane, or rectangular coordinate system, commonly known as the *xy*-plane, is shown below. The *x*-axis and *y*-axis intersect at the origin *O*, and they partition the plane into four quadrants. Each point in the *xy*-plane has coordinates (*x*, *y*) that give its location with respect to the axes; for example, the point *P*(2, −8) is located 2 units to the right of the *y*-axis and 8 units below the *x*-axis. The units on the *x*-axis have the same length as the units on the *y*-axis, unless otherwise noted.

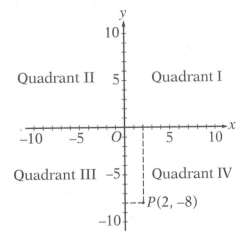

- Intermediate grid lines or tick marks in a coordinate system are evenly spaced unless otherwise noted.
- The term *x-intercept* refers to the *x*-coordinate of the point at which a graph in the *xy*-plane intersects the *x*-axis; it does not refer to the point itself. The term *y-intercept* is used analogously.

Sets, Lists, and Sequences

- Sets of numbers or other elements appear in some questions. Some sets are infinite, such as the set of integers; other sets are finite and may have all of their elements listed within curly brackets, such as the set {2, 4, 6, 8}. When the elements of a set are given, repetitions are *not* counted as additional elements and the order of the elements is *not* relevant. Elements are also called *members*. A set with one or more members is called *nonempty*; there is a set with no members, called the *empty set* and denoted by $\varnothing$. If *A* and *B* are sets, then the *intersection* of *A* and *B*, denoted by $A \cap B$, is the set of elements that are in both *A* and *B*, and the *union* of *A* and *B*, denoted by $A \cup B$, is the set of elements that are in either *A* or *B* or both. If all of the elements in *A* are also in *B*, then *A* is a *subset* of *B*. By convention, the empty set is a subset of every set. If *A* and *B* have no elements in common, they are called *disjoint* sets or *mutually exclusive* sets.
- Lists of numbers or other elements are also used in the test. When the elements of a list are given, repetitions *are* counted as additional elements and the order of the elements *is* relevant. For example, the list 3, 1, 2, 3, 3 contains five numbers, and the first, fourth, and last numbers in the list are each 3.
- The terms *data set* and *set of data* are not sets in the mathematical sense given above. Rather they refer to a list of data because there may be repetitions in the data, and if there are repetitions, they would be relevant.
- Sequences are lists that often have an infinite number of elements, or terms. The terms of a sequence are often represented by a fixed letter along with a subscript that indicates the order of a term in the sequence. For example, $a_1, a_2, a_3, \ldots, a_n, \ldots$ represents an infinite sequence in which the first term is a_1, the second term is a_2, and more generally, the *n*th term is a_n for every positive integer *n*. Sometimes the *n*th term of a sequence is given by a formula, such as $b_n = 2^n + 1$. Sometimes the first few terms of a sequence are given explicitly, as in the following sequence of consecutive even negative integers: $-2, -4, -6, -8, -10, \ldots$.
- Sets of consecutive integers are sometimes described by indicating the first and last integer, as in "the integers from 0 to 9, inclusive." This phrase refers to 10 integers, with or without "inclusive" at the end. Thus, the phrase "during the years from 1985 to 2005" refers to 21 years.

Data and Statistics

- Numerical data are sometimes given in lists and sometimes displayed in other ways, such as in tables, bar graphs, or circle graphs. Various statistics, or measures of data, appear in questions: measures of central tendency—mean, median, and mode; measures of position—quartiles and percentiles; and measures of dispersion—standard deviation, range, and interquartile range.
- The term *average* is used in two ways, with and without the qualification "(arithmetic mean)." For a list of data, the *average* (*arithmetic mean*) of the data is

the sum of the data divided by the number of data. The term *average* does not refer to either *median* or *mode* in the test. Without the qualification of "arithmetic mean," *average* can refer to a rate or the ratio of one quantity to another, as in "average number of miles per hour" or "average weight per truckload."

- When *mean* is used in the context of data, it means *arithmetic mean*.

- The *median* of an odd number of data is the middle number when the data are listed in increasing order; the *median* of an even number of data is the arithmetic mean of the two middle numbers when the data are listed in increasing order.

- For a list of data, the *mode* of the data is the most frequently occurring number in the list. Thus, there may be more than one mode for a list of data.

- For data listed in increasing order, the *first quartile*, *second quartile*, and *third quartile* of the data are three numbers that divide the data into four groups that are roughly equal in size. The first group of numbers is from the least number up to the first quartile. The second group is from the first quartile up to the second quartile, which is also the median of the data. The third group is from the second quartile up to the third quartile, and the fourth group is from the third quartile up to the greatest number. Note that the four groups themselves are sometimes referred to as quartiles—*first quartile*, *second quartile*, *third quartile*, and *fourth quartile*. The latter usage is clarified by the word "in" as in the phrase "the cow's weight is *in* the third quartile of the herd."

- For data listed in increasing order, the *percentiles* of the data are 99 numbers that divide the data into 100 groups that are roughly equal in size. The 25th percentile equals the first quartile; the 50th percentile equals the second quartile, or median; and the 75th percentile equals the third quartile.

- For a list of data, where the arithmetic mean is denoted by m, the *standard deviation* of the data refers to the nonnegative square root of the mean of the squared differences between m and each of the data. This statistic is also known as the *population standard deviation* and is not to be confused with the *sample standard deviation*.

- For a list of data, the *range* of the data is the greatest number in the list minus the least number. The *interquartile range* of the data is the third quartile minus the first quartile.

Data Distributions and Probability Distributions

- Some questions display data in *frequency distributions*, where discrete data values are repeated with various frequencies, or where preestablished intervals of possible values are assigned frequencies corresponding to the numbers of data in the intervals. For example, the lifetimes, rounded to the nearest hour, of 300 lightbulbs could be in the following 10 intervals: 501–550 hours, 551–600 hours, 601–650 hours, . . . , 951–1,000 hours; consequently, each of the intervals would have a number, or frequency, of lifetimes, and the sum of the 10 frequencies is 300.

- Questions may involve *relative frequency distributions*, where each frequency of a frequency distribution is divided by the total number of data in the distribution, resulting in a relative frequency. In the example above, the 10 frequencies of the 10 intervals would each be divided by 300, yielding 10 relative frequencies.

- Some questions describe *probability experiments*, or *random experiments*, that have a finite number of possible *outcomes*. In a random experiment, any particular set of outcomes is called an *event*, and every event E has a *probability*, denoted by $P(E)$, where $0 \leq P(E) \leq 1$. If each outcome of an experiment is equally likely, then the probability of an event E is defined as the following ratio:

$$P(E) = \frac{\text{The number of outcomes in the event } E}{\text{The number of possible outcomes in the experiment}}$$

- If E and F are two events in an experiment, then "E and F" is an event, which is the set of outcomes that are in the intersection of events E and F. Another event is "E or F," which is the set of outcomes that are in the union of events E and F.
- If E and F are two events and E and F are mutually exclusive, then $P(E \text{ and } F) = 0$.
- If E and F are two events such that the occurrence of either event does not affect the occurrence of the other, then E and F are said to be *independent* events. Events E and F are independent if and only if $P(E \text{ and } F) = P(E)P(F)$.
- A *random variable* is a variable that represents values resulting from a random experiment. The values of the random variable may be the actual outcomes of the experiment if the outcomes are numerical, or the random variable may be related to the outcomes more indirectly. In either case, random variables can be used to describe events in terms of numbers.
- A random variable from an experiment with only a finite number of possible outcomes also has only a finite number of values and is called a *discrete random variable*. When the values of a random variable form a continuous interval of real numbers, such as all of the numbers between 0 and 2, the random variable is called a *continuous random variable*.
- Every value of a discrete random variable X, say $X = a$, has a probability denoted by $P(a)$. A histogram (or a table) showing all of the values of X and their probabilities $P(X)$ is called the *probability distribution* of X. The *mean of the random variable* X is the sum of the products $XP(X)$ for all values of X.
- The mean of a random variable X is also called the *expected value* of X or the *mean of the probability distribution* of X.
- For a continuous random variable X, every interval of values, say $a \leq X \leq b$, has a probability, which is denoted by $P(a \leq X \leq b)$. The *probability distribution* of X can be described by a curve in the xy–plane that mimics the tops of the bars of a histogram, only smoother. The curve is the graph of a function f whose values are nonnegative and whose graph is therefore above the X-axis. The curve $y = f(X)$ is related to the probability of each interval $a \leq X \leq b$ in the following way: $P(a \leq X \leq b)$ is equal to the area of the region that is below the curve, above the X-axis, and between the vertical lines $X = a$ and $X = b$. The area of the entire region under the curve is 1.
- The *mean of a continuous random variable* X is the point m on the X-axis at which region under the distribution curve would perfectly balance if a fulcrum were placed at $X = m$. The *median* of X is the point M on the X-axis at which the line $X = M$ divides the region under the distribution curve into two regions of equal area.
- The *standard deviation of a random variable* X is a measure of dispersion, which indicates how spread out the probability distribution of X is from its mean. It is also called the *standard deviation of the probability distribution* of X.
- The most important probability distribution is the *normal distribution*, whose distribution curve is shaped like a bell. A random variable X with this distribution

is called *normally distributed*. The curve is symmetric about the line $X = m$, where m is the mean as well as the median. The right and left tails of the distribution become ever closer to the *X*-axis but never touch it.

● The *standard normal distribution* has mean 0 and standard deviation 1. The following figure shows the distribution, including approximate probabilities corresponding to the six intervals shown.

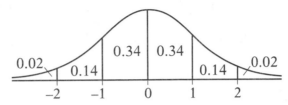

Graphical Representations of Data

● Graphical data presentations, such as bar graphs, circles graphs, and line graphs, **are** drawn to scale; therefore, you can read, estimate, or compare data values by sight or by measurement.

● Standard conventions apply to graphs of data unless otherwise indicated. For example, a circle graph represents 100 percent of the data indicated in the graph's title, and the areas of the individual sectors are proportional to the percents they represent. Scales, grid lines, dots, bars, shadings, solid and dashed lines, legends, etc., are used on graphs to indicate the data. Sometimes, scales that do not begin at 0 are used, and sometimes broken scales are used.

● In Venn diagrams, various sets of objects are represented by circular regions and by regions formed by intersections of the circles. In some Venn diagrams, all of the circles are inside a rectangular region that represents a universal set. A number placed in a region is the number of elements in the subset represented by the smallest region containing the number, unless otherwise noted. Sometimes a number is placed above a circle to indicate the number of elements in the entire circle.

Miscellaneous Guidelines for Interpreting and Using Information in Test Questions

● Numbers given in a question are to be used as exact numbers, even though in some real-life settings they are likely to have been rounded. For example, if a question states that "30 percent of the company's profit was from health products," then 30 is to be used as an exact number; it is not to be used as a rounded number obtained from, say, 29 or 30.1.

● An integer that is given as the number of certain objects, whether in a real-life or pure-math setting, is to be taken as the total number of such objects. For example, if a question states that "a bag contains 50 marbles, and 23 of the marbles are red," then 50 is to be taken as the total number of marbles in the bag and 23 is to be taken as the total number of red marbles in the bag, so that the other 27 marbles are not red. Fractions and percents are understood in a similar way, so "one-fifth, or 20 percent, of the 50 marbles in the bag are green" means 10 marbles in the bag are green and 40 marbles are not green.

- When a multiple-choice question asks for an approximate quantity without stipulating a degree of approximation, the correct answer is the choice that is closest in value to the quantity that can be computed from the information given.

- Unless otherwise indicated, the phrase "difference between two quantities" is assumed to mean "positive difference," that is, the greater quantity minus the lesser quantity. For example, "for which two consecutive years was the difference in annual rainfall least?" means "for which two consecutive years was the *absolute value of the difference* in annual rainfall least?"

- When the term *profit* is used in a question, it refers to *gross profit*, which is the sales revenue minus the cost of production. The profit does not involve any other amounts unless they are explicitly given.

- The common meaning of terms such as *months* and *years* and other everyday terms are assumed in questions where the terms appear.

- In questions involving real-life scenarios in which a variable is given to represent a number of existing objects or another nonnegative amount, the context implies that the variable is greater than 0. For example, "Jane sold x rugs and deposited her profit of y dollars into her savings account" implies that x and y are greater than 0.

- Some quantities may involve units, such as inches, pounds, and Celsius degrees, while other quantities are pure numbers. Any units of measurement, such as English units or metric units, may be used. However, if an answer to a question requires converting one unit of measurement to another, then the relationship between the units is given in the question, unless the relationship is a common one, such as the relationships between minutes and hours, dollars and cents, and metric units like centimeters and meters.

- In any question, there may be some information that is not needed for obtaining the correct answer.

- When reading questions, do not introduce unwarranted assumptions. For example, if a question describes a trip that begins and ends at certain times, the intended answer will assume that the times are unaffected by crossing time zones or by changes to the local time for daylight savings, unless those matters are explicitly mentioned. As another example, do not consider sales taxes on purchases unless explicitly mentioned.

- The display of data in a Data Interpretation set of questions is the same for each question in the set. Also, the display may contain more than one graph or table. Each question will refer to some of the data, but it may happen that some part of the data will have no question that refers to it.

- In a Data Interpretation set of questions, each question should be considered separately from the others. No information except what is given in the display of data should be carried over from one question to another.

- In many questions, mathematical expressions and words appear together in a phrase. In such a phrase, each mathematical expression should be interpreted *separately* from the words before it is interpreted *along with* the words. For example, if n is an integer, then the phrase "the sum of the first two consecutive integers greater than $n + 6$" means $(n + 7) + (n + 8)$; it does not mean "the sum of the first two consecutive integers greater than n" plus 6, or $(n + 1) + (n + 2) + 6$. That is, the expression $n + 6$ should be interpreted first, separately from the words. However, in a phrase like "the function g is defined for all $x \geq 0$," the phrase "for all $x \geq 0$" is a mathematical shorthand for "for all numbers x such that $x \geq 0$."

GRE® Quantitative Reasoning Practice Questions

This chapter contains four sets of GRE Quantitative Reasoning practice questions. Each of the first three practice sets consists of Quantitative Comparison questions, both types of Multiple-choice questions, and Numeric Entry questions. These three sets are arranged in order of increasing difficulty. The first is easy, the second is medium, and the third is hard. The fourth practice set consists of Data Interpretation questions of varying levels of difficulty.

Following the last set is an Answer Key for quick reference. Then, at the end of the chapter, you will find complete explanations for every question. Each explanation is presented with the corresponding question, so that you can easily see what was asked and what the various answer choices or Numeric Entry answer boxes were.

Sharpen your GRE Quantitative Reasoning skills by working your way through these question sets. For the Discrete question sets, begin with the easy sets and then move on to the medium and hard sets. Review the answers and explanations carefully, paying particular attention to explanations for questions that you answered incorrectly.

For the practice questions in this chapter, use the directions that begin on the following page.

General Directions

For each question, indicate the best answer, using the directions given.

Notes: All numbers used are real numbers.

All figures are assumed to lie in a plane unless otherwise indicated.

Geometric figures, such as lines, circles, triangles, and quadrilaterals, **are not necessarily** drawn to scale. That is, you should **not** assume that quantities such as lengths and angle measures are as they appear in a figure. You should assume, however, that lines shown as straight are actually straight, points on a line are in the order shown, and more generally, all geometric objects are in the relative positions shown. For questions with geometric figures, you should base your answers on geometric reasoning, not on estimating or comparing quantities by sight or by measurement.

Coordinate systems, such as *xy*-planes and number lines, **are** drawn to scale; therefore, you can read, estimate, or compare quantities in such figures by sight or by measurement.

Graphical data presentations, such as bar graphs, circles graphs, and line graphs, **are** drawn to scale; therefore, you can read, estimate, or compare data values by sight or by measurement.

Directions for Quantitative Comparison questions

Compare Quantity A and Quantity B, using additional information centered above the two quantities if such information is given. Select one of the following four answer choices and fill in the corresponding oval to the right of the question.

Ⓐ Quantity A is greater.
Ⓑ Quantity B is greater.
Ⓒ The two quantities are equal.
Ⓓ The relationship cannot be determined from the information given.

A symbol that appears more than once in a question has the same meaning throughout the question.

	Quantity A	Quantity B	Correct Answer
Example 1:	(2)(6)	2 + 6	⬤Ⓐ Ⓑ Ⓒ Ⓓ

	Quantity A	Quantity B	Correct Answer
Example 2:	PS	SR	Ⓐ Ⓑ Ⓒ ⬤Ⓓ

(since equal lengths cannot be assumed, even though *PS* and *SR* appear equal)

Directions for Numeric Entry questions

Enter your answer in the answer box(es) below the question.

- Your answer may be an integer, a decimal, or a fraction, and it may be negative.
- If a question asks for a fraction, there will be two boxes—one for the numerator and one for the denominator.
- Equivalent forms of the correct answer, such as 2.5 and 2.50, are all correct. Fractions do not need to be reduced to lowest terms.
- Enter the exact answer unless the question asks you to round your answer.

SET 1. Discrete Questions: Easy

Quantitative Comparison

For Questions 1 to 6, compare Quantity A and Quantity B, using additional information centered above the two quantities if such information is given. Select one of the following four answer choices and fill in the corresponding oval to the right of the question.

- Ⓐ Quantity A is greater.
- Ⓑ Quantity B is greater.
- Ⓒ The two quantities are equal.
- Ⓓ The relationship cannot be determined from the information given.

A symbol that appears more than once in a question has the same meaning throughout the question.

Emma spent $75 buying a used bicycle and $27 repairing it. Then she sold the bicycle for 40 percent more than the total amount she spent buying and repairing it.

	Quantity A	Quantity B	
1.	The price at which Emma sold the bicycle	$140	Ⓐ Ⓑ Ⓒ Ⓓ

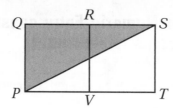

In the figure above, squares *PQRV* and *VRST* have sides of length 6.

Quantity A	Quantity B

2. The area of the shaded region | 36 | Ⓐ Ⓑ Ⓒ Ⓓ

In 2009 the property tax on each home in Town *X* was *p* percent of the assessed value of the home, where *p* is a constant. The property tax in 2009 on a home in Town *X* that had an assessed value of $125,000 was $2,500.

Quantity A	Quantity B

3. The property tax in 2009 on a home in Town *X* that had an assessed value of $160,000 | $3,000 | Ⓐ Ⓑ Ⓒ Ⓓ

$$x + y = -1$$

Quantity A	Quantity B

4. | *x* | *y* | Ⓐ Ⓑ Ⓒ Ⓓ

---

r, *s*, and *t* are three consecutive odd integers such that $r < s < t$.

Quantity A	Quantity B

5. | $r + s + 1$ | $s + t - 1$ | Ⓐ Ⓑ Ⓒ Ⓓ

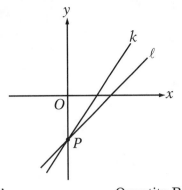

Quantity A	Quantity B	
6. The slope of line k	The slope of line ℓ	Ⓐ Ⓑ Ⓒ Ⓓ

Multiple-choice Questions—Select One Answer Choice

For Questions 7 to 11, select a single answer choice.

7. In the figure above, what is the value of $\dfrac{x + y + z}{45}$?

   Ⓐ 2

   Ⓑ 3

   Ⓒ 4

   Ⓓ 5

   Ⓔ 6

8. A certain store sells two types of pens: one type for $2 per pen and the other type for $3 per pen. If a customer can spend up to $25 to buy pens at the store and there is no sales tax, what is the greatest number of pens the customer can buy?

   Ⓐ   9

   Ⓑ 10

   Ⓒ 11

   Ⓓ 12

   Ⓔ 20

9. If $y = 3x$ and $z = 2y$, what is $x + y + z$ in terms of x ?

    (A) $10x$

    (B) $9x$

    (C) $8x$

    (D) $6x$

    (E) $5x$

10. A certain shipping service charges an insurance fee of $0.75 when shipping any package with contents worth $25.00 or less and an insurance fee of $1.00 when shipping any package with contents worth over $25.00. If Dan uses the shipping company to ship three packages with contents worth $18.25, $25.00, and $127.50, respectively, what is the total insurance fee that the company charges Dan to ship the three packages?

    (A) $1.75

    (B) $2.25

    (C) $2.50

    (D) $2.75

    (E) $3.00

11. If 55 percent of the people who purchase a certain product are female, what is the ratio of the number of females who purchase the product to the number of males who purchase the product?

    (A) 11 to 9

    (B) 10 to 9

    (C) 9 to 10

    (D) 9 to 11

    (E) 5 to 9

Numeric Entry

For Questions 12 and 13, enter your answer in the answer box(es) below the question.

- **Your answer may be an integer, a decimal, or a fraction, and it may be negative.**
- **If a question asks for a fraction, there will be two boxes—one for the numerator and one for the denominator.**
- **Equivalent forms of the correct answer, such as 2.5 and 2.50, are all correct. Fractions do not need to be reduced to lowest terms.**
- **Enter the exact answer unless the question asks you to round your answer.**

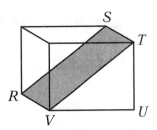

12. In the rectangular solid above, $TU = 3$, $UV = 4$, and $VR = 2$. What is the area of the shaded rectangular region?

13. A list of numbers has a mean of 8 and a standard deviation of 2.5. If x is a number in the list that is 2 standard deviations above the mean, what is the value of x ?

$x =$ ⬚

Multiple-choice Questions—Select One or More Answer Choices

For Question 14, select all the answer choices that apply.

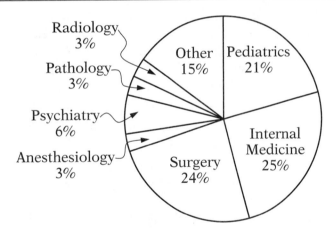

14. The circle graph above shows the distribution of 200,000 physicians by specialty. Which of the following sectors of the circle graph represent more than 40,000 physicians?

Indicate all such sectors.

- A Pediatrics
- B Internal Medicine
- C Surgery
- D Anesthesiology
- E Psychiatry

SET 2. Discrete Questions: Medium

Quantitative Comparison

> For Questions 1 to 5, compare Quantity A and Quantity B, using additional information centered above the two quantities if such information is given. Select one of the following four answer choices and fill in the corresponding oval to the right of the question.
>
> (A) Quantity A is greater.
> (B) Quantity B is greater.
> (C) The two quantities are equal.
> (D) The relationship cannot be determined from the information given.
>
> A symbol that appears more than once in a question has the same meaning throughout the question.

Machine R, working alone at a constant rate, produces x units of a product in 30 minutes, and machine S, working alone at a constant rate, produces x units of the product in 48 minutes, where x is a positive integer.

| Quantity A | Quantity B |

1. The number of units of the product that machine R, working alone at its constant rate, produces in 3 hours | The number of units of the product that machine S, working alone at its constant rate, produces in 4 hours

  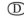 ⓓ

Frequency Distribution for List X

Number	1	2	3	5
Frequency	10	20	18	12

Frequency Distribution for List Y

Number	6	7	8	9
Frequency	24	17	10	9

List X and list Y each contain 60 numbers. Frequency distributions for each list are given above. The average (arithmetic mean) of the numbers in list X is 2.7, and the average of the numbers in list Y is 7.1. List Z contains 120 numbers: the 60 numbers in list X and the 60 numbers in list Y.

| Quantity A | Quantity B |

2. The average of the 120 numbers in list Z | The median of the 120 numbers in list Z

   ⓓ

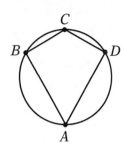

In the figure above, the diameter of the circle is 10.

	Quantity A	Quantity B	
3.	The area of quadrilateral *ABCD*	40	Ⓐ Ⓑ Ⓒ Ⓓ

$$x^2y > 0$$
$$xy^2 < 0$$

	Quantity A	Quantity B	
4.	*x*	*y*	Ⓐ Ⓑ Ⓒ Ⓓ

Among the 9,000 people attending a football game at College *C*, there were *x* students from College *C* and *y* students who were <u>not</u> from College *C*.

	Quantity A	Quantity B	
5.	The number of people attending the game who were <u>not</u> students	$9,000 - x - y$	Ⓐ Ⓑ Ⓒ Ⓓ

Multiple-choice Questions—Select One Answer Choice

For Questions 6 to 10, select a single answer choice.

6. If $x \neq 0$, which of the following is equivalent to $\dfrac{x(x^2)^3}{x^2}$?

   Ⓐ x^2
   Ⓑ x^3
   Ⓒ x^4
   Ⓓ x^5
   Ⓔ x^6

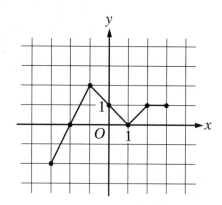

7. The figure above shows the graph of the function f in the xy-plane. What is the value of $f(f(-1))$?

    (A) −2

    (B) −1

    (C) 0

    (D) 1

    (E) 2

8. If $\dfrac{d - 3n}{7n - d} = 1$, which of the following statements describes d in terms of n?

    (A) d is 4 less than n.

    (B) d is 4 more than n.

    (C) d is $\dfrac{3}{7}$ of n.

    (D) d is 2 times n.

    (E) d is 5 times n.

9. By weight, liquid A makes up 8 percent of solution R and 18 percent of solution S. If 3 grams of solution R are mixed with 7 grams of solution S, then liquid A accounts for what percent of the weight of the resulting solution?

    (A) 10%

    (B) 13%

    (C) 15%

    (D) 19%

    (E) 26%

10. Of the 700 members of a certain organization, 120 are lawyers. Two members of the organization will be selected at random. Which of the following is closest to the probability that <u>neither</u> of the members selected will be a lawyer?

    (A) 0.5

    (B) 0.6

    (C) 0.7

    (D) 0.8

    (E) 0.9

Numeric Entry

> **For Questions 11 and 12, enter your answer in the answer box(es) below the question.**
>
> - **Your answer may be an integer, a decimal, or a fraction, and it may be negative.**
> - **If a question asks for a fraction, there will be two boxes—one for the numerator and one for the denominator.**
> - **Equivalent forms of the correct answer, such as 2.5 and 2.50, are all correct. Fractions do not need to be reduced to lowest terms.**
> - **Enter the exact answer unless the question asks you to round your answer.**

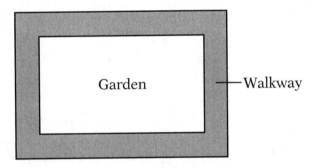

11. The figure above represents a rectangular garden with a walkway around it. The garden is 18 feet long and 12 feet wide. The walkway is uniformly 3 feet wide, and its edges meet at right angles. What is the area of the walkway?

    ▭ square feet

12. Line k lies in the xy-plane. The x-intercept of line k is -4, and line k passes through the midpoint of the line segment whose endpoints are $(2, 9)$ and $(2, 0)$. What is the slope of line k?

    Give your answer as a fraction.

Multiple-choice Questions—Select One or More Answer Choices

> **For Questions 13 and 14, select all the answer choices that apply.**

13. If the lengths of two sides of a triangle are 5 and 9, respectively, which of the following could be the length of the third side of the triangle?

Indicate <u>all</u> such lengths.

- A   3
- B   5
- C   8
- D   15

14. On the number line shown above, the tick marks are equally spaced. Which of the following statements about the numbers x, y, and z must be true?

Indicate <u>all</u> such statements.

- A $xyz < 0$
- B $x + z = y$
- C $z(y - x) > 0$

SET 3. Discrete Questions: Hard

Quantitative Comparison

For Questions 1 to 6, compare Quantity A and Quantity B, using additional information centered above the two quantities if such information is given. Select one of the following four answer choices and fill in the corresponding oval to the right of the question.

Ⓐ Quantity A is greater.

Ⓑ Quantity B is greater.

Ⓒ The two quantities are equal.

Ⓓ The relationship cannot be determined from the information given.

A symbol that appears more than once in a question has the same meaning throughout the question.

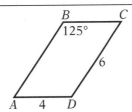

In the figure above, *ABCD* is a parallelogram.

Quantity A	Quantity B	
1.　The area of *ABCD*	24	Ⓐ　Ⓑ　Ⓒ　Ⓓ

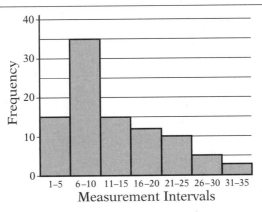

In the course of an experiment, 95 measurements were recorded, and all of the measurements were integers. The 95 measurements were then grouped into 7 measurement intervals. The graph above shows the frequency distribution of the 95 measurements by measurement interval.

Quantity A	Quantity B	
2.　The average (arithmetic mean) of the 95 measurements	The median of the 95 measurements	Ⓐ　Ⓑ　Ⓒ　Ⓓ

x is an integer greater than 1.

Quantity A	Quantity B	
3. 3^{x+1}	4^x	Ⓐ Ⓑ Ⓒ Ⓓ

A, B, and C are three rectangles. The length and width of rectangle A are 10 percent greater and 10 percent less, respectively, than the length and width of rectangle C. The length and width of rectangle B are 20 percent greater and 20 percent less, respectively, than the length and width of rectangle C.

Quantity A	Quantity B	
4. The area of rectangle A	The area of rectangle B	Ⓐ Ⓑ Ⓒ Ⓓ

The random variable X is normally distributed. The values 650 and 850 are at the 60th and 90th percentiles of the distribution of X, respectively.

Quantity A	Quantity B	
5. The value at the 75th percentile of the distribution of X	750	Ⓐ Ⓑ Ⓒ Ⓓ

Set S consists of all positive integers less than 81 that are <u>not</u> equal to the square of an integer.

Quantity A	Quantity B	
6. The number of integers in set S	72	Ⓐ Ⓑ Ⓒ Ⓓ

Multiple-choice Questions—Select One Answer Choice

For Questions 7 to 12, select a single answer choice.

7. A manager is forming a 6-person team to work on a certain project. From the 11 candidates available for the team, the manager has already chosen 3 to be on the team. In selecting the other 3 team members, how many different combinations of 3 of the remaining candidates does the manager have to choose from?

   Ⓐ   6
   Ⓑ   24
   Ⓒ   56
   Ⓓ   120
   Ⓔ   462

8. Which of the following could be the graph of all values of x that satisfy the inequality $2 - 5x \le -\dfrac{6x - 5}{3}$?

   Ⓐ
        0

   Ⓑ
        0

   Ⓒ
        0

   Ⓓ
        0

   Ⓔ
        0

9. If $1 + x + x^2 + x^3 = 60$, then the average (arithmetic mean) of x, x^2, x^3, and x^4 is equal to which of the following?

   Ⓐ $12x$
   Ⓑ $15x$
   Ⓒ $20x$
   Ⓓ $30x$
   Ⓔ $60x$

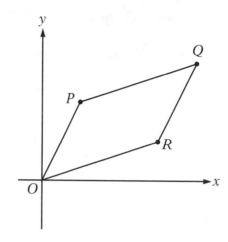

10. Parallelogram $OPQR$ lies in the xy-plane, as shown in the figure above. The coordinates of point P are $(2, 4)$ and the coordinates of point Q are $(8, 6)$. What are the coordinates of point R ?

    Ⓐ $(3, 2)$
    Ⓑ $(3, 3)$
    Ⓒ $(4, 4)$
    Ⓓ $(5, 2)$
    Ⓔ $(6, 2)$

11. The relationship between the area A of a circle and its circumference C is given by the formula $A = kC^2$, where k is a constant. What is the value of k ?

    Ⓐ $\dfrac{1}{4\pi}$

    Ⓑ $\dfrac{1}{2\pi}$

    Ⓒ $\dfrac{1}{4}$

    Ⓓ 2π

    Ⓔ $4\pi^2$

12. The sequence of numbers $a_1, a_2, a_3, \ldots, a_n, \ldots$ is defined by $a_n = \dfrac{1}{n} - \dfrac{1}{n+2}$ for each integer $n \geq 1$. What is the sum of the first 20 terms of this sequence?

    Ⓐ $\left(1 + \dfrac{1}{2}\right) - \dfrac{1}{20}$

    Ⓑ $\left(1 + \dfrac{1}{2}\right) - \left(\dfrac{1}{21} + \dfrac{1}{22}\right)$

    Ⓒ $1 - \left(\dfrac{1}{20} + \dfrac{1}{22}\right)$

    Ⓓ $1 - \dfrac{1}{22}$

    Ⓔ $\dfrac{1}{20} - \dfrac{1}{22}$

Numeric Entry

For Question 13, enter your answer in the answer box(es) below the question.

- Your answer may be an integer, a decimal, or a fraction, and it may be negative.
- If a question asks for a fraction, there will be two boxes—one for the numerator and one for the denominator.
- Equivalent forms of the correct answer, such as 2.5 and 2.50, are all correct. Fractions do not need to be reduced to lowest terms.
- Enter the exact answer unless the question asks you to round your answer.

Y	Frequency
$\dfrac{1}{2}$	2
$\dfrac{3}{4}$	7
$\dfrac{5}{4}$	8
$\dfrac{3}{2}$	8
$\dfrac{7}{4}$	9

13. The table above shows the frequency distribution of the values of a variable Y. What is the mean of the distribution?

    Give your answer to the <u>nearest 0.01</u>.

    [   ]

Multiple-choice Questions—Select One or More Answer Choices

For Questions 14 and 15, select all the answer choices that apply.

14. Let S be the set of all positive integers n such that n^2 is a multiple of both 24 and 108. Which of the following integers are divisors of every integer n in S ?

    Indicate <u>all</u> such integers.

    - [A] 12
    - [B] 24
    - [C] 36
    - [D] 72

15. The range of the heights of the female students in a certain class is 13.2 inches, and the range of the heights of the male students in the class is 15.4 inches.

Which of the following statements <u>individually</u> provide(s) sufficient additional information to determine the range of the heights of all the students in the class?

Indicate <u>all</u> such statements.

[A] The tallest male student in the class is 5.8 inches taller than the tallest female student in the class.

[B] The median height of the male students in the class is 1.1 inches greater than the median height of the female students in the class.

[C] The average (arithmetic mean) height of the male students in the class is 4.6 inches greater than the average height of the female students in the class.

SET 4. Data Interpretation Sets

For Questions 1 to 7, select a single answer choice unless otherwise directed.

Questions 1 to 3 are based on the following data.

PERCENT OF FEMALE FACULTY AND PERCENT OF MALE FACULTY
AT UNIVERSITY *X*, BY FIELD
Total female faculty: 200
Total male faculty: 250

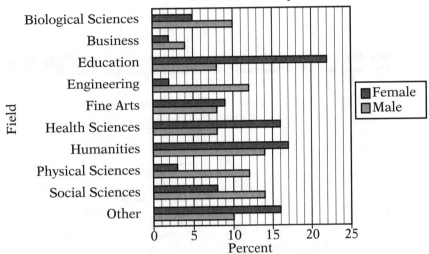

Medium Question

1. There are 275 students in the field of engineering at University *X*.
    Approximately what is the ratio of the number of students in engineering to
    the number of faculty in engineering?

    (A)   8 to 1

    (B)   10 to 1

    (C)   12 to 1

    (D)   14 to 1

    (E)   20 to 1

Medium Question

2. Approximately what percent of the faculty in humanities are male?

    (A)   35%

    (B)   38%

    (C)   41%

    (D)   45%

    (E)   51%

For Question 3, use the directions for Numeric Entry questions.

Hard Question

3. For the biological sciences and health sciences faculty combined, $\frac{1}{3}$ of the female and $\frac{2}{9}$ of the male faculty members are tenured professors. What fraction of all the faculty members in those two fields combined are tenured professors?

Questions 4 to 7 are based on the following data.

VALUE OF IMPORTS TO AND EXPORTS FROM COUNTRY *T,* 2000–2009
(in United States dollars)

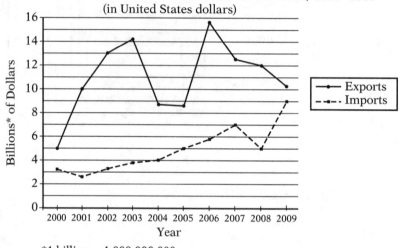

*1 billion = 1,000,000,000

For Question 4, select all the answer choices that apply.

Easy Question

4. For which of the eight years from 2001 to 2008 did exports exceed imports by more than $5 billion?

Indicate <u>all</u> such years.

- A 2001
- B 2002
- C 2003
- D 2004
- E 2005
- F 2006
- G 2007
- H 2008

Medium Question

5. Which of the following is closest to the average (arithmetic mean) of the 9 changes in the value of imports between consecutive years from 2000 to 2009 ?

   (A) $260 million

   (B) $320 million

   (C) $400 million

   (D) $480 million

   (E) $640 million

Medium Question

6. In 2008 the value of exports was approximately what percent greater than the value of imports?

   (A)   40%

   (B)   60%

   (C)   70%

   (D) 120%

   (E) 140%

Hard Question

7. If it were discovered that the value of imports shown for 2007 was incorrect and should have been $5 billion instead, then the average (arithmetic mean) value of imports per year for the 10 years shown would have been approximately how much less?

   (A) $200 million

   (B) $50 million

   (C) $20 million

   (D) $7 million

   (E) $5 million

ANSWER KEYS

SET 1. Discrete Questions: Easy

1. **Choice A**: Quantity A is greater.
2. **Choice C**: The two quantities are equal.
3. **Choice A**: Quantity A is greater.
4. **Choice D**: The relationship cannot be determined from the information given.
5. **Choice B**: Quantity B is greater.
6. **Choice A**: Quantity A is greater.
7. **Choice C**: 4
8. **Choice D**: 12
9. **Choice A**: $10x$
10. **Choice C**: $2.50
11. **Choice A**: 11 to 9
12. **10**
13. **13**
14. **Choice A**: Pediatrics
    AND
    Choice B: Internal Medicine
    AND
    Choice C: Surgery

SET 2. Discrete Questions: Medium

1. **Choice A**: Quantity A is greater.
2. **Choice B**: Quantity B is greater.
3. **Choice D**: The relationship cannot be determined from the information given.
4. **Choice B**: Quantity B is greater.
5. **Choice C**: The two quantities are equal.
6. **Choice D**: x^5
7. **Choice D**: 1
8. **Choice E**: d is 5 times n.
9. **Choice C**: 15%
10. **Choice C**: 0.7
11. **216**
12. $\frac{3}{4}$ (or any equivalent fraction)
13. **Choice B**: 5
    AND
    Choice C: 8
14. **Choice A**: $xyz < 0$
    AND
    Choice B: $x + z = y$
    AND
    Choice C: $z(y - x) > 0$

ANSWER KEYS

SET 3. Discrete Questions: Hard

1. **Choice B**: Quantity B is greater.
2. **Choice A**: Quantity A is greater.
3. **Choice D**: The relationship cannot be determined from the information given.
4. **Choice A**: Quantity A is greater.
5. **Choice B**: Quantity B is greater.
6. **Choice C**: The two quantities are equal.
7. **Choice C**: 56
8. **Choice C**:

9. **Choice B**: $15x$
10. **Choice E**: $(6, 2)$
11. **Choice A**: $\dfrac{1}{4\pi}$
12. **Choice B**: $\left(1 + \dfrac{1}{2}\right) - \left(\dfrac{1}{21} + \dfrac{1}{22}\right)$
13. **1.29**
14. **Choice A**: 12
    AND
    Choice C: 36
15. **Choice A**: The tallest male student in the class is 5.8 inches taller than the tallest female student in the class.

SET 4. Data Interpretation Sets

1. **Choice A**: 8 to 1
2. **Choice E**: 51%
3. $\dfrac{24}{87}$ (or any equivalent fraction)

4. **Choice A**: 2001
   AND
   Choice B: 2002
   AND
   Choice C: 2003
   AND
   Choice F: 2006
   AND
   Choice G: 2007
   AND
   Choice H: 2008
5. **Choice E**: $640 million
6. **Choice E**: 140%
7. **Choice A**: $200 million

Answers and Explanations

For the practice questions in this chapter, use the following directions.

General Directions

For each question, indicate the best answer, using the directions given.

Notes: All numbers used are real numbers.

All figures are assumed to lie in a plane unless otherwise indicated.

Geometric figures, such as lines, circles, triangles, and quadrilaterals, **are not necessarily** drawn to scale. That is, you should **not** assume that quantities such as lengths and angle measures are as they appear in a figure. You should assume, however, that lines shown as straight are actually straight, points on a line are in the order shown, and more generally, all geometric objects are in the relative positions shown. For questions with geometric figures, you should base your answers on geometric reasoning, not on estimating or comparing quantities by sight or by measurement.

Coordinate systems, such as xy-planes and number lines, **are** drawn to scale; therefore, you can read, estimate, or compare quantities in such figures by sight or by measurement.

Graphical data presentations, such as bar graphs, circles graphs, and line graphs, **are** drawn to scale; therefore, you can read, estimate, or compare data values by sight or by measurement.

Directions for Quantitative Comparison questions

> **Compare Quantity A and Quantity B, using additional information centered above the two quantities if such information is given. Select one of the following four answer choices and fill in the corresponding oval to the right of the question.**
>
> (A) **Quantity A is greater.**
> (B) **Quantity B is greater.**
> (C) **The two quantities are equal.**
> (D) **The relationship cannot be determined from the information given.**
>
> **A symbol that appears more than once in a question has the same meaning throughout the question.**

	Quantity A	Quantity B	Correct Answer
Example 1:	(2)(6)	2 + 6	(A) (B) (C) (D)

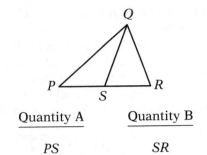

	Quantity A	Quantity B		Correct Answer

Example 2:   *PS*   *SR*

Ⓐ   Ⓑ   Ⓒ   ⬤Ⓓ
(since equal lengths cannot
be assumed, even though
PS and *SR* appear equal)

Directions for Numeric Entry questions

Enter your answer in the answer box(es) below the question.

- **Your answer may be an integer, a decimal, or a fraction, and it may be negative.**
- **If a question asks for a fraction, there will be two boxes—one for the numerator and one for the denominator.**
- **Equivalent forms of the correct answer, such as 2.5 and 2.50, are all correct. Fractions do not need to be reduced to lowest terms.**
- **Enter the exact answer unless the question asks you to round your answer.**

SET 1. Discrete Questions: Easy

Quantitative Comparison

For Questions 1 to 6, use the directions for Quantitative Comparison questions.

Emma spent $75 buying a used bicycle and $27
repairing it. Then she sold the bicycle for 40 percent
more than the total amount she spent buying and
repairing it.

     Quantity A   Quantity B

1.   The price at which Emma $140   Ⓐ   Ⓑ   Ⓒ   Ⓓ
     sold the bicycle

Explanation

In this question you are asked to compare the price at which Emma sold the
bicycle with $140. From the information given, you can conclude that Emma
spent a total of 75 + 27 = 102 dollars buying and repairing the bicycle and that
she sold it for 40 percent more than the $102 she spent buying and repairing it.
If you notice that 140 is 40 percent more than 100, you can conclude that 40
percent more than 102 is greater than 40 percent more than 100, and therefore,

Quantity A is greater than Quantity B. The correct answer is Choice A. (If you solve the problem in this way, you do not have to calculate the value of Quantity A.)

Another way to solve the problem is by explicitly calculating the value of Quantity A and comparing the result with $140 directly. Since 40 percent of 102 is $(0.4)(102) = 40.8$, it follows that Quantity A, the price at which Emma sold the bicycle, is $102.00 + 40.80 = 142.80$ dollars. Thus Quantity A, $142.80, is greater than Quantity B, $140, and the correct answer is **Choice A**.

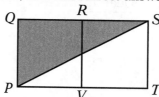

In the figure above, squares *PQRV* and *VRST* have sides of length 6.

Quantity A	Quantity B	
2. The area of the shaded region	36	Ⓐ Ⓑ Ⓒ Ⓓ

Explanation

In this question you are asked to compare the area of the shaded region with 36. You are given that both *PQRV* and *VRST* are squares with sides of length 6. Therefore, you can conclude that the length of *QS* is 12, and the area of the shaded right triangle *PQS* is $\frac{1}{2}(12)(6)$, or 36. Thus Quantity A is equal to Quantity B, and the correct answer is **Choice C**.

In 2009 the property tax on each home in Town *X* was *p* percent of the assessed value of the home, where *p* is a constant. The property tax in 2009 on a home in Town *X* that had an assessed value of $125,000 was $2,500.

Quantity A	Quantity B	
3. The property tax in 2009 on a home in Town *X* that had an assessed value of $160,000	$3,000	Ⓐ Ⓑ Ⓒ Ⓓ

Explanation

Before making the comparison in this problem, you need to analyze the information given to see what it tells you about the value of Quantity A, the property tax in 2009 on a home in Town *X* that had an assessed value of $160,000. One way of doing this is to determine the value of the constant *p* and then use that value to calculate the tax on the home that had an assessed value of $160,000.

Since it is given that a home that had an assessed value of $125,000 had a property tax of $2,500, you can conclude that *p* is equal to $\frac{2,500}{125,000}$, or 2%. Once you know that the property tax is 2% of the assessed value, you can determine that tax on the home that had an assessed value of $160,000 was 2% of 160,000, or 3,200. The correct answer is **Choice A**.

Another way to calculate the property tax on a home with an assessed value of $160,000 is by setting up a proportion. Because the tax rate is the same for each home in Town X, you can let the variable x represent the tax for the home assessed at $160,000 and solve for x as follows.

$$\frac{x}{160,000} = \frac{2,500}{125,000}$$
$$125,000x = (160,000)(2,500)$$
$$x = \frac{(160,000)(2,500)}{125,000}$$
$$x = 3,200$$

The correct answer is **Choice A**.

$$x + y = -1$$

Quantity A	Quantity B	
4. x	y	Ⓐ Ⓑ Ⓒ Ⓓ

Explanation

One way to approach this question is to plug in values for one of the variables and determine the corresponding value for the other variable.

One way to plug in: Plug in easy values. For example, you can plug in $x = 0$ and find that the corresponding value of y is -1; then you can plug in $y = 0$ and find that the corresponding value of x is -1. Since in the first case x is greater than y and in the second case y is greater than x, the correct answer is **Choice D**, the relationship cannot be determined from the information given.

A second way to plug in: If you prefer to always plug in values of x to determine corresponding values of y, you can begin by writing the equation $x + y = -1$ as $y = -x - 1$. Writing it in this form makes it easier to find the corresponding values of y.

You can start by plugging in the value $x = 0$. For this value of x, the corresponding value of y is $y = -1$, and therefore, x is greater than y. If you continue plugging in a variety of values of x, some negative and some positive, you will see that sometimes x is greater than y and sometimes y is greater than x.

If you inspect the equation $y = -x - 1$, you can conclude that since there is a negative sign in front of the x but not in front of the y, for each value of x that is greater than 0, the corresponding value of y is less than 0; therefore, for each $x > 0$, x is greater than y.

What about negative values of x? A quick inspection of the equation $y = -x - 1$ allows you to conclude that if $x < -1$, then $y > 0$, so y is greater than x.

So for some values of x and y that satisfy the equation, x is greater than y; and for other values, y is greater than x. Therefore, the relationship between the two quantities x and y cannot be determined from the information given, and the correct answer is **Choice D**.

r, s, and t are three consecutive odd integers such that $r < s < t$.

Quantity A	Quantity B	
5. $r + s + 1$	$s + t - 1$	Ⓐ Ⓑ Ⓒ Ⓓ

Explanation

You are given that three numbers, r, s, and t, are consecutive odd integers and that $r < s < t$. This means that if you express the three consecutive odd integers in terms of r, they are r, $r + 2$, and $r + 4$.

One way to approach this problem is to set up a placeholder relationship between the two quantities and simplify it to see what conclusions you can draw.

Simplification 1: Begin simplifying by expressing s and t in terms of r. The steps in this simplification can be done as follows.

$$r + s + 1 \;?\; s + t - 1$$
$$r + (r + 2) + 1 \;?\; (r + 2) + (r + 4) - 1$$
$$2r + 3 \;?\; 2r + 5$$
$$3 \;?\; 5$$

In the last step of the simplification, you can easily see that $3 < 5$. If you follow the simplification steps in reverse, you can see that the placeholder in each step remains unchanged, so you can conclude that Quantity B is greater than Quantity A, and the correct answer is **Choice B**.

Simplification 2: Since the number s appears in both quantities, you can begin the simplification by subtracting s from both sides of the relationship and then express t in terms of r. The steps in this simplification can be done as follows.

$$r + s + 1 \;?\; s + t - 1$$
$$r + 1 \;?\; t - 1$$
$$r + 1 \;?\; (r + 4) - 1$$
$$r + 1 \;?\; r + 3$$
$$1 \;?\; 3$$

In the last step of the simplification, you can easily see that $1 < 3$. If you follow the simplification steps in reverse, you can see that the placeholder in each step remains unchanged, so you can conclude that Quantity B is greater than Quantity A, and the correct answer is **Choice B**.

Note that in this solution, the fact that r is odd is not used; what is used is the fact that the consecutive odd integers differ by 2.

Quantity A	Quantity B	
6.　　The slope of line k	The slope of line ℓ	

Explanation

Note that the slope of each of the lines is positive, since each line rises as it goes to the right. Since the slopes of both lines are positive and line k rises faster (or is steeper) than line ℓ, line k has the greater slope, and the correct answer is **Choice A**.

You can also use the definition of the slope to arrive at the correct answer. Slope can be defined as the ratio of "rise" to "run" between any two points on a line, where the rise is the vertical distance between the points and the run is the horizontal distance, and the slope is respectively positive or negative depending on whether the line rises or falls when viewed from left to right. Because both lines pass through point P on the y-axis, they have the same rise from P to the x-axis. However, line ℓ intersects the x-axis at a greater value than line k. Thus, the run of line ℓ from the y-axis to the x-intercept is greater than the run of line k. When the slope is expressed as a ratio, both lines have the same numerator (rise), but line ℓ has a greater denominator (run). The greater denominator results in a lesser fraction and a lesser slope for line ℓ. Therefore, the correct answer is **Choice A**.

Multiple-choice Questions—Select One Answer Choice

For Questions 7 to 11, select a single answer choice.

7. In the figure above, what is the value of $\dfrac{x + y + z}{45}$?

   (A) 2
   (B) 3
   (C) 4
   (D) 5
   (E) 6

Explanation

The sum of the measures, in degrees, of the three interior angles of any triangle is 180°. As shown in the figure, the three angles of the triangle have measures of $x°$, $y°$, and $z°$, so $x + y + z = 180$. Therefore, $\dfrac{x + y + z}{45} = \dfrac{180}{45} = 4$, and the correct answer is **Choice C**.

8. A certain store sells two types of pens: one type for $2 per pen and the other type for $3 per pen. If a customer can spend up to $25 to buy pens at the store and there is no sales tax, what is the greatest number of pens the customer can buy?

    (A) 9
    (B) 10
    (C) 11
    (D) 12
    (E) 20

Explanation

It is fairly clear that the greatest number of pens that can be bought for $25 will consist mostly, if not entirely, of $2 pens. In fact, it is reasonable to begin by looking at how many of the $2 pens the customer can buy if the customer does not buy any $3 pens. It is easy to see that the customer could buy 12 of the $2 pens, with $1 left over.

If the customer bought 11 of the $2 pens, there would be $3 left over with which to buy a $3 pen. In this case, the customer could still buy 12 pens.

If the customer bought 10 of the $2 pens, there would be $5 left over. Only 1 of the $3 pens could be bought with the $5, so in this case, the customer could buy only 11 pens.

As the number of $2 pens decreases, the total number of pens that the customer can buy with $25 decreases as well. Thus the greatest number of pens the customer can buy with $25 is 12. The correct answer is **Choice D**.

9. If $y = 3x$ and $z = 2y$, what is $x + y + z$ in terms of x ?

    (A) $10x$
    (B) $9x$
    (C) $8x$
    (D) $6x$
    (E) $5x$

Explanation

It is not necessary to find the individual values of x, y, and z to answer the question. You are asked to rewrite the expression $x + y + z$ as an equivalent expression in terms of x. This means that you need to use the information provided about y and z to express them in terms of the variable x. The variable y is already given in terms of x; that is, $y = 3x$; and because $z = 2y$, it follows that $z = (2)(3x) = 6x$. Using substitution, you can rewrite the expression as follows.

$$\begin{aligned} x + y + z &= x + (3x) + (6x) \\ &= (1 + 3 + 6)x \\ &= 10x \end{aligned}$$

The correct answer is **Choice A**.

10. A certain shipping service charges an insurance fee of $0.75 when shipping any package with contents worth $25.00 or less and an insurance fee of $1.00 when shipping any package with contents worth over $25.00. If Dan uses the shipping company to ship three packages with contents worth $18.25, $25.00, and $127.50, respectively, what is the total insurance fee that the company charges Dan to ship the three packages?

   Ⓐ $1.75

   Ⓑ $2.25

   Ⓒ $2.50

   Ⓓ $2.75

   Ⓔ $3.00

Explanation

Note that two of the packages being shipped have contents that are worth $25.00 or less. Therefore, each of them has an insurance fee of $0.75, for a total of $1.50. The third package has contents worth over $25.00, and it has an insurance fee of $1.00. Therefore, the total insurance fee for the three packages is $1.50 + $1.00 = $2.50, and the correct answer is **Choice C**.

11. If 55 percent of the people who purchase a certain product are female, what is the ratio of the number of females who purchase the product to the number of males who purchase the product?

   Ⓐ 11 to 9

   Ⓑ 10 to 9

   Ⓒ   9 to 10

   Ⓓ   9 to 11

   Ⓔ   5 to 9

Explanation

Note that because 55 percent of the people who purchase the product are females, it follows that 45 percent of the people who purchase the product are males. Therefore, the ratio of the number of females who purchase the product to the number of males who purchase the product is 55 to 45, or 11 to 9, and the correct answer is **Choice A**.

Numeric Entry

For Questions 12 and 13, use the directions for Numeric Entry questions.

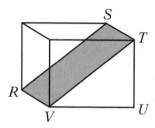

12. In the rectangular solid above, $TU = 3$, $UV = 4$, and $VR = 2$. What is the area of the shaded rectangular region?

Explanation

To find the area of the shaded rectangular region, you need to multiply the length of the rectangular region by its width. In this question you are given the lengths of three edges: $TU = 3$, $UV = 4$, and $VR = 2$. Note that VR is the length of the shaded rectangle. To find the width of the shaded rectangle, you need to find either RS or VT. Note that VT lies on the front face of the rectangular solid. It is the hypotenuse of right triangle VUT. You know that $UV = 4$ and $TU = 3$, so by the Pythagorean theorem you can conclude that $VT = \sqrt{3^2 + 4^2} = \sqrt{9 + 16} = \sqrt{25} = 5$. Therefore, the area of the shaded rectangular region is $(5)(2) = 10$. The correct answer is **10**.

13. A list of numbers has a mean of 8 and a standard deviation of 2.5. If x is a number in the list that is 2 standard deviations above the mean, what is the value of x?

$$x = \boxed{}$$

Explanation

You are given that x is 2 standard deviations above the mean, 8. Because the standard deviation of the numbers in the list is 2.5, it follows that x is $(2)(2.5)$, or 5 units above the mean 8. Therefore, $x = 8 + 5 = 13$, and the correct answer is **13**.

Multiple-choice Questions—Select One or More Answer Choices

For Question 14, select all the answer choices that apply.

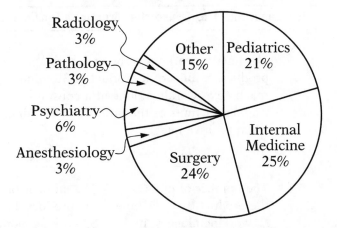

14. The circle graph above shows the distribution of 200,000 physicians by specialty. Which of the following sectors of the circle graph represent more than 40,000 physicians?

Indicate all such sectors.

- A Pediatrics
- B Internal Medicine
- C Surgery
- D Anesthesiology
- E Psychiatry

Explanation

One approach to solve this problem is to find out what percent of 200,000 is 40,000 and then compare this percent with the percents given in the circle graph. Because $\frac{40,000}{200,000} = 0.2$, it follows that 40,000 is 20% of 200,000, and any specialty that has more than 20% of the distribution has more than 40,000 physicians. This is true for the specialties of pediatrics, internal medicine, and surgery. The correct answer consists of **Choices A, B, and C**.

SET 2. Discrete Questions: Medium

Quantitative Comparison

For Questions 1 to 5, use the directions for Quantitative Comparison questions.

Machine R, working alone at a constant rate, produces x units of a product in 30 minutes, and machine S, working alone at a constant rate, produces x units of the product in 48 minutes, where x is a positive integer.

Quantity A	Quantity B

1. The number of units of the product that machine R, working alone at its constant rate, produces in 3 hours

   The number of units of the product that machine S, working alone at its constant rate, produces in 4 hours

Explanation

In this question you are given that machine R, working alone at its constant rate, produces x units of a product in 30 minutes. Since it is easy to see that 3 hours is 6 times 30 minutes, you can conclude that Quantity A is $6x$.

You can compare $6x$ with Quantity B in two ways.

One: In the additional information centered above the quantities, you are given that machine S, working alone at its constant rate, produces x units of the product in 48 minutes, so you can conclude that machine S can produce $6x$ units of the product in (6)(48) minutes, or 4.8 hours. So in 4 hours, machine S produces less than $6x$ units, and Quantity B is less than $6x$.

Two: First, convert 48 minutes to $\frac{4}{5}$ hour, then find the number of 48-minute periods there are in 4 hours by computing $\dfrac{4}{\left(\frac{4}{5}\right)} = (4)\left(\frac{5}{4}\right) = 5$. Thus, Quantity B is $5x$.

Either way, Quantity A is greater than Quantity B, and the correct answer is **Choice A**.

Frequency Distribution for List X

Number	1	2	3	5
Frequency	10	20	18	12

Frequency Distribution for List Y

Number	6	7	8	9
Frequency	24	17	10	9

List X and list Y each contain 60 numbers. Frequency distributions for each list are given above. The average (arithmetic mean) of the numbers in list X is 2.7, and the average of the numbers in list Y is 7.1. List Z contains 120 numbers: the 60 numbers in list X and the 60 numbers in list Y.

	Quantity A	Quantity B	
2.	The average of the 120 numbers in list Z	The median of the 120 numbers in list Z	Ⓐ Ⓑ Ⓒ Ⓓ

Explanation

In this problem you are asked to compare the average with the median of the 120 numbers in list Z. Since list Z consists of the numbers in lists X and Y combined, it is reasonable to try to use the information about lists X and Y to calculate the average and the median of the numbers in list Z.

To determine the average of the 120 numbers in list Z, you can use the information given about the individual averages of the numbers in lists X and Y. Because lists X and Y each contain 60 numbers, the average of the numbers in list Z is the average of the individual averages of the numbers in lists X and Y. Thus, the average of the numbers in list Z is $\dfrac{2.7 + 7.1}{2}$, or 4.9.

To determine the median of the 120 numbers in list Z, first note that list Z contains an even number of numbers, so the median of the numbers in list Z is the average of the middle two numbers when the numbers are listed in increasing order. If you look at the numbers in the two lists, you will see that the 60 numbers in list X are all less than or equal to 5, and the 60 numbers in list Y are all greater than or equal to 6. Thus, the two middle numbers in list Z are 5 and 6, and the average of these numbers is $\dfrac{5 + 6}{2}$, or 5.5. Therefore, the median of the numbers in list Z is 5.5, and this is greater than the average of 4.9. The correct answer is **Choice B**.

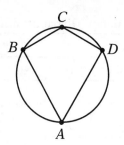

In the figure above, the diameter of the circle is 10.

Quantity A	Quantity B	
3. The area of quadrilateral *ABCD*	40	Ⓐ Ⓑ Ⓒ Ⓓ

Explanation

You are given that the circle has a diameter of 10, and from the figure you can assume that points *A*, *B*, *C*, and *D* lie on the circle in the order shown. However, because figures are not necessarily drawn to scale, you cannot assume anything else about the positions of points *A*, *B*, *C*, and *D* on the circle. Therefore, to get an idea of how various possible positions of these four points could affect the area of quadrilateral *ABCD*, it is a good idea to see how the figure can vary but still have points *A*, *B*, *C*, and *D* in the same order as in the figure above.

One way that you might vary the figure is to evenly space the four points along the circle, as shown below.

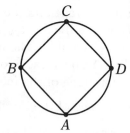

Another way is to draw points *A* and *C* opposite each other, with points *B* and *D* close to point *C*, as shown below.

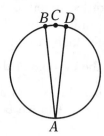

From these figures you can draw some basic conclusions about the area of *ABCD*.

If points *A* and *C* are opposite each other, with points *B* and *D* very close to point *C*, the area of quadrilateral *ABCD* is very close to 0. Clearly, the area can be less than 40 (Quantity B).

If points *A*, *B*, *C*, and *D* are evenly spaced, the area is not close to 0. How does the area compare with 40? To calculate the area of *ABCD*, draw the diameters *AC* and *BD* in the figure. The two diameters are perpendicular bisectors of each other, so they divide *ABCD* into 4 right triangles, as shown.

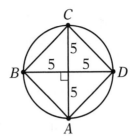

The area of each of the right triangles is $\left(\frac{1}{2}\right)(5)(5)$, or 12.5. Thus, the area of *ABCD* is (4)(12.5), or 50.

Since the area of the quadrilateral in the first figure is less than 40 and the area of the quadrilateral in the second figure is greater than 40, the relationship cannot be determined from the information given. The correct answer is **Choice D**.

$$x^2y > 0$$
$$xy^2 < 0$$

Quantity A	Quantity B	
4. x	y	Ⓐ Ⓑ Ⓒ Ⓓ

Explanation

You are given that $x^2y > 0$, which means that the product of the two numbers x^2 and y is positive. Recall that the product of two numbers is positive only if both numbers are positive or both numbers are negative. The square of a number is always greater than or equal to 0. In this case, x^2 cannot equal 0 because the product x^2y is not 0. Thus, x^2 is positive and it follows that y is also positive.

You are also given that $xy^2 < 0$, which means that the product of the two numbers x and y^2 is negative. The product of two numbers is negative only if one of the numbers is negative and the other number is positive. In this case, y^2 cannot be negative because it is the square of a number, and it cannot be 0 because the product x^2y is not 0. Thus, y^2 is positive and so x must be negative.

Because x is negative and y is positive, y must be greater than x, and the correct answer is **Choice B**.

Among the 9,000 people attending a football game at College *C*, there were x students from College *C* and y students who were <u>not</u> from College *C*.

Quantity A	Quantity B	
5. The number of people attending the game who were <u>not</u> students	$9{,}000 - x - y$	Ⓐ Ⓑ Ⓒ Ⓓ

Explanation

In this question you are not told whether all of the 9,000 people attending the game were students. Let z be the number of people attending the game who were not students. The people attending the game can be broken down into three groups: students from College C, students not from College C, and people who were not students. This can be expressed algebraically as $9{,}000 = x + y + z$, where x represents the number of students from College C attending the game and y represents the number of students attending the game who were not from College C. Therefore, $9{,}000 - x - y = z$ is the number of people attending the game who were not students. The correct answer is **Choice C**.

Multiple-choice Questions—Select One Answer Choice

For Questions 6 to 10, select a single answer choice.

6. If $x \neq 0$, which of the following is equivalent to $\dfrac{x(x^2)^3}{x^2}$?

(A) x^2

(B) x^3

(C) x^4

(D) x^5

(E) x^6

Explanation

To simplify $\dfrac{x(x^2)^3}{x^2}$, it can be helpful to write $(x^2)^3$ as $(x^2)(x^2)(x^2)$ in the given expression; that is, $\dfrac{x(x^2)^3}{x^2} = \dfrac{x(x^2)(x^2)(x^2)}{x^2}$. Because $x \neq 0$, both numerator and denominator can be divided by x^2, and the expression simplifies to $x(x^2)(x^2)$, which, by the rules of exponents, is equal to x^5.

Another way to simplify the expression using the rules of exponents directly is as follows.

$$\frac{x(x^2)^3}{x^2} = \frac{x(x^6)}{x^2} = \frac{x^7}{x^2} = x^5$$

The correct answer is **Choice D**.

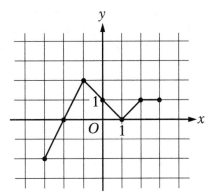

7. The figure above shows the graph of the function f in the xy-plane. What is the value of $f(f(-1))$?

    Ⓐ -2
    Ⓑ -1
    Ⓒ 0
    Ⓓ 1
    Ⓔ 2

Explanation

Note that to find $f(f(-1))$, you must apply the function f twice, first to find the value of $f(-1)$ and then to find the value of $f(f(-1))$. To find the value of $f(-1)$, find the point on the graph of the function f whose x-coordinate is $x = -1$. This point has y-coordinate $y = 2$. Therefore, the value of $f(-1)$ is 2, and $f(f(-1)) = f(2)$. Next you need to find the value of $f(2)$. To find the value of $f(2)$, find the point on the graph whose x-coordinate is $x = 2$. This point has y-coordinate $y = 1$. Therefore, $f(2) = 1$, and because $f(f(-1)) = f(2)$, you can conclude that $f(f(-1)) = 1$. The correct answer is **Choice D**.

8. If $\dfrac{d - 3n}{7n - d} = 1$, which of the following statements describes d in terms of n?

    Ⓐ d is 4 less than n.
    Ⓑ d is 4 more than n.
    Ⓒ d is $\dfrac{3}{7}$ of n.
    Ⓓ d is 2 times n.
    Ⓔ d is 5 times n.

Explanation

To describe d in terms of n, you need to solve the equation $\dfrac{d - 3n}{7n - d} = 1$ for d. To simplify the equation, you can begin by multiplying both sides by $7n - d$ and then proceed as follows.

$$(7n - d)\left(\frac{d - 3n}{7n - d}\right) = (7n - d)(1)$$
$$d - 3n = 7n - d$$
$$d = 10n - d$$
$$2d = 10n$$
$$d = 5n$$

The correct answer is **Choice E**.

9. By weight, liquid *A* makes up 8 percent of solution *R* and 18 percent of solution *S*. If 3 grams of solution *R* are mixed with 7 grams of solution *S*, then liquid *A* accounts for what percent of the weight of the resulting solution?

    (A) 10%

    (B) 13%

    (C) 15%

    (D) 19%

    (E) 26%

Explanation

Liquid *A* makes up 8 percent of the weight of solution *R* and 18 percent of the weight of solution *S*. Therefore, 3 grams of solution *R* contain (0.08)(3), or 0.24 gram of liquid *A*, and 7 grams of solution *S* contain (0.18)(7), or 1.26 grams of liquid *A*. When the two solutions are mixed, the resulting solution weighs 3 + 7, or 10 grams and contains 0.24 + 1.26, or 1.5 grams of liquid *A*. This means that liquid *A* makes up $\frac{1.5}{10}$, or $\frac{15}{100}$, or 15 percent of the weight of the resulting solution. The correct answer is **Choice C**.

10. Of the 700 members of a certain organization, 120 are lawyers. Two members of the organization will be selected at random. Which of the following is closest to the probability that <u>neither</u> of the members selected will be a lawyer?

    (A) 0.5

    (B) 0.6

    (C) 0.7

    (D) 0.8

    (E) 0.9

Explanation

The probability that neither of the members selected will be a lawyer is equal to the fraction

$$\frac{\text{the number of ways 2 members who are not lawyers can be selected}}{\text{the number of ways 2 members can be selected}}$$

where the order of selection does not matter.

Since there are 120 members who are lawyers, there must be 700 − 120, or 580 members who are not lawyers. There are 580 ways of selecting a first member who is not a lawyer and 579 ways of selecting a second member who is not a lawyer. Multiplying these two numbers gives the number of ways to select two members who are not lawyers. However, in the (580)(579) ways, each group of 2 members who are not lawyers is counted twice. You can see this by considering two members, *A* and *B*. The two members can be chosen in 2 ways: *A* first, followed by *B*, and *B* first, followed by *A*. To adjust for double counting, you need to divide (580)(579) by 2.

Similarly, the number of ways 2 members can be selected from among the 700 members is (700)(699) divided by 2. Thus, the desired probability is

$$\frac{\dfrac{(580)(579)}{2}}{\dfrac{(700)(699)}{2}} = \frac{(580)(579)}{(700)(699)}$$

Since the answer choices are all tenths, you need to approximate the value of this fraction to the nearest tenth. There are several ways to do this approximation. One way is to use your calculator to convert the fraction to a decimal and round the decimal to the nearest tenth.

Another way is to approximate the value of the fraction as follows.

$$\frac{(580)(579)}{(700)(699)} \approx \frac{(600)(600)}{(700)(700)} = \left(\frac{6}{7}\right)^2 = \frac{36}{49} \approx \frac{36}{50} = 0.72$$

Either way, the answer choice that is closest to the value of the fraction is 0.7. The correct answer is **Choice C**.

Another approach to this problem is to consider the random selections as two separate but successive events. The probability of selecting a first member who is not a lawyer is $\frac{580}{700}$, because there are 580 members out of the 700 members who are not lawyers. For the second selection, there are only 699 members left to select from, because one member has already been selected. If the first member selected is not a lawyer, then there are only 579 members left who are not lawyers. So the probability of selecting a second member who is not a lawyer, given the condition that the first member selected was not a lawyer, is $\frac{579}{699}$. The probability that both members selected will not be lawyers is the product of the two probabilities, or $\left(\frac{580}{700}\right)\left(\frac{579}{699}\right)$, which is approximated above as 0.72. The correct answer is **Choice C**.

Numeric Entry

For Questions 11 and 12, use the directions for Numeric Entry questions.

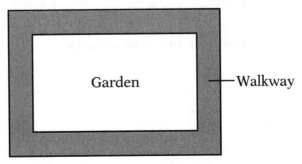

11. The figure above represents a rectangular garden with a walkway around it. The garden is 18 feet long and 12 feet wide. The walkway is uniformly 3 feet wide, and its edges meet at right angles. What is the area of the walkway?

    [   ] square feet

Explanation

You can see from the figure that the shaded region is the region between the two rectangles. Looking at the shaded region in this way suggests that the area of the walkway can be calculated as the difference between the area of the larger rectangle and the area of the smaller rectangle.

The region represented by the smaller rectangle is the garden. Since the garden is 18 feet long and 12 feet wide, its area is (18)(12), or 216 square feet.

The region represented by the larger rectangle is the garden and the walkway combined. The length of the region is the length of the garden plus twice the width of the walkway, or 18 + (2)(3) = 24 feet. The width of the region is the width of the garden plus twice the width of the walkway, or 12 + (2)(3) = 18 feet. Therefore, the area of the region represented by the larger rectangle is (24)(18), or 432 square feet, and the area of the walkway is 432 − 216, or 216 square feet.

Another way to approach this problem is to think of the walkway as being composed of four rectangles and four squares, as shown in the figure below.

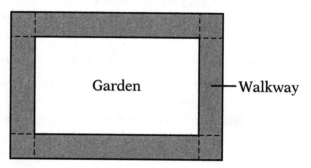

Each of the 4 squares is 3 feet long and 3 feet wide. The two rectangles running along the length of the garden are 18 feet long and 3 feet wide, and the two rectangles running along the width of the garden are 12 feet long and 3 feet wide. Thus, the area of the walkway is

$$4(3)(3) + 2(18)(3) + 2(12)(3) = 36 + 108 + 72 = 216 \text{ square feet}$$

The correct answer is **216**.

12. Line k lies in the xy-plane. The x-intercept of line k is −4, and line k passes through the midpoint of the line segment whose endpoints are $(2, 9)$ and $(2, 0)$. What is the slope of line k ?

    Give your answer as a fraction.

Explanation

You can calculate the slope of a line if you know the coordinates of two points on the line. In this question you are given information about two points on line k, namely,

- the point at which line k crosses the x-axis has x-coordinate −4;
- the midpoint of the line segment with endpoints at $(2, 9)$ and $(2, 0)$ is on line k.

The coordinates of the first point are $(-4, 0)$, since the x-coordinate is -4 and the y-coordinate of every point on the x-axis is 0. For the second point, the midpoint of the line segment is halfway between the endpoints $(2, 9)$ and $(2, 0)$. Thus, the midpoint has x-coordinate 2 and y-coordinate $\frac{9}{2}$, the number halfway between 9 and 0. Based on the coordinates $(-4, 0)$ and $\left(2, \frac{9}{2}\right)$, the slope of line k is

$$\frac{\frac{9}{2} - 0}{2 - (-4)} = \frac{\frac{9}{2}}{6} = \frac{3}{4}$$

The correct answer is $\frac{3}{4}$ (or any equivalent fraction).

Multiple-choice Questions—Select One or More Answer Choices

For Questions 13 and 14, select all the answer choices that apply.

13. If the lengths of two sides of a triangle are 5 and 9, respectively, which of the following could be the length of the third side of the triangle?

    Indicate <u>all</u> such lengths.

    [A] 3
    [B] 5
    [C] 8
    [D] 15

Explanation

A good way to approach this problem is to think about how much the length of the third side of a triangle with two fixed side lengths can vary. If you think about it a bit, you will see that the smaller the interior angle between the two sides of the triangle is, the smaller the length of the third side is; and the larger the interior angle between the two sides of the triangle is, the larger the length of the third side is. This suggests drawing two triangles, one in which the angle between the two sides is close to 0 degrees and one in which the angle between the two sides is close to 180 degrees, like the triangles below.

In the triangle in which the angle between the sides of length 5 and 9 is small, you can see that the length of the third side is a bit greater than $9 - 5$, or 4. If it were equal to 4, the triangle would degenerate into a line segment.

In the triangle in which the angle between the sides of length 5 and 9 is large, you can see that the length of the third side is a bit less than $9 + 5$, or 14. If it were equal to 14, the triangle would degenerate into a line segment.

Therefore, the length of the third side of the triangle must be greater than 4 and less than 14. Furthermore, it is intuitive that any length between these two numbers can be achieved by some triangle. The correct answer consists of **Choices B and C**.

14. On the number line shown above, the tick marks are equally spaced. Which of the following statements about the numbers x, y, and z must be true?

Indicate <u>all</u> such statements.

A $xyz < 0$

B $x + z = y$

C $z(y - x) > 0$

Explanation

You can see from their positions on the number line that x is less than 0 and both y and z are greater than 0. Because the tick marks are equally spaced, you can also see that $x = -y$ and $z = 2y$. You need to evaluate each answer choice separately to determine whether it must be true.

Choice A says that the product of the three numbers x, y, and z is less than 0. Recall that the product of three numbers is negative under either of the following two conditions.

- All three numbers are negative.
- One of the numbers is negative and the other two numbers are positive.

Choice A must be true, since x is negative and y and z are positive.

Choice B is the equation $x + z = y$. To see whether the equation must be true, it is a good idea to express two of the variables in terms of the third (that is, to "get rid of" two of the variables). The equations $x = -y$ and $z = 2y$ give x and z in terms of y, so the equation $x + z = y$ can be rewritten, substituting $-y$ for x and $2y$ for z, as $-y + 2y = y$. In this form you can quickly conclude that the equation must be true.

Choice C says that the product of the two numbers z and $y - x$ is greater than 0. Recall that the product of two numbers is positive under either of the following two conditions.

- Both numbers are positive.
- Both numbers are negative.

Since you already know that z is positive, you can conclude that the product $z(y - x)$ will be positive if $y - x$ is positive. By adding x to both sides of the inequality $y - x > 0$, you can see that it is equivalent to the inequality $y > x$, which is clearly true from the number line. Since $y - x$ is positive, the product $z(y - x)$ must be positive.

Therefore, the correct answer consists of **Choices A, B, and C**.

SET 3. Discrete Questions: Hard

Quantitative Comparison

For Questions 1 to 6, use the directions for Quantitative Comparison questions.

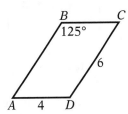

In the figure above, *ABCD* is a parallelogram.

	Quantity A	Quantity B	
1.	The area of *ABCD*	24	Ⓐ Ⓑ Ⓒ Ⓓ

Explanation

In this question you are asked to compare the area of a parallelogram with an area of 24, given two side lengths and the measure of one interior angle of the parallelogram. Since the measure of the interior angle given is 125°, you can conclude that the parallelogram is not a rectangle.

Recall that the area of a parallelogram is found by multiplying the length of a base by the height corresponding to the base. It is helpful to draw the vertical height from vertex *C* to base *AD* of the parallelogram, as shown in the figure below.

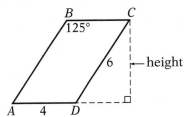

Note that the newly drawn height is a leg in a newly formed right triangle. The hypotenuse of the triangle is a side of the parallelogram and has length 6. Thus, the leg of the triangle, which is the height of the parallelogram, must be less than the hypotenuse 6. The area of the parallelogram is equal to the length of base *AD*, which is 4, times the height, which is less than 6. Since the product of 4 and a number less than 6 must be less than 24, the area of the parallelogram must be less than 24. Quantity B is greater than Quantity A, and the correct answer is **Choice B.**

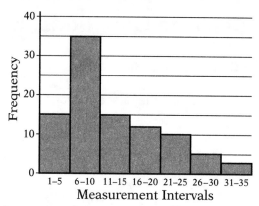

In the course of an experiment, 95 measurements were recorded, and all of the measurements were integers. The 95 measurements were then grouped into 7 measurement intervals. The graph above shows the frequency distribution of the 95 measurements by measurement interval.

Quantity A	Quantity B	
2. The average (arithmetic mean) of the 95 measurements	The median of the 95 measurements	Ⓐ Ⓑ Ⓒ Ⓓ

Explanation

From the histogram, you can observe that

- all of the measurement intervals are the same size,
- the distribution has a peak at the measurement interval 6–10, and
- more of the measurement intervals are to the right of the peak than are to the left of the peak.

Since in the histogram the 95 measurements have been grouped into intervals, you cannot calculate the exact value of either the average or the median; you must compare them without being able to determine the exact value of either one.

The median of the 95 measurements is the middle measurement when the measurements are listed in increasing order. The middle measurement is the 48th measurement. From the histogram, you can see that the measurement interval 1–5 contains the first 15 measurements, and the measurement interval 6–10 contains the next 35 measurements (that is, measurements 16 through 50). Therefore, the median is in the measurement interval 6–10 and could be 6, 7, 8, 9, or 10.

Estimating the average of the 95 measurements is more complicated.

Since you are asked to compare the average and the median, not necessarily to calculate them, you may ask yourself if you can tell whether the average is greater than or less than the median. Note that visually the measurements in the first three measurement intervals are symmetric around the measurement interval 6–10, so you would expect the average of the measurements in just these three measurement intervals to lie in the 6–10 measurement interval. The 30 measurements in the remaining four measurement intervals are all greater than 10, some significantly greater than 10. Therefore, the average of the 95 measurements is greater than the average of the measurements in the first three measurement intervals, probably greater than 10. At this point it seems likely that the average of the 95 measurements is greater than the median of the 95 measurements. It turns out that this is true.

To actually show that the average must be greater than 10, you can make the average as small as possible and see if the smallest possible average is greater than 10. To make the average as small as possible, assume that all of the measurements in each interval are as small as possible. That is to say, all 15 measurements in the measurement interval 1–5 are equal to 1, all 35 measurements in the measurement interval 6–10 are equal to 6, etc. Under this assumption, the average of the 95 measurements is

$$\frac{(1)(15) + (6)(35) + (11)(15) + (16)(12) + (21)(10) + (26)(5) + (31)(3)}{95} = \frac{990}{95}$$

The value of the smallest possible average, $\frac{990}{95}$, is greater than 10.

Therefore, since the average of the 95 measurements is greater than 10 and the median is in the measurement interval 6–10, it follows that the average is greater than the median, and the correct answer is **Choice A**.

x is an integer greater than 1.

	Quantity A	Quantity B	
3.	3^{x+1}	4^x	Ⓐ Ⓑ Ⓒ Ⓓ

Explanation

One way to approach this question is to plug in numbers for the variables and see what the relationship between the two quantities is for each of the numbers you plug in.

If you plug in $x = 2$, you see that Quantity A is $3^{x+1} = 3^3$, or 27, and Quantity B is $4^x = 4^2$, or 16. In this case, Quantity A is greater than Quantity B.

If you plug in $x = 3$, you see that Quantity A is $3^{x+1} = 3^4$, or 81, and Quantity B is $4^x = 4^3$, or 64. In this case, Quantity A is greater than Quantity B.

If you plug in $x = 4$, you see that Quantity A is $3^{x+1} = 3^5$, or 243, and Quantity B is $4^x = 4^4$, or 256. In this case, Quantity B is greater than Quantity A. Since for $x = 2$ and for $x = 3$, Quantity A is greater than Quantity B, and for $x = 4$, Quantity B is greater than Quantity A, it follows that the relationship between the two quantities cannot be determined. The correct answer is **Choice D**.

Since both quantities are algebraic expressions, another way to approach this problem is to set up a placeholder relationship between the two quantities and simplify it to see what conclusions you can draw.

$$3^{x+1} \;\boxed{?}\; 4^x$$
$$3(3^x) \;\boxed{?}\; 4^x$$
$$\frac{3(3^x)}{3^x} \;\boxed{?}\; \frac{4^x}{3^x}$$
$$3 \;\boxed{?}\; \left(\frac{4}{3}\right)^x$$

For any value of x, the value of 3^x is positive, so dividing by 3^x does not change any inequality that could be put in the placeholder. Since each step in this simplification is reversible, this reduces the problem to comparing 3 with $\left(\frac{4}{3}\right)^x$.

You can see that because $\frac{4}{3}$ is greater than 1, the value of $\left(\frac{4}{3}\right)^x$ becomes greater as x becomes larger. In particular, it is greater than 3 for large enough values of x. For the smallest value of x, $x = 2$, the relationship is $\left(\frac{4}{3}\right)^2 = \frac{16}{9} < 3$.

Since for $x = 2$, Quantity A is greater than Quantity B and for large values of x, Quantity B is greater than Quantity A, it follows that the relationship between the two quantities cannot be determined. The correct answer is **Choice D**.

> A, B, and C are three rectangles. The length and width of rectangle A are 10 percent greater and 10 percent less, respectively, than the length and width of rectangle C. The length and width of rectangle B are 20 percent greater and 20 percent less, respectively, than the length and width of rectangle C.

	Quantity A	Quantity B				
4.	The area of rectangle A	The area of rectangle B	Ⓐ	Ⓑ	Ⓒ	Ⓓ

Explanation

In this question you are asked to compare the area of rectangle A and the area of rectangle B. Since the information given relates the dimensions of both rectangle A and rectangle B to the corresponding dimensions of rectangle C, you can try to use the relationships to make the desired comparison.

If ℓ represents the length of rectangle C and w represents its width, then the length and width of rectangles A and B can be translated into algebraic expressions as follows.

- The length of rectangle A is 10 percent greater than the length of rectangle C, or 1.1ℓ.
- The width of rectangle A is 10 percent less than the width of rectangle C, or $0.9w$.
- The length of rectangle B is 20 percent greater than the length of rectangle C, or 1.2ℓ.
- The width of rectangle B is 20 percent less than the width of rectangle C, or $0.8w$.

In terms of ℓ and w, the area of rectangle A is $(1.1\ell)(0.9w)$, or $0.99\ell w$.
In terms of ℓ and w, the area of rectangle B is $(1.2\ell)(0.8w)$, or $0.96\ell w$.
Since $0.99\ell w$ is greater than $0.96\ell w$, Quantity A is greater than Quantity B, and the correct answer is **Choice A**.

> The random variable X is normally distributed. The values 650 and 850 are at the 60th and 90th percentiles of the distribution of X, respectively.

	Quantity A	Quantity B				
5.	The value at the 75th percentile of the distribution of X	750	Ⓐ	Ⓑ	Ⓒ	Ⓓ

Explanation

You are given that the distribution of random variable X is normal and that the values 650 and 850 are at the 60th and 90th percentiles of the distribution, respectively.

Both of the values 650 and 850 are greater than the mean of the distribution. If you draw a rough sketch of the graph of the normal distribution, the sketch could look something like the one below. Note that it is not necessary to know the exact location of 650 and 850, just that both values are above the mean.

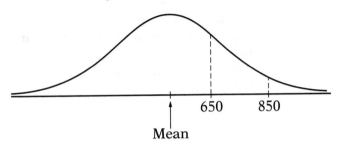

To say that the value 650 is at the 60th percentile of the distribution means, graphically, that 60 percent of the area between the normal curve and the horizontal axis lies to the left of the vertical line segment at 650. To say that 850 is at the 90th percentile of the distribution means that 90 percent of the area between the normal curve and the horizontal axis lies to the left of the vertical line segment at 850.

The value 750 is halfway between 650 and 850. However, because the curve is decreasing in that interval, the area between 650 and 750 is greater than the area between 750 and 850. Since the value at the 75th percentile should divide in half the <u>area</u> between the value at the 60th percentile (650) and the value at the 90th percentile (850), this value is closer to 650 than to 850. Thus you can conclude that Quantity A, the value at the 75th percentile of the distribution of X, is less than Quantity B. The correct answer is **Choice B**.

> Set S consists of all positive integers less than 81 that are <u>not</u> equal to the square of an integer.

Quantity A	Quantity B	
6. The number of integers in set S	72	Ⓐ Ⓑ Ⓒ Ⓓ

Explanation

Set S consists of all integers from 1 to 80, except those that are equal to the square of an integer. So, Quantity A, the number of integers in set S, is equal to the number of positive integers that are less than 81 minus the number of positive integers less than 81 that <u>are</u> equal to the square of an integer.

Clearly, there are 80 positive integers that are less than 81.

One way to determine the number of positive integers less than 81 that are squares of integers is by noticing that 81 is equal to 9^2 and concluding that the squares of the integers from 1 to 8 are all positive integers that are less than 81.

You can also draw this conclusion by squaring each of the positive integers, beginning with 1, until you get to an integer n such that n^2 is greater than or equal to 81. Either way, there are 8 positive integers less than 81 that are squares of integers.

Therefore, the number of integers in set S is $80 - 8$, or 72, which is equal to Quantity B. So Quantity A is equal to Quantity B, and the correct answer is **Choice C**.

Multiple-choice Questions—Select One Answer Choice

For Questions 7 to 12, select a single answer choice.

7. A manager is forming a 6-person team to work on a certain project. From the 11 candidates available for the team, the manager has already chosen 3 to be on the team. In selecting the other 3 team members, how many different combinations of 3 of the remaining candidates does the manager have to choose from?

   (A)   6

   (B)   24

   (C)   56

   (D)   120

   (E)   462

Explanation

To determine the number of different combinations of 3 of the remaining candidates that the manager has to choose from, you first have to know the number of remaining candidates. Since you know that the manager has already chosen 3 of the 11 candidates to be on the team, it is easy to see that there are 8 remaining candidates. Now you need to count how many different combinations of 3 objects can be chosen from a group of 8 objects.

If you remember the combinations formula, you know that the number of combinations is $\dfrac{8!}{3!(8-3)!}$ (which is denoted symbolically as $\binom{8}{3}$ or $_8C_3$). You can then calculate the number of different combinations of 3 of the remaining candidates as follows.

$$\frac{8!}{3!(8-3)!} = \frac{(8)(7)(6)(5!)}{(3!)(5!)} = \frac{(8)(7)(6)}{6} = 56$$

The correct answer is **Choice C**.

8. Which of the following could be the graph of all values of x that satisfy the inequality $2 - 5x \le -\dfrac{6x - 5}{3}$?

   (A)

   (B)

   (C)

   (D)

   (E)

Explanation

To determine which of the graphs is the correct answer, you first need to determine all values of x that satisfy the inequality. To do that you need to simplify the inequality until you isolate x.

You can begin by multiplying both sides of the inequality by 3 to obtain $(3)(2 - 5x) \le -(6x - 5)$. Note that when you multiply by 3, the right-hand side of the inequality becomes $-(6x - 5)$, not $-6x - 5$.

The rest of the simplification is as follows.

$$(3)(2 - 5x) \le -6x + 5$$
$$6 - 15x \le -6x + 5$$
$$-15x \le -6x - 1$$
$$-9x \le -1$$
$$x \ge \frac{1}{9}$$

Note that when an inequality is multiplied (or divided) by a negative number, the direction of the inequality reverses.

The graphs in the answer choices are number lines on which only the number 0 is indicated. Therefore, you do not need to locate $\frac{1}{9}$ on the number line; it is enough to know that $\frac{1}{9}$ is a positive number. Choice C is the only choice in which the shaded part of the line is equal to or greater than a positive number. Therefore, the correct answer is **Choice C**.

9. If $1 + x + x^2 + x^3 = 60$, then the average (arithmetic mean) of x, x^2, x^3, and x^4 is equal to which of the following?

Ⓐ $12x$
Ⓑ $15x$
Ⓒ $20x$
Ⓓ $30x$
Ⓔ $60x$

Explanation

A quick inspection of the answer choices shows that it is not necessary to solve the equation $1 + x + x^2 + x^3 = 60$ for x to answer this question. You are being asked to express the average of the four quantities x, x^2, x^3, and x^4 in terms of x. To express this average in terms of x, you need to add the 4 quantities and divide the result by 4; that is, $\frac{x + x^2 + x^3 + x^4}{4}$.

The only information given in the question is that the sum of the 4 quantities, $1 + x + x^2 + x^3$, is 60, so you need to think of a way to use this information to simplify the expression $\frac{x + x^2 + x^3 + x^4}{4}$.

Note that the numerator of the fraction is a sum of 4 quantities, each of which has an x term raised to a power. Thus, the expression in the numerator can be factored as $x + x^2 + x^3 + x^4 = x(1 + x + x^2 + x^3)$. By using the information in the question, you can make the following simplification.

$$\frac{x + x^2 + x^3 + x^4}{4} = \frac{x(1 + x + x^2 + x^3)}{4} = \frac{x(60)}{4} = 15x$$

Therefore, the correct answer is **Choice B**.

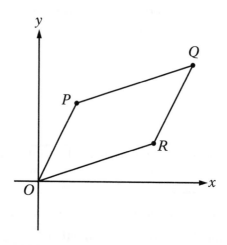

10. Parallelogram $OPQR$ lies in the xy-plane, as shown in the figure above. The coordinates of point P are $(2, 4)$ and the coordinates of point Q are $(8, 6)$. What are the coordinates of point R ?

Ⓐ $(3, 2)$

Ⓑ $(3, 3)$

Ⓒ $(4, 4)$

Ⓓ $(5, 2)$

Ⓔ $(6, 2)$

Explanation

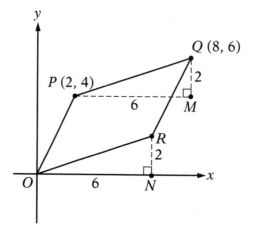

Since $OPQR$ is a parallelogram, line segments PQ and OR have the same length and the same slope. Therefore, in the figure above, PQM and ORN are congruent right triangles. From the coordinates of P and Q, the lengths of the legs of triangle PQM are $PM = 8 - 2 = 6$ and $QM = 6 - 4 = 2$. Thus, the lengths of the legs ON and RN of triangle ORN are also 6 and 2, respectively. So the coordinates of point R are $(6, 2)$. The correct answer is **Choice E**.

11. The relationship between the area A of a circle and its circumference C is given by the formula $A = kC^2$, where k is a constant. What is the value of k ?

    (A) $\dfrac{1}{4\pi}$

    (B) $\dfrac{1}{2\pi}$

    (C) $\dfrac{1}{4}$

    (D) 2π

    (E) $4\pi^2$

Explanation

One way to approach this problem is to realize that the value of the constant k is the same for all circles. Therefore, you can pick a specific circle and substitute the circumference and the area of that particular circle into the formula and calculate the value of k.

Say, for example, that you pick a circle with radius 1. The area of the circle is π and the circumference of the circle is 2π. Inserting these values into the formula gives $\pi = k(2\pi)^2$. Solving this equation for k gives $k = \dfrac{1}{4\pi}$, and the correct answer is **Choice A**.

Another way to approach the problem is to express A and C in terms of a common variable and then solve the resulting equation for k. Recall the commonly used formulas for the area and the circumference of a circle: $A = \pi r^2$ and $C = 2\pi r$. Note that in these formulas, both A and C are expressed in terms of the radius r. So, in the formula $A = kC^2$, you can substitute expressions for A and C in terms of r.

Substituting πr^2 for A and $2\pi r$ for C gives $\pi r^2 = k(2\pi r)^2$.

Now you can determine the value of k by solving the equation for k as follows.

$$\pi r^2 = k(2\pi r)^2$$
$$\pi r^2 = k(4\pi^2 r^2)$$
$$\pi = k(4\pi^2)$$
$$\frac{1}{4\pi} = k$$

The correct answer is **Choice A**.

12. The sequence of numbers $a_1, a_2, a_3, \ldots, a_n, \ldots$ is defined by $a_n = \dfrac{1}{n} - \dfrac{1}{n+2}$ for each integer $n \geq 1$. What is the sum of the first 20 terms of this sequence?

(A) $\left(1 + \dfrac{1}{2}\right) - \dfrac{1}{20}$

(B) $\left(1 + \dfrac{1}{2}\right) - \left(\dfrac{1}{21} + \dfrac{1}{22}\right)$

(C) $1 - \left(\dfrac{1}{20} + \dfrac{1}{22}\right)$

(D) $1 - \dfrac{1}{22}$

(E) $\dfrac{1}{20} - \dfrac{1}{22}$

Explanation

This question asks for the sum of the first 20 terms of the sequence. Obviously, it would be very time-consuming to write out the first 20 terms of the sequence and add them together, so it is reasonable to try to find a more efficient way to calculate the sum. Questions involving sequences can often be answered by looking for a pattern. Scanning the answer choices and noting that they contain fractions with denominators 2, 20, 21, and 22, and nothing in between, seems to confirm that looking for a pattern is a good approach to try.

To look for a pattern, begin by adding the first two terms of the sequence.

$$\left(\dfrac{1}{1} - \dfrac{1}{3}\right) + \left(\dfrac{1}{2} - \dfrac{1}{4}\right) = \left(\dfrac{1}{1} + \dfrac{1}{2}\right) - \left(\dfrac{1}{3} + \dfrac{1}{4}\right)$$

Now, if you add the first three terms of the sequence, you get

$$\left(\dfrac{1}{1} - \dfrac{1}{3}\right) + \left(\dfrac{1}{2} - \dfrac{1}{4}\right) + \left(\dfrac{1}{3} - \dfrac{1}{5}\right)$$

Note that you can simplify the sum by canceling the fraction $\dfrac{1}{3}$; that is, the sum of positive $\dfrac{1}{3}$ and negative $\dfrac{1}{3}$ is 0.

$$\left(\dfrac{1}{1} - \dfrac{\cancel{1}}{\cancel{3}}\right) + \left(\dfrac{1}{2} - \dfrac{1}{4}\right) + \left(\dfrac{\cancel{1}}{\cancel{3}} - \dfrac{1}{5}\right) = \left(\dfrac{1}{1} + \dfrac{1}{2}\right) - \left(\dfrac{1}{4} + \dfrac{1}{5}\right)$$

If you add the first four terms, you get

$$\left(\dfrac{1}{1} - \dfrac{1}{3}\right) + \left(\dfrac{1}{2} - \dfrac{1}{4}\right) + \left(\dfrac{1}{3} - \dfrac{1}{5}\right) + \left(\dfrac{1}{4} - \dfrac{1}{6}\right)$$

Again, you can simplify the sum by canceling. This time, you can cancel the fractions $\dfrac{1}{3}$ and $\dfrac{1}{4}$.

$$\left(\dfrac{1}{1} - \dfrac{\cancel{1}}{\cancel{3}}\right) + \left(\dfrac{1}{2} - \dfrac{\cancel{1}}{\cancel{4}}\right) + \left(\dfrac{\cancel{1}}{\cancel{3}} - \dfrac{1}{5}\right) + \left(\dfrac{\cancel{1}}{\cancel{4}} - \dfrac{1}{6}\right) = \left(\dfrac{1}{1} + \dfrac{1}{2}\right) - \left(\dfrac{1}{5} + \dfrac{1}{6}\right)$$

If you write out the next two sums and simplify them, you will see that they are

$$\left(\frac{1}{1}+\frac{1}{2}\right)-\left(\frac{1}{6}+\frac{1}{7}\right) \text{ and } \left(\frac{1}{1}+\frac{1}{2}\right)-\left(\frac{1}{7}+\frac{1}{8}\right)$$

Working with the sums makes it clear that this pattern continues to hold as you add more and more terms of the sequence together and that a formula for the sum of the first k terms of the sequence is

$$\left(\frac{1}{1}+\frac{1}{2}\right)-\left(\frac{1}{k+1}+\frac{1}{k+2}\right)$$

Therefore, the sum of the first 20 terms of the sequence is equal to

$$\left(\frac{1}{1}+\frac{1}{2}\right)-\left(\frac{1}{20+1}+\frac{1}{20+2}\right)=\left(1+\frac{1}{2}\right)-\left(\frac{1}{21}+\frac{1}{22}\right)$$

The correct answer is **Choice B**.

Numeric Entry

For Question 13, use the directions for Numeric Entry questions.

Y	Frequency
$\frac{1}{2}$	2
$\frac{3}{4}$	7
$\frac{5}{4}$	8
$\frac{3}{2}$	8
$\frac{7}{4}$	9

13. The table above shows the frequency distribution of the values of a variable Y. What is the mean of the distribution?

Give your answer to the <u>nearest 0.01</u>.

Explanation

The mean of distribution of the variable Y is the sum of all the values of Y divided by the number of values of Y. However, before you begin the summing process, you need to understand how the information is presented in the question. Information about the variable is given in a table, where any repetitions of values have been summarized in the column labeled "Frequency." Reading from the table, you can see that the value $\frac{1}{2}$ occurs twice, the value $\frac{3}{4}$ occurs seven times, and so on. To sum all the values of Y, you could add the value $\frac{1}{2}$ twice, add the value $\frac{3}{4}$ seven times, and continue the addition process in this manner. It is easier, however, to multiply the values by their corresponding frequencies and then sum the individual products, as shown below.

$$(2)\left(\frac{1}{2}\right) + (7)\left(\frac{3}{4}\right) + (8)\left(\frac{5}{4}\right) + (8)\left(\frac{3}{2}\right) + (9)\left(\frac{7}{4}\right) = \frac{4}{4} + \frac{21}{4} + \frac{40}{4} + \frac{48}{4} + \frac{63}{4}$$
$$= \frac{176}{4}$$
$$= 44$$

To find the average, you need to divide the sum, 44, by the number of values of Y. The number of values can be found by looking at the column of frequencies in the table. The sum of the numbers in this column, $2 + 7 + 8 + 8 + 9$, or 34, is the number of values of Y. Thus, the mean of the distribution is $\frac{44}{34}$, which, as a decimal, equals 1.2941…. Rounded to the nearest 0.01, the correct answer is **1.29**.

Multiple-choice Questions—Select One or More Answer Choices

> **For Questions 14 and 15, select all the answer choices that apply.**

14. Let S be the set of all positive integers n such that n^2 is a multiple of both 24 and 108. Which of the following integers are divisors of every integer n in S?

    Indicate all such integers.

    A 12
    B 24
    C 36
    D 72

Explanation

To determine which of the integers in the answer choices is a divisor of every positive integer n in S, you must first understand the integers that are in S. Note that in this question you are given information about n^2, not about n itself. Therefore, you must use the information about n^2 to derive information about n.

The fact that n^2 is a multiple of both 24 and 108 implies that n^2 is a multiple of the least common multiple of 24 and 108. To determine the least common multiple of 24 and 108, factor 24 and 108 into prime factors as $(2^3)(3)$ and $(2^2)(3^3)$, respectively. Because these are prime factorizations, you can conclude that the least common multiple of 24 and 108 is $(2^3)(3^3)$.

Knowing that n^2 must be a multiple of $(2^3)(3^3)$ does not mean that every multiple of $(2^3)(3^3)$ is a possible value of n^2, because n^2 must be the square of an integer. The prime factorization of a square number must contain only even exponents. Thus, the least multiple of $(2^3)(3^3)$ that is a square is $(2^4)(3^4)$. This is the least possible value of n^2, and so the least possible value of n is $(2^2)(3^2)$, or 36. Furthermore, since every value of n^2 is a multiple of $(2^4)(3^4)$, the values of n are the positive multiples of 36; that is, $S = \{36, 72, 108, 144, 180, \ldots\}$.

The question asks for integers that are divisors of every integer n in S, that is, divisors of every positive multiple of 36. Since Choice A, 12, is a divisor of 36, it is also a divisor of every multiple of 36. The same is true for Choice C, 36. Choices B and D, 24 and 72, are not divisors of 36, so they are not divisors of every integer in S. The correct answer consists of **Choices A and C**.

15. The range of the heights of the female students in a certain class is 13.2 inches, and the range of the heights of the male students in the class is 15.4 inches.

Which of the following statements <u>individually</u> provide(s) sufficient additional information to determine the range of the heights of all the students in the class?

Indicate <u>all</u> such statements.

A The tallest male student in the class is 5.8 inches taller than the tallest female student in the class.

B The median height of the male students in the class is 1.1 inches greater than the median height of the female students in the class.

C The average (arithmetic mean) height of the male students in the class is 4.6 inches greater than the average height of the female students in the class.

Explanation

Choice A tells you that the tallest male student is 5.8 inches taller than the tallest female student. You can combine this information with the given information about the male and female height ranges to place four students—the shortest male, the shortest female, the tallest male, and the tallest female—in relative order according to height, as shown in the figure below.

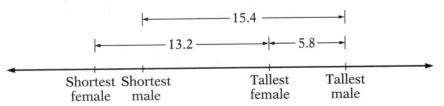

You can see from the figure that the tallest student must be a male and the shortest student must be a female. You can also see the difference in height between those two students, which is the range of the heights of the entire class. Therefore, Choice A provides sufficient additional information to determine the range.

Choice B provides information about one of the centers of the data—the median; it does not say anything about how spread out the data are around that center. You are given that the median height of the males is 1.1 inches greater than that of the females. First note that it is possible for two different sets of data to have the same median but have very different ranges. Choice B gives the difference between the medians of the male heights and the female heights, without giving the actual medians. However, even if you knew the medians, the fact that the ranges can vary widely indicates that the range of the heights of the entire class can also vary widely.

It is possible to construct examples of heights of students that satisfy all of the information in the question and in Choice B but have different ranges for the heights of the entire class. Here are two such examples, each of which has only three females and three males. Although the examples are small, they illustrate the fact that the range of the heights of the entire class can vary. In both examples, the range of female heights is 13.2, the range of male heights is 15.4, and the difference between the median heights is 1.1 inches.

Example 1
Female heights: 50.0   56.6   63.2   which have a median of 56.6
Male heights: 50.0   57.7   65.4   which have a median of 57.7
Range of heights of entire class: 15.4

Example 2
Female heights: 50.0   56.6   63.2   which have a median of 56.6
Male heights: 51.0   57.7   66.4   which have a median of 57.7
Range of heights of entire class: 16.4

Therefore, Choice B does not provide sufficient additional information to determine the range of the heights of the entire class.

Choice C provides information about another center of the data—the average. You are given that the average height of the males is 4.6 inches greater than that of the females. However, like Choice B, the statement gives no information about how spread out the data are around that center. Again, it is possible for two different sets of data to have the same average but have very different ranges. Examples similar to the two examples above can be constructed that satisfy all of the information in the question and in Choice C but have different ranges for the heights of the entire class. Therefore, Choice C does not provide sufficient additional information to determine the range of the heights of the entire class.

The correct answer consists of **Choice A**.

SET 4. Data Interpretation Sets

For Questions 1 to 7, select a single answer choice unless otherwise directed.

Questions 1 to 3 are based on the following data.

PERCENT OF FEMALE FACULTY AND PERCENT OF MALE FACULTY
AT UNIVERSITY *X*, BY FIELD

Total female faculty: 200
Total male faculty: 250

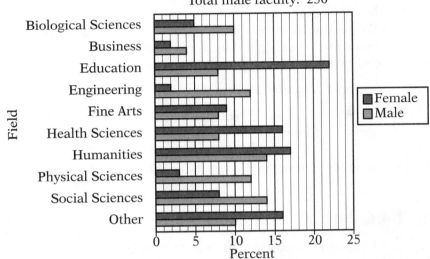

Medium Question

1. There are 275 students in the field of engineering at University *X*. Approximately what is the ratio of the number of students in engineering to the number of faculty in engineering?

   (A) 8 to 1
   (B) 10 to 1
   (C) 12 to 1
   (D) 14 to 1
   (E) 20 to 1

Explanation

According to the graph, 2 percent of the female faculty and 12 percent of the male faculty are in the engineering field. To determine the total number of faculty members in engineering, you need to add 2 percent of 200, which is 4, to 12 percent of 250, which is 30, to get 34. Thus, the ratio of the numbers of students to faculty in engineering is 275 to 34, which is approximately equal to 280 to 35, or 8 to 1. The correct answer is **Choice A**.

Medium Question

2. Approximately what percent of the faculty in humanities are male?

    Ⓐ 35%

    Ⓑ 38%

    Ⓒ 41%

    Ⓓ 45%

    Ⓔ 51%

Explanation

You need to determine the numbers of female and male faculty in the humanities field. According to the graph, 17 percent of the 200 females, or 34, and 14 percent of the 250 males, or 35, are in humanities. Thus, the fraction of humanities faculty who are male is $\frac{35}{34 + 35} = \frac{35}{69}$, or approximately 0.507. As a percent, the answer choice that is closest to 0.507 is 51 percent. The correct answer is **Choice E**.

For Question 3, use the directions for Numeric Entry questions.

Hard Question

3. For the biological sciences and health sciences faculty combined, $\frac{1}{3}$ of the female and $\frac{2}{9}$ of the male faculty members are tenured professors. What fraction of all the faculty members in those two fields combined are tenured professors?

Explanation

You need to determine the number of female faculty and the number of male faculty in the combined group. According to the graph, 5 percent of the female faculty, or 10, and 10 percent of the male faculty, or 25, are in the biological sciences. Similarly, 16 percent of the female faculty, or 32, and 8 percent of the male faculty, or 20, are in the health sciences. When you combine the groups, you get a total of 42 females (10 + 32) and 45 males (25 + 20), which is a total of 87 faculty. The tenured faculty are $\frac{1}{3}$ of the 42 females, or 14 females, and $\frac{2}{9}$ of the 45 males, or 10 males. Thus, there are 24 tenured faculty, and the fraction that are tenured professors is $\frac{24}{87}$. The correct answer is $\frac{24}{87}$ (or any equivalent fraction).

VALUE OF IMPORTS TO AND EXPORTS FROM COUNTRY *T*, 2000–2009
(in United States dollars)

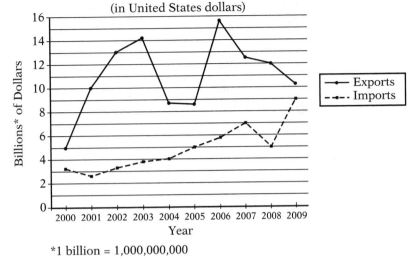

*1 billion = 1,000,000,000

For Question 4, select all the answer choices that apply.

Easy Question

4. For which of the eight years from 2001 to 2008 did exports exceed imports by more than $5 billion?

    Indicate all such years.

    [A] 2001
    [B] 2002
    [C] 2003
    [D] 2004
    [E] 2005
    [F] 2006
    [G] 2007
    [H] 2008

Explanation

Note that for all years shown, the dollar value of exports is greater than the dollar value of imports. For each year, the difference between the dollar value of exports and the dollar value of imports can be read directly from the graph. The difference was more than $5 billion for each of the years 2001, 2002, 2003, 2006, 2007, and 2008. The correct answer consists of **Choices A, B, C, F, G, and H**.

Medium Question

5. Which of the following is closest to the average (arithmetic mean) of the 9 changes in the value of imports between consecutive years from 2000 to 2009 ?

    (A) $260 million

    (B) $320 million

    (C) $400 million

    (D) $480 million

    (E) $640 million

Explanation

The average of the 9 changes in the value of imports between consecutive years can be represented as follows, where the function v(year) represents the value of imports for the indicated year.

$$\frac{(v(2001) - v(2000)) + (v(2002) - v(2001)) + (v(2003) - v(2002)) + \cdots + (v(2009) - v(2008))}{9}$$

Note that in the numerator of the fraction, each term, with the exception of $v(2000)$ and $v(2009)$, appears first as positive and then again as negative. The positive and negative pairs sum to 0, and the fraction simplifies to $\frac{v(2009) - v(2000)}{9}$.

Reading the values from the graph, you can approximate the value of the simplified fraction as $\frac{9.0 - 3.2}{9} = \frac{5.8}{9} \approx 0.644$ billion dollars. The answer choice that is closest to $0.644 billion is $640 million. The correct answer is **Choice E**.

Medium Question

6. In 2008 the value of exports was approximately what percent greater than the value of imports?

    (A) 40%

    (B) 60%

    (C) 70%

    (D) 120%

    (E) 140%

Explanation

The difference between the value of exports and the value of imports expressed as a percent of the value of imports is

$$\left(\frac{(\text{value of exports}) - (\text{value of imports})}{\text{value of imports}}\right)(100\%)$$

In 2008 the value of imports was approximately $5 billion and the value of exports was approximately $12 billion, so the value of the fraction is approximately $\frac{12 - 5}{5}$, or $\frac{7}{5}$.

Since the fraction is greater than 1, expressing it as a percent will give a percent greater than 100. The fraction is equal to 1.4, or 140 percent. The correct answer is **Choice E**.

Hard Question

7. If it were discovered that the value of imports shown for 2007 was incorrect and should have been $5 billion instead, then the average (arithmetic mean) value of imports per year for the 10 years shown would have been approximately how much less?

    Ⓐ $200 million

    Ⓑ $50 million

    Ⓒ $20 million

    Ⓓ $7 million

    Ⓔ $5 million

Explanation

To answer this question, you do not need to compute either of the two 10-year averages referred to in the question; you just need to calculate the difference between the two averages.

The average value of imports for the 10 years shown in the graph is found by adding the 10 values and then dividing the sum by 10. The value of imports in 2007 is $7 billion. If that amount were $5 billion instead, then the sum of the values would be $2 billion less. If the sum were $2 billion less than what it was, then the average would decrease by 2 billion divided by 10, or $\frac{2,000,000,000}{10} = 200,000,000$. The average would therefore be $200 million less, and the correct answer is **Choice A**.

A more algebraic approach to the problem is to let S represent the sum, in billions, of the 10 values of imports in the graph. The average of the 10 values is $\frac{S}{10}$. Note that $S - 2$ represents the sum, in billions, of the 10 values adjusted for the $2 billion correction for 2007. The average of the adjusted sum is $\frac{S - 2}{10}$. The difference between the two averages is

$$\frac{S}{10} - \frac{S - 2}{10} = \frac{S - (S - 2)}{10}$$
$$= \frac{S - S + 2}{10}$$
$$= \frac{2}{10}$$

The difference is 0.2 billion dollars, or $200 million. The correct answer is **Choice A**.

7 GRE® Math Review

This Math Review will familiarize you with the mathematical skills and concepts that are important to understand in order to solve problems and reason quantitatively on the Quantitative Reasoning measure of the GRE revised General Test. The following material includes many definitions, properties, and examples, as well as a set of exercises (with answers) at the end of each review section. Note, however, that this review is not intended to be all-inclusive—there may be some concepts on the test that are not explicitly presented in this review. If any topics in this review seem especially unfamiliar or are covered too briefly, we encourage you to consult appropriate mathematics texts for a more detailed treatment.

The Math Review covers the following topics:

1. ARITHMETIC

The review of arithmetic begins with integers, fractions, and decimals and progresses to the set of real numbers. The basic arithmetic operations of addition, subtraction, multiplication, and division are discussed, along with exponents and roots. The section ends with the concepts of ratio and percent.

1.1 Integers

The **integers** are the numbers 1, 2, 3, and so on, together with their negatives, -1, -2, $-3, \ldots$, and 0. Thus, the set of integers is $\{\ldots, -3, -2, -1, 0, 1, 2, 3, \ldots\}$.

The positive integers are greater than 0, the negative integers are less than 0, and 0 is neither positive nor negative. When integers are added, subtracted, or multiplied, the result is always an integer; division of integers is addressed below. The many elementary number facts for these operations, such as $7 + 8 = 15, 78 - 87 = -9$, $7 - (-18) = 25$, and $(7)(8) = 56$, should be familiar to you; they are not reviewed here. Here are some general facts regarding multiplication of integers.

- The product of two positive integers is a positive integer.
- The product of two negative integers is a positive integer.
- The product of a positive integer and a negative integer is a negative integer.

When integers are multiplied, each of the multiplied integers is called a **factor** or **divisor** of the resulting product. For example, $(2)(3)(10) = 60$, so 2, 3, and 10 are factors of 60. The integers 4, 15, 5, and 12 are also factors of 60, since $(4)(15) = 60$ and $(5)(12) = 60$. The positive factors of 60 are 1, 2, 3, 4, 5, 6, 10, 12, 15, 20, 30, and 60. The negatives of these integers are also factors of 60, since, for example, $(-2)(-30) = 60$. There are no other factors of 60. We say that 60 is a **multiple** of each of its factors and that 60 is **divisible** by each of its divisors. Here are some more examples of factors and multiples.

- The positive factors of 100 are 1, 2, 4, 5, 10, 20, 25, 50, and 100.
- 25 is a multiple of only six integers: 1, 5, 25, and their negatives.
- The list of positive multiples of 25 has no end: 0, 25, 50, 75, 100, 125, 150, etc.; likewise, every nonzero integer has infinitely many multiples.
- 1 is a factor of every integer; 1 is not a multiple of any integer except 1 and -1.
- 0 is a multiple of every integer; 0 is not a factor of any integer except 0.

The **least common multiple** of two nonzero integers a and b is the least positive integer that is a multiple of both a and b. For example, the least common multiple of 30 and 75 is 150. This is because the positive multiples of 30 are 30, 60, 90, 120, 150, 180, 210, 240, 270, 300, etc., and the positive multiples of 75 are 75, 150, 225, 300, 375, 450, etc. Thus, the *common* positive multiples of 30 and 75 are 150, 300, 450, etc., and the least of these is 150.

The **greatest common divisor** (or **greatest common factor**) of two nonzero integers a and b is the greatest positive integer that is a divisor of both a and b. For example, the greatest common divisor of 30 and 75 is 15. This is because the positive divisors of 30 are 1, 2, 3, 5, 6, 10, 15, and 30, and the positive divisors of 75 are 1, 3, 5, 15, 25, and 75. Thus, the *common* positive divisors of 30 and 75 are 1, 3, 5, and 15, and the greatest of these is 15.

When an integer a is divided by an integer b, where b is a divisor of a, the result is always a divisor of a. For example, when 60 is divided by 6 (one of its divisors), the result is 10, which is another divisor of 60. If b is *not* a divisor of a, then the result can be viewed in three different ways. The result can be viewed as a fraction or as a decimal, both of which are discussed later, or the result can be viewed as a **quotient** with a **remainder**, where both are integers. Each view is useful, depending on the context. Fractions and decimals are useful when the result must be viewed as a single number, while **quotients** with **remainders** are useful for describing the result in terms of integers only.

Regarding quotients with remainders, consider two positive integers a and b for which b is *not* a divisor of a; for example, the integers 19 and 7. When 19 is divided by 7, the result is greater than 2, since $(2)(7) < 19$, but less than 3, since $19 < (3)(7)$. Because 19 is 5 more than $(2)(7)$, we say that the result of 19 divided by 7 is the quotient 2 with remainder 5, or simply "2 remainder 5." In general, when a positive integer a is divided by a positive integer b, you first find the greatest multiple of b that is less than or equal to a. That multiple of b can be expressed as the product qb, where q is the quotient. Then the remainder is equal to a minus that multiple of b, or $r = a - qb$, where r is the remainder. The remainder is always greater than or equal to 0 and less than b.

Here are examples that illustrate a few different cases of division resulting in a quotient and remainder.

- 100 divided by 45 is 2 remainder 10, since the greatest multiple of 45 that's less than or equal to 100 is $(2)(45)$, or 90, which is 10 less than 100.
- 24 divided by 4 is 6 remainder 0, since the greatest multiple of 4 that's less than or equal to 24 is 24 itself, which is 0 less than 24. In general, the remainder is 0 if and only if a is divisible by b.
- 6 divided by 24 is 0 remainder 6, since the greatest multiple of 24 that's less than or equal to 6 is $(0)(24)$, or 0, which is 6 less than 6.

Here are some other examples.

- 100 divided by 3 is 33 remainder 1, since $100 = (33)(3) + 1$.
- 100 divided by 25 is 4 remainder 0, since $100 = (4)(25) + 0$.
- 80 divided by 100 is 0 remainder 80, since $80 = (0)(100) + 80$.
- When you divide 100 by 2, the remainder is 0.
- When you divide 99 by 2, the remainder is 1.

If an integer is divisible by 2, it is called an **even integer**; otherwise it is an **odd integer**. Note that when a positive odd integer is divided by 2, the remainder is always 1. The set of even integers is $\{\ldots, -6, -4, -2, 0, 2, 4, 6, \ldots\}$, and the set of odd integers is $\{\ldots, -5, -3, -1, 1, 3, 5, \ldots\}$. There are several useful facts regarding the sum and product of even and odd integers.

- The sum of two even integers is an even integer.
- The sum of two odd integers is an even integer.
- The sum of an even integer and an odd integer is an odd integer.
- The product of two even integers is an even integer.
- The product of two odd integers is an odd integer.
- The product of an even integer and an odd integer is an even integer.

A **prime number** is an integer greater than 1 that has only two positive divisors: 1 and itself. The first ten prime numbers are 2, 3, 5, 7, 11, 13, 17, 19, 23, and 29. The integer 14 is not a prime number, since it has four positive divisors: 1, 2, 7, and 14. The integer 1 is not a prime number, and the integer 2 is the only prime number that is even.

Every integer greater than 1 either is a prime number or can be uniquely expressed as a product of factors that are prime numbers, or **prime divisors**. Such an expression is called a **prime factorization**. Here are several examples of prime factorizations.

$$12 = (2)(2)(3) = (2^2)(3)$$
$$14 = (2)(7)$$
$$81 = (3)(3)(3)(3) = 3^4$$
$$338 = (2)(13)(13) = (2)(13^2)$$
$$800 = (2)(2)(2)(2)(2)(5)(5) = (2^5)(5^2)$$
$$1{,}155 = (3)(5)(7)(11)$$

An integer greater than 1 that is not a prime number is called a **composite number**. The first ten composite numbers are 4, 6, 8, 9, 10, 12, 14, 15, 16, and 18.

1.2 Fractions

A **fraction** is a number $\frac{a}{b}$, of the form where a and b are integers and $b \neq 0$. The integer a is called the **numerator** of the fraction, and b is called the **denominator**. For example, $\frac{-7}{5}$ is a fraction in which -7 is the numerator and 5 is the denominator. Such numbers are also called **rational numbers**.

If both the numerator a and denominator b are multiplied by the same nonzero integer, the resulting fraction will be equivalent to $\frac{a}{b}$. For example,

$$\frac{-7}{5} = \frac{(-7)(4)}{(5)(4)} = \frac{-28}{20}$$
$$\frac{-7}{5} = \frac{(-7)(-1)}{(5)(-1)} = \frac{7}{-5}$$

A fraction with a negative sign in either the numerator or denominator can be written with the negative sign in front of the fraction; for example, $\frac{-7}{5} = \frac{7}{-5} = -\frac{7}{5}$.

If both the numerator and denominator have a common factor, then the numerator and denominator can be factored and reduced to an equivalent fraction. For example,

$$\frac{40}{72} = \frac{(8)(5)}{(8)(9)} = \frac{5}{9}$$

To add two fractions with the same denominator, you add the numerators and keep the same denominator. For example,

$$-\frac{8}{11} + \frac{5}{11} = \frac{-8 + 5}{11} = \frac{-3}{11} = -\frac{3}{11}$$

To add two fractions with different denominators, first find a **common denominator**, which is a common multiple of the two denominators. Then convert both fractions to equivalent fractions with the same denominator. Finally, add the numerators and keep the common denominator. For example, to add the fractions $\frac{1}{3}$ and $-\frac{2}{5}$, use the common denominator 15:

$$\frac{1}{3} + \frac{-2}{5} = \left(\frac{1}{3}\right)\left(\frac{5}{5}\right) + \left(\frac{-2}{5}\right)\left(\frac{3}{3}\right) = \frac{5}{15} + \frac{-6}{15} = \frac{5 + (-6)}{15} = -\frac{1}{15}$$

The same method applies to subtraction of fractions.

To multiply two fractions, multiply the two numerators and multiply the two denominators. For example,

$$\left(\frac{10}{7}\right)\left(\frac{-1}{3}\right) = \frac{(10)(-1)}{(7)(3)} = \frac{-10}{21} = -\frac{10}{21}$$

$$\left(\frac{8}{3}\right)\left(\frac{7}{3}\right) = \frac{56}{9}$$

To divide one fraction by another, first **invert** the second fraction—that is, find its **reciprocal**—then multiply the first fraction by the inverted fraction. For example,

$$\frac{17}{8} \div \frac{3}{4} = \left(\frac{17}{8}\right)\left(\frac{4}{3}\right) = \left(\frac{4}{8}\right)\left(\frac{17}{3}\right) = \left(\frac{1}{2}\right)\left(\frac{17}{3}\right) = \frac{17}{6}$$

$$\frac{\dfrac{3}{10}}{\dfrac{7}{13}} = \left(\frac{3}{10}\right)\left(\frac{13}{7}\right) = \frac{39}{70}$$

An expression such as $4\frac{3}{8}$ is called a **mixed number**. It consists of an integer part and a fraction part; the mixed number $4\frac{3}{8}$ means $4 + \frac{3}{8}$. To convert a mixed number to an ordinary fraction, convert the integer part to an equivalent fraction and add it to the fraction part. For example,

$$4\frac{3}{8} = 4 + \frac{3}{8} = \left(\frac{4}{1}\right)\left(\frac{8}{8}\right) + \frac{3}{8} = \frac{32}{8} + \frac{3}{8} = \frac{35}{8}$$

Note that numbers of the form $\frac{a}{b}$, where either a or b is not an integer and $b \neq 0$, are fractional expressions that can be manipulated just like fractions. For example, the numbers $\frac{\pi}{2}$ and $\frac{\pi}{3}$ can be added together as follows.

$$\frac{\pi}{2} + \frac{\pi}{3} = \left(\frac{\pi}{2}\right)\left(\frac{3}{3}\right) + \left(\frac{\pi}{3}\right)\left(\frac{2}{2}\right) = \frac{3\pi}{6} + \frac{2\pi}{6} = \frac{5\pi}{6}$$

And the number $\dfrac{\dfrac{1}{\sqrt{2}}}{\dfrac{3}{\sqrt{5}}}$ can be simplified as follows.

$$\frac{\dfrac{1}{\sqrt{2}}}{\dfrac{3}{\sqrt{5}}} = \left(\frac{1}{\sqrt{2}}\right)\left(\frac{\sqrt{5}}{3}\right) = \frac{\sqrt{5}}{3\sqrt{2}}$$

1.3 Exponents and Roots

Exponents are used to denote the repeated multiplication of a number by itself; for example, $3^4 = (3)(3)(3)(3) = 81$ and $5^3 = (5)(5)(5) = 125$. In the expression 3^4, 3 is called the **base**, 4 is called the **exponent**, and we read the expression as "3 to the fourth power." So 5 to the third power is 125. When the exponent is 2, we call the process **squaring**. Thus, 6 squared is 36, $6^2 = (6)(6) = 36$, and 7 squared is 49, $7^2 = (7)(7) = 49$.

When negative numbers are raised to powers, the result may be positive or negative. For example, $(-3)^2 = (-3)(-3) = 9$, while $(-3)^5 = (-3)(-3)(-3)(-3)(-3) = -243$. A negative number raised to an even power is always positive, and a negative number raised to an odd power is always negative. Note that without the parentheses, the expression -3^2 means "the negative of '3 squared'"; that is, the exponent is applied before the negative sign. So $(-3)^2 = 9$, but $-3^2 = -9$.

Exponents can also be negative or zero; such exponents are defined as follows.

- For all nonzero numbers a, $a^0 = 1$. The expression 0^0 is undefined.

- For all nonzero numbers a, $a^{-1} = \dfrac{1}{a}$, $a^{-2} = \dfrac{1}{a^2}$, $a^{-3} = \dfrac{1}{a^3}$, etc. Note that

$$(a)(a^{-1}) = (a)\left(\frac{1}{a}\right) = 1.$$

A **square root** of a nonnegative number n is a number r such that $r^2 = n$. For example, 4 is a square root of 16 because $4^2 = 16$. Another square root of 16 is -4, since $(-4)^2 = 16$. All positive numbers have two square roots, one positive and one negative. The only square root of 0 is 0. The symbol $\sqrt{n}$ is used to denote the *nonnegative* square root of the nonnegative number n. Therefore, $\sqrt{100} = 10$, $-\sqrt{100} = -10$, and $\sqrt{0} = 0$. Square roots of negative numbers are not defined in the real number system.

Here are some important rules regarding operations with square roots, where $a > 0$ and $b > 0$.

Rule	Examples	
$\left(\sqrt{a}\right)^2 = a$	$\left(\sqrt{3}\right)^2 = 3$	$\left(\sqrt{\pi}\right)^2 = \pi$
$\sqrt{a^2} = a$	$\sqrt{4} = 2$	$\sqrt{\pi^2} = \pi$
$\sqrt{a}\sqrt{b} = \sqrt{ab}$	$\sqrt{3}\sqrt{10} = \sqrt{30}$	$\sqrt{24} = \sqrt{4}\sqrt{6} = 2\sqrt{6}$
$\dfrac{\sqrt{a}}{\sqrt{b}} = \sqrt{\dfrac{a}{b}}$	$\dfrac{\sqrt{5}}{\sqrt{15}} = \sqrt{\dfrac{5}{15}} = \sqrt{\dfrac{1}{3}}$	$\dfrac{\sqrt{18}}{\sqrt{2}} = \sqrt{\dfrac{18}{2}} = \sqrt{9} = 3$

A square root is a root of order 2. Higher-order roots of a positive number n are defined similarly. For orders 3 and 4, the **cube root** $\sqrt[3]{n}$ and **fourth root** $\sqrt[4]{n}$ represent numbers such that when they are raised to the powers 3 and 4, respectively, the result is n. These roots obey rules similar to those above (but with the exponent 2 replaced by 3 or 4 in the first two rules). There are some notable differences between odd-order roots and even-order roots (in the real number system):

- For odd-order roots, there is *exactly one* root for *every* number n, even when n is negative.
- For even-order roots, there are *exactly two* roots for every *positive* number n and *no* roots for any *negative* number n.

For example, 8 has exactly one cube root, $\sqrt[3]{8} = 2$, but 8 has two fourth roots: $\sqrt[4]{8}$ and $-\sqrt[4]{8}$; and -8 has exactly one cube root, $\sqrt[3]{-8} = -2$, but -8 has no fourth root, since it is negative.

1.4 Decimals

The decimal number system is based on representing numbers using powers of 10. The place value of each digit corresponds to a power of 10. For example, the digits of the number 7,532.418 have the following place values.

$$
\begin{array}{ccccccccc}
\text{Thousands} & & \text{Hundreds} & \text{Tens} & \text{Ones or Units} & & \text{Tenths} & \text{Hundredths} & \text{Thousandths} \\
7 & , & 5 & 3 & 2 & . & 4 & 1 & 8
\end{array}
$$

That is,

$$7{,}532.418 = 7(1{,}000) + 5(100) + 3(10) + 2(1) + 4\left(\frac{1}{10}\right) + 1\left(\frac{1}{100}\right) + 8\left(\frac{1}{1{,}000}\right)$$
$$= 7(10^3) + 5(10^2) + 3(10^1) + 2(10^0) + 4(10^{-1}) + 1(10^{-2}) + 8(10^{-3})$$

If there are a finite number of digits to the right of the decimal point, converting a decimal to an equivalent fraction with integers in the numerator and denominator is a straightforward process. Since each place value is a power of 10, every decimal can be converted to an integer divided by a power of 10. For example,

$$2.3 = 2 + \frac{3}{10} = \frac{23}{10}$$
$$90.17 = 90 + \frac{17}{100} = \frac{9{,}000 + 17}{100} = \frac{9{,}017}{100}$$
$$0.612 = \frac{612}{1{,}000} = \frac{153}{250}$$

Conversely, every fraction with integers in the numerator and denominator can be converted to an equivalent decimal by dividing the numerator by the denominator using long division (which is not in this review). The decimal that results from the long division will either **terminate**, as in $\frac{1}{4} = 0.25$ and $\frac{52}{25} = 2.08$, or the decimal will **repeat** without end, as in $\frac{1}{9} = 0.111\ldots$, $\frac{1}{22} = 0.0454545\ldots$, and $\frac{25}{12} = 2.08333\ldots$. One way to indicate the repeating part of a decimal that repeats without end is to use a bar over the digits that repeat. Here are some examples of fractions converted to decimals.

$$\frac{3}{8} = 0.375$$
$$\frac{259}{40} = 6 + \frac{19}{40} = 6.475$$
$$-\frac{1}{3} = -0.\overline{3}$$
$$\frac{15}{14} = 1.0\overline{714285}$$

Every fraction with integers in the numerator and denominator is equivalent to a decimal that terminates or repeats. That is, every rational number can be expressed as a terminating or repeating decimal. The converse is also true; that is, every terminating or repeating decimal represents a rational number.

Not all decimals are terminating or repeating; for instance, the decimal that is equivalent to $\sqrt{2}$ is 1.41421356237..., and it can be shown that this decimal does not terminate or repeat. Another example is 0.010110111011110111110..., which has groups of consecutive 1's separated by a 0, where the number of 1's in each successive group increases by one. Since these two decimals do not terminate or repeat, they are not rational numbers. Such numbers are called **irrational numbers**.

1.5 Real Numbers

The set of **real numbers** consists of all rational numbers and all irrational numbers. The real numbers include all integers, fractions, and decimals. The set of real numbers can be represented by a number line called the **real number line**.

Every real number corresponds to a point on the number line, and every point on the number line corresponds to a real number. On the number line, all numbers to the left of 0 are negative and all numbers to the right of 0 are positive. Only the number 0 is neither negative nor positive.

A real number x is **less than** a real number y if x is to the left of y on the number line, which is written as $x < y$. A real number y is **greater than** x if y is to the right of x on the number line, which is written as $y > x$. For example,

$$-\sqrt{5} < -2$$
$$\frac{1}{2} > 0$$
$$1 < \sqrt{2} < 2$$

To say that a real number x is between 2 and 3 on the number line means that $x > 2$ and $x < 3$, which can also be written as the double inequality $2 < x < 3$. The set of all real numbers that are between 2 and 3 is called an **interval**, and the double inequality $2 < x < 3$ is often used to represent that interval. Note that the endpoints of the interval, 2 and 3, are not included in the interval. Sometimes one or both of the endpoints are to be included in an interval. The following inequalities represent four types of intervals, depending on whether the endpoints are included.

$$2 < x < 3$$
$$2 \leq x < 3$$
$$2 < x \leq 3$$
$$2 \leq x \leq 3$$

There are also four types of intervals with only one endpoint, each of which consists of all real numbers to the right or to the left of the endpoint, perhaps including the endpoint. The following inequalities represent these types of intervals.

$$x < 4$$
$$x \leq 4$$
$$x > 4$$
$$x \geq 4$$

The entire real number line is also considered to be an interval.

The distance between a number x and 0 on the number line is called the **absolute value** of x, written as $|x|$. Therefore, $|3| = 3$ and $|-3| = 3$ because each of the numbers 3 and -3 is a distance of 3 from 0. Note that if x is positive, then $|x| = x$; if x is negative, then $|x| = -x$; and lastly, $|0| = 0$. It follows that the absolute value of any nonzero number is positive. Here are some examples.

$$|\sqrt{5}| = \sqrt{5}$$
$$|-23| = -(-23) = 23$$
$$|-10.2| = 10.2$$

There are several general properties of real numbers that are used frequently. If a, b, and c are real numbers, then

- $a + b = b + a$ and $ab = ba$.
  For example, $8 + 2 = 2 + 8 = 10$ and $(-3)(17) = (17)(-3) = -51$.
- $(a + b) + c = a + (b + c)$ and $(ab)c = a(bc)$.
  For example, $(7 + 3) + 8 = 7 + (3 + 8) = 18$ and $\left(7\sqrt{2}\right)\sqrt{2} = 7\left(\sqrt{2}\sqrt{2}\right) = (7)(2) = 14$.
- $a(b + c) = ab + bc$
  For example, $5(3 + 16) = (5)(3) + (5)(16) = 95$.
- $a + 0 = a$, $(a)(0) = 0$, and $(a)(1) = a$.
- If $ab = 0$, then either $a = 0$ or $b = 0$ or both.
  For example, if $-2b = 0$, then $b = 0$.
- Division by 0 is not defined; for example, $5 \div 0$, $\dfrac{-7}{0}$, and $\dfrac{0}{0}$ are undefined.

- If both a and b are positive, then both $a + b$ and ab are positive.
- If both a and b are negative, then $a + b$ is negative and ab is positive.
- If a is positive and b is negative, then ab is negative.
- $|a + b| \leq |a| + |b|$. This is known as the **triangle inequality.**
  For example, if $a = 5$ and $b = -2$, then $|5 + (-2)| = |5-2| = |3| = 3$ and $|5| + |-2| = 5 + 2 = 7$. Therefore, $|5 + (-2)| \leq |5| + |-2|$.
- $|a||b| = |ab|$. For example, $|5||-2| = |(5)(-2)| = |-10| = 10$.
- If $a > 1$, then $a^2 > a$. If $0 < b < 1$, then $b^2 < b$.
  For example, $5^2 = 25 > 5$, but $\left(\dfrac{1}{5}\right)^2 = \dfrac{1}{25} < \dfrac{1}{5}$.

1.6 Ratio

The **ratio** of one quantity to another is a way to express their relative sizes, often in the form of a fraction, where the first quantity is the numerator and the second quantity is the denominator. Thus, if s and t are positive quantities, then the ratio of s to t can be written as the fraction $\dfrac{s}{t}$. The notation "s to t" or "$s:t$" is also used to express this ratio. For example, if there are 2 apples and 3 oranges in a basket, we can say that the ratio of the number of apples to the number of oranges is $\dfrac{2}{3}$ or that it is 2 to 3 or that it is 2:3. Like fractions, ratios can be reduced to lowest terms. For example, if there are 8 apples and 12 oranges in a basket, then the ratio of the numbers of apples to oranges is still 2 to 3. Similarly, the ratio 9 to 12 is equivalent to the ratio 3 to 4.

If three or more positive quantities are being considered, say r, s, and t, then their relative sizes can also be expressed as a ratio with the notation "r to s to t." For example, if there are 5 apples, 30 pears, and 20 oranges in a basket, then the ratio of the numbers of apples to pears to oranges is 5 to 30 to 20. This ratio can be reduced to 1 to 6 to 4 by dividing each number by the greatest common divisor of 5, 30, and 20, which is 5.

A **proportion** is an equation relating two ratios; for example, $\frac{9}{12} = \frac{3}{4}$. To solve a problem involving ratios, you can often write a proportion and solve it by **cross multiplication**.

Example 1.6.1: To find a number x so that the ratio of x to 49 is the same as the ratio of 3 to 21, you can write

$$\frac{x}{49} = \frac{3}{21}$$

Then cross multiply to get $21x = (3)(49)$, and solve for x to get $x = \frac{(3)(49)}{21} = 7$.

1.7 Percent

The term **percent** means *per hundred*, or *hundredths*. Percents are ratios that are often used to represent *parts of a whole*, where the whole is considered as having 100 parts.

- 1 percent means 1 part out of 100 parts, or $\frac{1}{100}$.

- 32 percent means 32 parts out of 100 parts, or $\frac{32}{100}$.

- 50 percent means 50 parts out of 100 parts, or $\frac{1}{2}$.

Note that the *part* is the numerator of the ratio and the *whole* is the denominator. Percents are often written with the % symbol; fractional and decimal equivalents are often used as well but without the % symbol, as follows.

$$1\% = \frac{1}{100} = 0.01$$
$$100\% = \frac{100}{100} = 1$$
$$32\% = \frac{32}{100} = 0.32$$
$$50\% = \frac{50}{100} = 0.5$$
$$0.3\% = \frac{0.3}{100} = 0.003$$

Be careful not to confuse 0.01 with 0.01%. The percent symbol matters. For example, $0.01 = 1\%$ but $0.01\% = \frac{0.01}{100} = 0.0001$.

- To compute a *percent*, given the *part* and the *whole*, divide the part by the whole. The result will be the decimal equivalent, so multiply the result by 100 to convert to percent.

Example 1.7.1: If the whole is 20 and the part is 13, you can find the percent as follows.

$$\frac{part}{whole} = \frac{13}{20} = 0.65 = 65\%$$

Example 1.7.2: What percent of 150 is 12.9?

Solution: Here the whole is 150 and the part is 12.9.

$$\frac{part}{whole} = \frac{12.9}{150} = 0.086 = 8.6\%$$

● To find the *part* that is a certain *percent* of a *whole*, you can either multiply the *whole* by the decimal equivalent of the percent or set up a proportion to find the part.

Example 1.7.3: To find 30% of 350, multiply 350 by the decimal equivalent of 30%, or 0.3, as follows.

$$x = (350)(0.3) = 105$$

To use a proportion, you need to find the number of parts of 350 that yields the same ratio as 30 out of 100 parts. You want a number x that satisfies the proportion

$$\frac{part}{whole} = \frac{30}{100}$$

$$\frac{x}{350} = \frac{30}{100}$$

Solving for x yields $x = \frac{(30)(350)}{100} = 105$, so 30% of 350 is 105.

● Given the *percent* and the *part*, you can calculate the *whole*. To do this you can either use the decimal equivalent of the percent or you can set up a proportion and solve it.

Example 1.7.4: 15 is 60% of what number?

Solution: Use the decimal equivalent of 60%. Because 60% of some number z is 15, multiply z by the decimal equivalent of 60%, or 0.6.

$$0.6z = 15$$

Now solve for z by dividing both sides of the equation by 0.6 as follows.

$$z = \frac{15}{0.6} = 25$$

Using a proportion, look for a number z such that

$$\frac{part}{whole} = \frac{60}{100}$$

$$\frac{15}{z} = \frac{60}{100}$$

Hence, $60z = (15)(100)$, and therefore, $z = \frac{(15)(100)}{60} = \frac{1,500}{60} = 25$. That is, 15 is 60% of 25.

Although the discussion about percent so far assumes a context of a *part* and a *whole*, it is not necessary that the part be less than the whole. In general, the whole is called the **base** of the percent. When the numerator of a percent is greater than the base, the percent is greater than 100%. For example, 15 is 300% of 5, since

$$\frac{15}{5} = \frac{300}{100}$$

and 250% of 16 is $\left(\frac{250}{100}\right)(16) = (2.5)(16) = 40$. Note that the decimal equivalent of 250% is 2.5.

It is also not necessary for the part to be related to the whole at all, as in the question, "a teacher's salary is what percent of a banker's salary?"

When a quantity changes from an initial positive amount to another positive amount, for example, an employee's salary that is raised, you can compute the amount of change as a percent of the initial amount. This is called **percent change**. If a quantity increases from 600 to 750, then the **percent increase** is found by dividing the amount of increase, 150, by the base, 600, which is the initial number given:

$$\frac{amount\ of\ increase}{base} = \frac{750 - 600}{600} = \frac{150}{600} = \frac{25}{100} = 0.25 = 25\%$$

We say the percent increase is 25%. Sometimes this computation is written as

$$\left(\frac{750 - 600}{600}\right)(100\%) = \left(\frac{150}{600}\right)(100\%) = 25\%$$

If a quantity doubles in size, then the percent increase is 100%. For example, if a quantity changes from 150 to 300, then the percent increase is

$$\frac{change}{base} = \frac{300 - 150}{150} = \frac{150}{150} = 100\%$$

If a quantity decreases from 500 to 400, calculate the **percent decrease** as follows.

$$\frac{change}{base} = \frac{500 - 400}{500} = \frac{100}{500} = \frac{20}{100} = 0.20 = 20\%$$

The quantity decreased by 20%.

When computing a percent *increase*, the base is the *smaller* number. When computing a percent *decrease*, the base is the *larger* number. In either case, the base is the initial number, before the change.

Example 1.7.5: An investment in a mutual fund increased by 12% in a single day. If the value of the investment before the increase was $1,300, what was the value after the increase?

Solution: The percent increase is 12%. Therefore, the value of the increase is 12% of $1,300, or, using the decimal equivalent, the increase is (0.12)($1,300) = $156. Thus, the value of the investment after the change is

$$\$1,300 + \$156 = \$1,456$$

Because the final result is the sum of the initial investment—100% of $1,300—and the increase—12% of $1,300—the final result is 100% + 12% = 112% of $1,300.

Thus, another way to get the final result is to multiply the value of the investment by the decimal equivalent of 112%, which is 1.12:

$$(\$1,300)(1.12) = \$1,456$$

A quantity may have several successive percent changes. The base of each successive percent change is the result of the preceding percent change.

Example 1.7.6: The monthly enrollment at a preschool decreased by 8% during one month and increased by 6% during the next month. What was the cumulative percent change for the two months?

Solution: If E is the enrollment before the first month, then the enrollment as a result of the 8% decrease can be found by multiplying the base E by the decimal equivalent of $100\% - 8\% = 92\%$, which is 0.92:

$$0.92E$$

The enrollment as a result of the second percent change—the 6% increase—can be found by multiplying the *new* base $0.92E$ by the decimal equivalent of $100\% + 6\% = 106\%$, which is 1.06:

$$(1.06)(0.92)E = 0.9752E$$

The percent equivalent of 0.9752 is 97.52%, which is 2.48% less than 100%. Thus, the cumulative percent change in the enrollment for the two months is a 2.48% decrease.

ARITHMETIC EXERCISES

1. Evaluate the following.

   (a) $15 - (6 - 4)(-2)$
   (b) $(2 - 17) \div 5$
   (c) $(60 \div 12) - (-7 + 4)$
   (d) $(3)^4 - (-2)^3$

   (e) $(-5)(-3) - 15$
   (f) $(-2)^4(15 - 18)^4$
   (g) $(20 \div 5)^2(-2 + 6)^3$
   (h) $(-85)(0) - (-17)(3)$

2. Evaluate the following.

   (a) $\dfrac{1}{2} - \dfrac{1}{3} + \dfrac{1}{12}$

   (b) $\left(\dfrac{3}{4} + \dfrac{1}{7}\right)\left(\dfrac{-2}{5}\right)$

   (c) $\left(\dfrac{7}{8} - \dfrac{4}{5}\right)^2$

   (d) $\left(\dfrac{3}{-8}\right) \div \left(\dfrac{27}{32}\right)$

3. Which of the integers 312, 98, 112, and 144 are divisible by 8?

4. (a) What is the prime factorization of 372?
   (b) What are the positive divisors of 372?

5. (a) What are the prime divisors of 100?
   (b) What are the prime divisors of 144?

6. Which of the integers 2, 9, 19, 29, 30, 37, 45, 49, 51, 83, 90, and 91 are prime numbers?

7. What is the prime factorization of 585?

8. Which of the following statements are true?

   (a) $-5 < 3.1$
   (b) $\sqrt{16} = 4$
   (c) $7 \div 0 = 0$
   (d) $0 < \left| -\dfrac{1}{7} \right|$
   (e) $0.3 < \dfrac{1}{3}$
   (f) $(-1)^{87} = -1$

   (g) $\sqrt{(-3)^2} < 0$
   (h) $\dfrac{21}{28} = \dfrac{3}{4}$
   (i) $-|-23| = 23$
   (j) $\dfrac{1}{2} > \dfrac{1}{17}$
   (k) $(59)^3 (59)^2 = 59^6$
   (l) $-\sqrt{25} < -4$

9. Find the following.

   (a) 40% of 15
   (b) 150% of 48
   (c) 0.6% of 800

   (d) 15 is 30% of which number?
   (e) 11 is what percent of 55?

10. If a person's salary increased from $200 per week to $234 per week, what was the percent increase in the person's salary?

11. If an athlete's weight decreased from 160 pounds to 152 pounds, what was the percent decrease in the athlete's weight?

12. A particular stock is valued at $40 per share. If the value increases by 20 percent and then decreases by 25 percent, what will be the value of the stock per share after the decrease?

13. If the ratio of the number of men to the number of women on a committee of 20 members is 3 to 2, how many members of the committee are women?

14. The integer a is even and the integer b is odd. For each of the following integers, indicate whether the integer is even or odd.

Integer	Even	Odd
$a + 2b$		
$2a + b$		
ab		
a^b		
$(a + b)^2$		
$a^2 - b^2$		

15. When the positive integer n is divided by 3, the remainder is 2 and when n is divided by 5, the remainder is 1. What is the least possible value of n?

ANSWERS TO ARITHMETIC EXERCISES

1. (a) 19
   (b) −3
   (c) 8
   (d) 89

   (e) 0
   (f) 1,296
   (g) 1,024
   (h) 51

2. (a) $\dfrac{1}{4}$ (c) $\dfrac{9}{1,600}$

    (b) $-\dfrac{5}{14}$ (d) $-\dfrac{4}{9}$

3. 312, 112, and 144

4. (a) $372 = (2^2)(3)(31)$

    (b) The positive divisors of 372 are 1, 2, 3, 4, 6, 12, 31, 62, 93, 124, 186, and 372.

5. (a) $100 = (2^2)(5^2)$, so the prime divisors are 2 and 5.

    (b) $144 = (2^4)(3^2)$, so the prime divisors are 2 and 3.

6. 2, 19, 29, 37, and 83

7. $585 = (3^2)(5)(13)$

8. (a) True   (g) False; $\sqrt{(-3)^2} = \sqrt{9} = 3 > 0$

    (b) True   (h) True

    (c) False; division by 0 is undefined   (i) False; $-|-23| = -23$

    (d) True   (j) True

    (e) True   (k) False; $(59)^3(59)^2 = 59^{3+2} = 59^5$

    (f) True   (l) True

9. (a) 6   (d) 50

    (b) 72   (e) 20%

    (c) 4.8

10. 17%

11. 5%

12. $36 per share

13. 8 women

14.

Integer	Even	Odd
$a + 2b$	✓	
$2a + b$		✓
ab	✓	
a^b	✓	
$(a + b)^2$		✓
$a^2 - b^2$		✓

15. 11

2. ALGEBRA

Basic algebra can be viewed as an extension of arithmetic. The main concept that distinguishes algebra from arithmetic is that of a **variable**, which is a letter that represents a quantity whose value is unknown. The letters x and y are often used as variables, although any letter can be used. Variables enable you to present a word problem in terms of unknown quantities by using algebraic expressions, equations, inequalities, and functions. This section reviews these algebraic tools and then progresses to several examples of applying them to solve real-life word problems. The section ends with coordinate geometry and graphs of functions as other important algebraic tools for solving problems.

2.1 Operations with Algebraic Expressions

An **algebraic expression** has one or more variables and can be written as a single **term** or as a sum of terms. Here are some examples of algebraic expressions.

$$2x \qquad y - \frac{1}{4} \qquad w^3z + 5z^2 - z^2 + 6 \qquad \frac{8}{n+p}$$

In the examples above, $2x$ is a single term, $y - \frac{1}{4}$ has two terms,

$w^3z + 5z^2 - z^2 + 6$ has four terms, and $\frac{8}{n+p}$ has one term. In the expression

$w^3z + 5z^2 - z^2 + 6$, the terms $5z^2$ and $-z^2$ are called **like terms** because they have the same variables, and the corresponding variables have the same exponents. A term that has no variable is called a **constant** term. A number that is multiplied by variables is called the **coefficient** of a term. For example, in the expression $2x^2 + 7x - 5$, 2 is the coefficient of the term $2x^2$, 7 is the coefficient of the term $7x$, and -5 is a constant term.

The same rules that govern operations with numbers apply to operations with algebraic expressions. One additional rule, which helps in simplifying algebraic expressions, is that like terms can be combined by simply adding their coefficients, as the following examples show.

$$2x + 5x = 7x$$

$$w^3z + 5z^2 - z^2 + 6 = w^3z + 4z^2 + 6$$

$$3xy + 2x - xy - 3x = 2xy - x$$

A number or variable that is a factor of each term in an algebraic expression can be factored out, as the following examples show.

$$4x + 12 = 4(x + 3)$$

$$15y^2 - 9y = 3y(5y - 3)$$

$$\frac{7x^2 + 14x}{2x + 4} = \frac{7x(x + 2)}{2(x + 2)} = \frac{7x}{2} \quad \text{(where } x \neq -2 \text{, since division by 0 is not defined)}$$

To multiply two algebraic expressions, each term of the first expression is multiplied by each term of the second expression, and the results are added, as the following examples show.

$$(x + 2)(3x - 7) = x(3x) + x(-7) + 2(3x) + 2(-7)$$

$$= 3x^2 - 7x + 6x - 14$$

$$= 3x^2 - x - 14$$

A statement of equality between two algebraic expressions that is true for all possible values of the variables involved is called an **identity**. All of the statements above are identities. Here are some standard identities that are useful.

$$(a + b)^2 = a^2 + 2ab + b^2$$

$$(a - b)^3 = a^3 - 3a^2b + 3ab^2 - b^3$$

$$a^2 - b^2 = (a + b)(a - b)$$

All of the identities above can be used to modify and simplify algebraic expressions. For example, the identity $a^2 - b^2 = (a + b)(a-b)$ can be used to simplify the following algebraic expression.

$$\frac{x^2 - 9}{4x - 12} = \frac{(x + 3)(x - 3)}{4(x - 3)} = \frac{x + 3}{4} \quad (\text{where } x \neq 3)$$

A statement of equality between two algebraic expressions that is true for only certain values of the variables involved is called an **equation**. The values are called the **solutions** of the equation.

The following are examples of some basic types of equations.

$$3x + 5 = -2 \quad \text{A \textbf{linear equation in one variable}, } x$$

$$x - 3y = 10 \quad \text{A \textbf{linear equation in two variables}, } x \text{ and } y$$

$$20y^2 + 6y - 17 = 0 \quad \text{A \textbf{quadratic equation in one variable}, } y$$

2.2 Rules of Exponents

In the algebraic expression x^a, where x is raised to the power a, x is called a **base** and a is called an **exponent**. Here are the basic rules of exponents, where the bases x and y are nonzero real numbers and the exponents a and b are integers.

1. $x^{-a} = \dfrac{1}{x^a}$

    Examples: $4^{-3} = \dfrac{1}{4^3} = \dfrac{1}{64}$, $x^{-10} = \dfrac{1}{x^{10}}$, and $\dfrac{1}{2^{-a}} = 2^a$

2. $(x^a)(x^b) = x^{a+b}$

    Examples: $(3^2)(3^4) = 3^{2+4} = 3^6 = 729$ and $(y^3)(y^{-1}) = y^2$

3. $\dfrac{x^a}{x^b} = x^{a-b} = \dfrac{1}{x^{b-a}}$

    Examples: $\dfrac{5^7}{5^4} = 5^{7-4} = 5^3 = 125$ and $\dfrac{t^3}{t^8} = t^{-5} = \dfrac{1}{t^5}$

4. $x^0 = 1$

    Examples: $7^0 = 1$ and $(-3)^0 = 1$. Note that 0^0 is not defined.

5. $(x^a)(y^a) = (xy)^a$

    Examples: $(2^3)(3^3) = 6^3 = 216$ and $(10z)^3 = 10^3z^3 = 1,000z^3$

6. $\left(\dfrac{x}{y}\right)^a = \dfrac{x^a}{y^a}$

   Examples: $\left(\dfrac{3}{4}\right)^2 = \dfrac{3^2}{4^2} = \dfrac{9}{16}$ and $\left(\dfrac{r}{4t}\right)^3 = \dfrac{r^3}{64t^3}$

7. $(x^a)^b = x^{ab}$

   Examples: $(2^5)^2 = 2^{10} = 1{,}024$ and $(3y^6)^2 = (3^2)(y^6)^2 = 9y^{12}$

The rules above are identities that are used to simplify expressions. Sometimes algebraic expressions look like they can be simplified in similar ways, but in fact they cannot. Here are several pairs of expressions that are *commonly mistaken* to be identities.

- $x^a y^b \neq (xy)^{a+b}$

  Note that the bases are not the same.

- $(x^a)^b \neq x^a x^b$

  Instead, $(x^a)^b = x^{ab}$ and $x^a x^b = x^{a+b}$; for example, $(4^2)^3 = 4^6$ and $4^2 4^3 = 4^5$.

- $(x + y)^a \neq x^a + y^a$

  Recall that $(x + y)^2 = x^2 + 2xy + y^2$; that is, the correct expansion contains terms such as $2xy$.

- $(-x)^2 \neq -x^2$

  Instead, $(-x)^2 = x^2$. Note carefully where each minus sign appears.

- $\sqrt{x^2 + y^2} \neq x + y$

- $\dfrac{a}{x + y} \neq \dfrac{a}{x} + \dfrac{a}{y}$

  But it *is* true that $\dfrac{x + y}{a} = \dfrac{x}{a} + \dfrac{y}{a}$.

2.3 Solving Linear Equations

To **solve an equation** means to find the values of the variables that make the equation true; that is, the values that **satisfy the equation**. Two equations that have the same solutions are called **equivalent equations**. For example, $x + 1 = 2$ and $2x + 2 = 4$ are equivalent equations; both are true when $x = 1$ and are false otherwise. The general method for solving an equation is to find successively simpler equivalent equations so that the simplest equivalent equation makes the solutions obvious.

The following rules are important for producing equivalent equations.

- When the same constant is added to or subtracted from both sides of an equation, the equality is preserved and the new equation is equivalent to the original equation.
- When both sides of an equation are multiplied or divided by the same nonzero constant, the equality is preserved and the new equation is equivalent to the original equation.

A **linear equation** is an equation involving one or more variables in which each term in the equation is either a constant term or a variable multiplied by a coefficient. None of the variables are multiplied together or raised to a power greater than 1. For example, $2x + 1 = 7x$ and $10x - 9y - z = 3$ are linear equations, but $x + y^2 = 0$ and $xz = 3$ are not.

Linear Equations in One Variable

To solve a linear equation in one variable, simplify each side of the equation by combining like terms. Then use the rules for producing simpler equivalent equations.

Example 2.3.1:

$$11x - 4 - 8x = 2(x + 4) - 2x$$
$$3x - 4 = 2x + 8 - 2x \quad \text{(like terms combined)}$$
$$3x - 4 = 8 \quad \text{(simplified)}$$
$$3x - 4 + 4 = 8 + 4 \quad \text{(4 added to both sides)}$$
$$3x = 12$$
$$\frac{3x}{3} = \frac{12}{3} \quad \text{(both sides divided by 3)}$$
$$x = 4$$

You can always check your solution by substituting it into the original equation.

Note that it is possible for a linear equation to have no solutions. For example, the equation $2x + 3 = 2(7 + x)$ has no solution, since it is equivalent to the equation $3 = 14$, which is false. Also, it is possible that what looks to be a linear equation turns out to be an identity when you try to solve it. For example, $3x - 6 = -3(2 - x)$ is true for all values of x, so it is an identity.

Linear Equations in Two Variables

A linear equation in two variables, x and y, can be written in the form

$$ax + by = c$$

where a, b, and c are real numbers and a and b are not both zero. For example, $3x + 2y = 8$ is a linear equation in two variables.

A solution of such an equation is an **ordered pair** of numbers (x, y) that makes the equation true when the values of x and y are substituted into the equation. For example, both $(2, 1)$ and $(-\frac{2}{3}, 5)$ are solutions of the equation $3x + 2y = 8$, but $(1, 2)$ is not a solution. A linear equation in two variables has infinitely many solutions. If another linear equation in the same variables is given, it is usually possible to find a unique solution of both equations. Two equations with the same variables are called a **system of equations**, and the equations in the system are called **simultaneous equations**. To solve a system of two equations means to find an ordered pair of numbers that satisfies *both* equations in the system.

There are two basic methods for solving systems of linear equations, by **substitution** or by **elimination**. In the substitution method, one equation is manipulated to express one variable in terms of the other. Then the expression is substituted in the other equation. For example, to solve the system of equations

$$4x + 3y = 13$$
$$x + 2y = 2$$

you can express x in the second equation in terms of y as $x = 2 - 2y$. Then substitute $2 - 2y$ for x in the first equation to find the value of y.

$$4(2 - 2y) + 3y = 13$$
$$8 - 8y + 3y = 13$$
$$-8y + 3y = 5 \quad \text{(8 subtracted from both sides)}$$
$$-5y = 5 \quad \text{(like terms combined)}$$
$$y = -1 \quad \text{(both sides divided by} -5)$$

Then -1 can be substituted for y in either equation to find the value of x. We use the second equation:

$$x + 2y = 2$$
$$x + 2(-1) = 2$$
$$x - 2 = 2$$
$$x = 4 \quad \text{(2 added to both sides)}$$

In the elimination method, the object is to make the coefficients of one variable the same in both equations so that one variable can be eliminated either by adding the equations together or by subtracting one from the other. In the example above, multiplying both sides of the second equation by 4 yields $4(x + 2y) = 4(2)$, or $4x + 8y = 8$. Now you have two equations with the same coefficient of x.

$$4x + 3y = 13$$
$$4x + 8y = 8$$

If you subtract the second equation from the first, the result is $-5y = 5$. Thus, $y = -1$, and substituting -1 for y in either of the original equations yields $x = 4$.

By either method, the solution of the system is $x = 4$ and $y = -1$, or $(x, y) = (4, -1)$.

2.4 Solving Quadratic Equations

A **quadratic equation** in the variable x is an equation that can be written in the form

$$ax^2 + bx + c = 0$$

where a, b, and c are real numbers and $a \neq 0$. When such an equation has solutions, they can be found using the **quadratic formula**:

$$x = \frac{-b \pm \sqrt{b^2 - 4ac}}{2a}$$

where the notation $\pm$ is shorthand for indicating two solutions—one that uses the plus sign and the other that uses the minus sign.

Example 2.4.1: In the quadratic equation $2x^2 - x - 6 = 0$, we have $a = 2$, $b = -1$, and $c = -6$. Therefore, the quadratic formula yields

$$x = \frac{-(-1) \pm \sqrt{(-1)^2 - 4(2)(-6)}}{2(2)}$$
$$= \frac{1 \pm \sqrt{49}}{4}$$
$$= \frac{1 \pm 7}{4}$$

Hence the two solutions are $x = \dfrac{1 + 7}{4} = 2$ and $x = \dfrac{1 - 7}{4} = -\dfrac{3}{2}$.

Quadratic equations have at most two real solutions, as in the example above. However, some quadratic equations have only one real solution. For example, the quadratic equation $x^2 + 4x + 4 = 0$ has only one solution, which is $x = -2$. In this case, the expression under the square root symbol in the quadratic formula is equal to 0, and so adding or subtracting 0 yields the same result. Other quadratic equations have no real solutions; for example, $x^2 + x + 5 = 0$. In this case, the expression under the square root symbol is negative, so the entire expression is not a real number.

Some quadratic equations can be solved more quickly by factoring. For example, the quadratic equation $2x^2 - x - 6 = 0$ in example 2.4.1 can be factored as $(2x + 3)(x - 2) = 0$. When a product is equal to 0, at least one of the factors must be equal to 0, which leads to two cases: either $2x + 3 = 0$ or $x - 2 = 0$. Therefore,

$$2x + 3 = 0$$
$$2x = -3 \qquad \text{OR} \qquad \begin{aligned} x - 2 &= 0 \\ x &= 2 \end{aligned}$$
$$x = -\frac{3}{2}$$

and the solutions are $-\dfrac{3}{2}$ and 2.

Example 2.4.2: Here is another example of a quadratic equation that can be easily factored.

$$5x^2 + 3x - 2 = 0$$
$$(5x - 2)(x + 1) = 0$$

Therefore,

$$\begin{aligned} 5x - 2 &= 0 \\ x &= \frac{2}{5} \end{aligned} \qquad \text{OR} \qquad \begin{aligned} x + 1 &= 0 \\ x &= -1 \end{aligned}$$

2.5 Solving Linear Inequalities

A mathematical statement that uses one of the following inequality signs is called an **inequality**.

$<$	less than
$>$	greater than
$\leq$	less than or equal to
$\geq$	greater than or equal to

Inequalities can involve variables and are similar to equations, except that the two sides are related by one of the inequality signs instead of the equality sign used in equations. For example, the inequality $4x - 1 \leq 7$ is a linear inequality in one variable, which states that "$4x - 1$ is less than or equal to 7." To **solve an inequality** means to find the set of all values of the variable that make the inequality true. This set of values is also known as the **solution set** of an inequality. Two inequalities that have the same solution set are called **equivalent inequalities**.

The procedure used to solve a linear inequality is similar to that used to solve a linear equation, which is to simplify the inequality by isolating the variable on one side of the inequality, using the following two rules.

- When the same constant is added to or subtracted from both sides of an inequality, the direction of the inequality is preserved and the new inequality is equivalent to the original.
- When both sides of the inequality are multiplied or divided by the same nonzero constant, the direction of the inequality is *preserved if the constant is positive* but the direction is *reversed if the constant is negative*. In either case, the new inequality is equivalent to the original.

Example 2.5.1: The inequality $-3x + 5 \le 17$ can be solved as follows.

$$-3x + 5 \le 17$$
$$-3x \le 12 \qquad \text{(5 subtracted from both sides)}$$
$$\frac{-3x}{-3} \ge \frac{12}{-3} \qquad \text{(both sides divided by } -3\text{, which reverses}$$
$$\text{the direction of the inequality)}$$
$$x \ge -4$$

Therefore, the solution set of $-3x + 5 \le 17$ consists of all real numbers greater than or equal to -4.

Example 2.5.2:

$$\frac{4x + 9}{11} < 5$$
$$4x + 9 < 55 \qquad \text{(both sides multiplied by 11)}$$
$$4x < 46 \qquad \text{(9 subtracted from both sides)}$$
$$x < \frac{46}{4} \qquad \text{(both sides divided by 4)}$$
$$x < 11.5$$

Therefore, the solution set of $\dfrac{4x + 9}{11} < 5$ consists of all real numbers less than 11.5.

2.6 Functions

An algebraic expression in one variable can be used to define a **function** of that variable. Functions are usually denoted by letters such as f, g, and h. For example, the algebraic expression $3x + 5$ can be used to define a function f by

$$f(x) = 3x + 5$$

where $f(x)$ is called the value of f at x and is obtained by substituting the value of x in the expression above. For example, if $x = 1$ is substituted in the expression above, the result is $f(1) = 8$.

It might be helpful to think of a function f as a machine that takes an input, which is a value of the variable x, and produces the corresponding output, $f(x)$. For any function, each input x gives exactly one output $f(x)$. However, more than one value of x can give the same output $f(x)$. For example, if g is the function defined by $g(x) = x^2 - 2x + 3$, then $g(0) = 3$ and $g(2) = 3$.

The **domain** of a function is the set of all permissible inputs, that is, all permissible values of the variable x. For the functions f and g defined above, the domain is the set of all real numbers. Sometimes the domain of the function is given explicitly and is restricted to a specific set of values of x. For example, we can define the function h by $h(x) = x^2 - 4$ for $-2 \leq x \leq 2$. Without an explicit restriction, the domain is assumed to be the set of all values of x for which $f(x)$ is a real number.

Example 2.6.1: Let f be the function defined by $f(x) = \dfrac{2x}{x - 6}$. In this case, f is not defined at $x = 6$ because $\dfrac{12}{0}$ is not defined. Hence, the domain of f consists of all real numbers except for 6.

Example 2.6.2: Let g be the function defined by $g(x) = x^3 + \sqrt{x + 2} - 10$. In this case, $g(x)$ is not a real number if $x < -2$. Hence, the domain of g consists of all real numbers x such that $x \geq -2$.

Example 2.6.3: Let h be the function defined by $h(x) = |x|$, the **absolute value** of x, which is the distance between x and 0 on the number line (see section 1.5). The domain of h is the set of all real numbers. Also, $h(x) = h(-x)$ for all real numbers x, which reflects the property that on the number line the distance between x and 0 is the same as the distance between $-x$ and 0.

2.7 Applications

Translating verbal descriptions into algebraic expressions is an essential initial step in solving word problems. Some examples are given below.

- If the square of the number x is multiplied by 3, and then 10 is added to that product, the result can be represented by $3x^2 + 10$.
- If John's present salary s is increased by 14 percent, then his new salary is $1.14s$.
- If y gallons of syrup are to be distributed among 5 people so that one particular person gets 1 gallon and the rest of the syrup is divided equally among the remaining 4, then each of those 4 people will get $\dfrac{y - 1}{4}$ gallons of syrup.

Here are several examples of using algebraic techniques to solve word problems.

Example 2.7.1: Ellen has received the following scores on 3 exams: 82, 74, and 90. What score will Ellen need to receive on the next exam so that the average (arithmetic mean) score for the 4 exams will be 85?

Solution: Let x represent the score on Ellen's next exam. This initial step of assigning a variable to the quantity that is sought is an important beginning to solving the problem. Then in terms of x, the average of the 4 exams is

$$\frac{82 + 74 + 90 + x}{4}$$

which is supposed to equal 85. Now simplify the expression and set it equal to 85:

$$\frac{82 + 74 + 90 + x}{4} = \frac{246 + x}{4} = 85$$

Solving the resulting linear equation for x, you get

$$246 + x = 340$$
$$x = 94$$

Therefore, Ellen will need to attain a score of 94 on the next exam.

Example 2.7.2: A mixture of 12 ounces of vinegar and oil is 40 percent vinegar, where all of the measurements are by weight. How many ounces of oil must be added to the mixture to produce a new mixture that is only 25 percent vinegar?

Solution: Let x represent the number of ounces of oil to be added. Then the total number of ounces of the new mixture will be $12 + x$, and the total number of ounces of vinegar in the new mixture will be $(0.40)(12)$. Since the new mixture must be 25 percent vinegar,

$$\frac{(0.40)(12)}{12 + x} = 0.25$$

Therefore,

$$(0.40)(12) = (12 + x)(0.25)$$
$$4.8 = 3 + 0.25x$$
$$1.8 = 0.25x$$
$$7.2 = x$$

Thus, 7.2 ounces of oil must be added to produce a new mixture that is 25 percent vinegar.

Example 2.7.3: In a driving competition, Jeff and Dennis drove the same course at average speeds of 51 miles per hour and 54 miles per hour, respectively. If it took Jeff 40 minutes to drive the course, how long did it take Dennis?

Solution: Let x be the time, in minutes, that it took Dennis to drive the course. The distance d, in miles, is equal to the product of the rate r, in miles per hour, and the time t, in hours; that is,

$$d = rt$$

Note that since the rates are given in miles per *hour*, it is necessary to express the times in hours; for example, 40 minutes equals $\frac{40}{60}$ of an hour. Thus, the distance traveled by Jeff is the product of his speed and his time, $(51)\left(\frac{40}{60}\right)$ miles, and the distance traveled by Dennis is similarly represented by $(54)\left(\frac{x}{60}\right)$ miles. Since the distances are equal,

$$(51)\left(\frac{40}{60}\right) = (54)\left(\frac{x}{60}\right)$$
$$(51)(40) = 54x$$
$$x = \frac{(51)(40)}{54} \approx 37.8$$

Thus, it took Dennis approximately 37.8 minutes to drive the course.

Example 2.7.4: Working alone at its constant rate, machine A takes 3 hours to produce a batch of identical computer parts. Working alone at its constant rate, machine B takes 2 hours to produce an identical batch of parts. How long will it take the two machines, working simultaneously at their respective constant rates, to produce an identical batch of parts?

Solution: Since machine A takes 3 hours to produce a batch, machine A can produce $\frac{1}{3}$ of the batch in 1 hour. Similarly, machine B can produce $\frac{1}{2}$ of the batch in 1 hour. If we let x represent the number of hours it takes both machines, working simultaneously, to produce the batch, then the two machines will produce $\frac{1}{x}$ of the job in 1 hour. When the two machines work together, adding their individual production rates, $\frac{1}{3}$ and $\frac{1}{2}$, gives their combined production rate $\frac{1}{x}$. Therefore,

$$\frac{1}{3} + \frac{1}{2} = \frac{1}{x}$$
$$\frac{2}{6} + \frac{3}{6} = \frac{1}{x}$$
$$\frac{5}{6} = \frac{1}{x}$$
$$\frac{6}{5} = x$$

Thus, working together, the machines will take $\frac{6}{5}$ hours, or 1 hour 12 minutes, to produce a batch of parts.

Example 2.7.5: At a fruit stand, apples can be purchased for $0.15 each and pears for $0.20 each. At these rates, a bag of apples and pears was purchased for $3.80. If the bag contained 21 pieces of fruit, how many of the pieces were pears?

Solution: If a represents the number of apples purchased and p represents the number of pears purchased, the information can be translated into the following system of equations.

$$0.15a + 0.20p = 3.80 \qquad \text{(total cost)}$$
$$a + p = 21 \qquad \text{(total number of fruit)}$$

From the second equation, $a = 21 - p$. Substituting $21 - p$ into the first equation for a gives

$$0.15(21 - p) + 0.20p = 3.80$$
$$(0.15)(21) - 0.15p + 0.20p = 3.80$$
$$3.15 - 0.15p + 0.20p = 3.80$$
$$0.05p = 0.65$$
$$p = 13$$

Thus, of the 21 pieces of fruit, 13 were pears.

Example 2.7.6: To produce a particular radio model, it costs a manufacturer $30 per radio, and it is assumed that if 500 radios are produced, all of them will be sold. What must be the selling price per radio to ensure that the profit (revenue from the sales minus the total production cost) on the 500 radios is greater than $8,200 ?

Solution: If y represents the selling price per radio, then the profit is $500(y - 30)$. Therefore, we set

$$500(y - 30) > 8,200$$

Solving the inequality, we get

$$500y - 15,000 > 8,200$$
$$500y > 23,200$$
$$y > 46.4$$

Thus, the selling price must be greater than $46.40 to ensure that the profit is greater than $8,200.

Some applications involve computing **interest** earned on an investment during a specified time period. The interest can be computed as simple interest or compound interest.

Simple interest is based only on the initial deposit, which serves as the amount on which interest is computed, called the **principal**, for the entire time period. If the amount P is invested at a *simple annual interest rate of r percent*, then the value V of the investment at the end of t years is given by the formula

$$V = P\left(1 + \frac{rt}{100}\right)$$

where P and V are in dollars.

In the case of **compound interest**, interest is added to the principal at regular time intervals, such as annually, quarterly, and monthly. Each time interest is added to the principal, the interest is said to be compounded. After each compounding, interest is earned on the new principal, which is the sum of the preceding principal and the interest just added. If the amount P is invested at an *annual interest rate of r percent, compounded annually*, then the value V of the investment at the end of t years is given by the formula

$$V = P\left(1 + \frac{r}{100}\right)^t$$

If the amount P is invested at an *annual interest rate of r percent, compounded n times per year*, then the value V of the investment at the end of t years is given by the formula

$$V = P\left(1 + \frac{r}{100n}\right)^{nt}$$

Example 2.7.7: If $10,000 is invested at a simple annual interest rate of 6 percent, what is the value of the investment after half a year?

Solution: According to the formula for simple interest, the value of the investment after $\frac{1}{2}$ year is

$$\$10,000\left(1 + 0.06\left(\frac{1}{2}\right)\right) = \$10,000(1.03) = \$10,300$$

Example 2.7.8: If an amount P is to be invested at an annual interest rate of 3.5 percent, compounded annually, what should be the value of P so that the value of the investment is \$1,000 at the end of 3 years?

Solution: According to the formula for 3.5 percent annual interest, compounded annually, the value of the investment after 3 years is

$$P(1 + 0.035)^3$$

and we set it to be equal to \$1,000

$$P(1 + 0.035)^3 = \$1,000$$

To find the value of P, we divide both sides of the equation by $(1 + 0.035)^3$.

$$P = \frac{\$1,000}{(1 + 0.035)^3} \approx \$901.94$$

Thus, an amount of approximately \$901.94 should be invested.

Example 2.7.9: A college student expects to earn at least \$1,000 in interest on an initial investment of \$20,000. If the money is invested for one year at interest compounded quarterly, what is the least annual interest rate that would achieve the goal?

Solution: According to the formula for r percent annual interest, compounded quarterly, the value of the investment after 1 year is

$$\$20,000\left(1 + \frac{r}{400}\right)^4$$

By setting this value greater than or equal to \$21,000 and solving for r, we get

$$\$20,000\left(1 + \frac{r}{400}\right)^4 \geq \$21,000$$

$$\left(1 + \frac{r}{400}\right)^4 \geq 1.05$$

We can use the fact that taking the positive fourth root of each side of an inequality preserves the direction of the inequality. This is also true for the positive square root or any other positive root.

$$1 + \frac{r}{400} \geq \sqrt[4]{1.05}$$

$$r \geq 400\left(\sqrt[4]{1.05} - 1\right)$$

To compute the fourth root, we can use the fact that $\sqrt[4]{x} = \sqrt{\sqrt{x}}$ for $x \geq 0$; that is, we can compute a fourth root by taking a square root twice:

$$r \geq 400\left(\sqrt[4]{1.05} - 1\right) = 400\left(\sqrt{\sqrt{1.05}} - 1\right) \approx 4.91$$

So the least annual interest rate is approximately 4.91 percent.

2.8 Coordinate Geometry

Two real number lines that are perpendicular to each other and that intersect at their respective zero points define a **rectangular coordinate system**, often called the **xy-coordinate system** or **xy-plane**. The horizontal number line is called the **x-axis** and the vertical number line is called the **y-axis**. The point where the two axes intersect is called the **origin**, denoted by O. The positive half of the x-axis is to the right of the origin, and the positive half of the y-axis is above the origin. The two axes divide the plane into four regions called **quadrants I, II, III**, and **IV**, as shown in the figure below.

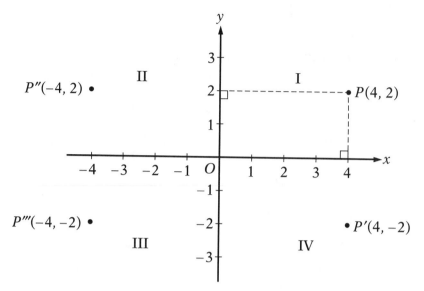

Each point P in the xy-plane can be identified with an ordered pair (x, y) of real numbers and is denoted by $P(x, y)$. The first number is called the **x-coordinate**, and the second number is called the **y-coordinate**. A point with coordinates (x, y) is located $|x|$ units to the right of the y-axis if x is positive or to the left of the y-axis if x is negative. Also, the point is located $|y|$ units above the x-axis if y is positive or below the x-axis if y is negative. If $x = 0$, the point lies on the y-axis, and if $y = 0$, the point lies on the x-axis. The origin has coordinates $(0, 0)$. Unless otherwise noted, the units used on the x-axis and the y-axis are the same.

In the figure above, the point $P(4, 2)$ is 4 units to the right of the y-axis and 2 units above the x-axis, and the point $P'''(-4, -2)$ is 4 units to the left of the y-axis and 2 units below the x-axis.

Note that the three points $P'(4, -2)$, $P''(-4, 2)$, and $P'''(-4, -2)$ have the same coordinates as P except for the sign. These points are geometrically related to P as follows.

- P' is the **reflection of P about the x-axis**, or P' and P are **symmetric about the x-axis**.
- P'' is the **reflection of P about the y-axis**, or P'' and P are **symmetric about the y-axis**.
- P''' is the **reflection of P about the origin**, or P''' and P are **symmetric about the origin**.

The distance between two points in the xy-plane can be found by using the Pythagorean theorem. For example, the distance between the two points $Q(-2, -3)$ and $R(4, 1.5)$ in the figure at the top of the following page is the length of line segment QR. To find this distance, construct a right triangle (indicated by the dashed lines) and then note that the two shorter sides of the triangle have lengths $QS = 4 - (-2) = 6$ and $RS = 1.5 - (-3) = 4.5$.

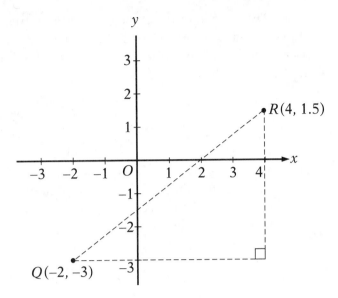

Since line segment QR is the hypotenuse of the triangle, you can apply the Pythagorean theorem:

$$QR = \sqrt{6^2 + 4.5^2} = \sqrt{56.25} = 7.5$$

(For a discussion of right triangles and the Pythagorean theorem, see section 3.3.)

Equations in two variables can be represented as graphs in the coordinate plane. In the xy-plane, the **graph of an equation** in the variables x and y is the set of all points whose ordered pairs (x, y) satisfy the equation.

The graph of a linear equation of the form $y = mx + b$ is a straight line in the xy-plane, where m is called the **slope** of the line and b is called the **y-intercept**.

The **x-intercepts** of a graph are the x-values of the points at which the graph intersects the x-axis. Similarly, the **y-intercepts** of a graph are the y-values of the points at which the graph intersects the y-axis.

The slope of a line passing through two points $Q(x_1, y_1)$ and $R(x_2, y_2)$, where $x_1 \neq x_2$, is defined as

$$\frac{y_2 - y_1}{x_2 - x_1}$$

This ratio is often called "rise over run," where *rise* is the change in y when moving from Q to R and *run* is the change in x when moving from Q to R. A horizontal line has a slope of 0, since the rise is 0 for any two points on the line. So the equation of every horizontal line has the form $y = b$, where b is the y-intercept. The slope of a vertical line is not defined, since the run is 0. The equation of every vertical line has the form $x = a$, where a is the x-intercept.

Two lines are **parallel** if their slopes are equal. Two lines are **perpendicular** if their slopes are negative reciprocals of each other. For example, the line with equation $y = 2x + 5$ is perpendicular to the line with equation $y = -\frac{1}{2}x + 9$.

Example 2.8.1: In the xy-plane above, the slope of the line passing through the points $Q(-2, -3)$ and $R(4, 1.5)$ is

$$\frac{1.5 - (-3)}{4 - (-2)} = \frac{4.5}{6} = 0.75$$

Line QR appears to intersect the y-axis close to the point $(0, -1.5)$, so the y-intercept of the line must be close to -1.5. To get the exact value of the y-intercept, substitute the coordinates of any point on the line, say $Q(-2, -3)$, into the equation $y = 0.75x + b$, and solve it for b as follows.

$$y = 0.75x + b$$
$$-3 = (0.75)(-2) + b$$
$$b = -3 + (0.75)(2)$$
$$b = -1.5$$

Therefore, the equation of line QR is $y = 0.75x - 1.5$.

You can see from the graph that the x-intercept of line QR is 2, since QR passes through the point $(2, 0)$. More generally, you can find the x-intercept by setting $y = 0$ in an equation of the line and solving it for x as follows.

$$0 = 0.75x - 1.5$$
$$1.5 = 0.75x$$
$$x = \frac{1.5}{0.75} = 2$$

Graphs of linear equations can be used to illustrate solutions of systems of linear equations and inequalities.

Example 2.8.2: Consider the system of linear equations in two variables in section 2.3:

$$4x + 3y = 13$$
$$x + 2y = 2$$

Solving each equation for y in terms of x yields

$$y = -\frac{4}{3}x + \frac{13}{3}$$
$$y = -\frac{1}{2}x + 1$$

The graphs of the two equations are below, and the solution of the system of equations is the point at which the two graphs intersect, which is $(4, -1)$.

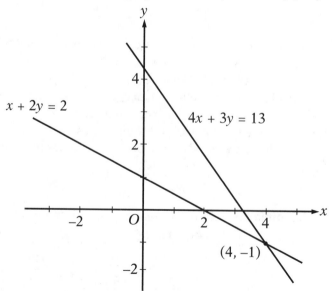

Example 2.8.3: Consider the following system of linear inequalities.

$$x - 3y \geq -6$$
$$2x + y \geq -1$$

Solving each inequality for y in terms of x yields

$$y \leq \frac{1}{3}x + 2$$
$$y \geq -2x - 1$$

Each point (x, y) that satisfies the first inequality $y \leq \frac{1}{3}x + 2$ is either on the line $y = \frac{1}{3}x + 2$ or *below* the line because the y-coordinate is either equal to or *less than* $\frac{1}{3}x + 2$. Therefore, the graph of $y \leq \frac{1}{3}x + 2$ consists of the line $y = \frac{1}{3}x + 2$ and the entire region below it. Similarly, the graph of $y \geq -2x - 1$ consists of the line $y = -2x - 1$ and the entire region *above* it. Thus, the solution set of the system of inequalities consists of all of the points that lie in the shaded region shown in the figure below, which is the intersection of the two regions described.

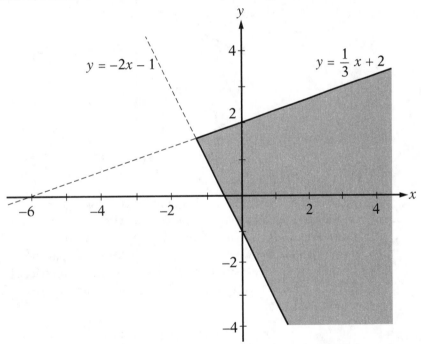

Symmetry with respect to the x-axis, the y-axis, and the origin is mentioned above. Another important symmetry is symmetry with respect to the line with equation $y = x$. The line $y = x$ passes through the origin, has a slope of 1, and makes a 45-degree angle with each axis. For any point with coordinates (a, b), the point with interchanged coordinates (b, a) is the reflection of (a, b) about the line $y = x$; that is, (a, b) and (b, a) are symmetric about the line $y = x$. It follows that interchanging x and y in the equation of any graph yields another graph that is the reflection of the original graph about the line $y = x$.

Example 2.8.4: Consider the line whose equation is $y = 2x + 5$. Interchanging x and y in the equation yields $x = 2y + 5$. Solving this equation for y yields $y = \frac{1}{2}x - \frac{5}{2}$. The line $y = 2x + 5$ and its reflection $y = \frac{1}{2}x - \frac{5}{2}$ are graphed below.

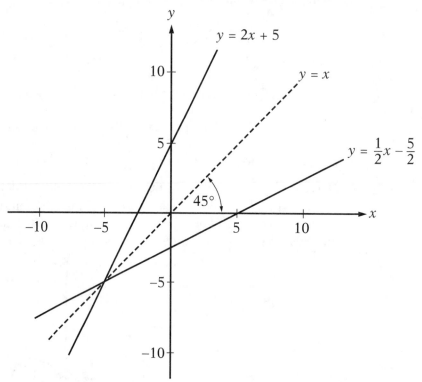

The line $y = x$ is a **line of symmetry** for the graphs of $y = 2x + 5$ and $y = \frac{1}{2}x - \frac{5}{2}$.

The graph of a quadratic equation of the form $y = ax^2 + bx + c$, where a, b, and c are constants and $a \neq 0$, is a **parabola**. The x-intercepts of the parabola are the solutions of the equation $ax^2 + bx + c = 0$. If a is positive, the parabola opens upward and the **vertex** is its lowest point. If a is negative, the parabola opens downward and the vertex is the highest point. Every parabola is symmetric with itself about the vertical line that passes through its vertex. In particular, the two x-intercepts are equidistant from this line of symmetry.

Example 2.8.5: The equation $y = x^2 - 2x - 3$ has the following graph.

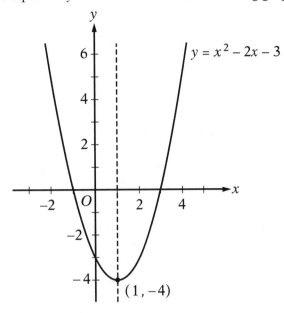

The graph indicates that the x-intercepts of the parabola are -1 and 3. The values of the x-intercepts can be confirmed by solving the quadratic equation $x^2 - 2x - 3 = 0$ to get $x = -1$ and $x = 3$. The point $(1, -4)$ is the vertex of the parabola, and the line $x = 1$ is its line of symmetry. The y-intercept is the y-coordinate of the point on the parabola at which $x = 0$, which is $y = 0^2 - 2(0) - 3 = -3$.

The graph of an equation of the form $(x - a)^2 + (y - b)^2 = r^2$ is a **circle** with its center at the point (a, b) and with radius r.

Example 2.8.6: The graph of $x^2 + y^2 = 100$ is a circle with its center at the origin and with radius 10, as shown in the figure below. The smaller circle has center $(6, -5)$ and radius 3, so its equation is $(x - 6)^2 + (y + 5)^2 = 9$.

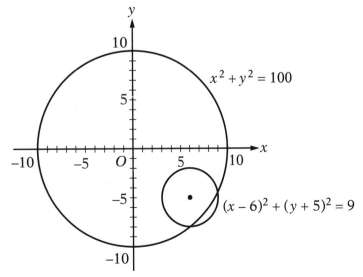

2.9 Graphs of Functions

The coordinate plane can be used for graphing functions. To graph a function in the xy-plane, you represent each input x and its corresponding output $f(x)$ as a point (x, y), where $y = f(x)$. In other words, you use the x-axis for the input and the y-axis for the output.

Below are several examples of graphs of elementary functions.

Example 2.9.1: Consider the linear function defined by $f(x) = -\frac{1}{2}x + 1$. Its graph in the xy-plane is the line with the linear equation $y = -\frac{1}{2}x + 1$, as shown in the figure below.

Example 2.9.2: Consider the quadratic function defined by $g(x) = x^2$. The graph of g is the parabola with the quadratic equation $y = x^2$, as shown in the figure below.

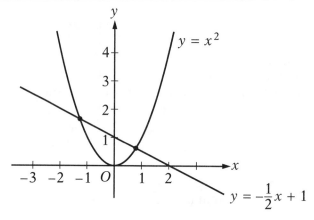

Note that the graphs of f and g from the two examples above intersect at two points. These are the points at which $g(x) = f(x)$. We can find these points algebraically by setting

$$g(x) = f(x)$$
$$x^2 = -\frac{1}{2}x + 1$$

and solving for x, using the quadratic formula, as follows.

$$x^2 = -\frac{1}{2}x + 1$$
$$x^2 + \frac{1}{2}x - 1 = 0$$
$$2x^2 + x - 2 = 0$$

We get $x = \dfrac{-1 \pm \sqrt{1 + 16}}{4}$, which represent the x-coordinates of the two solutions

$$x = \frac{-1 + \sqrt{17}}{4} \approx 0.78 \quad \text{and} \quad x = \frac{-1 - \sqrt{17}}{4} \approx -1.28$$

With these input values, the corresponding y-coordinates can be found using either f or g:

$$g\left(\frac{-1+\sqrt{17}}{4}\right) = \left(\frac{-1+\sqrt{17}}{4}\right)^2 \approx 0.61 \quad \text{and} \quad g\left(\frac{-1-\sqrt{17}}{4}\right) = \left(\frac{-1-\sqrt{17}}{4}\right)^2 \approx 1.64$$

Thus, the two intersection points can be approximated by $(0.78, 0.61)$ and $(-1.28, 1.64)$.

Example 2.9.3: Consider the absolute value function defined by $h(x) = |x|$. By using the definition of absolute value (see section 1.5), h can be expressed as a **piecewise-defined** function:

$$h(x) = \begin{cases} x, & x \geq 0 \\ -x, & x < 0 \end{cases}$$

The graph of this function is V-shaped and consists of two linear pieces, $y = x$ and $y = -x$, joined at the origin, as shown in the figure below.

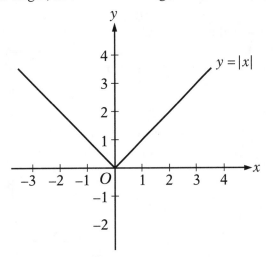

Example 2.9.4: Consider the positive square-root function defined by $j(x) = \sqrt{x}$ for $x \geq 0$, whose graph is half of a parabola lying on its side. Also consider the negative square-root function defined by $k(x) = -\sqrt{x}$ for $x \geq 0$, whose graph is the other half of the parabola lying on its side—the dashed curve below the x-axis. Both graphs are shown in the figure below, along with the parabola $y = x^2$ (with its left half dashed).

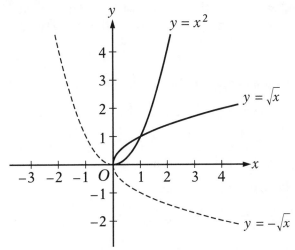

The graphs of $y = \sqrt{x}$ and $y = -\sqrt{x}$ are halves of a parabola because they are reflections of the right and left halves, respectively, of the parabola $y = x^2$ about the line $y = x$. This follows from squaring both sides of the two square root equations to get $y^2 = x$ and then interchanging x and y to get $y = x^2$.

Also note that $y = -\sqrt{x}$ is the reflection of $y = \sqrt{x}$ about the x-axis. In general, for any function h, the graph of $y = -h(x)$ is the **reflection** of the graph of $y = h(x)$ about the x-axis.

Example 2.9.5: Consider the functions defined by $f(x) = |x| + 2$ and $g(x) = (x + 1)^2$. These functions are related to the absolute value function $|x|$ and the quadratic function x^2, respectively, in simple ways.

The graph of f is the graph of $|x|$ shifted upward by 2 units, as shown in the figure below. Similarly, the graph of the function $|x| - 5$ is the graph of $|x|$ shifted downward by 5 units (not shown).

The graph of g is the graph of x^2 shifted to the left by 1 unit, as shown in the figure below. Similarly, the graph of the function $(x - 4)^2$ is the graph of x^2 shifted to the right by 4 units (not shown). To double-check the direction of the shift, you can plot some corresponding values of the original function and the shifted function.

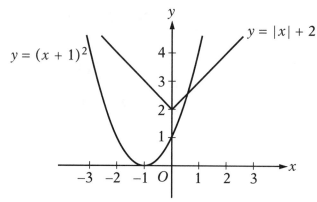

In general, for any function $h(x)$ and any positive number c, the following are true.

- The graph of $h(x) + c$ is the graph of $h(x)$ **shifted upward** by c units.
- The graph of $h(x) - c$ is the graph of $h(x)$ **shifted downward** by c units.
- The graph of $h(x + c)$ is the graph of $h(x)$ **shifted to the left** by c units.
- The graph of $h(x - c)$ is the graph of $h(x)$ **shifted to the right** by c units.

Example 2.9.6: Consider the functions defined by $f(x) = 2|x - 1|$ and $g(x) = -\dfrac{x^2}{4}$.

These functions are related to the absolute value function $|x|$ and the quadratic function x^2, respectively, in more complicated ways than in the preceding example.

The graph of f is the graph of $|x|$ shifted to the right by 1 unit and then stretched vertically away from the x-axis by a factor of 2, as shown in the figure below. Similarly, the graph of the function $\dfrac{1}{2}|x - 1|$ is the graph of $|x|$ shifted to the right by 1 unit and then shrunk vertically toward the x-axis by a factor of $\dfrac{1}{2}$ (not shown).

The graph of g is the graph of x^2 shrunk vertically by a factor of $\frac{1}{4}$ and then reflected in the x-axis, as shown in the figure below.

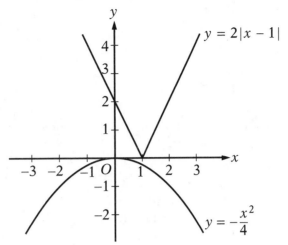

In general, for any function $h(x)$ and any positive number c, the following are true.

- The graph of $ch(x)$ is the graph of $h(x)$ **stretched vertically** by a factor of c if $c > 1$.
- The graph of $ch(x)$ is the graph of $h(x)$ **shrunk vertically** by a factor of c if $0 < c < 1$.

ALGEBRA EXERCISES

1. Find an algebraic expression to represent each of the following.
   (a) The square of y is subtracted from 5, and the result is multiplied by 37.
   (b) Three times x is squared, and the result is divided by 7.
   (c) The product of $(x + 4)$ and y is added to 18.

2. Simplify each of the following algebraic expressions.
   (a) $3x^2 - 6 + x + 11 - x^2 + 5x$
   (b) $3(5x - 1) - x + 4$
   (c) $\dfrac{x^2 - 16}{x - 4}$, where $x \neq 4$
   (d) $(2x + 5)(3x - 1)$

3. (a) What is the value of $f(x) = 3x^2 - 7x + 23$ when $x = -2$?
   (b) What is the value of $h(x) = x^3 - 2x^2 + x - 2$ when $x = 2$?
   (c) What is the value of $k(x) = \dfrac{5}{3}x - 7$ when $x = 0$?

4. If the function g is defined for all nonzero numbers y by $g(y) = \dfrac{y}{|y|}$, find the value of each of the following.
   (a) $g(2)$
   (b) $g(-2)$
   (c) $g(2) - g(-2)$

5. Use the rules of exponents to simplify the following.

   (a) $(n^5)(n^{-3})$

   (b) $(s^7)(t^7)$

   (c) $\dfrac{r^{12}}{r^4}$

   (d) $\left(\dfrac{2a}{b}\right)^5$

   (e) $(w^5)^{-3}$

   (f) $(5^0)(d^3)$

   (g) $\dfrac{(x^{10})(y^{-1})}{(x^{-5})(y^5)}$

   (h) $\left(\dfrac{3x}{y}\right)^2 \div \left(\dfrac{1}{y}\right)^5$

6. Solve each of the following equations for x.
   (a) $5x - 7 = 28$
   (b) $12 - 5x = x + 30$
   (c) $5(x + 2) = 1 - 3x$
   (d) $(x + 6)(2x - 1) = 0$
   (e) $x^2 + 5x - 14 = 0$
   (f) $x^2 - x - 1 = 0$

7. Solve each of the following systems of equations for x and y.

   (a) $\begin{array}{l} x + y = 24 \\ x - y = 18 \end{array}$

   (b) $\begin{array}{l} 3x - y = -5 \\ x + 2y = 3 \end{array}$

   (c) $\begin{array}{l} 15x - 18 - 2y = -3x + y \\ 10x + 7y + 20 = 4x + 2 \end{array}$

8. Solve each of the following inequalities for x.
   (a) $-3x > 7 + x$
   (b) $25x + 16 \geq 10 - x$
   (c) $16 + x > 8x - 12$

9. For a given two-digit positive integer, the tens digit is 5 more than the units digit. The sum of the digits is 11. Find the integer.

10. If the ratio of $2x$ to $5y$ is 3 to 4, what is the ratio of x to y?

11. Kathleen's weekly salary was increased by 8 percent to $237.60. What was her weekly salary before the increase?

12. A theater sells children's tickets for half the adult ticket price. If 5 adult tickets and 8 children's tickets cost a total of $27, what is the cost of an adult ticket?

13. Pat invested a total of $3,000. Part of the money was invested in a money market account that paid 10 percent simple annual interest, and the remainder of the money was invested in a fund that paid 8 percent simple annual interest. If the interest earned at the end of the first year from these investments was $256, how much did Pat invest at 10 percent and how much at 8 percent?

14. Two cars started from the same point and traveled on a straight course in opposite directions for exactly 2 hours, at which time they were 208 miles apart. If one car traveled, on average, 8 miles per hour faster than the other car, what was the average speed of each car for the 2-hour trip?

15. A group can charter a particular aircraft at a fixed total cost. If 36 people charter the aircraft rather than 40 people, then the cost per person is greater by $12.
    (a) What is the fixed total cost to charter the aircraft?
    (b) What is the cost per person if 40 people charter the aircraft?

16. An antiques dealer bought c antique chairs for a total of x dollars. The dealer sold each chair for y dollars.
    (a) Write an algebraic expression for the profit, P, earned from buying and selling the chairs.
    (b) Write an algebraic expression for the profit <u>per chair</u>.

17. In the coordinate system below, find the following.
    (a) Coordinates of point Q
    (b) Lengths of PQ, QR, and PR
    (c) Perimeter of $\triangle PQR$
    (d) Area of $\triangle PQR$
    (e) Slope, y-intercept, and equation of the line passing through points P and R

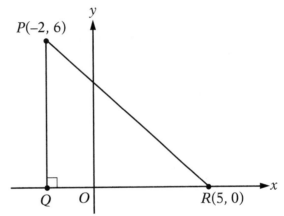

18. In the xy-plane, find the following.
    (a) Slope and y-intercept of the line with equation $2y + x = 6$
    (b) Equation of the line passing through the point $(3, 2)$ with y-intercept 1
    (c) The y-intercept of a line with slope 3 that passes through the point $(-2, 1)$
    (d) The x-intercepts of the graphs in (a), (b), and (c)

19. For the parabola $y = x^2 - 4x - 12$ in the xy-plane, find the following.
    (a) The x-intercepts
    (b) The y-intercept
    (c) Coordinates of the vertex

20. For the circle $(x - 1)^2 + (y + 1)^2 = 20$ in the xy-plane, find the following.
    (a) Coordinates of the center
    (b) Radius
    (c) Area

21. For each of the following functions, give the domain and a description of the graph $y = f(x)$ in the xy-plane, including its shape, and the x- and y-intercepts.
    (a) $f(x) = -4$
    (b) $f(x) = 100 - 900x$
    (c) $f(x) = 5 - (x + 20)^2$
    (d) $f(x) = \sqrt{x + 2}$
    (e) $f(x) = x + |x|$

ANSWERS TO ALGEBRA EXERCISES

1. (a) $37(5 - y)^2$, or $185 - 37y^2$
    (b) $\dfrac{(3x)^2}{7}$, or $\dfrac{9x^2}{7}$
    (c) $18 + (x + 4)(y)$, or $18 + xy + 4y$

2. (a) $2x^2 + 6x + 5$ (c) $x + 4$
    (b) $14x + 1$ (d) $6x^2 + 13x - 5$

3. (a) 49   (b) 0   (c) -7

4. (a) 1   (b) -1 (c) 2

5. (a) n^2 (e) $\dfrac{1}{w^{15}}$
    (b) $(st)^7$ (f) d^3
    (c) r^8 (g) $\dfrac{x^{15}}{y^6}$
    (d) $\dfrac{32a^5}{b^5}$ (h) $9x^2y^3$

6. (a) 7   (d) $-6, \dfrac{1}{2}$
    (b) -3 (e) $-7, 2$
    (c) $-\dfrac{9}{8}$ (f) $\dfrac{1 + \sqrt{5}}{2}, \dfrac{1 - \sqrt{5}}{2}$

7. (a) $\begin{matrix} x = 21 \\ y = 3 \end{matrix}$ (b) $\begin{matrix} x = -1 \\ y = 2 \end{matrix}$ (c) $\begin{matrix} x = \dfrac{1}{2} \\ y = -3 \end{matrix}$

8. (a) $x < -\dfrac{7}{4}$
    (b) $x \geq -\dfrac{3}{13}$
    (c) $x < 4$

9. 83

10. 15 to 8

11. $220

12. $3

13. $800 at 10% and $2,200 at 8%

14. 48 mph and 56 mph

15. (a) $4,320   (b) $108

16. (a) $P = cy - x$ (b) Profit per chair: $\dfrac{P}{c} = \dfrac{cy - x}{c} = y - \dfrac{x}{c}$

17. (a) $(-2, 0)$
    (b) $PQ = 6$, $QR = 7$, $PR = \sqrt{85}$
    (c) $13 + \sqrt{85}$
    (d) 21
    (e) Slope: $-\dfrac{6}{7}$; y-intercept: $\dfrac{30}{7}$; equation of line: $y = -\dfrac{6}{7}x + \dfrac{30}{7}$, or
       $7y + 6x = 30$

18. (a) Slope: $-\dfrac{1}{2}$; y-intercept: 3
    (b) $y = \dfrac{x}{3} + 1$
    (c) 7
    (d) $6, -3, -\dfrac{7}{3}$

19. (a) $x = -2$ and $x = 6$
    (b) $y = -12$
    (c) $(2, -16)$

20. (a) $(1, -1)$
    (b) $\sqrt{20}$
    (c) 20π

21. (a) Domain: the set of all real numbers. The graph is a horizontal line with y-intercept -4 and no x-intercept.
    (b) Domain: the set of all real numbers. The graph is a line with slope -900, y-intercept 100, and x-intercept $\dfrac{1}{9}$.
    (c) Domain: the set of all real numbers. The graph is a parabola opening downward with vertex at $(-20, 5)$, line of symmetry $x = -20$, y-intercept -395, and x-intercepts $-20 \pm \sqrt{5}$.
    (d) Domain: the set of numbers greater than or equal to -2. The graph is half a parabola opening to the right with vertex at $(-2, 0)$, x-intercept -2, and y-intercept $\sqrt{2}$.
    (e) Domain: the set of all real numbers. The graph is two half-lines joined at the origin: one half-line is the negative x-axis and the other is a line starting at the origin with slope 2. Every nonpositive number is an x-intercept, and the y-intercept is 0. The function is equal to the following piecewise-defined function

$$f(x) = \begin{cases} 2x, & x \geq 0 \\ 0, & x < 0 \end{cases}$$

3. GEOMETRY

The review of geometry begins with lines and angles and progresses to other plane figures, such as polygons, triangles, quadrilaterals, and circles. The section ends with some basic three-dimensional figures. Coordinate geometry is covered in the Algebra section

3.1 Lines and Angles

Plane geometry is devoted primarily to the properties and relations of plane figures, such as angles, triangles, other polygons, and circles. The terms "point," "line," and "plane" are familiar intuitive concepts. A **point** has no size and is the simplest geometric figure. All geometric figures consist of points. A **line** is understood to be a straight line that extends in both directions without ending. A **plane** can be thought of as a floor or a tabletop, except that a plane extends in all directions without ending and has no thickness

Given any two points on a line, a **line segment** is the part of the line that contains the two points and all the points between them. The two points are called **endpoints**. Line segments that have equal lengths are called **congruent line segments**. The point that divides a line segment into two congruent line segments is called the **midpoint** of the line segment.

In the figure below, A, B, C, and D are points on line ℓ.

Line segment AB consists of points A and B and all the points on the line between A and B. Sometimes the notation AB denotes line segment AB, and sometimes it denotes the **length** of line segment AB. The meaning of the notation can be determined from the context. According to the figure above, the lengths of line segments AB, BC, and CD are 8, 6, and 6, respectively. Hence, line segments BC and CD are congruent. Since C is halfway between B and D, point C is the midpoint of line segment BD.

When two lines intersect at a point, they form four **angles**, as indicated below. Each angle has a **vertex** at point P, which is the point of intersection of the two lines.

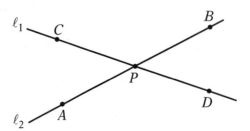

In the figure, angles APC and BPD are called **opposite angles**, also known as **vertical angles**. Angles APD and CPB are also opposite angles. Opposite angles have equal measures, and angles that have equal measures are called **congruent angles**. Hence, opposite angles are congruent. The sum of the measures of the four angles is 360°.

Sometimes the angle symbol ∠ is used instead of the word "angle." For example, angle APC can be written as ∠APC.

Two lines that intersect to form four congruent angles are called **perpendicular lines**. Each of the four angles has a measure of 90°. An angle with a measure of 90° is called a **right angle**. The figure below shows two lines, ℓ_1 and ℓ_2, that are perpendicular, denoted by $\ell_1 \perp \ell_2$.

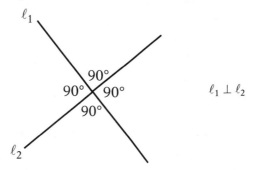

$\ell_1 \perp \ell_2$

A common way to indicate that an angle is a right angle is to draw a small square at the vertex of the angle, as shown below, where *PON* is a right angle

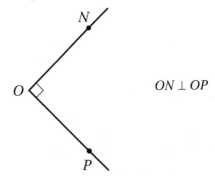

$ON \perp OP$

An angle with a measure less than 90° is called an **acute angle**, and an angle with measure between 90° and 180° is called an **obtuse angle**.

Two lines in the same plane that do not intersect are called **parallel lines**. The figure below shows two lines, ℓ_1 and ℓ_2, that are parallel, denoted by $\ell_1 \| \ell_2$. The two lines are intersected by a third line, ℓ_3, forming eight angles. Note that four of the angles have the measure $x°$, and the remaining four angles have the measure $y°$, where $x + y = 180$.

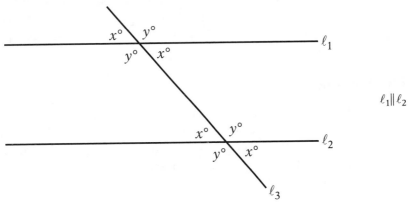

$\ell_1 \| \ell_2$

3.2 Polygons

A **polygon** is a closed figure formed by three or more line segments, called **sides**. Each side is joined to two other sides at its endpoints, and the endpoints are called **vertices**. In this discussion, the term "polygon" means "convex polygon," that is, a polygon in which the measure of each interior angle is less than 180°. The figures below are examples of such polygons.

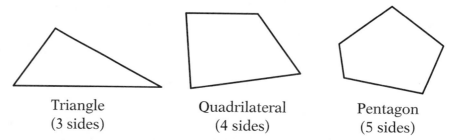

Triangle   Quadrilateral   Pentagon
(3 sides)   (4 sides)   (5 sides)

The simplest polygon is a **triangle**. Note that a **quadrilateral** can be divided into 2 triangles, and a **pentagon** can be divided into 3 triangles, as shown below.

If a polygon has n sides, it can be divided into $n - 2$ triangles. Since the sum of the measures of the interior angles of a triangle is 180°, it follows that the sum of the measures of the interior angles of an n-sided polygon is $(n - 2)(180°)$. For example, the sum for a quadrilateral ($n = 4$) is $(4 - 2)(180°) = 360°$, and the sum for a **hexagon** ($n = 6$) is $(6 - 2)(180°) = 720°$.

A polygon in which all sides are congruent and all interior angles are congruent is called a **regular polygon**. For example, in a **regular octagon** (8 sides), the sum of the measures of the interior angles is $(8 - 2)(180°) = 1,080°$. Therefore, the measure of each angle is $\frac{1,080°}{8} = 135°$.

The **perimeter** of a polygon is the sum of the lengths of its sides. The **area** of a polygon refers to the area of the region enclosed by the polygon.

In the next two sections, we will look at some basic properties of triangles and quadrilaterals.

3.3 Triangles

Every triangle has three sides and three interior angles. The measures of the interior angles add up to 180°. The length of each side must be less than the sum of the lengths of the other two sides. For example, the sides of a triangle could not have the lengths 4, 7, and 12 because 12 is greater than 4 + 7.

The following are special triangles.

- A triangle with three congruent sides is called an **equilateral triangle**. The measures of the three interior angles of such a triangle are also equal, and each measure is 60°.
- A triangle with at least two congruent sides is called an **isosceles triangle**. If a triangle has two congruent sides, then the angles opposite the two sides are

congruent. The converse is also true. For example, in $\triangle ABC$ below, since both $\angle A$ and $\angle C$ have measure $50°$, it follows that $AB = BC$. Also, since $50 + 50 + x = 180$, the measure of $\angle B$ is $80°$.

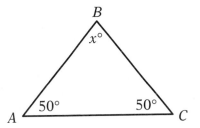

- A triangle with an interior right angle is called a **right triangle**. The side opposite the right angle is called the **hypotenuse**; the other two sides are called **legs**.

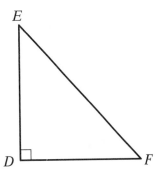

In right triangle DEF above, EF is the hypotenuse and DE and DF are legs. The **Pythagorean theorem** states that in a right triangle, the square of the length of the hypotenuse is equal to the sum of the squares of the lengths of the legs. Thus, for triangle DEF above,

$$(EF)^2 = (DE)^2 + (DF)^2$$

This relationship can be used to find the length of one side of a right triangle if the lengths of the other two sides are known. For example, if one leg of a right triangle has length 5 and the hypotenuse has length 8, then the length of the other side can be determined as follows.

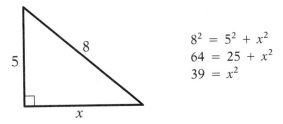

$$8^2 = 5^2 + x^2$$
$$64 = 25 + x^2$$
$$39 = x^2$$

Since $x^2 = 39$ and x must be positive, it follows that $x = \sqrt{39}$, or approximately 6.2.

The Pythagorean theorem can be used to determine the ratios of the sides of two special right triangles. One special right triangle is an isosceles right triangle. Applying the Pythagorean theorem to such a triangle shows that the lengths of its sides are in the ratio 1 to 1 to $\sqrt{2}$, as indicated below.

$$y^2 = x^2 + x^2$$
$$y^2 = 2x^2$$
$$y = \sqrt{2}x$$

The other special right triangle is a 30°- 60°- 90° right triangle, which is half of an equilateral triangle, as indicated below.

Note that the length of the shortest side, x, is one-half the length of the longest side, $2x$. By the Pythagorean theorem, the ratio of x to y is 1 to $\sqrt{3}$ because

$$x^2 + y^2 = (2x)^2$$
$$x^2 + y^2 = 4x^2$$
$$y^2 = 4x^2 - x^2$$
$$y^2 = 3x^2$$
$$y = \sqrt{3}x$$

Hence, the ratio of the lengths of the three sides of such a triangle is 1 to $\sqrt{3}$ to 2.

The **area** A of a triangle equals one-half the product of the length of a base and the height corresponding to the base. In the figure below, the base is denoted by b and the corresponding height is denoted by h.

$$A = \frac{bh}{2}$$

Any side of a triangle can be used as a base; the height that corresponds to the base is the perpendicular line segment from the opposite vertex to the base (or to an extension of the base). The examples below show three different configurations of a base and the corresponding height.

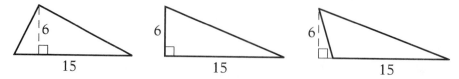

In all three triangles above, the area is $\dfrac{(15)(6)}{2}$, or 45.

Two triangles that have the same shape and size are called **congruent triangles**. More precisely, two triangles are congruent if their vertices can be matched up so that the corresponding angles and the corresponding sides are congruent.

The following three propositions can be used to determine whether two triangles are congruent by comparing only some of their sides and angles.

- If the three sides of one triangle are congruent to the three sides of another triangle, then the triangles are congruent.
- If two sides and the included angle of one triangle are congruent to two sides and the included angle of another triangle, then the triangles are congruent.
- If two angles and the included side of one triangle are congruent to two angles and the included side of another triangle, then the triangles are congruent.

Two triangles that have the same shape but not necessarily the same size are called **similar triangles**. More precisely, two triangles are similar if their vertices can be matched up so that the corresponding angles are congruent or, equivalently, the lengths of corresponding sides have the same ratio, called the scale factor of similarity. For example, all 30°- 60°- 90° right triangles, discussed above, are similar triangles, though they may differ in size.

When we say that triangles ABC and DEF are similar, it is assumed that angles A and D are congruent, angles B and E are congruent, and angles C and F are congruent, as shown in the figure below. In other words, the order of the letters indicates the correspondences.

Since triangles ABC and DEF are similar, we have $\dfrac{AB}{DE} = \dfrac{BC}{EF} = \dfrac{AC}{DF}$. By cross multiplication, we can obtain other proportions, such as $\dfrac{AB}{BC} = \dfrac{DE}{EF}$.

3.4 Quadrilaterals

Every quadrilateral has four sides and four interior angles. The measures of the interior angles add up to 360°. The following are special quadrilaterals.

- A quadrilateral with four right angles is called a **rectangle**. Opposite sides of a rectangle are parallel and congruent, and the two diagonals are also congruent.

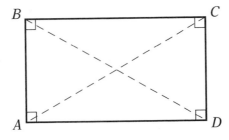

$$AB \| CD \text{ and } AD \| BC$$
$$AB = CD \text{ and } AD = BC$$
$$AC = BD$$

- A rectangle with four congruent sides is called a **square**.

- A quadrilateral in which both pairs of opposite sides are parallel is called a **parallelogram**. In a parallelogram, opposite sides are congruent and opposite angles are congruent.

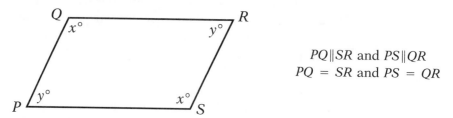

$$PQ\|SR \text{ and } PS\|QR$$
$$PQ = SR \text{ and } PS = QR$$

- A quadrilateral in which two opposite sides are parallel is called a **trapezoid**.

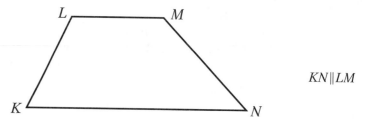

$$KN\|LM$$

For all parallelograms, including rectangles and squares, the **area** A equals the product of the length of a base b and the corresponding height h; that is,

$$A = bh$$

Any side can be used as a base. The height corresponding to the base is the perpendicular line segment from any point of a base to the opposite side (or an extension of that side). Below are examples of finding the areas of a rectangle and a parallelogram.

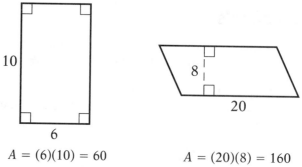

$$A = (6)(10) = 60 \qquad A = (20)(8) = 160$$

The **area** A of a trapezoid equals half the product of the sum of the lengths of the two parallel sides b_1 and b_2 and the corresponding height h; that is,

$$A = \frac{1}{2}(b_1 + b_2)(h)$$

For example, for the trapezoid below with bases of length 10 and 18 and a height of 7.5, the area is

$$A = \frac{1}{2}(10 + 18)(7.5) = 105$$

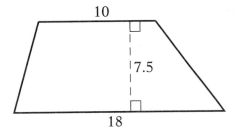

3.5 Circles

Given a point O in a plane and a positive number r, the set of points in the plane that are a distance of r units from O is called a **circle**. The point O is called the **center** of the circle and the distance r is called the **radius** of the circle. The **diameter** of the circle is twice the radius. Two circles with equal radii are called **congruent circles**.

Any line segment joining two points on the circle is called a **chord**. The terms "radius" and "diameter" can also refer to line segments: A **radius** is any line segment joining a point on the circle and the center of the circle, and a **diameter** is a chord that passes through the center of the circle. In the figure below, O is the center of the circle, r is the radius, PQ is a chord, and ST is a diameter.

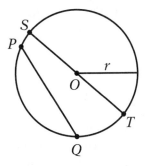

The distance around a circle is called the **circumference** of the circle, which is analogous to the perimeter of a polygon. The ratio of the circumference C to the diameter d is the same for all circles and is denoted by the Greek letter π; that is,

$$\frac{C}{d} = \pi$$

The value of π is approximately 3.14 and can also be approximated by the fraction $\frac{22}{7}$.

If r is the radius of a circle, then $\frac{C}{d} = \frac{C}{2r} = \pi$, and so the circumference is related to the radius as follows.

$$C = 2\pi r$$

For example, if a circle has a radius of 5.2, then its circumference is

$$(2)(\pi)(5.2) = (10.4)(\pi) \approx (10.4)(3.14)$$

which is approximately 32.7.

Given any two points on a circle, an **arc** is the part of the circle containing the two points and all the points between them. Two points on a circle are always the endpoints of two arcs. It is customary to identify an arc by three points to avoid ambiguity. In the figure below, arc ABC is the shorter arc between A and C, and arc ADC is the longer arc between A and C.

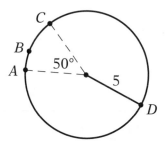

A **central angle** of a circle is an angle with its vertex at the center of the circle. The **measure of an arc** is the measure of its central angle, which is the angle formed by two radii that connect the center of the circle to the two endpoints of the arc. An entire circle is considered to be an arc with measure 360°. In the figure above, the measure of arc ABC is 50° and the measure of arc ADC is 310°.

To find the **length of an arc** of a circle, note that the ratio of the length of an arc to the circumference is equal to the ratio of the degree measure of the arc to 360°. The circumference of the circle above is 10π. Therefore,

$$\frac{\text{length of arc } ABC}{10\pi} = \frac{50}{360}$$

$$\text{length of arc } ABC = \left(\frac{50}{360}\right)(10\pi) = \frac{25\pi}{18} \approx \frac{(25)(3.14)}{18} \approx 4.4$$

The **area** of a circle with radius r is equal to πr^2. For example, the area of the circle above with radius 5 is $\pi(5)^2 = 25\pi$.

A **sector** of a circle is a region bounded by an arc of the circle and two radii. In the circle above, the region bounded by arc ABC and the two dashed radii is a sector with central angle 50°. Just as in the case of the length of an arc, the ratio of the area of a sector of a circle to the area of the entire circle is equal to the ratio of the degree measure of its arc to 360°. Therefore, if S represents the area of the sector with central angle 50°, then

$$\frac{S}{25\pi} = \frac{50}{360}$$

$$S = \left(\frac{50}{360}\right)(25\pi) = \frac{125\pi}{36} \approx \frac{(125)(3.14)}{36} \approx 10.9$$

A **tangent** to a circle is a line that intersects the circle at exactly one point, called the **point of tangency**, denoted by P in the figure at the top of the following page. If a line is tangent to a circle, then a radius drawn to the point of tangency is perpendicular to the tangent line. The converse is also true; that is, if a line is perpendicular to a radius at its endpoint on the circle, then the line is a tangent to the circle at that endpoint.

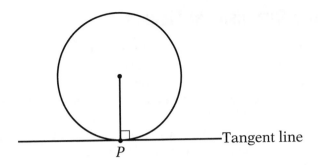

Tangent line

A polygon is **inscribed** in a circle if all its vertices lie on the circle, or equivalently, the circle is **circumscribed** about the polygon. Triangles *RST* and *XYZ* below are inscribed in the circles with centers *O* and *W*, respectively.

 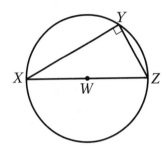

If one side of an inscribed triangle is a diameter of the circle, as in triangle *XYZ* above, then the triangle is a right triangle. Conversely, if an inscribed triangle is a right triangle, then one of its sides is a diameter of the circle.

A polygon is circumscribed about a circle if each side of the polygon is tangent to the circle, or equivalently, the circle is inscribed in the polygon. In the figure below, quadrilateral *ABCD* is circumscribed about the circle with center *O*.

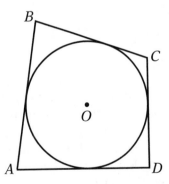

Two or more circles with the same center are called **concentric circles**, as shown in the figure below.

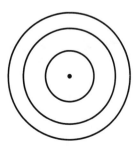

3.6 Three-Dimensional Figures

Basic three-dimensional figures include rectangular solids, cubes, cylinders, spheres, pyramids, and cones. In this section, we look at some properties of rectangular solids and right circular cylinders.

A **rectangular solid** has six rectangular surfaces called **faces**, as shown in the figure below. Adjacent faces are perpendicular to each other. Each line segment that is the intersection of two faces is called an **edge**, and each point at which the edges intersect is called a **vertex**. There are 12 edges and 8 vertices. The dimensions of a rectangular solid are the length ℓ, the width w, and the height h.

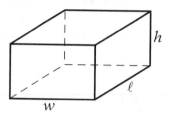

A rectangular solid with six square faces is called a **cube**, in which case $\ell = w = h$. The **volume** V of a rectangular solid is the product of its three dimensions, or

$$V = \ell wh$$

The **surface area** A of a rectangular solid is the sum of the areas of the six faces, or

$$A = 2(\ell w + \ell h + wh)$$

For example, if a rectangular solid has length 8.5, width 5, and height 10, then its volume is

$$V = (8.5)(5)(10) = 425$$

and its surface area is

$$A = 2((8.5)(5) + (8.5)(10) + (5)(10)) = 355$$

A **circular cylinder** consists of two bases that are congruent circles and a **lateral surface** made of all line segments that join points on the two circles and that are parallel to the line segment joining the centers of the two circles. The latter line segment is called the **axis** of the cylinder. A **right circular cylinder** is a circular cylinder whose axis is perpendicular to its bases.

The right circular cylinder shown in the figure below has circular bases with centers P and Q. Line segment PQ is the axis of the cylinder and is perpendicular to both bases. The length of PQ is called the height of the cylinder.

The **volume** V of a right circular cylinder that has height h and a base with radius r is the product of the height and the area of the base, or

$$V = \pi r^2 h$$

The **surface area** A of a right circular cylinder is the sum of the areas of the two bases and the lateral area, or

$$A = 2(\pi r^2) + 2\pi rh$$

For example, if a right circular cylinder has height 6.5 and a base with radius 3, then its volume is

$$V = \pi(3)^2(6.5) = 58.5\pi$$

and its surface area is

$$A = (2)(\pi)(3)^2 + (2)(\pi)(3)(6.5) = 57\pi$$

GEOMETRY EXERCISES

1. Lines ℓ and m below are parallel. Find the values of x and y.

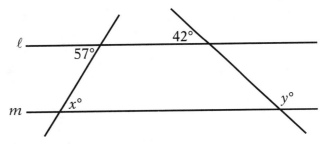

2. In the figure below, $AC = BC$. Find the values of x and y.

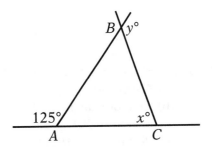

3. In the figure below, what is the relationship between x, y, and z?

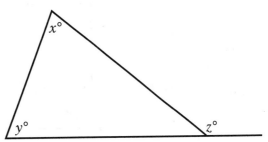

4. What is the sum of the measures of the interior angles of a decagon (10-sided polygon)?

5. If the polygon in question 4 is regular, what is the measure of each interior angle?

6. The lengths of two sides of an isosceles triangle are 15 and 22, respectively. What are the possible values of the perimeter?

7. Triangles *PQR* and *XYZ* are similar. If *PQ* = 6, *PR* = 4, and *XY* = 9, what is the length of side *XZ*?

8. What are the lengths of sides *NO* and *OP* in triangle *NOP* below?

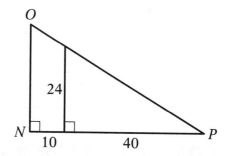

9. In the figure below, *AB* = *BC* = *CD*. If the area of triangle *CDE* is 42, what is the area of triangle *ADG*?

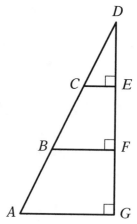

10. In rectangle *ABCD* below, *AB* = 5, *AF* = 7, and *FD* = 3. Find the following.
    (a) Area of *ABCD*
    (b) Area of triangle *AEF*
    (c) Length of *BD*
    (d) Perimeter of *ABCD*

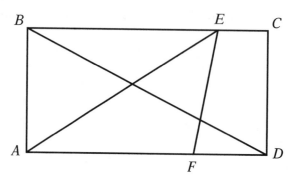

11. In parallelogram *ABCD* below, find the following.
     (a) Area of *ABCD*
     (b) Perimeter of *ABCD*
     (c) Length of diagonal *BD*

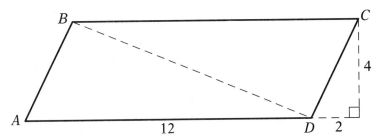

12. The circle with center *O* below has radius 4. Find the following.
     (a) Circumference of the circle
     (b) Length of arc *ABC*
     (c) Area of the shaded region

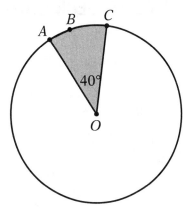

13. The figure below shows two concentric circles, each with center *O*. Given that the larger circle has radius 12 and the smaller circle has radius 7, find the following.
     (a) Circumference of the larger circle
     (b) Area of the smaller circle
     (c) Area of the shaded region

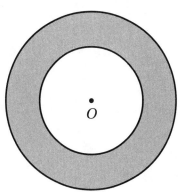

14. For the rectangular solid below, find the following.
    (a) Surface area of the solid
    (b) Length of diagonal *AB*

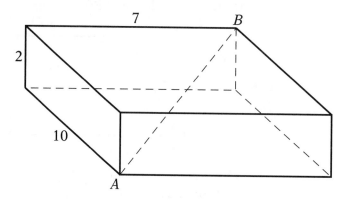

ANSWERS TO GEOMETRY EXERCISES

1. $x = 57$ and $y = 138$

2. $x = 70$ and $y = 125$

3. $z = x + y$

4. $1,440°$

5. $144°$

6. 52 and 59

7. 6

8. $NO = 30$ and $OP = 10\sqrt{34}$

9. 378

10. (a) 50
    (b) 17.5
    (c) $5\sqrt{5}$
    (d) 30

11. (a) 48
    (b) $24 + 4\sqrt{5}$
    (c) $2\sqrt{29}$

12. (a) 8π
    (b) $\dfrac{8\pi}{9}$
    (c) $\dfrac{16\pi}{9}$

13. (a) 24π
    (b) 49π
    (c) 95π

14. (a) 208
    (b) $3\sqrt{17}$

4. DATA ANALYSIS

The goal of data analysis is to understand data well enough to describe past and present trends, predict future events, and make good decisions. In this limited review of data analysis, we begin with tools for describing data; follow with tools for understanding counting and probability; review the concepts of distributions of data, random variables, and probability distributions; and end with examples of interpreting data.

4.1 Graphical Methods for Describing Data

Data can be organized and summarized using a variety of methods. Tables are commonly used, and there are many graphical and numerical methods as well. The appropriate type of representation for a collection of data depends in part on the nature of the data, such as whether the data are numerical or nonnumerical. In this section, we review some common graphical methods for describing and summarizing data.

Variables play a major role in algebra because a variable serves as a convenient name for many values at once, and it also can represent a particular value in a given problem to solve. In data analysis, variables also play an important role but with a somewhat different meaning. In data analysis, a **variable** is any characteristic that can vary for the population of individuals or objects being analyzed. For example, both gender and age represent variables among people.

Data are collected from a population after observing either a single variable or observing more than one variable simultaneously. The distribution of a variable, or **distribution of data**, indicates the values of the variable and how frequently the values are observed in the data.

Frequency Distributions

The **frequency**, or **count**, of a particular category or numerical value is the number of times that the category or value appears in the data. A **frequency distribution** is a table or graph that presents the categories or numerical values along with their associated frequencies. The **relative frequency** of a category or a numerical value is the associated frequency divided by the total number of data. Relative frequencies may be expressed in terms of percents, fractions, or decimals. A **relative frequency distribution** is a table or graph that presents the relative frequencies of the categories or numerical values.

Example 4.1.1: A survey was taken to find the number of children in each of 25 families. A list of the values collected in the survey follows.

1 2 0 4 1 3 3 1 2 0 4 5 2 3 2 3 2 4 1 2 3 0 2 3 1

Here are the resulting frequency and relative frequency distributions of the data.

Frequency Distribution

Number of Children	Frequency
0	3
1	5
2	7
3	6
4	3
5	1
Total	25

Relative Frequency Distribution

Number of Children	Relative Frequency
0	12%
1	20%
2	28%
3	24%
4	12%
5	4%
Total	100%

Note that the total for the relative frequencies is 100%. If decimals were used instead of percents, the total would be 1. The sum of the relative frequencies in a relative frequency distribution is always 1.

Bar Graphs

A commonly used graphical display for representing frequencies, or counts, is a **bar graph**, or bar chart. In a bar graph, rectangular bars are used to represent the categories of the data, and the height of each bar is proportional to the corresponding frequency or relative frequency. All of the bars are drawn with the same width, and the bars can be presented either vertically or horizontally. Bar graphs enable comparisons across several categories, making it easy to identify frequently and infrequently occurring categories.

Example 4.1.2:

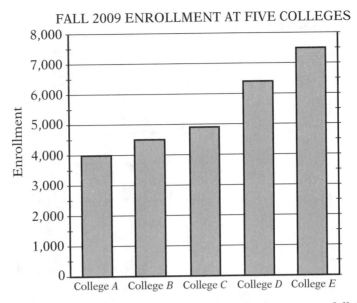

FALL 2009 ENROLLMENT AT FIVE COLLEGES

From the graph, we can conclude that the college with the greatest fall 2009 enrollment was College *E*, and the college with the least enrollment was College *A*. Also, we can estimate that the enrollment for College *D* was about 6,400.

A **segmented bar graph** is used to show how different subgroups or subcategories contribute to an entire group or category. In a segmented bar graph, each bar represents a category that consists of more than one subcategory. Each bar is divided into segments that represent the different subcategories. The height of each segment is proportional to the frequency or relative frequency of the subcategory that the segment represents.

Example 4.1.3:

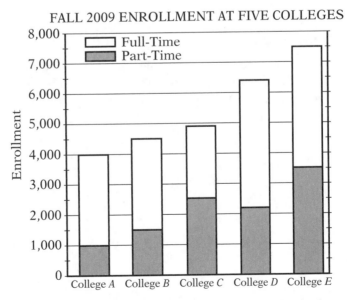

FALL 2009 ENROLLMENT AT FIVE COLLEGES

Different values can be estimated from the segmented bar graph above. For example, for College *D*, the total enrollment was approximately 6,400 students, the part-time enrollment was approximately 2,200, and the full-time enrollment was approximately 6,400 − 2,200, or 4,200 students.

Bar graphs can also be used to compare different groups using the same categories.

Example 4.1.4:

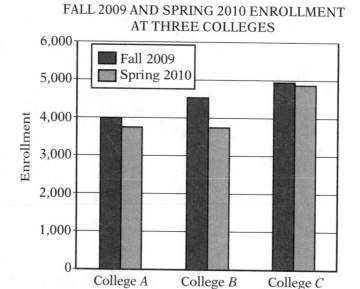

FALL 2009 AND SPRING 2010 ENROLLMENT
AT THREE COLLEGES

Observe that for all three colleges, the fall 2009 enrollment was greater than the spring 2010 enrollment. Also, the greatest decrease in the enrollment from fall 2009 to spring 2010 occurred at College *B*.

Although bar graphs are commonly used to compare frequencies, as in the examples above, they are sometimes used to compare numerical data that could be displayed in a table, such as temperatures, dollar amounts, percents, heights, and weights. Also, the categories sometimes are numerical in nature, such as years or other time intervals.

Circle Graphs

Circle graphs, often called pie charts, are used to represent data with a relatively small number of categories. They illustrate how a whole is separated into parts. The area of the circle graph representing each category is proportional to the part of the whole that the category represents.

Example 4.1.5:

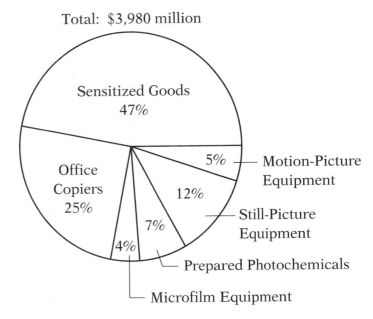

UNITED STATES PRODUCTION OF PHOTOGRAPHIC
EQUIPMENT AND SUPPLIES IN 1971

Total: $3,980 million

The graph shows that of all United States production of photographic equipment and supplies in 1971, Sensitized Goods was the category with the greatest dollar value.

Each part of a circle graph is called a **sector**. Because the area of each sector is proportional to the percent of the whole that the sector represents, the measure of the central angle of a sector is proportional to the percent of 360 degrees that the sector represents. For example, the measure of the central angle of the sector representing the category Prepared Photochemicals is 7 percent of 360 degrees, or 25.2 degrees.

Histograms

When a list of data is large and contains many different values of a numerical variable, it is useful to organize it by grouping the values into intervals, often called classes. To do this, divide the entire interval of values into smaller intervals of equal length and then count the values that fall into each interval. In this way, each interval has a frequency and a relative frequency. The intervals and their frequencies (or relative frequencies) are often displayed in a **histogram**. Histograms are graphs of frequency distributions that are similar to bar graphs, but they have a number line for the horizontal axis. Also, in a histogram, there are no regular spaces between the bars. Any spaces between bars in a histogram indicate that there are no data in the intervals represented by the spaces.

Example 4.5.1 in section 4.5 illustrates a histogram with 50 bars. Numerical variables with just a few values can also be displayed using histograms, where the frequency or relative frequency of each value is represented by a bar centered over the value, as in the histogram in the following example.

Example 4.1.6: The relative frequency distribution in example 4.1.1 can be displayed as a histogram.

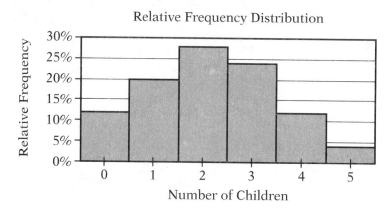

Histograms are useful for identifying the general shape of a distribution of data. Also evident are the "center" and degree of "spread" of the distribution, as well as high-frequency and low-frequency intervals. From the histogram above, you can see that the distribution is shaped like a mound with one peak; that is, the data are frequent in the middle and sparse at both ends. The central values are 2 and 3, and the distribution is close to being symmetric about those values. Because the bars all have the same width, the area of each bar is proportional to the amount of data that the bar represents. Thus, the areas of the bars indicate where the data are concentrated and where they are not.

Finally, note that because each bar has a width of 1, the sum of the areas of the bars equals the sum of the relative frequencies, which is 100% or 1, depending on whether percents or decimals are used. This fact is central to the discussion of probability distributions in section 4.5.

Scatterplots

All examples used thus far have involved data resulting from a single characteristic or variable. These types of data are referred to as **univariate**; that is, data observed for one variable. Sometimes data are collected to study two different variables in the same population of individuals or objects. Such data are called **bivariate** data. We might want to study the variables separately or investigate a relationship between the two variables. If the variables were to be analyzed separately, each of the graphical methods for univariate numerical data presented above could be applied.

To show the relationship between two numerical variables, the most useful type of graph is a **scatterplot**. In a scatterplot, the values of one variable appear on the horizontal axis of a rectangular coordinate system and the values of the other variable appear on the vertical axis. For each individual or object in the data, an ordered pair of numbers is collected, one number for each variable, and the pair is represented by a point in the coordinate system.

A scatterplot makes it possible to observe an overall pattern, or **trend**, in the relationship between the two variables. Also, the strength of the trend as well as striking deviations from the trend are evident. In many cases, a line or a curve that best represents the trend is also displayed in the graph and is used to make predictions about the population.

Example 4.1.7: A bicycle trainer studied 50 bicyclists to examine how the finishing time for a certain bicycle race was related to the amount of physical training in the three months before the race. To measure the amount of training, the trainer developed a training index, measured in "units" and based on the intensity of each bicyclist's training. The data and the trend of the data, represented by a line, are displayed in the scatterplot below.

In addition to the given trend line, you can see how scattered or close the data are to the trend line; or to put it another way, you can see how well the trend line fits the data. You can also see that the finishing times generally decrease as the training indices increase and that three or four data are relatively far from the trend.

Several types of predictions can be based on the trend line. For example, it can be predicted, based on the trend line, that a bicyclist with a training index of 70 units would finish the race in approximately 4 hours. This value is obtained by noting that the vertical line at the training index of 70 units intersects the trend line very close to 4 hours.

Another prediction based on the trend line is the number of minutes that a bicyclist can expect to lower his or her finishing time for each increase of 10 training index units. This prediction is basically the ratio of the change in finishing time to the change in training index, or the slope of the trend line. Note that the slope is negative. To estimate the slope, estimate the coordinates of any two points on the line—for instance, the points at the extreme left and right ends of the line: $(0, 5.8)$ and $(100, 3.2)$. The slope is

$$\frac{3.2 - 5.8}{100 - 0} = \frac{-2.6}{100} = -0.026$$

which is measured in hours per unit. The slope can be interpreted as follows: the finishing time is predicted to decrease 0.026 hours for every unit by which the training index increases. Since we want to know how much the finishing time decreases for an increase of *10 units*, we multiply the rate by 10 to get 0.26 hour per 10 units. To compute the decrease in *minutes* per 10 units, we multiply 0.26 by 60 to get approximately 16 minutes. Based on the trend line, the bicyclist can expect to decrease the finishing time by 16 minutes for every increase of 10 training index units.

Time Plots

Sometimes data are collected in order to observe changes in a variable over time. For example, sales for a department store may be collected monthly or yearly. A **time plot** (sometimes called a time series) is a graphical display useful for showing changes in data collected at regular intervals of time. A time plot of a variable plots each observation corresponding to the time at which it was measured. A time plot uses a coordinate plane similar to a scatterplot, but the time is always on the horizontal axis, and the variable measured is always on the vertical axis. Additionally, consecutive observations are connected by a line segment to emphasize increases and decreases over time.

Example 4.1.8:

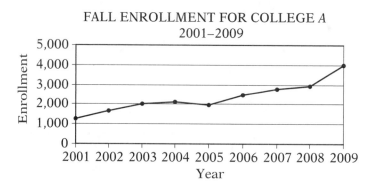

FALL ENROLLMENT FOR COLLEGE *A*
2001–2009

You can observe from the graph that the greatest increase in fall enrollment between consecutive years occurred from 2008 to 2009. One way to determine this is by noting that the slope of the line segment joining the values for 2008 and 2009 is greater than the slopes of the line segments joining all other consecutive years, because the time intervals are regular.

Although time plots are commonly used to compare frequencies, as in the example above, they can be used to compare any numerical data as the data change over time, such as temperatures, dollar amounts, percents, heights, and weights.

4.2 Numerical Methods for Describing Data

Data can be described numerically by various **statistics**, or **statistical measures**. These statistical measures are often grouped in three categories: measures of central tendency, measures of position, and measures of dispersion.

Measures of Central Tendency

Measures of **central tendency** indicate the "center" of the data along the number line and are usually reported as values that represent the data. There are three common measures of central tendency: (i) the **arithmetic mean**—usually called the **average** or simply the **mean**, (ii) the **median**, and (iii) the **mode**.

To calculate the **mean** of n numbers, take the sum of the n numbers and divide it by n.

Example 4.2.1: For the five numbers 6, 4, 7, 10, and 4, the mean is

$$\frac{6 + 4 + 7 + 10 + 4}{5} = \frac{31}{5} = 6.2$$

When several values are repeated in a list, it is helpful to think of the mean of the numbers as a **weighted mean** of only those values in the list that are *different*.

Example 4.2.2: Consider the following list of 16 numbers.

$$2, 4, 4, 5, 7, 7, 7, 7, 7, 7, 8, 8, 9, 9, 9, 9$$

There are only 6 different values in the list: 2, 4, 5, 7, 8, and 9. The mean of the numbers in the list can be computed as

$$\frac{1(2) + 2(4) + 1(5) + 6(7) + 2(8) + 4(9)}{1 + 2 + 1 + 6 + 2 + 4} = \frac{109}{16} = 6.8125$$

The number of times a value appears in the list, or the frequency, is called the **weight** of that value. So the mean of the 16 numbers is the weighted mean of the values 2, 4, 5, 7, 8, and 9, where the respective weights are 1, 2, 1, 6, 2, and 4. Note that the sum of the weights is the number of numbers in the list, 16.

The mean can be affected by just a few values that lie far above or below the rest of the data, because these values contribute directly to the sum of the data and therefore to the mean. By contrast, the **median** is a measure of central tendency that is fairly unaffected by unusually high or low values relative to the rest of the data.

To calculate the median of n numbers, first order the numbers from least to greatest. If n is odd, then the median is the middle number in the ordered list of numbers. If n is even, then there are *two* middle numbers, and the median is the average of these two numbers.

Example 4.2.3: The five numbers in example 4.2.1 listed in increasing order are 4, 4, 6, 7, 10, so the median is 6, the middle number. Note that if the number 10 in the list is replaced by the number 24, the mean increases from 6.2 to

$$\frac{4 + 4 + 6 + 7 + 24}{5} = \frac{45}{5} = 9$$

but the median remains equal to 6. This example shows how the median is relatively unaffected by an unusually large value.

The median, as the "middle value" of an ordered list of numbers, divides the list into roughly two equal parts. However, if the median is equal to one of the data values and it is repeated in the list, then the numbers of data above and below the median may be rather different. See example 4.2.2, where the median is 7, but four of the data are less than 7 and six of the data are greater than 7.

The **mode** of a list of numbers is the number that occurs most frequently in the list.

Example 4.2.4: The mode of the numbers in the list 1, 3, 6, 4, 3, 5 is 3. A list of numbers may have more than one mode. For example, the list 1, 2, 3, 3, 3, 5, 7, 10, 10, 10, 20 has two modes, 3 and 10.

Measures of Position

The three most basic **positions**, or locations, in a list of data ordered from least to greatest are the beginning, the end, and the middle. It is useful here to label these as L for the least, G for the greatest, and M for the median. Aside from these, the most common measures of position are **quartiles** and **percentiles**. Like the median M, quartiles and percentiles are numbers that divide the data into roughly equal groups after the data have been ordered from the least value L to the greatest value G. There are three quartile numbers that divide the data into four roughly equal groups, and there are 99 percentile numbers that divide the data into 100 roughly equal groups. As with the mean and median, the quartiles and percentiles may or may not themselves be values in the data.

The **first quartile** Q_1, the **second quartile** Q_2 (which is simply the median M), and the **third quartile** Q_3 divide a group of data into four roughly equal groups as follows. After the data are listed in increasing order, the first group consists of the data from L to Q_1, the second group is from Q_1 to M, the third group is from M to Q_3, and the fourth group is from Q_3 to G. Because the number of data in a list may not be divisible by 4, there are various rules to determine the exact values of Q_1 and Q_3 and some statisticians use different rules, but in all cases $Q_2 = M$. We use perhaps the most common rule, in which $Q_2 = M$ divides the data into two equal parts—the lesser numbers and the greater numbers—and then Q_1 is the median of the lesser numbers and Q_3 is the median of the greater numbers.

Example 4.2.5: To find the quartiles for the list of 16 numbers 2, 4, 4, 5, 7, 7, 7, 7, 7, 7, 8, 8, 9, 9, 9, 9 (already listed in order), first divide the data into two groups of 8 numbers each. The first group is 2, 4, 4, 5, 7, 7, 7, 7 and the second group is 7, 7, 8, 8, 9, 9, 9, 9, so that the second quartile, or median, is $Q_2 = M = 7$. To find the other quartiles, you can take each of the two smaller groups and find *its* median: the first quartile is $Q_1 = 6$ (the average of 5 and 7) and the third quartile is $Q_3 = 8.5$ (the average of 8 and 9).

In example 4.2.5, note that the number 4 is in the lowest 25 percent of the distribution of data. There are different ways to describe this. We can say that 4 is *below* the first quartile, that is, below Q_1; we can also say that 4 is *in* the first quartile. The phrase "*in* a quartile" refers to being *in* one of the four groups determined by Q_1, Q_2, and Q_3.

Percentiles are mostly used for very large lists of numerical data ordered from least to greatest. Instead of dividing the data into four groups, the 99 percentiles P_1, $P_2, P_3, \ldots, P_{99}$ divide the data into 100 groups. Consequently, $Q_1 = P_{25}$, $M = Q_2 = P_{50}$, and $Q_3 = P_{75}$. Because the number of data in a list may not be divisible by 100, statisticians apply various rules to determine values of percentiles.

Measures of Dispersion

Measures of **dispersion** indicate the degree of "spread" of the data. The most common statistics used as measures of dispersion are the range, the interquartile range, and the standard deviation. These statistics measure the spread of the data in different ways.

The **range** of the numbers in a group of data is the difference between the greatest number G in the data and the least number L in the data; that is, $G - L$. For example, given the list 11, 10, 5, 13, 21, the range of the numbers is $21 - 5 = 16$.

The simplicity of the range is useful in that it reflects that maximum spread of the data. However, sometimes a data value is so unusually small or so unusually large in comparison with the rest of the data that it is viewed with suspicion when the data are analyzed—the value could be erroneous or accidental in nature. Such data are called **outliers** because they lie so far out that in most cases, they are ignored when analyzing the data. Unfortunately, the range is directly affected by outliers.

A measure of dispersion that is not affected by outliers is the **interquartile range**. It is defined as the difference between the third quartile and the first quartile, that is, $Q_3 - Q_1$. Thus, the interquartile range measures the spread of the middle half of the data.

Example 4.2.6: In the list of 16 numbers 2, 4, 4, 5, 7, 7, 7, 7, 7, 7, 8, 8, 9, 9, 9, 9, the range is $9 - 2 = 7$, the first quartile is $Q_1 = 6$, and the third quartile is $Q_3 = 8.5$. So the interquartile range for the numbers in this list is $8.5 - 6 = 2.5$.

One way to summarize a group of numerical data and to illustrate its center and spread is to use the five numbers L, Q_1, Q_2, Q_3, and G. These five numbers can be plotted along a number line to show where the four quartile groups lie. Such plots are called **boxplots** or **box-and-whisker plots**, because a box is used to identify each of the two middle quartile groups of data, and "whiskers" extend outward from the boxes to the least and greatest values. The following graph shows the boxplot for the list of 16 numbers in example 4.2.6.

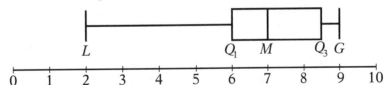

There are a few variations in the way boxplots are drawn—the position of the ends of the boxes can vary slightly, and some boxplots identify outliers with certain symbols—but all boxplots show the center of the data at the median and illustrate the spread of the data in each of the four quartile groups. As such, boxplots are useful for comparing sets of data side by side.

Example 4.2.7: Two large lists of numerical data, list I and list II, are summarized by the following boxplots.

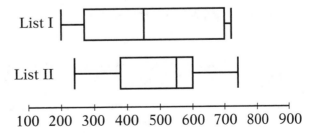

Based on the boxplots, several different comparisons of the two lists can be made. First, the median of list II, which is approximately 550, is greater than the median of list I, which is approximately 450. Second, the two measures of spread, range and interquartile range, are greater for list I than for list II. For list I, these measures are approximately 520 and 430, respectively; and for list II, they are approximately 500 and 220, respectively.

Unlike the range and the interquartile range, the **standard deviation** is a measure of spread that depends on each number in the list. Using the mean as the center of the data, the standard deviation takes into account how much each value differs from the mean and then takes a type of average of these differences. As a result, the more the data are spread away from the mean, the greater the standard deviation; and the more the data are clustered around the mean, the lesser the standard deviation.

The standard deviation of a group of n numerical data is computed by (1) calculating the mean of the n values, (2) finding the difference between the mean and each of the n values, (3) squaring each of the differences, (4) finding the average of the n squared differences, and (5) taking the nonnegative square root of the average squared difference.

Example 4.2.8: For the five data 0, 7, 8, 10, and 10, the standard deviation can be computed as follows. First, the mean of the data is 7, and the squared differences from the mean are

$$(7 - 0)^2, (7 - 7)^2, (7 - 8)^2, (7 - 10)^2, (7 - 10)^2$$

or 49, 0, 1, 9, 9. The average of the five squared differences is $\frac{68}{5}$, or 13.6, and the positive square root of 13.6 is approximately 3.7.

Note on terminology: The term "standard deviation" defined above is slightly different from another measure of dispersion, the **sample standard deviation**. The latter term is qualified with the word "sample" and is computed by dividing the sum of the squared differences by $n - 1$ instead of n. The sample standard deviation is only slightly different from the standard deviation but is preferred for technical reasons for a sample of data that is taken from a larger population of data. Sometimes the standard deviation is called the **population standard deviation** to help distinguish it from the sample standard deviation.

Example 4.2.9: Six hundred applicants for several post office jobs were rated on a scale from 1 to 50 points. The ratings had a mean of 32.5 points and a standard deviation of 7.1 points. How many standard deviations above or below the mean is a rating of 48 points? A rating of 30 points? A rating of 20 points?

Solution: Let d be the standard deviation, so $d = 7.1$ points. Note that 1 standard deviation above the mean is

$$32.5 + d = 32.5 + 7.1 = 39.6$$

and 2 standard deviations above the mean is

$$32.5 + 2d = 32.5 + 2(7.1) = 46.7$$

So 48 is a little more than 2 standard deviations above the mean. Since 48 is actually 15.5 points above the mean, the number of standard deviations that 48 is above the mean is $\frac{15.5}{7.1} \approx 2.2$. Thus, to answer the question, we first found the difference from the mean and then we divided by the standard deviation. The number of standard deviations that a rating of 30 is away from the mean is

$$\frac{30 - 32.5}{7.1} = \frac{-2.5}{7.1} \approx -0.4$$

where the negative sign indicates that the rating is 0.4 standard deviation *below* the mean.

The number of standard deviations that a rating of 20 is away from the mean is

$$\frac{20 - 32.5}{7.1} = \frac{-12.5}{7.1} \approx -1.8$$

where the negative sign indicates that the rating is 1.8 standard deviations *below* the mean.

To summarize:

- 48 points is 15.5 points above the mean, or approximately 2.2 standard deviations above the mean.
- 30 points is 2.5 points below the mean, or approximately 0.4 standard deviation below the mean.
- 20 points is 12.5 points below the mean, or approximately 1.8 standard deviations below the mean.

One more instance, which may seem trivial, is important to note:

- 32.5 points is 0 points from the mean, or approximately 0 standard deviations from the mean.

Example 4.2.9 shows that for a group of data, each value can be located with respect to the mean by using the standard deviation as a ruler. The process of subtracting the mean from each value and then dividing the result by the standard deviation is called **standardization**. Standardization is a useful tool because for each data value, it provides a measure of position relative to the rest of the data independently of the variable for which the data was collected and the units of the variable.

Note that the standardized values 2.2, −0.4, and −1.8 from example 4.2.9 are all between −3 and 3; that is, the corresponding ratings 48, 30, and 20 are all within 3 standard deviations above or below the mean. This is not surprising, based on the following fact about the standard deviation.

*In **any group of data**, most of the data are within about **3** standard deviations above or below the mean.*

Thus, when *any group of data* are standardized, most of the data are transformed to an interval on the number line centered about 0 and extending from about −3 to 3. The mean is always transformed to 0.

4.3 Counting Methods

Uncertainty is part of the process of making decisions and predicting outcomes. Uncertainty is addressed with the ideas and methods of probability theory. Since elementary probability requires an understanding of counting methods, we now turn to a discussion of counting objects in a systematic way before reviewing probability.

When a set of objects is small, it is easy to list the objects and count them one by one. When the set is too large to count that way, and when the objects are related in a patterned or systematic way, there are some useful techniques for counting the objects without actually listing them.

Sets and Lists

The term **set** has been used informally in this review to mean a collection of objects that have some property, whether it is the collection of all positive integers, all points in a circular region, or all students in a school that have studied French. The objects of a set are called **members** or **elements**. Some sets are **finite**, which means that their members can be completely counted. Finite sets can, in principle, have all of their members listed, using curly brackets, such as the set of even digits $\{0, 2, 4, 6, 8\}$. Sets that are not finite are called **infinite** sets, such as the set of all integers. A set that has no members is called the **empty set** and is denoted by the symbol $\varnothing$. A set with one or more members is called **nonempty**. If A and B are sets and all of the members of A are also members of B, then A is a **subset** of B. For example, $\{2, 8\}$ is a subset of $\{0, 2, 4, 6, 8\}$. Also, by convention, $\varnothing$ is a subset of every set.

A **list** is like a finite set, having members that can all be listed, but with two differences. In a list, the members are ordered; that is, rearranging the members of a list makes it a different list. Thus, the terms "first element," "second element," etc., make sense in a list. Also, elements can be repeated in a list and the repetitions matter. For example, the lists 1, 2, 3, 2 and 1, 2, 2, 3 are different lists, each with four elements, and they are both different from the list 1, 2, 3, which has three elements.

In contrast to a list, when the elements of a set are given, repetitions are not counted as additional elements and the order of the elements does not matter. For example, the sets $\{1, 2, 3, 2\}$ and $\{3, 1, 2\}$ are the same set, which has three elements. For any finite set S, the number of elements of S is denoted by $|S|$. Thus, if $S = \{6.2, -9, \pi, 0.01, 0\}$, then $|S| = 5$. Also, $|\varnothing| = 0$.

Sets can be formed from other sets. If S and T are sets, then the **intersection** of S and T is the set of all elements that are in both S and T and is denoted by $S \cap T$. The **union** of S and T is the set of all elements that are in either S or T or both and is denoted by $S \cup T$. If sets S and T have no elements in common, they are called **disjoint** or **mutually exclusive**.

A useful way to represent two or three sets and their possible intersections and unions is a **Venn diagram**. In a Venn diagram, sets are represented by circular regions that overlap if they have elements in common but do not overlap if they are disjoint. Sometimes the circular regions are drawn inside a rectangular region, which represents a **universal set**, of which all other sets involved are subsets.

Example 4.3.1: The sets A, B, and C are represented in the Venn diagram below, where U represents a universal set.

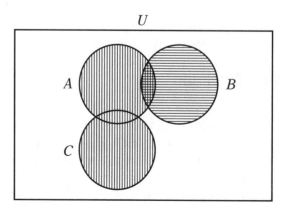

The regions with vertical stripes represent the set $A \cup C$. The regions with horizontal stripes represent the set B. The region with both kinds of stripes represents the set $A \cap B$. The sets B and C are mutually exclusive, often written $B \cap C = \varnothing$.

The example above can be used to illustrate an elementary counting principle involving intersecting sets, called the **inclusion-exclusion principle** for two sets. This principle relates the numbers of elements in the union and intersection of two finite sets: The number of elements in the union of two sets equals the sum of their individual numbers of elements minus the number of elements in their intersection. If the sets in example 4.3.1 are finite, then we have for the union of A and B,

$$|A \cup B| = |A| + |B| - |A \cap B|$$

Because $A \cap B$ is a subset of both A and B, the subtraction is necessary to avoid counting the elements in $A \cap B$ twice. For the union of B and C, we have

$$|B \cup C| = |B| + |C|$$

because $B \cap C = \varnothing$.

Multiplication Principle

Suppose there are two choices to be made sequentially and that the second choice is independent of the first choice. Suppose also that there are k different possibilities for the first choice and m different possibilities for the second choice. The **multiplication principle** states that under those conditions, there are km different possibilities for the pair of choices.

For example, suppose that a meal is to be ordered from a restaurant menu and that the meal consists of one entrée and one dessert. If there are 5 entrées and 3 desserts on the menu, then there are $(5)(3) = 15$ different meals that can be ordered from the menu.

The multiplication principle applies in more complicated situations as well. If there are more than two independent choices to be made, then the number of different possible outcomes of all of the choices is the product of the numbers of possibilities for each choice.

Example 4.3.2: Suppose that a computer password consists of four characters such that the first character is one of the 10 digits from 0 to 9 and each of the next 3 characters is any one of the uppercase letters from the 26 letters of the English alphabet. How many different passwords are possible?

Solution: The description of the password allows repetitions of letters. Thus, there are 10 possible choices for the first character in the password and 26 possible choices for each of the next 3 characters in the password. Therefore, applying the multiplication principle, the number of possible passwords is $(10)(26)(26)(26) = 175{,}760$.

Note that if repetitions of letters are *not* allowed in the password, then the choices are not all independent, but a modification of the multiplication principle can still be applied. There are 10 possible choices for the first character in the password, 26 possible choices for the second character, 25 for the third character because the first letter cannot be repeated, and 24 for the fourth character because the first two letters cannot be repeated. Therefore, the number of possible passwords is $(10)(26)(25)(24) = 156{,}000$.

Example 4.3.3: Each time a coin is tossed, there are 2 possible outcomes—either it lands heads up or it lands tails up. Using this fact and the multiplication principle, you can conclude that if a coin is tossed 8 times, there are $(2)(2)(2)(2)(2)(2)(2)(2) = 2^8 = 256$ possible outcomes.

Permutations and Factorials

Suppose you want to determine the number of different ways the 3 letters A, B, and C can be placed in order from 1st to 3rd. The following is a list of all the possible orders in which the letters can be placed.

$$ABC \quad ACB \quad BAC \quad BCA \quad CAB \quad CBA$$

There are 6 possible orders for the 3 letters.

Now suppose you want to determine the number of different ways the 4 letters A, B, C, and D can be placed in order from 1st to 4th. Listing all of the orders for 4 letters is time-consuming, so it would be useful to be able to count the possible orders without listing them.

To order the 4 letters, one of the 4 letters must be placed first, one of the remaining 3 letters must be placed second, one of the remaining 2 letters must be placed third, and the last remaining letter must be placed fourth. Therefore, applying the multiplication principle, there are (4)(3)(2)(1), or 24, ways to order the 4 letters.

More generally, suppose n objects are to be ordered from 1st to nth, and we want to count the number of ways the objects can be ordered. There are n choices for the first object, $n - 1$ choices for the second object, $n - 2$ choices for the third object, and so on, until there is only 1 choice for the nth object. Thus, applying the multiplication principle, the number of ways to order the n objects is equal to the product

$$n(n - 1)(n - 2)\cdots(3)(2)(1)$$

Each order is called a **permutation**, and the product above is called the number of permutations of n objects.

Because products of the form $n(n - 1)(n - 2)\cdots(3)(2)(1)$ occur frequently when counting objects, a special symbol $n!$, called **n factorial**, is used to denote this product.

For example,

$$1! = 1$$
$$2! = (2)(1) = 2$$
$$3! = (3)(2)(1) = 6$$
$$4! = (4)(3)(2)(1) = 24$$

As a special definition, $0! = 1$.

Note that $n! = n(n - 1)! = n(n - 1)(n - 2)! = n(n - 1)(n - 2)(n - 3)!$ and so on.

Example 4.3.4: Suppose that 10 students are going on a bus trip, and each of the students will be assigned to one of the 10 available seats. Then the number of possible different seating arrangements of the students on the bus is

$$10! = (10)(9)(8)(7)(6)(5)(4)(3)(2)(1) = 3{,}628{,}800$$

Now suppose you want to determine the number of ways in which you can select 3 of the 5 letters A, B, C, D, and E and place them in order from 1st to 3rd. Reasoning as in the preceding examples, you find that there are (5)(4)(3), or 60, ways to select and order them.

More generally, suppose that k objects will be selected from a set of n objects, where $k \leq n$, and the k objects will be placed in order from 1st to kth. Then there are n choices for the first object, $n - 1$ choices for the second object, $n - 2$ choices for the third object, and so on, until there are $n - k + 1$ choices for the kth object. Thus, applying the multiplication principle, the number of ways to select and order k objects from a set of n objects is $n(n-1)(n-2)\cdots(n-k+1)$. It is useful to note that

$$n(n-1)(n-2)\cdots(n-k+1) = n(n-1)(n-2)\cdots(n-k+1)\frac{(n-k)!}{(n-k)!}$$

$$= \frac{n!}{(n-k)!}$$

This expression represents the number of **permutations of n objects taken k at a time**; that is, the number of ways to select and order k objects out of n objects.

Example 4.3.5: How many different five-digit positive integers can be formed using the digits 1, 2, 3, 4, 5, 6, and 7 if none of the digits can occur more than once in the integer?

Solution: This example asks how many ways there are to order 5 integers chosen from a set of 7 integers. According to the counting principle above, there are $(7)(6)(5)(4)(3) = 2{,}520$ ways to do this. Note that this is equal to

$$\frac{7!}{(7-5)!} = \frac{(7)(6)(5)(4)(3)(2!)}{2!} = (7)(6)(5)(4)(3).$$

Combinations

Given the five letters A, B, C, D, and E, suppose that you want to determine the number of ways in which you can select 3 of the 5 letters, but unlike before, you do not want to count different orders for the 3 letters. The following is a list of all of the ways in which 3 of the 5 letters can be selected without regard to the order of the letters.

ABC   ABD   ABE   ACD   ACE   ADE   BCD   BCE   BDE   CDE

There are 10 ways of selecting the 3 letters without order. There is a relationship between selecting with order and selecting without order.

The number of ways to select 3 of the 5 letters without order, which is 10, *multiplied by* the number of ways to order the 3 letters, which is 3!, or 6, *is equal to* the number of ways to select 3 of the 5 letters and order them, which is $\frac{5!}{2!} = 60$. In short,

(number of ways to select without order) $\times$ (number of ways to order)

$\qquad\qquad\qquad\qquad\qquad$ = (number of ways to select with order)

This relationship can also be described as follows.

(number of ways to select without order) $= \dfrac{\text{(number of ways to select with order)}}{\text{(number of ways to order)}}$

$$= \frac{\frac{5!}{2!}}{3!} = \frac{5!}{3!2!} = 10$$

More generally, suppose that k objects will be chosen from a set of n objects, where $k \le n$, but that the k objects will *not* be put in order. The number of ways in which this can be done is called the number of **combinations of n objects taken k at a time** and is given by the formula $\dfrac{n!}{k!(n-k)!}$.

Another way to refer to the number of combinations of n objects taken k at a time is n **choose** k, and two notations commonly used to denote this number are $_nC_k$ and $\binom{n}{k}$.

Example 4.3.6: Suppose you want to select a 3-person committee from a group of 9 students. How many ways are there to do this?

Solution: Since the 3 students on the committee are not ordered, you can use the formula for the combination of 9 objects taken 3 at a time, or "9 choose 3":

$$\frac{9!}{3!(9-3)!} = \frac{9!}{3!6!} = \frac{(9)(8)(7)}{(3)(2)(1)} = 84$$

Using the terminology of sets, given a set S consisting of n elements, n choose k is simply the number of subsets of S that consist of k elements. The formula $\frac{n!}{k!(n-k)!}$ also holds when $k = 0$ and $k = n$.

- n choose 0 is $\frac{n!}{0!n!} = 1$, which corresponds to the fact that there is only one subset of S with 0 elements, namely the empty set.

- n choose n is $\frac{n!}{n!0!} = 1$, since there is only one subset of S with n elements, namely the set S itself.

Finally, note that n choose k is always equal to n choose $n - k$, because

$$\frac{n!}{(n-k)!(n-(n-k))!} = \frac{n!}{(n-k)!k!} = \frac{n!}{k!(n-k)!}$$

4.4 Probability

Probability is a way of describing uncertainty in numerical terms. In this section we review some of the terminology used in elementary probability theory.

A **probability experiment**, also called a **random experiment**, is an experiment for which the result, or **outcome**, is uncertain. We assume that all of the possible outcomes of an experiment are known before the experiment is performed, but which outcome will actually occur is unknown. The set of all possible outcomes of a random experiment is called the **sample space**, and any particular set of outcomes is called an **event**. For example, consider a cube with faces numbered 1 to 6, called a 6-sided die. Rolling the die once is an experiment in which there are 6 possible outcomes—either 1, 2, 3, 4, 5, or 6 will appear on the top face. The sample space for this experiment is the set of numbers 1, 2, 3, 4, 5, and 6. Two examples of events for this experiment are (i) rolling the number 4, which has only one outcome, and (ii) rolling an odd number, which has three outcomes.

The **probability** of an event is a number from 0 to 1, inclusive, that indicates the likelihood that the event occurs when the experiment is performed. The greater the number, the more likely the event.

Example 4.4.1: Consider the following experiment. A box contains 15 pieces of paper, each of which has the name of one of the 15 students in a class consisting of 7 male and 8 female students, all with different names. The instructor will shake the box for a while and then, without looking, choose a piece of paper at random and read the name. Here the sample space is the set of 15 names. The assumption of **random selection** means that each of the names is **equally likely** to be selected. If this assumption is made, then the probability that any one particular name is selected is equal to $\frac{1}{15}$. For any event E, the probability that E occurs, denoted by $P(E)$, is defined by the ratio

$$P(E) = \frac{\text{the number of names in the event } E}{15}$$

If M is the event that the student selected is male, then $P(M) = \frac{7}{15}$.

In general, for a random experiment with a finite number of possible outcomes, if each outcome is equally likely to occur, then the probability that an event E occurs is defined by the ratio

$$P(E) = \frac{\text{the number of outcomes in the event } E}{\text{the number of possible outcomes in the experiment}}$$

In the case of rolling a 6-sided die, if the die is "fair," then the 6 outcomes are equally likely. So the probability of rolling a 4 is $\frac{1}{6}$, and the probability of rolling an odd number—rolling a 1, 3, or 5—can be calculated as $\frac{3}{6} = \frac{1}{2}$.

The following are general facts about probability.

- If an event E is certain to occur, then $P(E) = 1$.
- If an event E is certain *not* to occur, then $P(E) = 0$.
- If an event E is possible but not certain to occur, then $0 < P(E) < 1$.
- The probability that an event E will not occur is equal to $1 - P(E)$.
- If E is an event, then the probability of E is the sum of the probabilities of the outcomes in E.
- The sum of the probabilities of all possible outcomes of an experiment is 1.

If E and F are two events of an experiment, we consider two other events related to E and F.

- The event that both E and F occur; that is, outcomes in the set $E \cap F$.
- The event that E or F or both occur; that is, outcomes in the set $E \cup F$.

Events that cannot occur at the same time are said to be **mutually exclusive**. For example, if a 6-sided die is rolled once, the event of rolling an odd number and the event of rolling an even number are mutually exclusive. But rolling a 4 and rolling an even number are not mutually exclusive, since 4 is an outcome that is common to both events.

For events E and F, we have the following rules.

- P (either E or F or both occur) $= P(E) + P(F) - P$(both E and F occur), which is the inclusion-exclusion principle applied to probability.
- If E and F are mutually exclusive, then P (both E and F occur) $= 0$, and therefore, P(either E or F or both occur) $= P(E) + P(F)$.
- E and F are said to be **independent** if the occurrence of either event does not affect the occurrence of the other. If two events E and F are independent, then P(both E and F occur) $= P(E)P(F)$. For example, if a fair 6-sided die is rolled twice, the event E of rolling a 3 on the first roll and the event F of rolling a 3 on the second roll are independent, and the probability of rolling a 3 on both rolls is $P(E)P(F) = \left(\frac{1}{6}\right)\left(\frac{1}{6}\right) = \frac{1}{36}$. In this example, the experiment is actually

"rolling the die twice," and each outcome is an ordered pair of results like "4 on the first roll and 1 on the second roll." But event E restricts only the first roll—to a 3—having no effect on the second roll; similarly, event F restricts only the second roll—to a 3—having no effect on the first roll.

Note that if $P(E) \neq 0$ and $P(F) \neq 0$, then events E and F cannot be both mutually exclusive and independent. For if E and F are independent, then $P(\text{both } E \text{ and } F \text{ occur}) = P(E)P(F) \neq 0$; but if E and F are mutually exclusive, then $P(\text{both } E \text{ and } F \text{ occur}) = 0$.

It is common to use the shorter notation "E and F" instead of "both E and F occur" and use "E or F" instead of "E or F or both occur." With this notation, we have the following rules.

- $P(E \text{ or } F) = P(E) + P(F) - P(E \text{ and } F)$
- $P(E \text{ or } F) = P(E) + P(F)$ if E and F are mutually exclusive.
- $P(E \text{ and } F) = P(E)P(F)$ if E and F are independent.

Example 4.4.2: If a fair 6-sided die is rolled once, let E be the event of rolling a 3 and let F be the event of rolling an odd number. These events are *not* independent. This is because rolling a 3 makes certain that the event of rolling an odd number occurs. Note that $P(E \text{ and } F) \neq P(E)P(F)$, since

$$P(E \text{ and } F) = P(E) = \frac{1}{6} \quad \text{and} \quad P(E)P(F) = \left(\frac{1}{6}\right)\left(\frac{1}{2}\right) = \frac{1}{12}$$

Example 4.4.3: A 12-sided die, with faces numbered 1 to 12, is to be rolled once, and each of the 12 possible outcomes is equally likely to occur. The probability of rolling a 4 is $\frac{1}{12}$, so the probability of rolling a number that is *not* a 4 is $1 - \frac{1}{12} = \frac{11}{12}$. The probability of rolling a number that is either a multiple of 5—a 5 or a 10—or an odd number—a 1, 3, 5, 7, 9, or 11—is equal to

$$P(\text{multiple of 5}) + P(\text{odd}) - P(\text{multiple of 5 and odd}) = \frac{2}{12} + \frac{6}{12} - \frac{1}{12}$$

$$= \frac{7}{12}$$

Another way to calculate this probability is to notice that rolling a number that is either a multiple of 5 (5 or 10) or an odd number (1, 3, 5, 7, 9, or 11) is the same as rolling one of 1, 3, 5, 7, 9, 10, and 11, which are 7 equally likely outcomes. So by using the ratio formula to calculate the probability, the required probability is $\frac{7}{12}$.

Example 4.4.4: Consider an experiment with events A, B, and C for which $P(A) = 0.23$, $P(B) = 0.40$, and $P(C) = 0.85$. Suppose that events A and B are mutually exclusive and events B and C are independent. What are the probabilities $P(A \text{ or } B)$ and $P(B \text{ or } C)$?

Solution: Since A and B are mutually exclusive,

$$P(A \text{ or } B) = P(A) + P(B) = 0.23 + 0.40 = 0.63$$

Since B and C are independent, $P(B \text{ and } C) = P(B)P(C)$. So,

$$P(B \text{ or } C) = P(B) + P(C) - P(B \text{ and } C) = P(B) + P(C) - P(B)P(C)$$

Therefore,

$$P(B \text{ or } C) = 0.40 + 0.85 - (0.40)(0.85) = 1.25 - 0.34$$
$$= 0.91$$

Example 4.4.5: Suppose that there is a 6-sided die that is weighted in such a way that each time the die is rolled, the probabilities of rolling any of the numbers from 1 to 5 are all equal, but the probability of rolling a 6 is twice the probability of rolling a 1. When you roll the die once, the 6 outcomes are *not equally likely*. What are the probabilities of the 6 outcomes?

Solution: Using the notation $P(1)$ for the probability of rolling a 1, let $p = P(1)$. Then each of the probabilities of rolling a 2, 3, 4, or 5 is equal to p, and the probability of rolling a 6 is $2p$. Therefore, since the sum of the probabilities of all possible outcomes is 1, it follows that

$$1 = P(1) + P(2) + P(3) + P(4) + P(5) + P(6) = p + p + p + p + p + 2p$$
$$= 7p$$

So the probability of rolling each of the numbers from 1 to 5 is $p = \dfrac{1}{7}$, and the probability of rolling a 6 is $\dfrac{2}{7}$.

Example 4.4.6: Suppose that you roll the weighted 6-sided die from example 4.4.5 twice. What is the probability that the first roll will be an odd number and the second roll will be an even number?

Solution: To calculate the probability that the first roll will be odd and the second roll will be even, note that these two events are independent. To calculate the probability that both occur, you must multiply the probabilities of the two independent events. First compute the individual probabilities.

$$P(\text{odd}) = P(1) + P(3) + P(5) = \frac{3}{7}$$

$$P(\text{even}) = P(2) + P(4) + P(6) = \frac{4}{7}$$

Then, $P(\text{first roll is odd and second roll is even}) = P(\text{odd})P(\text{even}) = \left(\dfrac{3}{7}\right)\left(\dfrac{4}{7}\right) = \dfrac{12}{49}$.

Two events that happen sequentially are not always independent. The occurrence of one event may affect the occurrence of a following event. In this case, the probability that *both* events happen is equal to the probability that the first event happens multiplied by the probability that *given that the first event has already happened*, the second event happens as well.

Example 4.4.7: A box contains 5 orange disks, 4 red disks, and 1 blue disk. You are to select two disks at random and without replacement from the box. What is the probability that the first disk you select will be red and the second disk you select will be orange?

Solution: To solve, you need to calculate the following two probabilities and then multiply them

- The probability that the first disk selected from the box will be red
- The probability that the second disk selected from the box will be orange, given that the first disk selected from the box is red

The probability that the first disk you select will be red is $\frac{4}{10} = \frac{2}{5}$. If the first disk you select is red, there will be 5 orange disks, 3 red disks, and 1 blue disk left in the box, for a total of 9 disks. Therefore, the probability that the second disk you select will be orange, given that the first disk you selected is red, is $\frac{5}{9}$. Multiply the two probabilities to get $\left(\frac{2}{5}\right)\left(\frac{5}{9}\right) = \frac{2}{9}$.

4.5 Distributions of Data, Random Variables, and Probability Distributions

In data analysis, variables whose values depend on chance play an important role in linking distributions of data to probability distributions. Such variables are called random variables. We begin with a review of distributions of data.

Distributions of Data

Recall that relative frequency distributions given in a table or histogram are a common way to show how numerical data are distributed. In a histogram, the areas of the bars indicate where the data are concentrated. The histogram in example 4.1.6 illustrates a small group of data, with only 6 possible values and only 25 data altogether. Many groups of data are much larger than 25 and have many more than 6 possible values, which are often measurements of quantities like length, money, and time.

Example 4.5.1: The lifetimes of 800 electric devices were measured. Because the lifetimes had many different values, the measurements were grouped into 50 intervals, or **classes**, of 10 hours each: 601–610 hours, 611–620 hours, . . . , 1,091–1,100 hours. The resulting relative frequency distribution, as a histogram, has 50 thin bars and many different bar heights, as shown below.

Relative Frequency Distribution for Lifetimes of 800 Electric Devices

Note that the tops of the bars of the histogram have a relatively smooth appearance and begin to look like a curve. In general, histograms that represent very large data sets with many classes appear to have smooth shapes. Consequently, the distribution can be modeled by a smooth curve that is close to the tops of the bars. Such a model retains the shape of the distribution but is independent of classes.

Recall from example 4.1.6 that the sum of the areas of the bars of a relative frequency histogram is 1. Although the units on the horizontal axis of a histogram vary from one data set to another, the vertical scale can be adjusted (stretched or shrunk) so that the sum of the areas of the bars is 1. With this vertical scale adjustment, the area under the curve that models the distribution is also 1. This model curve is called a **distribution curve**, but it has other names as well, including **density curve** and **frequency curve**.

The purpose of the distribution curve is to give a good illustration of a large distribution of numerical data that doesn't depend on specific classes. To achieve this, the main property of a distribution curve is that the area under the curve in any vertical slice, just like a histogram bar, represents the proportion of the data that lies in the corresponding interval on the horizontal axis, which is at the base of the slice.

Before leaving this histogram, note that the mean m and the median M of the data are marked on the horizontal axis. Also, several standard deviations above and below the mean are marked, where d is the standard deviation of the data. The standard deviation marks show how most of the data are within about 3 standard deviations above or below the mean (that is, between the numbers $m - 3d$ (not shown) and $m + 3d$).

Finally, regarding the mean and the median, recall that the median splits the data into a lower half and an upper half, so that the sum of the areas of the bars to the left of M is the same as the sum of the areas to the right. On the other hand, m takes into account the exact value of each of the data, not just whether a value is high or low. The nature of the mean is such that if an imaginary fulcrum were placed somewhere under the horizontal axis in order to balance the distribution perfectly, the balancing position would be exactly at m. That is why m is somewhat to the right of M. The balance point at m takes into account *how high* the few very high values are (to the far right), while M just counts them as "high." To summarize, the median is the "halving point," and the mean is the "balance point."

Random Variables

When analyzing data, it is common to choose a value of the data at random and consider that choice as a random experiment, as introduced in section 4.4. Then, the probabilities of events involving the randomly chosen value may be determined. Given a distribution of data, a variable, say X, may be used to represent a randomly chosen value from the distribution. Such a variable X is an example of a **random variable**, which is a variable whose value is a numerical outcome of a random experiment.

Example 4.5.2: In the data from example 4.1.1 consisting of numbers of children, let X represent the number of children in a randomly chosen family among the 25 families. What is the probability that $X = 3$? That $X > 3$? That X is less than the mean of the distribution?

Solution: For convenience, here is the frequency distribution of the data.

Number of Children	Frequency
0	3
1	5
2	7
3	6
4	3
5	1
Total	25

Since there are 6 families with 3 children and each of the 25 families is equally likely to be chosen, the probability that a family with 3 children will be chosen is $\frac{6}{25}$. That is, $X = 3$ is an event, and its probability is $P(X = 3) = \frac{6}{25}$, or 0.24. It is common to use the shorter notation $P(3)$ instead of $P(X = 3)$, so you could write $P(3) = 0.24$. Note that in the histogram, shown below, the area of the bar corresponding to $X = 3$ as a proportion of the combined areas of all of the bars is equal to this probability. This indicates how probability is related to area in a histogram for a relative frequency distribution.

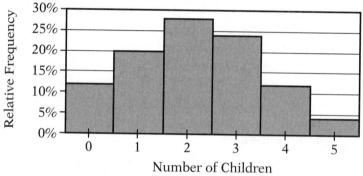

As for the event $X > 3$, it is the same as the event "$X = 4$ or $X = 5$". Because $X = 4$ and $X = 5$ are mutually exclusive events, we can use the rules of probability from section 4.4.

$$P(X > 3) = P(4) + P(5) = \frac{3}{25} + \frac{1}{25} = 0.12 + 0.04 = 0.16$$

For the last question, first compute the mean of the distribution.

$$\frac{0(3) + 1(5) + 2(7) + 3(6) + 4(3) + 5(1)}{25} = \frac{54}{25} = 2.16$$

Then,

$$P(X < 2.16) = P(0) + P(1) + P(2) = \frac{3}{25} + \frac{5}{25} + \frac{7}{25} = \frac{15}{25} = 0.6$$

A table showing all 6 possible values of X and their probabilities is called the **probability distribution** of the random variable X.

Probability Distribution of the Random Variable X

X	$P(X)$
0	0.12
1	0.20
2	0.28
3	0.24
4	0.12
5	0.04

Note that the probabilities are simply the relative frequencies of the 6 possible values expressed as decimals instead of percents. The following statement indicates a fundamental link between data distributions and probability distributions.

For a random variable that represents a randomly chosen value from a distribution of data, the probability distribution of the random variable is the same as the relative frequency distribution of the data.

Because the probability distribution and the relative frequency distribution are essentially the same, the probability distribution can be represented by a histogram. Also, all of the descriptive statistics—such as mean, median, and standard deviation—that apply to the distribution of data also apply to the probability distribution. For example, we say that the probability distribution above has a mean of 2.16, a median of 2, and a standard deviation of about 1.3, since the 25 data values have these statistics, as you can check.

These statistics are similarly defined for the random variable X above. Thus, we would say that the **mean of the random variable X** is 2.16. Another name for the mean of a random variable is **expected value**. So we would also say that the expected value of X is 2.16. Note that the mean of X can be expressed in terms of probabilities as follows.

$$\frac{0(3) + 1(5) + 2(7) + 3(6) + 4(3) + 5(1)}{25} = 0\left(\frac{3}{25}\right) + 1\left(\frac{5}{25}\right) + 2\left(\frac{7}{25}\right) + 3\left(\frac{6}{25}\right) + 4\left(\frac{3}{25}\right) + 5\left(\frac{1}{25}\right)$$

$$= 0P(0) + 1P(1) + 2P(2) + 3P(3) + 4P(4) + 5P(5)$$

which is the sum of the products $XP(X)$; that is, the sum of each value of X multiplied by its corresponding probability $P(X)$.

The preceding example involves a common type of random variable—one that represents a randomly chosen value from a distribution of data. However, the concept of a random variable is more general. A random variable can be any quantity whose value is the result of a random experiment. The possible values of the random variable are the same as the outcomes of the experiment. So any random experiment with numerical outcomes naturally has a random variable associated with it, as in the following example.

Example 4.5.3: Let Y represent the outcome of the experiment in example 4.4.5 of rolling a weighted 6-sided die. Then Y is a random variable with 6 possible values, the numbers 1 through 6. Each value of Y has a probability, which is listed in the probability distribution of the random variable Y and is shown in a histogram for Y.

Probability Distribution of the Random Variable Y

Y	1	2	3	4	5	6
$P(Y)$	$\dfrac{1}{7}$	$\dfrac{1}{7}$	$\dfrac{1}{7}$	$\dfrac{1}{7}$	$\dfrac{1}{7}$	$\dfrac{2}{7}$

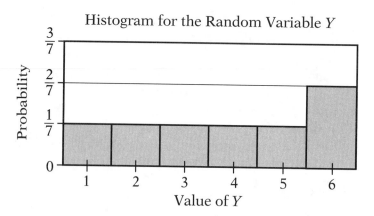

Histogram for the Random Variable Y

The mean, or expected value, of Y can be computed as

$$P(1) + 2P(2) + 3P(3) + 4P(4) + 5P(5) + 6P(6) = \left(\frac{1}{7}\right) + 2\left(\frac{1}{7}\right) + 3\left(\frac{1}{7}\right) + 4\left(\frac{1}{7}\right) + 5\left(\frac{1}{7}\right) + 6\left(\frac{2}{7}\right)$$

$$= \frac{1}{7} + \frac{2}{7} + \frac{3}{7} + \frac{4}{7} + \frac{5}{7} + \frac{12}{7}$$

$$= \frac{27}{7} \approx 3.86$$

Both of the random variables X and Y above are examples of **discrete random variables** because their values consist of discrete points on a number line.

A basic fact about probability from section 4.4 is that the sum of the probabilities of all possible outcomes of an experiment is 1, which can be confirmed by adding all of the probabilities in each of the probability distributions for the random variables X and Y above. Also, the sum of the areas of the bars in a histogram for the probability distribution of a random variable is 1. This fact is related to a fundamental link between the areas of the bars of a histogram and the probabilities of a discrete random variable.

In the histogram for a random variable, the area of each bar is proportional to the probability represented by the bar.

If the die in example 4.4.5 were a fair die instead of weighted, then the probability of each of the outcomes would be $\dfrac{1}{6}$, and consequently, each of the bars in the histogram would have the same height. Such a flat histogram indicates a **uniform distribution**, since the probability is distributed uniformly over all possible outcomes.

The Normal Distribution

Many natural processes yield data that have a relative frequency distribution shaped somewhat like a bell, as in the distribution below with mean m and standard deviation d.

Approximately Normal Relative Frequency Distribution

$m - 3d$ $m - 2d$ $m - d$ m $m + d$ $m + 2d$ $m + 3d$

Such data are said to be **approximately normally distributed** and have the following properties.

- The mean, median, and mode are all nearly equal.
- The data are grouped fairly symmetrically about the mean.
- About two-thirds of the data are within 1 standard deviation of the mean.
- Almost all of the data are within 2 standard deviations of the mean.

As stated above, you can always associate a random variable X with a distribution of data by letting X be a randomly chosen value from the distribution. If X is such a random variable for the distribution above, we say that X is approximately normally distributed.

As described in example 4.5.1, relative frequency distributions are often approximated using a smooth curve—a distribution curve or density curve—for the tops of the bars in the histogram. The region below such a curve represents a distribution, called a **continuous probability distribution**. There are many different continuous probability distributions, but the most important one is the **normal distribution**, which has a bell-shaped curve like the one shown in the figure below.

Normal Distribution

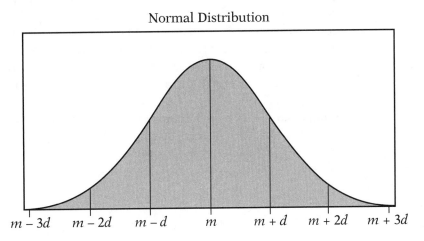

$m - 3d$ $m - 2d$ $m - d$ m $m + d$ $m + 2d$ $m + 3d$

Just as a data distribution has a mean and standard deviation, the normal probability distribution has a mean and standard deviation. Also, the properties listed above for the approximately normal distribution of data hold for the normal distribution, except that the mean, median, and mode are exactly the same and the distribution is perfectly symmetric about the mean.

A normal distribution, though always shaped like a bell, can be centered around any mean and can be spread out to a greater or lesser degree, depending on the standard deviation. Below are three normal distributions that have different centers and spreads. From left to right, the means of the three distributions are −10, 1, and 20; and the standard deviations are 5, 10, and 2.

Three Normal Distributions

As mentioned earlier, areas of the bars in a histogram for a discrete random variable correspond to probabilities for the values of the random variable; the sum of the areas is 1 and the sum of the probabilities is 1. This is also true for a continuous probability distribution: the area of the region under the curve is 1, and the areas of vertical slices of the region—similar to the bars of a histogram—are equal to probabilities of a random variable associated with the distribution. Such a random variable is called a **continuous random variable**, and it plays the same role as a random variable that represents a randomly chosen value from a distribution of data. The main difference is that we seldom consider the event in which a continuous random variable is equal to a single value like $X = 3$; rather, we consider events that are described by intervals of values such as $1 < X < 3$ and $X > 10$. Such events correspond to vertical slices under a continuous probability distribution, and the areas of the vertical slices are the probabilities of the corresponding events. (Consequently, the probability of an event such as $X = 3$ would correspond to the area of a line segment, which is 0.)

Example 4.5.4: If W is a random variable that is normally distributed with a mean of 5 and a standard deviation of 2, what is $P(W > 5)$? Approximately what is $P(3 < W < 7)$? Which of the four numbers 0.5, 0.1, 0.05, or 0.01 is the best estimate of $P(W < -1)$?

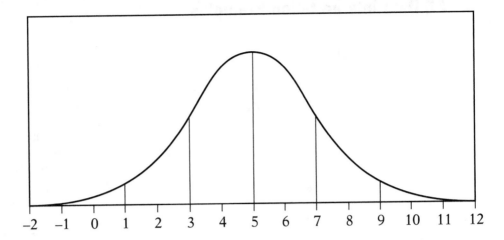

Solution: Since the mean of the distribution is 5, and the distribution is symmetric about the mean, the event $W > 5$ corresponds to exactly half of the area under the normal distribution. So $P(W > 5) = \dfrac{1}{2}$.

For the event $3 < W < 7$, note that since the standard deviation of the distribution is 2, the values 3 and 7 are one standard deviation below and above the mean, respectively. Since about two-thirds of the area is within one standard deviation of the mean, $P(3 < W < 7)$ is approximately $\dfrac{2}{3}$.

For the event $W < -1$, note that -1 is 3 standard deviations below the mean. Since the graph makes it fairly clear that the area of the region under the normal curve to the left of -1 is much less than 5 percent of all of the area, the best of the four estimates given for $P(W < -1)$ is 0.01.

The **standard normal distribution** is a normal distribution with a mean of 0 and standard deviation equal to 1. To transform a normal distribution with a mean of m and a standard deviation of d to a standard normal distribution, you standardize the values (as explained below example 4.2.9); that is, you subtract m from any observed value of the normal distribution and then divide the result by d.

Very precise values for probabilities associated with normal distributions can be computed using calculators, computers, or statistical tables for the standard normal distribution. For example, more precise values for $P(3 < W < 7)$ and $P(W < -1)$ are 0.683 and 0.0013. Such calculations are beyond the scope of this review.

4.6 Data Interpretation Examples

Example 4.6.1:

DISTRIBUTION OF CUSTOMER COMPLAINTS
RECEIVED BY AIRLINE *P*, 2003 AND 2004

Category	2003	2004
Flight problem	20.0%	22.1%
Baggage	18.3	21.8
Customer service	13.1	11.3
Oversales of seats	10.5	11.8
Refund problem	10.1	8.1
Fare	6.4	6.0
Reservation and ticketing	5.8	5.6
Tours	3.3	2.3
Smoking	3.2	2.9
Advertising	1.2	1.1
Credit	1.0	0.8
Special passenger accommodation	0.9	0.9
Other	6.2	5.3
Total	100.0%	100.0%
Total number of complaints	22,998	13,278

(a) Approximately how many complaints concerning credit were received by Airline *P* in 2003?

(b) By approximately what percent did the total number of complaints decrease from 2003 to 2004?

(c) Based on the information in the table, which of the following statements are true?

  I. In each of the years 2003 and 2004, complaints about flight problems, baggage, and customer service together accounted for more than 50 percent of all customer complaints received by Airline *P*.

  II. The number of special passenger accommodation complaints was unchanged from 2003 to 2004.

  III. From 2003 to 2004, the number of flight problem complaints increased by more than 2 percent.

Solutions:

(a) According to the table, in 2003, 1 percent of the total number of complaints concerned credit. Therefore, the number of complaints concerning credit is equal to 1 percent of 22,998. By converting 1 percent to its decimal equivalent, you obtain that the number of complaints in 2003 is equal to (0.01)(22,998), or about 230.

(b) The decrease in the total number of complaints from 2003 to 2004 was 22,998 − 13,278, or 9,720. Therefore, the percent decrease was $\left(\dfrac{9,720}{22,998}\right)(100\%)$, or approximately 42 percent.

(c) Since 20.0 + 18.3 + 13.1 and 22.1 + 21.8 + 11.3 are both greater than 50, statement I is true. For statement II, the *percent* of special passenger accommodation complaints *did* remain the same from 2003 to 2004, but the *number* of such complaints decreased because the total number of complaints decreased. Thus, statement II is false. For statement III, the *percents* shown in the table for flight problems do in fact increase by more than 2 percentage points, but the bases of the percents are different. The total number of complaints in 2004 was much lower than the total number of complaints in 2003, and clearly 20 percent of 22,998 is greater than 22.1 percent of 13,278. So, the number of flight problem complaints actually decreased from 2003 to 2004, and statement III is false.

Example 4.6.2:

UNITED STATES PRODUCTION OF PHOTOGRAPHIC EQUIPMENT AND SUPPLIES IN 1971

Total: $3,980 million

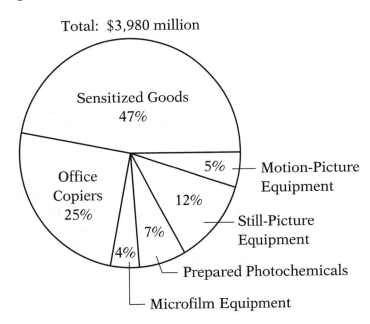

(a) Approximately what was the ratio of the value of sensitized goods to the value of still-picture equipment produced in 1971 in the United States?

(b) If the value of office copiers produced in 1971 was 30 percent greater than the corresponding value in 1970, what was the value of office copiers produced in 1970 ?

Solutions:

(a) The ratio of the value of sensitized goods to the value of still-picture equipment is equal to the ratio of the corresponding percents shown because the percents have the same base, which is the total value. Therefore, the ratio is 47 to 12, or approximately 4 to 1.

(b) The value of office copiers produced in 1971 was 0.25 times $3,980 million, or $995 million. Therefore, if the corresponding value in 1970 was x million dollars, then $1.3x = 995$ million. Solving for x yields $x = \dfrac{995}{1.3} \approx 765$, so the value of office copiers produced in 1970 was approximately $765 million.

Example 4.6.3:

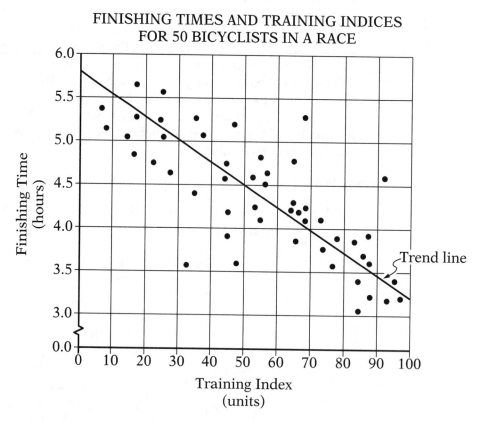

FINISHING TIMES AND TRAINING INDICES FOR 50 BICYCLISTS IN A RACE

A bicycle trainer studied 50 bicyclists to examine how the finishing time for a certain bicycle race was related to the amount of physical training in the three months before the race. To measure the amount of training, the trainer developed a training index, measured in "units" and based on the intensity of each bicyclist's training. The data and the trend of the data, represented by a line, are displayed in the scatterplot above.

(a) How many of the 50 bicyclists had both a training index less than 50 units and a finishing time less than 4.5 hours?

(b) What percent of the 10 fastest bicyclists in the race had a training index less than 90 units?

Solutions:

(a) The number of bicyclists who had both a training index less than 50 units and a finishing time less than 4.5 hours is equal to the number of points on the graph to the left of 50 and below 4.5. Since there are five data points that are both to the left of 50 units and below 4.5 hours, the correct answer is five.

(b) The 10 lowest data points represent the 10 fastest bicyclists. Of these 10 data points, 3 points are to the right of 90 units, so the number of points to the left of 90 units is 7, which represents 70 percent of the 10 fastest bicyclists.

Example 4.6.4:

TRAVELERS SURVEYED: 250

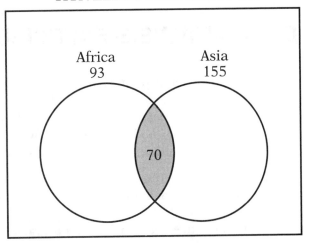

In a survey of 250 European travelers, 93 have traveled to Africa, 155 have traveled to Asia, and of these two groups, 70 have traveled to both continents, as illustrated in the Venn diagram above.

(a) How many of the travelers surveyed have traveled to Africa but <u>not</u> to Asia?

(b) How many of the travelers surveyed have traveled to <u>at least one</u> of the two continents of Africa and Asia?

(c) How many of the travelers surveyed have traveled <u>neither</u> to Africa <u>nor</u> to Asia?

Solutions: In the Venn diagram, the rectangular region represents the set of all travelers surveyed; the two circular regions represent the two sets of travelers to Africa and Asia, respectively; and the shaded region represents the subset of those who have traveled to both continents.

(a) The set described here is represented by *the part of the left circle that is not shaded*. This description suggests that the answer can be found by taking the shaded part away from the first circle—in effect, subtracting the 70 from the 93, to get 23 travelers who have traveled to Africa but not to Asia.

(b) The set described here is represented by that part of the rectangle that is *in at least one of the two circles*. This description suggests adding the two numbers 93 and 155. But the 70 travelers who have traveled to both continents would be counted twice in the sum 93 + 155. To correct the double counting, subtract 70 from the sum so that these 70 travelers are counted only once:

$$93 + 155 - 70 = 178$$

(c) The set described here is represented by the part of the rectangle that is *not in either circle*. Let N be the number of these travelers. Note that the entire rectangular region has two main non-overlapping parts: the part *outside* the circles and the part *inside* the circles. The first part represents N travelers and the second part represents $93 + 155 - 70 = 178$ travelers (from question (b)). Therefore,

$$250 = N + 178$$

and solving for N yields

$$N = 250 - 178 = 72$$

DATA ANALYSIS EXERCISES

1. The daily temperatures, in degrees Fahrenheit, for 10 days in May were 61, 62, 65, 65, 65, 68, 74, 74, 75, and 77.
   (a) Find the mean, median, mode, and range of the temperatures.
   (b) If each day had been 7 degrees warmer, what would have been the mean, median, mode, and range of those 10 temperatures?

2. The numbers of passengers on 9 airline flights were 22, 33, 21, 28, 22, 31, 44, 50, and 19. The standard deviation of these 9 numbers is approximately equal to 10.2.
   (a) Find the mean, median, mode, range, and interquartile range of the 9 numbers.
   (b) If each flight had had 3 times as many passengers, what would have been the mean, median, mode, range, interquartile range, and standard deviation of the nine numbers?
   (c) If each flight had had 2 fewer passengers, what would have been interquartile range and standard deviation of the nine numbers?

3. A group of 20 values has a mean of 85 and a median of 80. A different group of 30 values has a mean of 75 and a median of 72.
   (a) What is the mean of the 50 values?
   (b) What is the median of the 50 values?

4. Find the mean and median of the values of the random variable X, whose relative frequency distribution is given in the table below.

X	Relative Frequency
0	0.18
1	0.33
2	0.10
3	0.06
4	0.33

5. Eight hundred insects were weighed, and the resulting measurements, in milligrams, are summarized in the boxplot below.

(a) What are the range, the three quartiles, and the interquartile range of the measurements?
(b) If the 80th percentile of the measurements is 130 milligrams, about how many measurements are between 126 milligrams and 130 milligrams?

6. In how many different ways can the letters in the word STUDY be ordered?

7. Martha invited 4 friends to go with her to the movies. There are 120 different ways in which they can sit together in a row of 5 seats, one person per seat. In how many of those ways is Martha sitting in the middle seat?

8. How many 3-digit positive integers are odd and do not contain the digit 5 ?

9. From a box of 10 lightbulbs, you are to remove 4. How many different sets of 4 lightbulbs could you remove?

10. A talent contest has 8 contestants. Judges must award prizes for first, second, and third places, with no ties.
(a) In how many different ways can the judges award the 3 prizes?
(b) How many different groups of 3 people can get prizes?

11. If an integer is randomly selected from all positive 2-digit integers, what is the probability that the integer chosen has
(a) a 4 in the tens place?
(b) at least one 4 in the tens place or the units place?
(c) no 4 in either place?

12. In a box of 10 electrical parts, 2 are defective.
(a) If you choose one part at random from the box, what is the probability that it is not defective?
(b) If you choose two parts at random from the box, without replacement, what is the probability that both are defective?

13. The table shows the distribution of a group of 40 college students by gender and class.

	Sophomores	Juniors	Seniors
Males	6	10	2
Females	10	9	3

If one student is randomly selected from this group, find the probability that the student chosen is
(a) not a junior
(b) a female or a sophomore
(c) a male sophomore or a female senior

14. Let A, B, C, and D be events for which $P(A \text{ or } B) = 0.6$, $P(A) = 0.2$, $P(C \text{ or } D) = 0.6$, and $P(C) = 0.5$. The events A and B are mutually exclusive, and the events C and D are independent.
   (a) Find $P(B)$
   (b) Find $P(D)$

15. Lin and Mark each attempt independently to decode a message. If the probability that Lin will decode the message is 0.80 and the probability that Mark will decode the message is 0.70, find the probability that
   (a) both will decode the message
   (b) at least one of them will decode the message
   (c) neither of them will decode the message

16.

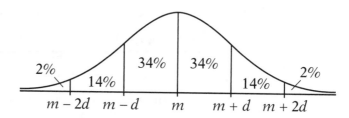

The figure shows a normal distribution with mean m and standard deviation d, including approximate percents of the distribution corresponding to the six regions shown.

Suppose the heights of a population of 3,000 adult penguins are approximately normally distributed with a mean of 65 centimeters and a standard deviation of 5 centimeters.
   (a) Approximately how many of the adult penguins are between 65 centimeters and 75 centimeters tall?
   (b) If an adult penguin is chosen at random from the population, approximately what is the probability that the penguin's height will be less than 60 centimeters? Give your answer to the nearest 0.05.

17.

PUBLIC AND PRIVATE SCHOOL EXPENDITURES
1987–2001
(in billions of dollars)

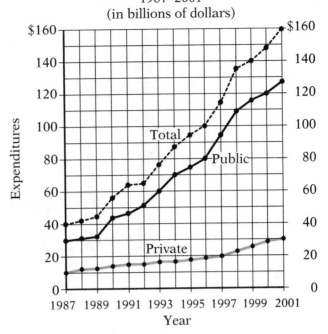

(a) For which year did total expenditures increase the most from the year before?

(b) For 2001, private school expenditures were approximately what percent of total expenditures?

18.

DISTRIBUTION OF WORKFORCE BY OCCUPATIONAL CATEGORY
FOR REGION *Y* IN 2001 AND PROJECTED FOR 2015

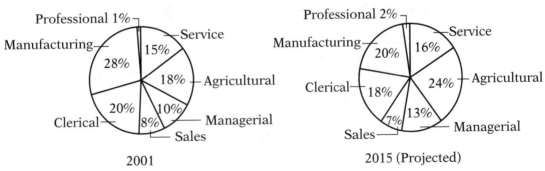

(a) In 2001, how many categories each comprised more than 25 million workers?

(b) What is the ratio of the number of workers in the Agricultural category in 2001 to the projected number of such workers in 2015 ?

(c) From 2001 to 2015, there is a projected increase in the number of workers in which of the following categories?

I. Sales   II. Service   III. Clerical

19.

A FAMILY'S EXPENDITURES AND SAVINGS
AS A PERCENT OF ITS GROSS ANNUAL INCOME*

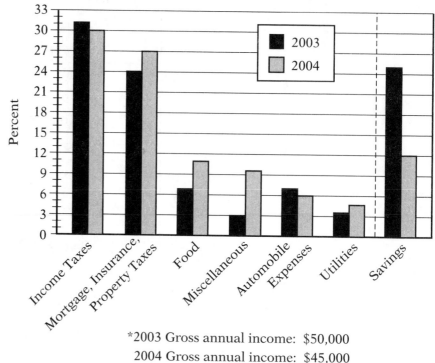

*2003 Gross annual income: $50,000
2004 Gross annual income: $45,000

(a) In 2003 the family used a total of 49 percent of its gross annual income for two of the categories listed. What was the total amount of the family's income used for those same categories in 2004?

(b) Of the seven categories listed, which category of expenditure had the greatest percent increase from 2003 to 2004 ?

ANSWERS TO DATA ANALYSIS EXERCISES

1. In degrees Fahrenheit, the statistics are
    (a) mean = 68.6, median = 66.5, mode = 65, range = 16
    (b) mean = 75.6, median = 73.5, mode = 72, range = 16

2. (a) mean = 30, median = 28, mode = 22,
        range = 31, interquartile range = 17
    (b) mean = 90, median = 84, mode = 66,
        range = 93, interquartile range = 51,

    standard deviation $= 3\sqrt{\dfrac{940}{9}} \approx 30.7$

    (c) interquartile range = 17, standard deviation ≈ 10.2

3. (a) mean = 79
    (b) The median cannot be determined from the information given.

4. mean = 2.03, median = 1

5. (a) range = 41, $Q_1 = 114$, $Q_2 = 118$, $Q_3 = 126$, interquartile range = 12
    (b) 40 measurements

6. $5! = 120$

7. 24

8. 288

9. 210

10. (a) 336   (b) 56

11. (a) $\frac{1}{9}$ (b) $\frac{1}{5}$ (c) $\frac{4}{5}$

12. (a) $\frac{4}{5}$ (b) $\frac{1}{45}$

13. (a) $\frac{21}{40}$ (b) $\frac{7}{10}$ (c) $\frac{9}{40}$

14. (a) 0.4   (b) 0.2

15. (a) 0.56   (b) 0.94   (c) 0.06

16. (a) 1,440   (b) 0.15

17. (a) 1998   (b) 19%

18. (a) Three   (b) 9 to 14, or $\frac{9}{14}$ (c) I, II, and III

19. (a) $17,550   (b) Miscellaneous

Authentic GRE® Practice Test

Your goals for this chapter	◥ Take a full-length authentic GRE revised General Test under actual test time limits. ◥ Review the test directions. ◥ Check your test answers and read explanations for every question. ◥ Use your results to identify your strengths and weaknesses.

Taking the Practice Test

N ow that you have become familiar with the three measures of the revised General Test, it is time to take the practice revised General Test to see how well you do. The test begins on the following pages. The total time that you should allow for this practice test is 3 hours and 30 minutes. The time allotted for each section appears at the beginning of that section.

Try to take the Practice Test under actual test conditions. Find a quiet place to work, and set aside enough time to complete the test without being disturbed. Work on only one section at a time. Use your watch or a timer to keep track of the time limits for each section.

For the Verbal Reasoning and Quantitative Reasoning portions of this test, you will mark your answers directly in this book. However, when you take the real GRE General Test on computer, you will click on your answer choices. For the Analytical Writing sections of this test, how you respond will depend on how you plan to take the actual test. If you plan to take the actual test on computer, you should type your responses. If you plan to take the paper-based test, you should handwrite your responses on paper. You will need a supply of blank paper for this task.

At the end of the test you will find an Answer Key. Check your answers against the Key, then follow the instructions for calculating your raw score. You will also find explanations for each test question. Review the explanations, paying particular attention to the ones for the questions that you answered incorrectly.

Once you have worked your way through this Practice Test, you will have a better idea of how ready you are to take the actual GRE revised General Test. You will also have a better sense of whether you are able to work fast enough to finish each section within the time allowed, or whether you need to improve your test-taking speed. After you have evaluated your test-taking performance, you can determine what type of additional preparation you might want to do for the test. For additional test-preparation materials and suggestions, visit the GRE website at **www.ets.org/gre/revised/prepare** for other preparation materials and suggestions.

The Graduate Record Examinations®

SECTION 1
Analytical Writing

ANALYZE AN ISSUE

30 minutes

You will be given a brief quotation that states or implies an issue of general interest and specific instructions on how to respond to that issue. You will then have 30 minutes to plan and compose a response according to the specific instructions. A response to any other issue will receive a score of zero.

Make sure that you respond according to the specific instructions and support your position on the issue with reasons and examples drawn from such areas as your reading, experience, observations, and/or academic studies.

Trained GRE readers will read your response and evaluate its overall quality, based on how well you:

- Respond to the specific instructions
- Consider the complexities of the issue
- Organize, develop, and express your ideas
- Support your ideas with relevant reasons and/or examples
- Control the elements of standard written English

Before you begin writing, you may want to think for a few minutes about the issue and instructions and then plan your response. Be sure to develop your position fully and organize it coherently, but leave time to reread what you have written and make any revisions you think are necessary.

Issue Topic

The best way to teach is to praise positive actions and ignore negative ones.

Write a response in which you discuss the extent to which you agree or disagree with the recommendation and explain your reasoning for the position you take. In developing and supporting your position, describe specific circumstances in which adopting the recommendation would or would not be advantageous and explain how these examples shape your position.

The Graduate Record Examinations®

SECTION 2
Analytical Writing

ANALYZE AN ARGUMENT

30 minutes

You will be given a short passage that presents an argument and specific instructions on how to respond to that passage. You will have 30 minutes to plan and compose a response in which you evaluate the passage according to the specific instructions. A response to any other argument will receive a score of zero.

Note that you are NOT being asked to present your own views on the subject. Make sure that you respond according to the specific instructions and support your evaluation with relevant reasons and/or examples.

Trained GRE readers will read your response and evaluate its overall quality, based on how well you:

- Respond to the specific instructions
- Identify and analyze important features of the passage
- Organize, develop, and express your evaluation
- Support your evaluation with relevant reasons and/or examples
- Control the elements of standard written English

Before you begin writing, you may want to think a few minutes about the passage and the instructions and then plan your response. Be sure to develop your evaluation fully and organize it coherently, but leave time to read what you have written and make any revisions that you think are necessary.

Argument Topic

The following appeared in an article written by Dr. Karp, an anthropologist.

"Twenty years ago, Dr. Field, a noted anthropologist, visited the island of Tertia and concluded from his observations that children in Tertia were reared by an entire village rather than by their own biological parents. However, my recent interviews with children living in the group of islands that includes Tertia show that these children spend much more time talking about their biological parents than about other adults in the village. This research of mine proves that Dr. Field's conclusion about Tertian village culture is invalid and thus that the observation-centered approach to studying cultures is invalid as well. The interview-centered method that my team of graduate students is currently using in Tertia will establish a much more accurate understanding of child-rearing traditions there and in other island cultures."

Write a response in which you discuss what specific evidence is needed to evaluate the argument and explain how the evidence would weaken or strengthen the argument.

NO TEST MATERIAL ON THIS PAGE

SECTION 3
Verbal Reasoning
Time—35 minutes
25 Questions

> For each of Questions 1 to 4, select <u>one</u> answer choice unless otherwise instructed.

Questions 1 to 3 are based on the following reading passage.

Whether the languages of the ancient American peoples were used for expressing abstract universal concepts can be clearly answered in the case of Nahuatl. Nahuatl, like Greek and German, is a language that allows the formation of extensive com-
line   pounds. By the combination of radicals or semantic elements, single compound words
5   can express complex conceptual relations, often of an abstract universal character.

The *tlamatinime* (those who know) were able to use this rich stock of abstract terms to express the nuances of their thought. They also availed themselves of other forms of expression with metaphorical meaning, some probably original, some derived from Toltec coinages. Of these forms, the most characteristic in Nahuatl is the juxtaposition
10   of two words that, because they are synonyms, associated terms, or even contraries, complement each other to evoke one single idea. Used metaphorically, the juxtaposed terms connote specific or essential traits of the being they refer to, introducing a mode of poetry as an almost habitual form of expression.

For the following question, consider each of the choices separately and select all that apply.

1. Which of the following can be inferred from the passage regarding present-day research relating to Nahuatl?

   A Some record or evidence of the thought of the *tlamatinime* is available.

   B For at least some Nahuatl expressions, researchers are able to trace their derivation from another ancient American language.

   C Researchers believe that in Nahuatl, abstract universal concepts are always expressed metaphorically.

2. Select the sentence in the passage in which the author introduces a specific Nahuatl mode of expression that is not identified as being shared with certain European languages.

3. In the context in which it appears, "coinages" (line 9) most nearly means

   Ⓐ adaptations
   Ⓑ creations
   Ⓒ idiosyncrasies
   Ⓓ pronunciations
   Ⓔ currencies

GO ON TO NEXT PAGE ↘

At a certain period in Earth's history, its atmosphere contained almost no oxygen, although plants were producing vast quantities of oxygen. As a way of reconciling these two facts, scientists have hypothesized that nearly all of the oxygen being produced was taken up by iron on Earth's surface. Clearly, however, **this explanation is inadequate**. New studies show that **the amount of iron on Earth's surface was not sufficient to absorb anywhere near as much oxygen as was being produced**. Therefore, something in addition to the iron on Earth's surface must have absorbed much of the oxygen produced by plant life.

4. In the argument given, the two portions in **boldface** play which of the following roles?

    (A) The first is a claim made by the argument in support of a certain position; the second is that position.

    (B) The first is a judgment made by the argument about a certain explanation; the second is that explanation.

    (C) The first expresses the argument's dismissal of an objection to the position it seeks to establish; the second is that position.

    (D) The first sums up the argument's position with regard to a certain hypothesis; the second provides grounds for that position.

    (E) The first is a concession by the argument that its initial formulation of the position it seeks to establish requires modification; the second presents that position in a modified form.

For Questions 5 to 8, select one entry for each blank from the corresponding column of choices. Fill all blanks in the way that best completes the text.

---

5. In her later years, Bertha Pappenheim was an apostle of noble but already (i)_____ notions, always respected for her integrity, her energy, and her resolve but increasingly out of step and ultimately (ii)_____ even her own organization.

Blank (i)	Blank (ii)
(A) anachronistic	(D) emulated by
(B) accepted	(E) appreciated by
(C) exotic	(F) alienated from

6. The reception given to Kimura's radical theory of molecular evolution shows that when _____ fights orthodoxy to a draw, then novelty has seized a good chunk of space from convention.

(A) imitation
(B) reaction
(C) dogmatism
(D) invention
(E) caution

7. The (i)_____ of Vladimir Nabokov as one of North America's literary giants has thrown the spotlight on his peripheral activities and has thus served to (ii)_____ his efforts as an amateur entomologist.

Blank (i)	Blank (ii)
(A) stigmatization	(D) foreground
(B) lionization	(E) transcend
(C) marginalization	(F) obscure

8. Mathematicians have a distinctive sense of beauty: they strive to present their ideas and results in a clear and compelling fashion, dictated by _____ as well as by logic.

(A) caprice
(B) aesthetics
(C) obligation
(D) methodologies
(E) intellect

GO ON TO NEXT PAGE ↘

For each of Questions 9 to 13, select **one** answer choice unless otherwise instructed.

Questions 9 to 12 are based on the following reading passage.

Animal signals, such as the complex songs of birds, tend to be costly. A bird, by singing, may forfeit time that could otherwise be spent on other important behaviors such as foraging or resting. Singing may also advertise an individual's location to rivals or pred-
line   ators and impair the ability to detect their approach. Although these types of cost may
5   be important, discussions of the cost of singing have generally focused on energy costs. Overall the evidence is equivocal: for instance, while Eberhardt found increases in energy consumption during singing for Carolina wrens, Chappell found no effect of crowing on energy consumption in roosters.

To obtain empirical data regarding the energy costs of singing, Thomas examined
10   the relationship between song rate and overnight changes in body mass of male nightingales. Birds store energy as subcutaneous fat deposits or "body reserves"; changes in these reserves can be reliably estimated by measuring changes in body mass. If singing has important energy costs, nightingales should lose more body mass on nights when their song rate is high. Thomas found that nightingales reached a sig-
15   nificantly higher body mass at dusk and lost more mass overnight on nights when their song rate was high.

These results suggest that there may be several costs of singing at night associated with body reserves. The increased metabolic cost of possessing higher body mass contributes to the increased overnight mass loss. The strategic regulation of evening body
20   reserves is also likely to incur additional costs, as nightingales must spend more time foraging in order to build up larger body reserves. The metabolic cost of singing itself may also contribute to increased loss of reserves. This metabolic cost may arise from the muscular and neural activity involved in singing or from behaviors associated with singing. For example, birds may expend more of their reserves on thermoregulation if
25   they spend the night exposed to the wind on a song post than if they are in a sheltered roost site. Thomas's data therefore show that whether or not singing per se has an important metabolic cost, metabolic costs associated with singing can have an important measurable effect on a bird's daily energy budget, at least in birds with high song rates such as nightingales.

9. The primary purpose of the passage is to
    (A) compare the different types of cost involved for certain birds in singing
    (B) question a hypothesis regarding the energy costs of singing for certain birds
    (C) present evidence suggesting that singing has an important energy cost for certain birds
    (D) discuss the benefits provided to an organism by a behavior that is costly in energy
    (E) describe an experiment that supports an alternative model of how birdsong functions

For the following question, consider each of the choices separately and select all that apply.

10. The passage implies that during the day before a night on which a male nightingale's song rate is high, that nightingale probably does which of the following?

    A Expends less of its reserves on thermoregulation than on other days
    B Stores more energy as body reserves than on other days
    C Hides to avoid predators

11. Select the sentence in the first or second paragraph that presents empirical results in support of a hypothesis about the energy costs of singing.

For the following question, consider each of the choices separately and select all that apply.

12. It can be inferred from the passage that compared with other costs of singing, which of the following is true of the energy costs of singing?

    A They are the single greatest cost to an individual bird.
    B They have generally received more attention from scientists.
    C They vary less from one bird species to another.

Question 13 is based on the following reading passage.

In the past ten years, there have been several improvements in mountain-climbing equipment. These improvements have made the sport both safer and more enjoyable for experienced climbers. Despite these improvements, however, the rate of mountain-climbing injuries has doubled in the past ten years.

13. Which of the following, if true, best reconciles the apparent discrepancy presented in the passage?

    (A) Many climbers, lulled into a false sense of security, use the new equipment to attempt climbing feats of which they are not capable.
    (B) Some mountain-climbing injuries are caused by unforeseeable weather conditions.
    (C) Mountain climbing, although a dangerous sport, does not normally result in injury to the experienced climber.
    (D) In the past ten years there have been improvements in mountain-climbing techniques as well as in mountain-climbing equipment.
    (E) Although the rate of mountain-climbing injuries has increased, the rate of mountain-climbing deaths has not changed.

GO ON TO NEXT PAGE ↘

For Questions 14 to 17, select one entry for each blank from the corresponding column of choices. Fill all blanks in the way that best completes the text.

14. Unenlightened authoritarian managers rarely recognize a crucial reason for the low levels of serious conflict among members of democratically run work groups: a modicum of tolerance for dissent often prevents _____.

Ⓐ demur
Ⓑ schism
Ⓒ cooperation
Ⓓ compliance
Ⓔ shortsightedness

15. The novelist devotes so much time to avid descriptions of his characters' clothes that the reader soon feels that such _____ concerns, although worthy of attention, have superseded any more directly literary aims.

Ⓐ didactic
Ⓑ syntactical
Ⓒ irrelevant
Ⓓ sartorial
Ⓔ frivolous

16. Belanger dances with an (i)_____ that draws one's attention as if by seeking to (ii)_____ it; through finesse and understatement, he manages to seem at once intensely present and curiously detached.

Blank (i)	Blank (ii)
Ⓐ undemonstrative panache	Ⓓ focus
Ⓑ unrestrained enthusiasm	Ⓔ overwhelm
Ⓒ unattractive gawkiness	Ⓕ deflect

17. The most striking thing about the politician is how often his politics have been (i)_____ rather than ideological, as he adapts his political positions at any particular moment to the political realities that constrain him. He does not, however, piously (ii)_____ political principles only to betray them in practice. Rather, he attempts in subtle ways to balance his political self-interest with a (iii)_____, viewing himself as an instrument of some unchanging higher purpose.

Blank (i)	Blank (ii)	Blank (iii)
Ⓐ quixotic	Ⓓ brandish	Ⓖ profound cynicism
Ⓑ self-righteous	Ⓔ flout	Ⓗ deeply felt moral code
Ⓒ strategic	Ⓕ follow	Ⓘ thoroughgoing pragmatism

For each of Questions 18 to 20, select **one** answer choice unless otherwise instructed.

Questions 18 to 20 are based on the following reading passage.

The condition of scholarship devoted to the history of women in photography is confounding. Recent years have witnessed the posthumous inflation of the role of the
hobbyist Alice Austen into that of a pioneering documentarian while dozens of notable
line   senior figures — Marion Palfi, whose photographs of civil-rights activities in the South
5   served as early evidence of the need for protective legislation, to name one — received
scant attention from scholars. And, while Naomi Rosenblum's synoptic *History of
Women Photographers* covers the subject through 1920 in a generally useful fashion,
once she reaches the 1920s, when the venues, forms, applications, and movements of
the medium expanded exponentially, she resorts to an increasingly terse listing of un-
10   familiar names, with approaches and careers summarized in a sentence or two.

18. The author of the passage cites Rosenblum's book most likely in order to
    (A) suggest that the works documented most thoroughly by historians of
        women in photography often do not warrant that attention
    (B) offer an explanation for the observation that not all aspects of the history
        of women in photography have received the same level of attention
    (C) provide an example of a way in which scholarship on the history of
        women in photography has been unsatisfactory
    (D) suggest that employing a strictly chronological approach when studying
        the history of women in photography may be unproductive
    (E) provide support for the notion that certain personalities in women's
        photography have attained undue prominence

For the following question, consider each of the choices separately and select all that apply.

19. Which of the following statements about Marion Palfi is supported by the
    passage?
    [A] Marion Palfi's photographs would have received greater recognition from
        historians had her work been done in an era when most aspects of
        photography were static rather than in a state of transition.
    [B] Alice Austen has achieved greater notoriety than has Marion Palfi
        primarily because the subjects that Austen photographed were more
        familiar to her contemporaries.
    [C] In addition to providing a record of certain historical events, Marion
        Palfi's photographs played a role in subsequent events.

20. In the context in which it appears, "inflation" (line 2) most nearly means
    (A) exaggeration
    (B) acquisition
    (C) evaluation
    (D) distortion
    (E) attenuation

GO ON TO NEXT PAGE ◥

For Questions 21 to 25, select the <u>two</u> answer choices that, when used to complete the sentence, fit the meaning of the sentence as a whole <u>and</u> produce completed sentences that are alike in meaning.

21. The plan, which the engineers said would save the aquifer by reducing pumping to _____ levels, has passed a governmental environmental review but faces opposition from outdoor and environmental groups.

    A innocuous

    B feasible

    C practicable

    D minimal

    E remedial

    F benign

22. Though feminist in its implications, Yvonne Rainer's 1974 film _____ the filmmaker's active involvement in feminist politics.

    A antedated

    B cloaked

    C portrayed

    D preceded

    E renewed

    F represented

23. Congress is having great difficulty developing a consensus on energy policy, primarily because the policy objectives of various members of Congress rest on such _____ assumptions.

    A commonplace

    B disparate

    C divergent

    D fundamental

    E trite

    F trivial

24. During the opera's most famous aria, the tempo chosen by the orchestra's conductor seemed _____, without necessary relation to what had gone before.

    [A] arbitrary

    [B] capricious

    [C] cautious

    [D] compelling

    [E] exacting

    [F] meticulous

25. Because they had expected the spacecraft Voyager 2 to be able to gather data only about the planets Jupiter and Saturn, scientists were _____ the wealth of information it sent back from Neptune twelve years after leaving Earth.

    [A] anxious for

    [B] confident in

    [C] thrilled about

    [D] keen on

    [E] elated by

    [F] eager for

STOP. This is the end of Section 3.

SECTION 4
Verbal Reasoning
Time — 35 minutes
25 Questions

> **For Questions 1 to 4, select the <u>two</u> answer choices that, when used to complete the sentence, fit the meaning of the sentence as a whole and produce completed sentences that are alike in meaning.**

1. Only by ignoring decades of mismanagement and inefficiency could investors conclude that a fresh infusion of cash would provide anything other than a _____ solution to the company's financial woes.

   A complete

   B fleeting

   C momentary

   D premature

   E trivial

   F total

2. Some scientists argue that carbon compounds play such a central role in life on Earth because of the possibility of _____ resulting from the carbon atom's ability to form an unending series of different molecules.

   A diversity

   B deviation

   C variety

   D reproduction

   E stability

   F invigoration

3. Given the flood of information presented by the mass media, the only way for someone to keep abreast of the news is to rely on _____ accounts.

   A synoptic

   B abridged

   C sensational

   D copious

   E lurid

   F understated

4. Always circumspect, she was reluctant to make judgments, but once arriving at a conclusion, she was _____ in its defense.

    A deferential

    B intransigent

    C lax

    D negligent

    E obsequious

    F resolute

GO ON TO NEXT PAGE ↘

For each of Questions 5 to 9, select one answer choice unless otherwise instructed.

Questions 5 and 6 are based on the following reading passage.

When marine organisms called phytoplankton photosynthesize, they absorb carbon dioxide dissolved in seawater, potentially causing a reduction in the concentration of atmospheric carbon dioxide, a gas that contributes to global warming. However, phy-

line

5 toplankton flourish only in surface waters where iron levels are sufficiently high. Martin therefore hypothesized that adding iron to iron-poor regions of the ocean could help alleviate global warming. While experiments subsequently confirmed that such a procedure increases phytoplankton growth, field tests have shown that such growth does not significantly lower atmospheric carbon dioxide. When phytoplankton utilize carbon dioxide for photosynthesis, the carbon becomes a building block for organic

10 matter, but the carbon leaks back into the atmosphere when predators consume the phytoplankton and respire carbon dioxide.

For the following question, consider each of the choices separately and select all that apply.

5. It can be inferred from the passage that Martin's hypothesis includes which of the following elements?

A A correct understanding of how phytoplankton photosynthesis utilizes carbon dioxide

B A correct prediction about how the addition of iron to iron-poor waters would affect phytoplankton growth

C An incorrect prediction about how phytoplankton growth would affect the concentration of atmospheric carbon dioxide

6. It can be inferred that the author of the passage mentions predators (line 10) primarily in order to

Ⓐ help explain why Martin's hypothesis is incorrect

Ⓑ identify one effect of adding iron to iron-poor waters

Ⓒ indicate how some carbon dioxide is converted to solid organic matter

Ⓓ help account for differences in the density of phytoplankton between different regions of the ocean

Ⓔ point out a factor that was not anticipated by the scientists who conducted the field tests mentioned in the passage

Sparva, unlike Treland's other provinces, requires automobile insurers to pay for any medical treatment sought by someone who has been involved in an accident; in the other provinces, insurers pay for nonemergency treatment only if they preapprove the treatment. Clearly, Sparva's less restrictive policy must be the explanation for the fact that altogether insurers there pay for far more treatments after accidents than insurers in other provinces, even though Sparva does not have the largest population.

7. Which of the following, if true, most strengthens the argument?

(A) Car insurance costs more in Sparva than in any other province.

(B) The cost of medical care in Sparva is higher than the national average.

(C) Different insurance companies have different standards for determining what constitutes emergency treatment.

(D) Fewer insurance companies operate in Sparva than in any other province.

(E) There are fewer traffic accidents annually in Sparva than in any of the provinces of comparable or greater population.

GO ON TO NEXT PAGE ➘

Elements of the Philosophy of Newton, published by Voltaire in 1738, was an early attempt to popularize the scientific ideas of Isaac Newton. In the book's frontispiece, Voltaire is seen writing at his desk, and over him a shaft of light from heaven, the light of truth, passes through Newton to Voltaire's collaborator Madame du Châtelet; she reflects that light onto the inspired Voltaire. Voltaire's book commanded a wide audience, according to Feingold, because "he was neither a mathematician nor a physicist, but a literary giant aloof from the academic disputes over Newtonian ideas." In other words, Voltaire's amateurism in science "was a source of his contemporary appeal, demonstrating for the first time the accessibility of Newton's ideas to nonspecialists."

For the following question, consider each of the choices separately and select all that apply.

8. Which of the following statements about Voltaire's *Elements of the Philosophy of Newton* can be inferred from the passage?

    A   Voltaire's literary stature helped secure a large audience for this attempt to popularize Newton's ideas.

    B   Voltaire's status as a nonscientist was an advantage in this effort to bring Newtonian science to the attention of the general public.

    C   The frontispiece of the book implies that Voltaire's understanding of Newton's ideas was not achieved without assistance.

9. Select the sentence that describes an allegory for Voltaire's acquisition of knowledge concerning Newton's ideas.

For Questions 10 to 13, select one entry for each blank from the corresponding column of choices. Fill all blanks in the way that best completes the text.

10. Ironically, the writer so wary of (i)_____ was (ii)_____ with ink and paper, his novel running to 2,500 shagreen-bound folio pages — a fortune in stationery at the time.

Blank (i)	Blank (ii)
Ⓐ probity	Ⓓ acquisitive
Ⓑ extravagance	Ⓔ illiberal
Ⓒ disapprobation	Ⓕ profligate

11. What readers most commonly remember about John Stuart Mill's classic exploration of the liberty of thought and discussion concerns the danger of (i)_____: in the absence of challenge, one's opinions, even when they are correct, grow weak and flabby. Yet Mill had another reason for encouraging the liberty of thought and discussion: the danger of partiality and incompleteness. Since one's opinions, even under the best circumstances, tend to (ii)_____, and because opinions opposed to one's own rarely turn out to be completely (iii)_____, it is crucial to supplement one's opinions with alternative points of view.

Blank (i)	Blank (ii)	Blank (iii)
Ⓐ tendentiousness	Ⓓ embrace only a portion of the truth	Ⓖ erroneous
Ⓑ complacency	Ⓔ change over time	Ⓗ antithetical
Ⓒ fractiousness	Ⓕ focus on matters close at hand	Ⓘ immutable

12. Just as the authors' book on eels is often a key text for courses in marine vertebrate zoology, their ideas on animal development and phylogeny _____ teaching in this area.

Ⓐ prevent
Ⓑ defy
Ⓒ replicate
Ⓓ inform
Ⓔ use

13. Mechanisms develop whereby every successful species can _____ its innate capacity for population growth with the constraints that arise through its interactions with the natural environment.

Ⓐ enhance
Ⓑ replace
Ⓒ produce
Ⓓ surpass
Ⓔ reconcile

GO ON TO NEXT PAGE ↘

For each of Questions 14 to 16, select __one__ answer choice unless otherwise instructed.

Questions 14 to 16 are based on the following reading passage.

It would be expected that a novel by a figure as prominent as W. E. B. DuBois would attract the attention of literary critics. Additionally, when the novel subtly engages the issue of race, as DuBois' *The Quest of the Silver Fleece* (1911) does, it would be a surprise not to encounter an abundance of scholarly work about that text. But though valuable scholarship has examined DuBois' political and historical thought, his novels have received scant attention. Perhaps DuBois the novelist must wait his turn behind DuBois the philosopher, historian, and editor. But what if the truth lies elsewhere: what if his novels do not speak to current concerns?

14. Which of the following can be inferred from the passage regarding DuBois' *The Quest of the Silver Fleece*?

(A) The lack of attention devoted to *The Quest of the Silver Fleece* can be attributed to the fact that it was DuBois' first novel.

(B) Among DuBois' novels, *The Quest of the Silver Fleece* is unusual in that it has received scant attention from scholars.

(C) *The Quest of the Silver Fleece* has at least one feature that typically would attract the attention of literary scholars.

(D) *The Quest of the Silver Fleece*, given its subtle exploration of race, is probably the best novel written by DuBois.

(E) Much of the scholarly work that has focused on *The Quest of the Silver Fleece* has been surprisingly critical of it.

15. In the fourth sentence ("Perhaps DuBois . . . editor."), the author of the passage is most likely suggesting that

(A) scholars will find that DuBois' novels are more relevant to current concerns than is his work as philosopher, historian, and editor

(B) more scholarly attention will be paid to *The Quest of the Silver Fleece* than to DuBois' other novels

(C) DuBois' novels will come to overshadow his work as philosopher, historian, and editor

(D) DuBois' novels may eventually attract greater scholarly interest than they have to date

(E) it will be shown that DuBois' work as philosopher, historian, and editor had an important influence on his work as novelist

16. Which of the following best describes the central issue with which the passage is concerned?

    Ⓐ The perfunctoriness of much of the critical work devoted to DuBois' novels

    Ⓑ The nature of DuBois' engagement with the issue of race in *The Quest of the Silver Fleece*

    Ⓒ Whether DuBois' novels are of high quality and relevant to current concerns

    Ⓓ The relationship between DuBois the novelist and DuBois the philosopher, historian, and editor

    Ⓔ The degree of consideration that has been given to DuBois' novels, including *The Quest of the Silver Fleece*

For Questions 17 to 20, select one entry for each blank from the corresponding column of choices. Fill all blanks in the way that best completes the text.

---

17. In the midst of so many evasive comments, this forthright statement, whatever its intrinsic merit, plainly stands out as _____.

Ⓐ a paradigm
Ⓑ a misnomer
Ⓒ a profundity
Ⓓ an inaccuracy
Ⓔ an anomaly

18. The activists' energetic work in the service of both woman suffrage and the temperance movement in the late nineteenth century (i)_____ the assertion that the two movements were (ii)_____.

Blank (i)	Blank (ii)
Ⓐ undermines	Ⓓ diffuse
Ⓑ supports	Ⓔ inimical
Ⓒ underscores	Ⓕ predominant

19. There is nothing quite like this movie, and indeed I am not altogether sure there is much more to it than its lovely (i)_____. At a moment when so many films strive to be as (ii)_____ as possible, it is gratifying to find one that is so subtle and puzzling.

Blank (i)	Blank (ii)
Ⓐ peculiarity	Ⓓ indirect
Ⓑ pellucidity	Ⓔ assertive
Ⓒ conventionality	Ⓕ enigmatic

GO ON TO NEXT PAGE ↘

20. Wills argues that certain malarial parasites are especially (i)_____ because they have more recently entered humans than other species and therefore have had (ii)_____ time to evolve toward (iii)_____. Yet there is no reliable evidence that the most harmful *Plasmodium* species has been in humans for a shorter time than less harmful species.

Blank (i)	Blank (ii)	Blank (iii)
Ⓐ populous	Ⓓ ample	Ⓖ virulence
Ⓑ malignant	Ⓔ insufficient	Ⓗ benignity
Ⓒ threatened	Ⓕ adequate	Ⓘ variability

For each of Questions 21 to 25, select <u>one</u> answer choice unless otherwise instructed.

Question 21 is based on the following reading passage.

Saturn's giant moon Titan is the only planetary satellite with a significant atmosphere and the only body in the solar system other than Earth that has a thick atmosphere dominated by molecular nitrogen. For a long time, the big question about Titan's
line atmosphere was how it could be so thick, given that Jupiter's moons Ganymede and
5 Callisto, which are the same size as Titan, have none. The conditions for acquiring and retaining a thick nitrogen atmosphere are now readily understood. The low temperature of the protosaturnian nebula enabled Titan to acquire the moderately volatile compounds methane and ammonia (later converted to nitrogen) in addition to water. The higher temperatures of Jupiter's moons, which were closer to the Sun, prevented them
10 from acquiring such an atmosphere.

21. According to the passage, Titan differs atmospherically from Ganymede and Callisto because of a difference in
   Ⓐ rate of heat loss
   Ⓑ proximity to the Sun
   Ⓒ availability of methane and ammonia
   Ⓓ distance from its planet
   Ⓔ size

Question 22 is based on the following reading passage.

Observations of the Arctic reveal that the Arctic Ocean is covered by less ice each summer than the previous summer. If this warming trend continues, within 50 years the Arctic Ocean will be ice free during the summer months. This occurrence would in itself have little or no effect on global sea levels, since the melting of ice floating in water does not affect the water level. However, serious consequences to sea levels would eventually result, because _____.

22. Which of the following most logically completes the passage?

    (A) large masses of floating sea ice would continue to form in the wintertime

    (B) significant changes in Arctic sea temperatures would be accompanied by changes in sea temperatures in more temperate parts of the world

    (C) such a warm Arctic Ocean would trigger the melting of massive land-based glaciers in the Arctic

    (D) an ice-free Arctic Ocean would support a very different ecosystem than it does presently

    (E) in the spring, melting sea ice would cause more icebergs to be created and to drift south into shipping routes

GO ON TO NEXT PAGE ⬖

In a recent study, David Cressy examines two central questions concerning English immigration to New England in the 1630s: what kinds of people immigrated and why? Using contemporary literary evidence, shipping lists, and customs records, Cressy finds *line* that most adult immigrants were skilled in farming or crafts, were literate, and were 5 organized in families. Each of these characteristics sharply distinguishes the 21,000 people who left for New England in the 1630s from most of the approximately 377,000 English people who had immigrated to America by 1700.

With respect to their reasons for immigrating, Cressy does not deny the frequently noted fact that some of the immigrants of the 1630s, most notably the organizers and 10 clergy, advanced religious explanations for departure, but he finds that such explanations usually assumed primacy only in retrospect. When he moves beyond the principal actors, he finds that religious explanations were less frequently offered, and he concludes that most people immigrated because they were recruited by promises of material improvement.

For the following question, consider each of the choices separately and select all that apply.

23. The passage indicates that Cressy would agree with which of the following statements about the organizers among the English immigrants to New England in the 1630s?

   [A] Some of them offered a religious explanation for their immigration.
   [B] They did not offer any reasons for their immigration until some time after they had immigrated.
   [C] They were more likely than the average immigrant to be motivated by material considerations.

24. Select the sentence that provides Cressy's opinion about what motivated English immigrants to go to New England in the 1630s.

25. In the passage, the author is primarily concerned with
   (A) summarizing the findings of an investigation
   (B) analyzing a method of argument
   (C) evaluating a point of view
   (D) hypothesizing about a set of circumstances
   (E) establishing categories

STOP. This is the end of Section 4.

SECTION 5
Quantitative Reasoning
Time—40 minutes
25 Questions

For each question, indicate the best answer, using the directions given.

Notes: All numbers used are real numbers.

All figures are assumed to lie in a plane unless otherwise indicated.

Geometric figures, such as lines, circles, triangles, and quadrilaterals, **are not necessarily** drawn to scale. That is, you should **not** assume that quantities such as lengths and angle measures are as they appear in a figure. You should assume, however, that lines shown as straight are actually straight, points on a line are in the order shown, and more generally, all geometric objects are in the relative positions shown. For questions with geometric figures, you should base your answers on geometric reasoning, not on estimating or comparing quantities by sight or by measurement.

Coordinate systems, such as xy-planes and number lines, **are** drawn to scale; therefore, you can read, estimate, or compare quantities in such figures by sight or by measurement.

Graphical data presentations, such as bar graphs, circles graphs, and line graphs, **are** drawn to scale; therefore, you can read, estimate, or compare data values by sight or by measurement.

For each of Questions 1 to 9, compare Quantity A and Quantity B, using additional information centered above the two quantities if such information is given. Select one of the following four answer choices and fill in the corresponding oval to the right of the question.

ⒶQuantity A is greater.
ⒷQuantity B is greater.
ⒸThe two quantities are equal.
ⒹThe relationship cannot be determined from the information given.

A symbol that appears more than once in a question has the same meaning throughout the question.

	Quantity A	Quantity B	Correct Answer
Example 1:	(2)(6)	2 + 6	Ⓐ Ⓑ Ⓒ Ⓓ

- -

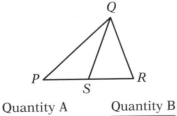

	Quantity A	Quantity B	Correct Answer
Example 2:	PS	SR	Ⓐ Ⓑ Ⓒ Ⓓ

(since equal lengths cannot be assumed, even though *PS* and *SR* appear equal)

Ⓐ **Quantity A is greater.**

Ⓑ **Quantity B is greater.**

Ⓒ **The two quantities are equal.**

Ⓓ **The relationship cannot be determined from the information given.**

O is the center of the circle above.

Quantity A	Quantity B	
1.	x	5	Ⓐ Ⓑ Ⓒ Ⓓ

Runner A ran $\frac{4}{5}$ kilometer and Runner B ran 800 meters.

	Quantity A	Quantity B	
2.	The distance that A ran	The distance that B ran	Ⓐ Ⓑ Ⓒ Ⓓ

$$x < y < z$$

	Quantity A	Quantity B	
3.	$\dfrac{x + y + z}{3}$	y	Ⓐ Ⓑ Ⓒ Ⓓ

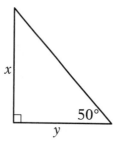

	Quantity A	Quantity B	
4.	$\dfrac{x}{y}$	1	Ⓐ Ⓑ Ⓒ Ⓓ

> (A) Quantity A is greater.
> (B) Quantity B is greater.
> (C) The two quantities are equal.
> (D) The relationship cannot be determined from the information given.

$$0 < x < y < 1$$

	Quantity A	Quantity B	
5.	$1 - y$	$y - x$	(A) (B) (C) (D)

---

p is the probability that event E will occur, and s is the probability that event E will <u>not</u> occur.

	Quantity A	Quantity B	
6.	$p + s$	ps	(A) (B) (C) (D)

X is the set of all integers n that satisfy the inequality $2 \le |n| \le 5$.

	Quantity A	Quantity B	
7.	The absolute value of the greatest integer in X	The absolute value of the least integer in X	(A) (B) (C) (D)

---

x and m are positive numbers, and m is a multiple of 3.

	Quantity A	Quantity B	
8.	$\dfrac{x^m}{x^3}$	$x^{m/3}$	(A) (B) (C) (D)

A random variable Y is normally distributed with a mean of 200 and a standard deviation of 10.

	Quantity A	Quantity B	
9.	The probability of the event that the value of Y is greater than 220	$\dfrac{1}{6}$	(A) (B) (C) (D)

GO ON TO THE NEXT PAGE ↘

Questions 10 to 25 have several different formats. Unless otherwise directed, select a single answer choice. For Numeric Entry questions, follow the instructions below.

Numeric Entry Questions
Enter your answer in the answer box(es) below the question.

- Your answer may be an integer, a decimal, or a fraction, and it may be negative.
- If a question asks for a fraction, there will be two boxes—one for the numerator and one for the denominator.
- Equivalent forms of the correct answer, such as 2.5 and 2.50, are all correct. Fractions do not need to be reduced to lowest terms.
- Enter the exact answer unless the question asks you to round your answer.

10. The ratio of $\frac{1}{3}$ to $\frac{3}{8}$ is equal to the ratio of

   Ⓐ 1 to 8
   Ⓑ 8 to 1
   Ⓒ 8 to 3
   Ⓓ 8 to 9
   Ⓔ 9 to 8

11. A reading list for a humanities course consists of 10 books, of which 4 are biographies and the rest are novels. Each student is required to read a selection of 4 books from the list, including 2 or more biographies. How many selections of 4 books satisfy the requirements?

   Ⓐ   90
   Ⓑ 115
   Ⓒ 130
   Ⓓ 144
   Ⓔ 195

For the following question, enter your answer in the box.

12. In a graduating class of 236 students, 142 took algebra and 121 took chemistry. What is the greatest possible number of students that could have taken both algebra and chemistry?

   [＿＿＿＿] students

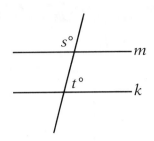

13. In the figure above, if $m \parallel k$ and $s = t + 30$, then $t =$

 (A) 30
 (B) 60
 (C) 75
 (D) 80
 (E) 105

14. If $2x = 3y = 4z = 20$, then $12xyz =$

 (A) 16,000
 (B) 8,000
 (C) 4,000
 (D) 800
 (E) 10

For the following question, select all the answer choices that apply.

15. The total amount that Mary paid for a book was equal to the price of the book plus a sales tax that was 4 percent of the price of the book. Mary paid for the book with a $10 bill and received the correct change, which was less than $3.00. Which of the following statements must be true?

 Indicate <u>all</u> such statements.

 A The price of the book was less than $9.50.
 B The price of the book was greater than $6.90.
 C The sales tax was less than $0.45.

16. If $\dfrac{1}{(2^{11})(5^{17})}$ is expressed as a terminating decimal, how many nonzero digits will the decimal have?

 (A) One
 (B) Two
 (C) Four
 (D) Six
 (E) Eleven

GO ON TO THE NEXT PAGE ↘

Questions 17 to 20 are based on the following data.

VARIATION IN THE AMOUNT OF CAFFEINE IN COMMON BEVERAGES AND DRUGS*

*Based on 5-ounce cups of coffee, tea, and cocoa; 12-ounce cups of soft drinks; and single doses of drugs.

17. The least amount of caffeine in a 5-ounce cup of drip-brewed coffee exceeds the greatest amount of caffeine in a 5-ounce cup of cocoa by approximately how many milligrams?

(A) 160

(B) 80

(C) 60

(D) 40

(E) 20

For the following question, enter your answer in the box.

18. For how many of the 11 categories of beverages and drugs listed in the graph can the amount of caffeine in the given serving size be less than 50 milligrams?

[ ] categories

19. Approximately what is the minimum amount of caffeine, in milligrams, consumed per day by a person who daily drinks two 10-ounce mugs of percolated coffee and one 12-ounce cup of a caffeinated soft drink?

(A) 230

(B) 190

(C) 140

(D) 110

(E)   70

20. Which of the following shows the four types of coffee listed in order according to the range of the amounts of caffeine in a 5-ounce cup, from the least range to the greatest range?

    (A) Decaffeinated, instant, percolated, drip-brewed

    (B) Decaffeinated, instant, drip-brewed, percolated

    (C) Instant, decaffeinated, drip-brewed, percolated

    (D) Instant, drip-brewed, decaffeinated, percolated

    (E) Instant, percolated, drip-brewed, decaffeinated

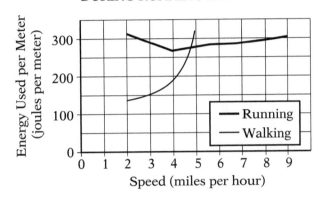

ENERGY USED PER METER VERSUS SPEED
DURING RUNNING AND WALKING

21. If s is a speed, in miles per hour, at which the energy used per meter during running is twice the energy used per meter during walking, then, according to the graph above, s is between

    (A) 2.5 and 3.0

    (B) 3.0 and 3.5

    (C) 3.5 and 4.0

    (D) 4.0 and 4.5

    (E) 4.5 and 5.0

22. If $n = 2^3$, then $n^n =$

    (A) 2^6

    (B) 2^{11}

    (C) 2^{18}

    (D) 2^{24}

    (E) 2^{27}

GO ON TO THE NEXT PAGE ↘

For the following question, select all the answer choices that apply.

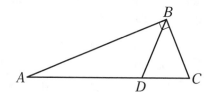

The length of AB is $10\sqrt{3}$.

23. Which of the following statements <u>individually</u> provide(s) sufficient additional information to determine the area of triangle ABC above?

    Indicate <u>all</u> such statements.

    A DBC is an equilateral triangle.
    B ABD is an isosceles triangle.
    C The length of BC is equal to the length of AD.
    D The length of BC is 10.
    E The length of AD is 10.

For the following question, enter your answer in the box.

$$a_1, a_2, a_3, \ldots, a_n, \ldots$$

24. In the sequence above, each term after the first term is equal to the preceding term plus the constant c. If $a_1 + a_3 + a_5 = 27$, what is the value of $a_2 + a_4$?

    $a_2 + a_4 = \boxed{}$

25. A desert outpost has a water supply that is sufficient to last 21 days for 15 people. At the same average rate of water consumption per person, how many days would the water supply last for 9 people?

    Ⓐ 28.0
    Ⓑ 32.5
    Ⓒ 35.0
    Ⓓ 37.5
    Ⓔ 42.0

STOP. This is the end of Section 5.

SECTION 6
Quantitative Reasoning
Time—40 minutes
25 Questions

For each question, indicate the best answer, using the directions given.

Notes: All numbers used are real numbers.

All figures are assumed to lie in a plane unless otherwise indicated.

Geometric figures, such as lines, circles, triangles, and quadrilaterals, **are not necessarily** drawn to scale. That is, you should **not** assume that quantities such as lengths and angle measures are as they appear in a figure. You should assume, however, that lines shown as straight are actually straight, points on a line are in the order shown, and more generally, all geometric objects are in the relative positions shown. For questions with geometric figures, you should base your answers on geometric reasoning, not on estimating or comparing quantities by sight or by measurement.

Coordinate systems, such as *xy*-planes and number lines, **are** drawn to scale; therefore, you can read, estimate, or compare quantities in such figures by sight or by measurement.

Graphical data presentations, such as bar graphs, circles graphs, and line graphs, **are** drawn to scale; therefore, you can read, estimate, or compare data values by sight or by measurement.

For each of Questions 1 to 9, compare Quantity A and Quantity B, using additional information centered above the two quantities if such information is given. Select one of the following four answer choices and fill in the corresponding oval to the right of the question.

Ⓐ **Quantity A is greater.**
Ⓑ **Quantity B is greater.**
Ⓒ **The two quantities are equal.**
Ⓓ **The relationship cannot be determined from the information given.**

A symbol that appears more than once in a question has the same meaning throughout the question.

	Quantity A	Quantity B	Correct Answer
Example 1:	(2)(6)	2 + 6	Ⓐ Ⓑ Ⓒ Ⓓ

	Quantity A	Quantity B	Correct Answer
Example 2:	*PS*	*SR*	Ⓐ Ⓑ Ⓒ Ⓓ

(since equal lengths cannot be assumed, even though *PS* and *SR* appear equal)

Country	Value of 1 United States Dollar
Argentina	0.93 peso
Kenya	32.08 shillings

Quantity A | Quantity B

1. The dollar value of 1 Argentine peso according to the table above | The dollar value of 1 Kenyan shilling according to the table above | Ⓐ Ⓑ Ⓒ Ⓓ

---

k is a digit in the decimal $1.3k5$, and $1.3k5$ is less than 1.33.

Quantity A | Quantity B

2. k | 1 | Ⓐ Ⓑ Ⓒ Ⓓ

AB is a diameter of the circle above.

Quantity A | Quantity B

3. The length of AB | The average (arithmetic mean) of the lengths of AC and AD | Ⓐ Ⓑ Ⓒ Ⓓ

$$st = \sqrt{10}$$

Quantity A | Quantity B

4. s^2 | $\dfrac{10}{t^2}$ | Ⓐ Ⓑ Ⓒ Ⓓ

> (A) Quantity A is greater.
> (B) Quantity B is greater.
> (C) The two quantities are equal.
> (D) The relationship cannot be determined from the information given.

Three consecutive integers have a sum of -84.

Quantity A	Quantity B	
5. The least of the three integers	-28	(A) (B) (C) (D)

In the xy-plane, the equation of line k is $3x - 2y = 0$.

Quantity A	Quantity B	
6. The x-intercept of line k	The y-intercept of line k	(A) (B) (C) (D)

---

n is a positive integer that is divisible by 6.

Quantity A	Quantity B	
7. The remainder when n is divided by 12	The remainder when n is divided by 18	(A) (B) (C) (D)

$$\frac{1-x}{x-1} = \frac{1}{x}$$

Quantity A	Quantity B	
8. x	$-\dfrac{1}{2}$	(A) (B) (C) (D)

In a set of 24 positive integers, 12 of the integers are less than 50. The rest are greater than 50.

Quantity A	Quantity B	
9. The median of the 24 integers	50	(A) (B) (C) (D)

GO ON TO THE NEXT PAGE ↘

Questions 10 to 25 have several different formats. Unless otherwise directed, select a single answer choice. For Numeric Entry questions, follow the instructions below.

Numeric Entry Questions

Enter your answer in the answer box(es) below the question.

- Your answer may be an integer, a decimal, or a fraction, and it may be negative.
- If a question asks for a fraction, there will be two boxes—one for the numerator and one for the denominator.
- Equivalent forms of the correct answer, such as 2.5 and 2.50, are all correct. Fractions do not need to be reduced to lowest terms.
- Enter the exact answer unless the question asks you to round your answer.

10. The fabric needed to make 3 curtains sells for $8.00 per yard and can be purchased only by the full yard. If the length of fabric required for each curtain is 1.6 yards and all of the fabric is purchased as a single length, what is the total cost of the fabric that needs to be purchased for the 3 curtains?

    Ⓐ $40.00

    Ⓑ $38.40

    Ⓒ $24.00

    Ⓓ $16.00

    Ⓔ $12.80

For the following question, select all the answer choices that apply.

11. In the xy-plane, line k is a line that does <u>not</u> pass through the origin.

    Which of the following statements <u>individually</u> provide(s) sufficient additional information to determine whether the slope of line k is negative?

    Indicate <u>all</u> such statements.

    [A] The x-intercept of line k is twice the y-intercept of line k.

    [B] The product of the x-intercept and the y-intercept of line k is positive.

    [C] Line k passes through the points (a, b) and (r, s), where $(a - r)(b - s) < 0$.

	Distance from Centerville (miles)
Freight train	$-10t + 115$
Passenger train	$-20t + 150$

12. The expressions in the table above give the distance from Centerville to each of two trains t hours after 12:00 noon. At what time after 12:00 noon will the trains be equidistant from Centerville?

    (A)   1:30
    (B)   3:30
    (C)   5:10
    (D)   8:50
    (E)   11:30

13. The company at which Mark is employed has 80 employees, each of whom has a different salary. Mark's salary of $43,700 is the second-highest salary in the first quartile of the 80 salaries. If the company were to hire 8 new employees at salaries that are less than the lowest of the 80 salaries, what would Mark's salary be with respect to the quartiles of the 88 salaries at the company, assuming no other changes in the salaries?

    (A)   The fourth-highest salary in the first quartile
    (B)   The highest salary in the first quartile
    (C)   The second-lowest salary in the second quartile
    (D)   The third-lowest salary in the second quartile
    (E)   The fifth-lowest salary in the second quartile

For the following question, enter your answer in the box.

14. In the xy-plane, the point with coordinates $(-6, -7)$ is the center of circle C. The point with coordinates $(-6, 5)$ lies inside C, and the point with coordinates $(8, -7)$ lies outside C. If m is the radius of C and m is an integer, what is the value of m ?

    $$m = \boxed{}$$

15. If $-\dfrac{m}{19}$ is an even integer, which of the following must be true?

    (A) m is a negative number.
    (B) m is a positive number.
    (C) m is a prime number.
    (D) m is an odd integer.
    (E) m is an even integer.

GO ON TO THE NEXT PAGE ➘

For the following question, select all the answer choices that apply.

16. The integer v is greater than 1. If v is the square of an integer, which of the following numbers must also be the square of an integer?

    Indicate <u>all</u> such numbers.

    A $81v$
    B $25v + 10\sqrt{v} + 1$
    C $4v^2 + 4\sqrt{v} + 1$

Questions 17 to 20 are based on the following data.

DISTANCE TRAVELED BY A CAR ACCORDING TO THE CAR'S SPEED WHEN THE DRIVER IS SIGNALED TO STOP

Distance Traveled During Reaction Time*

Distance Traveled After Brakes Have Been Applied

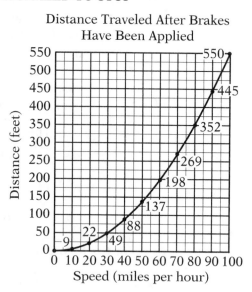

*Reaction time is the time period that begins when the driver is signaled to stop and ends when the driver applies the brakes.

<u>Note:</u> Total stopping distance is the sum of the distance traveled during reaction time and the distance traveled after brakes have been applied.

17. The speed, in miles per hour, at which the car travels a distance of 52 feet during reaction time is closest to which of the following?

    (A) 43
    (B) 47
    (C) 51
    (D) 55
    (E) 59

18. Approximately what is the total stopping distance, in feet, if the car is traveling at a speed of 40 miles per hour when the driver is signaled to stop?

    (A) 130
    (B) 110
    (C) 90
    (D) 70
    (E) 40

19. Of the following, which is the greatest speed, in miles per hour, at which the car can travel and stop with a total stopping distance of less than 200 feet?

    (A) 50
    (B) 55
    (C) 60
    (D) 65
    (E) 70

20. The total stopping distance for the car traveling at 60 miles per hour is approximately what percent greater than the total stopping distance for the car traveling at 50 miles per hour?

    (A) 22%
    (B) 30%
    (C) 38%
    (D) 45%
    (E) 52%

21. What is the least positive integer that is <u>not</u> a factor of 25! and is <u>not</u> a prime number?

    (A) 26
    (B) 28
    (C) 36
    (D) 56
    (E) 58

22. If $0 < a < 1 < b$, which of the following is true about the reciprocals of a and b ?

    (A) $1 < \dfrac{1}{a} < \dfrac{1}{b}$

    (B) $\dfrac{1}{a} < 1 < \dfrac{1}{b}$

    (C) $\dfrac{1}{a} < \dfrac{1}{b} < 1$

    (D) $\dfrac{1}{b} < 1 < \dfrac{1}{a}$

    (E) $\dfrac{1}{b} < \dfrac{1}{a} < 1$

GO ON TO THE NEXT PAGE ↘

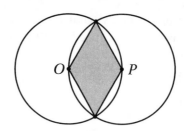

23. In the figure above, O and P are the centers of the two circles. If each circle has radius r, what is the area of the shaded region?

    (A) $\dfrac{\sqrt{2}}{2}r^2$

    (B) $\dfrac{\sqrt{3}}{2}r^2$

    (C) $\sqrt{2}r^2$

    (D) $\sqrt{3}r^2$

    (E) $2\sqrt{3}r^2$

For the following question, enter your answer in the boxes.

24. Of the 20 lightbulbs in a box, 2 are defective. An inspector will select 2 lightbulbs simultaneously and at random from the box. What is the probability that neither of the lightbulbs selected will be defective?

    Give your answer as a fraction.

25. What is the perimeter, in meters, of a rectangular playground 24 meters wide that has the same area as a rectangular playground 64 meters long and 48 meters wide?

    (A) 112

    (B) 152

    (C) 224

    (D) 256

    (E) 304

STOP. This is the end of Section 6.

Evaluating Your Performance

Now that you have completed the practice GRE revised General Test in this book, it is time to evaluate your performance. Because the new Verbal Reasoning and Quantitative Reasoning score scales for the GRE revised General Test were not yet available when this book went to press, we are providing estimates of your performance on the Verbal Reasoning and Quantitative Reasoning measures based on the previous 200–800 GRE scale.

Analytical Writing Measure

One way to evaluate your performance on the Issue and Argument topics you answered on the practice test is to compare your essay responses to the scored sample essay responses for these topics and review the reader commentary for these sample essay responses. Scored sample essay responses and reader commentary are presented starting on page 355 for the one Issue topic and one Argument topic presented in the Analytical Writing sections of the test.

The final scores on each of the two essays (Issue and Argument) are averaged and rounded up to the nearest half-point interval. A single score is reported for the Analytical Writing measure. You should review the score level descriptions on page 41 to better understand the analytical writing abilities characteristic of particular score levels.

Verbal and Quantitative Measures

The tables that follow contain information to help you evaluate your performance on the Verbal Reasoning and Quantitative Reasoning measures. An Answer Key with the correct answers to the questions in the Verbal Reasoning and Quantitative Reasoning sections begins on page 347. Compare your answers to the correct answers given in the table, crossing out questions you answered incorrectly or omitted. Partially correct answers should be treated as incorrect. Knowing which questions you answered incorrectly or omitted can help you identify content areas in which you need more practice or review.

The Answer Key contains additional information to help you evaluate your performance. With each answer, the Key provides a number, the P+. The P+ is the percent of a group of actual GRE takers who were administered that same question at a previous test administration and who answered it correctly. P+ is used to gauge the relative difficulty of a test question. The higher the P+, the easier the test question. You can use the P+ to compare your performance on each test question to the performance of other test takers on that same question. The P+ to compare your performance on each test question to the performance of other test takers on that same question.

To calculate your scores:

- Add the number of correct answers in Sections 3 and 4 to obtain your raw Verbal Reasoning score.
- Add the number of correct answers in Sections 5 and 6 to obtain your raw Quantitative Reasoning score.
- Once you have calculated your raw scores, refer to the score conversion table on pages 351–352 to find the scaled score ranges corresponding to your raw scores on both Verbal Reasoning and Quantitative Reasoning.

The scaled score ranges are based on the previous 200–800 GRE General Test reporting scales. They are provided as an estimate of your performance because the new score scale was not yet available when this book went to press. Beginning in November 2011, you can obtain information about how the scores on the previous 200–800 scales correspond to the new 130–170 scales at **www.ets.org/gre/revised_ general**. These scaled score ranges should give you a general idea of how you might perform on the GRE revised General Test, but they are not precise predictions of your future test performance. The score ranges can help guide your test preparation.

To give you a general indication of your level of performance compared to others who have taken the General Test, percentile ranks based upon the most recent norms for the 200–800 scale are also provided in the table on pages 353–354. The percentile rank is the percent of test takers who earned lower scores. To evaluate your level of performance on the practice test, find the percentile ranks associated with the scaled scores in your score range. These percentile ranks are only meant to provide you with a general indication of your performance and may not be identical to the actual norms for the GRE revised General Test scheduled to be published in November 2011.

Answer Key

Section 3. Verbal Reasoning

Question Number	P+	Correct Answer
1	39	**Choice A:** Some record or evidence of the thought of the *tlamatinime* is available. AND **Choice B:** For at least some Nahuatl expressions, researchers are able to trace their derivation from another ancient American language.
2	54	**Sentence 6:** Of these forms, the most characteristic in Nahuatl is the juxtaposition of two words that, because they are synonyms, associated terms, or even contraries, complement each other to evoke one single idea
3	49	**Choice B:** creations
4	48	**Choice D:** The first sums up the argument's position with regard to a certain hypothesis; the second provides grounds for that position.
5	57	**Choice A:** anachronistic; **Choice F:** alienated from
6	63	**Choice D:** invention
7	20	**Choice B:** lionization; **Choice D:** foreground
8	58	**Choice B:** aesthetics
9	69	**Choice C:** present evidence suggesting that singing has an important energy cost for certain birds
10	66	**Choice B:** Stores more energy as body reserves than on other days
11	65	**Sentence 9:** Thomas found that nightingales reached a significantly higher body mass at dusk and lost more mass overnight on nights when their song rate was high.
12	14	**Choice B:** They have generally received more attention from scientists.
13	86	**Choice A:** Many climbers, lulled into a false sense of security, use the new equipment to attempt climbing feats of which they are not capable.
14	46	**Choice B:** schism
15	10	**Choice D:** sartorial
16	36	**Choice A:** undemonstrative panache; **Choice F:** deflect
17	18	**Choice C:** strategic; **Choice D:** brandish; **Choice H:** deeply felt moral code
18	47	**Choice C:** provide an example of a way in which scholarship on the history of women in photography has been unsatisfactory
19	37	**Choice C:** In addition to providing a record of certain historical events, Marion Palfi's photographs played a role in subsequent events.
20	72	**Choice A:** exaggeration
21	24	**Choice A:** innocuous AND **Choice F:** benign
22	39	**Choice A:** antedated AND **Choice D:** preceded
23	61	**Choice B:** disparate AND **Choice C:** divergent
24	67	**Choice A:** arbitrary AND **Choice B:** capricious
25	85	**Choice C:** thrilled about AND **Choice E:** elated by

Answer Key

Section 4. Verbal Reasoning

Question Number	P+	Correct Answer
1	70	**Choice B:** fleeting; AND **Choice C:** momentary
2	80	**Choice A:** diversity; AND **Choice C:** variety
3	49	**Choice A:** synoptic; AND **Choice B:** abridged
4	68	**Choice B:** intransigent; AND **Choice F:** resolute
5	26	**Choice A:** A correct understanding of how phytoplankton photosynthesis utilizes carbon dioxide AND **Choice B:** A correct prediction about how the addition of iron to iron-poor waters would affect phytoplankton growth AND **Choice C:** An incorrect prediction about how phytoplankton growth would affect the concentration of atmospheric carbon dioxide
6	26	**Choice A:** help explain why Martin's hypothesis is incorrect
7	31	**Choice E:** There are fewer traffic accidents annually in Sparva than in any of the provinces of comparable or greater population.
8	23	**Choice A:** Voltaire's literary stature helped secure a large audience for this attempt to popularize Newton's ideas. AND **Choice B:** Voltaire's status as a nonscientist was an advantage in this effort to bring Newtonian science to the attention of the general public. AND **Choice C:** The frontispiece of the book implies that Voltaire's understanding of Newton's ideas was not achieved without assistance.
9	82	**Sentence 2:** In the book's frontispiece, Voltaire is seen writing at his desk, and over him a shaft of light from heaven, the light of truth, passes through Newton to Voltaire's collaborator Madame du Châtelet; she reflects that light onto the inspired Voltaire
10	60	**Choice B:** extravagance; **Choice F:** profligate
11	37	**Choice B:** complacency; **Choice D:** embrace only a portion of the truth; **Choice G:** erroneous
12	35	**Choice D:** inform
13	43	**Choice E:** reconcile
14	54	**Choice C:** *The Quest of the Silver Fleece* has at least one feature that typically would attract the attention of literary scholars.
15	68	**Choice D:** DuBois' novels may eventually attract greater scholarly interest than they have to date
16	49	**Choice E:** The degree of consideration that has been given to DuBois' novels, including *The Quest of the Silver Fleece*
17	50	**Choice E:** an anomaly
18	19	**Choice A:** undermines; **Choice E:** inimical
19	54	**Choice A:** peculiarity; **Choice E:** assertive
20	23	**Choice B:** malignant; **Choice E:** insufficient; **Choice H:** benignity
21	53	**Choice B:** proximity to the Sun
22	59	**Choice C:** such a warm Arctic Ocean would trigger the melting of massive land-based glaciers in the Arctic

Answer Key

Question Number	P+	Correct Answer
23	33	**Choice A:** Some of them offered a religious explanation for their immigration.
24	94	**Sentence 5:** When he moves beyond the principal actors, he finds that religious explanations were less frequently offered, and he concludes that most people immigrated because they were recruited by promises of material improvement.
25	64	**Choice A:** summarizing the findings of an investigation

Section 5. Quantitative Reasoning

Question Number	P+	Correct Answer
1	65	**Choice B:** Quantity B is greater.
2	83	**Choice C:** The two quantities are equal.
3	62	**Choice D:** The relationship cannot be determined from the information given.
4	48	**Choice A:** Quantity A is greater.
5	47	**Choice D:** The relationship cannot be determined from the information given.
6	36	**Choice A:** Quantity A is greater.
7	26	**Choice C:** The two quantities are equal.
8	34	**Choice D:** The relationship cannot be determined from the information given.
9	46	**Choice B:** Quantity B is greater.
10	62	**Choice D:** 8 to 9
11	26	**Choice B:** 115
12	51	**121**
13	52	**Choice C:** 75
14	60	**Choice C:** 4,000
15	18	**Choice C:** The sales tax was less than $0.45.
16	19	**Choice B:** Two
17	69	**Choice D:** 40
18	63	**9**
19	41	**Choice B:** 190
20	60	**Choice B:** Decaffeinated, instant, drip-brewed, percolated
21	70	**Choice A:** 2.5 and 3.0
22	35	**Choice D:** 2^{24}
23	17	**Choice A:** *DBC* is an equilateral triangle. AND **Choice D:** The length of *BC* is 10.
24	51	**18**
25	34	**Choice C:** 35.0

Answer Key

Section 6. Quantitative Reasoning

Question Number	P+	Correct Answer
1	66	**Choice A:** Quantity A is greater.
2	73	**Choice D:** The relationship cannot be determined from the information given.
3	52	**Choice A:** Quantity A is greater.
4	46	**Choice C:** The two quantities are equal.
5	48	**Choice B:** Quantity B is greater.
6	33	**Choice C:** The two quantities are equal.
7	40	**Choice D:** The relationship cannot be determined from the information given.
8	26	**Choice B:** Quantity B is greater.
9	31	**Choice D:** The relationship cannot be determined from the information given.
10	67	**Choice A:** $40.00
11	10	**Choice A:** The x-intercept of line k is twice the y-intercept of line k. AND **Choice B:** The product of the x-intercept and the y-intercept of line k is positive. AND **Choice C:** Line k passes through the points (a, b) and (r, s), where $(a - r)(b - s) < 0$.
12	49	**Choice B:** 3:30
13	27	**Choice E:** The fifth-lowest salary in the second quartile
14	38	**13**
15	40	**Choice E:** m is an even integer.
16	21	**Choice A:** $81v$ AND **Choice B:** $25v + 10\sqrt{v} + 1$
17	79	**Choice B:** 47
18	44	**Choice A:** 130
19	41	**Choice A:** 50
20	30	**Choice C:** 38%
21	11	**Choice E:** 58
22	58	**Choice D:** $\dfrac{1}{b} < 1 < \dfrac{1}{a}$
23	24	**Choice B:** $\dfrac{\sqrt{3}}{2} r^2$
24	15	$\dfrac{153}{190}$ (or any equivalent fraction)
25	30	**Choice E:** 304

Score Conversion Table

Raw Score	Verbal Scaled Range	Quantitative Scaled Range
50	750–800	750–800
49	750–800	750–800
48	750–800	750–800
47	750–800	750–800
46	750–800	750–800
45	750–800	750–800
44	750–800	750–800
43	740–800	750–800
42	710–800	750–800
41	700–800	750–800
40	680–780	750–800
39	660–760	750–800
38	650–750	750–800
37	630–730	750–800
36	620–720	740–800
35	590–690	730–800
34	580–680	720–800
33	570–670	710–800
32	540–640	700–800
31	530–630	690–790
30	520–620	680–780
29	510–610	660–760
28	490–590	650–750
27	480–580	630–730
26	470–570	620–720
25	460–560	590–690
24	440–540	580–680
23	430–530	570–670
22	420–520	560–660
21	410–510	540–640
20	390–490	510–610
19	380–480	500–600
18	370–470	470–570
17	360–460	450–550
16	340–440	440–540

Score Conversion Table

Raw Score	Verbal Scaled Range	Quantitative Scaled Range
15	330–430	410–510
14	310–410	390–490
13	290–390	380–480
12	280–380	340–440
11	270–370	330–430
10	260–360	310–410
9	250–350	280–380
8	240–340	260–360
7	220–320	250–350
6	220–320	230–330
5	200–300	210–310
4	200–290	200–280
3	200–290	200–260
2	200–270	200–250
1	200–260	200–250
0	200	200

Percentile Ranks

Percent of Examinees Scoring Lower Than Selected Scaled Scores

(Based on the performance of all examinees who tested between July 1, 2006, and June 30, 2009)

Scaled Score	Verbal Reasoning	Quantitative Reasoning
800		94
790		91
780		89
770		87
760		84
750		82
740		80
730	99	77
720	98	75
710	98	72
700	97	70
690	97	68
680	96	66
670	95	63
660	94	61
650	93	59
640	92	56
630	91	54
620	89	52
610	88	49
600	86	47
590	84	45
580	82	43
570	80	40
560	78	38
550	75	36
540	73	34
530	70	32
520	68	30
510	65	28
500	63	27

Percentile Ranks

Scaled Score	Verbal Reasoning	Quantitative Reasoning
490	60	25
480	57	23
470	55	22
460	52	20
450	49	19
440	46	17
430	43	16
420	41	15
410	38	14
400	35	12
390	32	11
380	29	10
370	27	9
360	24	8
350	21	8
340	19	7
330	16	6
320	13	5
310	10	5
300	8	4
290	6	3
280	5	3
270	3	2
260	2	2
250	1	2
240		1
230		
220		
210		
200		

Analytical Writing Sample Responses and Reader Commentaries

SECTION 1
Analytical Writing

ANALYZE AN ISSUE

The best way to teach is to praise positive actions and ignore negative ones.

Write a response in which you discuss the extent to which you agree or disagree with the recommendation and explain your reasoning for the position you take. In developing and supporting your position, describe specific circumstances in which adopting the recommendation would or would not be advantageous and explain how these examples shape your position.

*Score 6 Response *

The recommendation presents a view that I would agree is successful most of the time, but one that I cannot fully support due to the "all or nothing" impression it gives.

Certainly as an educator I agree fully that the best way to elicit positive response from students is to make use of students' positive energy and then encourage actions that you would like to see repeated. It is human nature that we all want to be accepted and achieve on some level, and when people in authority provide feedback that we have done something well, the drive to repeat the action that was praised is bound to be particularly strong.

This blanket statement would obviously pay dividends in situations in which a teacher desires to have students repeat particular behaviors. For example, if an educator is attempting to teach students proper classroom etiquette, it would be appropriate to openly praise a student who raises his or her hand when wishing to speak or address the class. In such cases, the teacher may also help shape positive behaviors by ignoring a student who is trying to interject without approval from the teacher. In fact, the decision to ignore students who are exhibiting inappropriate behaviors of this type could work very well in this situation, as the stakes are not very high and the intended outcome can likely be achieved by such a method. However, it is important to note here that this tactic would only be effective in such a "low-stakes" situation, as when a student speaks without raising her hand first. As we will discuss below, ignoring a student who hits another student, or engages in more serious misbehaviors, would not be effective or prudent.

To expand on this point, it is important for teachers to be careful when working with

---

NOTE: All responses are reproduced exactly as written, including errors, misspellings, etc., if any.

the second half of this statement, only ignoring negative actions that are not serious. Take for instance a student who is misbehaving just by chatting with a fellow class-mate. This student might not be presenting much of a problem and may be simply seeking attention. Ignoring the student might, in fact, be the best solution. Now assume the negative action is the improper administering of chemicals in a science experiment or the bullying of a fellow student. To ignore these negative actions would be absurd and negligent. Now you are allowing a problem to persist, one that could potentially lead to much bigger and more dangerous issues. In a more serious situation, addressing the negative actions quickly and properly could stop the problem it in its tracks. It is for reasons like this that I do not advocate the idea that a teacher can be successful by simply ignoring negative actions.

I do, however, greatly support the idea that the central focus of teaching should be to build on and encourage positive actions. However, the author's all-encompassing statement leaves too many negative possibilities for the classroom. Perhaps a better way to phrase this statement would be to say, "The best way to teach is to praise positive actions and ignore negative ones that are not debilitating to class efficiency or the safety of any individual".

Thus, in the original statement, there are indeed some good intentions, and there could be a lot of merit in adopting its basic principles. Data proves that positive support can substantially increase motivation and desire in students and contribute to positive achievements. In fact, most studies of teaching efficacy indicate that praising positive actions and ignoring negative ones can create a more stable and efficient classroom. It needs to be stressed, however, that this tool is only effective at certain levels of misbehavior. As mentioned above, when the behavior is precipitated by feelings of revenge, power or total self-worthlessness, this methodology will likely not work. It is likely to be very successful, however, when the drive behind the misbehavior is simple attention seeking. In many of these instances, if the teacher demonstrates clearly that inappropriate behavior does not result in the gaining of attention, students are more likely to seek attention by behaving properly. Should the student choose this path, then the ignoring has worked and when the positive behavior is exhibited, then the teacher can utilize the first part of the theory and support or praise this behavior. Now it is much more likely to be repeated. If the student does not choose this path and instead elects to raise the actions to a higher level that presents a more serious issue, then ignorance alone cannot work and other methods must be employed.

In conclusion, one can appreciate the credo expressed in this instance, but surely we all can see the potential error of following it through to the extreme.

Reader Commentary

This response receives a 6 for its well-articulated, insightful analysis of the issue. Rather than simply rejecting or accepting the prompt, the writer argues that the recommendation made by the prompt can often be true but is too "all or nothing" to be endorsed without qualification. The writer turns this idea into an insightful position by providing examples and evidence to fully and persuasively support its nuanced argument. The response offers nicely detailed situations that provide compelling support for a claim that the recommendation can, in fact, work. At the same time, it also highlights the recommendation's limits using additional specific, detailed examples. Particularly persuasive is the fourth paragraph, in which the writer compares the impact of ignoring minor behavioral problems like talking in class to the potential costs of ignoring more serious issues like bullying. Thus, the writer recognizes that the prompt's claim, as well as his/her own, is inevitably dependent on the specific context for its success or failure. Throughout the response, the writer demonstrates the ability to convey ideas fluently and precisely, using effective vocabulary and sentence variety. This sentence demonstrates the level of language facility seen throughout the response: "It is human nature that we all want to be accepted and achieve on some level, and when people in authority provide feedback that we have done something well, the drive to repeat the action that was praised is bound to be particularly strong."

Score 5 Response

I partially agree with the statement "The best way to teach is to praise positive actions and ignore negative ones". Children should be rewarded when they perform well; however, they should not be ignored for performing sub-optimally. For purposes of this essay, the term "actions" is defined as behaviors within the classroom.

Utilizing positive reinforcements, such as tangible rewards, can be a good method to teach children. If the teacher praises children for actions that are desirable, then the children are more likely to repeat those actions. For example, a student who completes an assignment on time and does a good job is likely to want to do a good job on the next assignment if he gets positive feedback. Likewise, the children who are not currently engaging in the desirable actions may be more inclined to do so in order to recieve the positive reinforcement.

Conversely, children should not be ignored for negative actions. If a child is not exhibiting appropriate behavior in the classroom, then it is the teacher's responsibility to encourage the child to perform optimally. Ignoring something doesn't make it go away, actions and consequences do. A student who is being disruptive in class will continue to be disruptive unless the teacher does something about it. However, the teacher's actions need be appropriate.

Before the teacher attempts to modify a child's behavior, the teacher needs to try and identify the reason behind the behavior. For instance, children who leave their seat often, stare in to space, or call out of turn may be initially viewed as having poor behavior. However, the teacher may suspect that the child has an attentional problem, and request that the child be tested. If the child does have an attentional problem, then the teacher can work with a related service, such as occupational therapy, to alter the classroom environment in order to cater to the needs of the child. For instance, the teacher could remove some of the stimulating bulliten board displays to make the room more calming to the child. If the child becomes more attentive in class then the teacher was able to assist the child without scorning them or ignoring them. The teacher met the needs of the child and created an enviornment to enable the child to optimally perform in the educational setting.

On the other hand, if the child is tested, and does not have any areas of concern that may be impacting the educational performance in the classroom, then the negative behavior may strictly be due to defiance. In such a case, the teacher still should not ignore the child, because the negative actions may hinder the learning opportunity for the remaining children in the class. As a result, a child who is being disruptive to the learning process of the class should be set apart from the class so that they do not receive the positive reinforcement of peer attention.

The teacher should not ignore the student who is misbehaving, but that does not mean that the teacher just needs to punish. It is better to address the child privately and make sure the child is aware of the negative actions. Once the child is aware, then the teacher should once again try to determine the reason why the child is behaving in a negative manner. Perhaps the child's parents are in the middle of a divorce and the child is outwardly expressing his frustration in the classroom. Or the academic content of the class may not be challenging enough for the child and so he is misbehaving out of boredom. Whatever the reason behind the behavior, the key factor is that the teacher works with the child to try and identify it. Simply punnishing or ignoring the child would not solve the problem, whereas working to create a plan for success in the classroom would. Likewise, rather than punnishing and defeating the child, the teacher is working with and empowering the child; a much more positive outcome to the situation.

Reader Commentary

This strong response presents a thoughtful and well-developed analysis of the issue. In this case the writer argues that teachers need to modify their approach based on context and observation, meaning that a blanket approach cannot be successful. The writer supports this position with relevant reasons and examples that present logically sound support. Note that the task instructions ask writers to discuss situations in which the statement might or might not hold true, and this response does that quite clearly. In the second paragraph, the writer gives an example of a student who completes an assignment on time and receives positive feedback, showing how the recommendation could hold true. Other examples show situations in which it might not hold true, and these various points are brought together to support the writer's position that teachers have to look at the context of the situation and cannot rely on simply ignoring negative actions. This response also demonstrates facility with language, using appropriate vocabulary and sentence variety. Sentences like this one demonstrate the writer's command of the conventions of standard written English: "If the child does have an attentional problem, then the teacher can work with a related service, such as occupational therapy, to alter the classroom environment in order to cater to the needs of the child." There are some minor errors, but overall the response demonstrates strong control of language. Although the response is clearly stronger than a 4, which would simply present a clear position on the issue according to the task instructions, it does not reach the level of a 6 because it does not develop its points in a way that creates a cogent and insightful position. It does, however, present a generally thoughtful and well-developed analysis of the issue, leading to a score of 5.

Score 4 Response

I absolutely agree with the first section of the statement above, but find fault with the latter half.

There is no doubt that praising positive actions is an excellent way to teach, and this method is most clearly exemplified when dealing with much younger children. When a young child is learning basic social behavior, it is imperative that he is encouraged to repeat positive actions. For example, when a child voluntarily shares his toys with another, if a teacher rewards that behavior, the child will understand that this is a good practice, and likely share again in the future.

In contrast, if a child displays negative behavior by stealing a toy away from his playmate, it would be very dangerous for the teacher to ignore this action, for then the child may never recognize that this is unacceptable. In this instance, the child has not learned from the situation at all. So what should a teacher do when faced with such a situation? Punishment is not necessarily the optimal choice, either. Rather than scolding a child for mistreating his playmates and sending him off to a corner, a teacher would be wise to demonstrate the positive alternative: to share his toys instead. In this case, rather than ignoring or punishing negative actions, the teacher could seize the opportunity to reinforce positive behavior, and further extend the child's learning experience.

In summary, positive reinforcement is certainly an excellent method for teaching new methods or behaviors, and encouraging a student to learn more. However to ignore, rather than recognize and correct negative actions, would be a disservice to the student, for he would not know what conclusion to draw from his action.

Reader Commentary

This adequate response follows the task directions and presents a clear position on the issue, supporting its main points with examples that are relevant, if only adequately developed. For instance, the discussion in the second paragraph of a teacher who reinforces the positive behavior of sharing a toy is certainly relevant and on-task (i.e., it describes a situation in which adopting the recommendation would be advantageous). However, the development of this idea does not lead to generally thoughtful or insightful analysis. Instead, it is simply presented as an example. In addition to its adequate development, this response also demonstrates sufficient control of the conventions of standard written English, and its main points are made with reasonable clarity. Some of the sentences demonstrate the syntactical variety normally seen in responses that receive higher scores (e.g., "Rather than scolding a child for mistreating his playmates and sending him off to a corner, a teacher would be wise to demonstrate the positive alternative: to share his toys instead"). However, the overall use of language in this response is merely adequate.

Score 3 Response

Praising postive actions and ignoring negative ones may be a good way to teach but not the best way. Ignoring negative actions could negate all the postive praises given to an individual, having negative actions go unchecked will lead to habits formed that would overwhelm any positive actions that are complementary to an individuals learning process.

For instance, in a classroom full of eight-year old kids; if during a lesson they are making alot of noise, having this ignored would tell the kids that it is okay to be disruptive in class. The individuals in that class would develop the habit of being distruptive hence hindering their learning process. However if the eight-year old kids were immediately told to stop the distruption then it will never become a habit.

Every action needs to have a related consequence follow in a learning environment. In the early years of education, the way they are taught becomes a lifelong habit which is hard to change in later years. If negative actions are not assigned a related consequences then teaching becomes ineffective because the students negative actions soon diminish the ability to do well in school. The way postive actions are dealt with should also be done with negative actions rather than being ignored which in turn enhance the learning environment.

Reader Commentary

Although this response has minor errors in its use of language, it receives a 3 primarily for insufficient overall clarity and for the limited development of its claims. The writer does make an attempt to follow the specific task instructions, and the response has a clear position on the issue, arguing that it is not acceptable practice to ignore negative behaviors. However, the development provided in support of that position is limited. The example of "eight-year old kids" making noise during class can be seen as a situation in which following the recommendation is not advantageous. Instead of developing that point in a logically persuasive way, however, the writer proceeds to make an unsupported assertion about the consequences of following the recommendation ("The individuals in that class would develop the habit of being disruptive hence hindering their learning process"). Another issue that keeps this response at the 3 level is a lack of clarity, particularly in the final paragraph. The final sentence demonstrates this problem with clarity: "The way postive actions are dealt with should also be done with negative actions rather than being ignored which in turn enhance the learning environment." Problems with the structure of this sentence make it difficult to determine the writer's intended meaning.

Score 2 Response

I don't agree with this afirmation, because I think is very important to praise positive actions but also is important to sign the negative ones, in some situations acording to the students level, grade, etc., could be better to put more emphasis in the positive things and if not ignore all the negative ones, do not give so much importance to them, this is particulary important in the lowest levels of education.

But in another situations you must sign the negative things, trying to avoid that the students can repeat them in the future, because I think you can also learn from the negative situations.

For this reason I believe that is important to praise positive actions but is also important no to ignore the negative ones, because in a given situation the student can have troubles recongnising what is right and what is wrong. And finally as a conclusion I think that the best way to teach is combination of praise positive things but also to sign the negative ones.

Reader Commentary

This response clearly fits several characteristics of a 2, as defined by the scoring guide. It is seriously limited in its development, organization, and focus. The response repeats itself rather than developing any of its statements, pointing to an inability to organize a response capable of supporting any specific claims with relevant reasons or examples. Additionally, serious language control problems frequently interfere with meaning. Thus, even though the writer does seem to be making an attempt to respond to the specific task instructions, the response merits a score of 2.

Score 1 Response

Write a response in which you disuss the extent to which you agree or disagree with the recommendation and explain your reasoning for the position you take. In developing and supporting position, describe specific circumstances in which adopting the recommendation would or would not be advantageous and explain how these examples shape your position.

Author says that The best way to teach is to praise positive actions and ignore negative ones. I agree to this recommendation. Explaining, I strongly believe that the best way to teach is not to praise positive action and ignore negative ones but is makeing everyone to be a good ones. Specific crimstances lead me which adopting the recommendation as the following:

First, we will lost the good children who have negative maner if we ignore them. Children are future, not all. Praise in negative should not be, teaching to children to best way. I strongly believe adopting this recommeindation would be not advantages.

second, negative ones in today may be a great people in the future. Not only ones behave do worse they are teenage. Teenage in today is not easy for all! Negative ones can not better, if only prainse positive actions, ignore negativeone. Negative ones may not positive be having, but if we praise them only, they not think they should be positive person later.

conclusion, specific circumstances are which adopting the recommendation would not be advantage, I am not agree to the the recommendation. Ignore negative manor when they will not be positive behavrio in futre. But they can, if do not ignore them. we should not ignor negative person but should make them think that they can be a good man future like positive person.

Reader Commentary

This response has severe and pervasive problems in language and sentence structure that, as stated in the scoring guide, consistently interfere with meaning and result in incoherence. The response begins by repeating the prompt, but then the severe problems with language control and organization undermine any evidence of the ability to understand the prompt or to present and develop a clear position. For example, it is not clear what the writer means by the claim that the best way to teach is "makeing everyone to be a good ones." Severe problems with language control in that sentence and throughout the response prevent it from developing a coherent position on the issue or responding to the specific task instructions. Although the writer makes an attempt at organization, with points marked as first, second, and conclusion, the response actually exhibits little or no evidence of the ability to develop any potential understanding of the prompt into a logical position on the issue.

SECTION 2
Analytical Writing

ANALYZE AN ARGUMENT

The following appeared in an article written by Dr. Karp, an anthropologist.

"Twenty years ago, Dr. Field, a noted anthropologist, visited the island of Tertia and concluded from his observations that children in Tertia were reared by an entire village rather than by their own biological parents. However, my recent interviews with children living in the group of islands that includes Tertia show that these children spend much more time talking about their biological parents than about other adults in the village. This research of mine proves that Dr. Field's conclusion about Tertian village culture is invalid and thus that the observation-centered approach to studying cultures is invalid as well. The interview-centered method that my team of graduate students is currently using in Tertia will establish a much more accurate understanding of child-rearing traditions there and in other island cultures."

Write a response in which you discuss what specific evidence is needed to evaluate the argument and explain how the evidence would weaken or strengthen the argument.

Score 6 Response

It might seem logical, at first glance, to agree with the argument in Dr. Karp's article that children in Tertia actually are raised by their biological parents (and perhaps even, by implication, that an observation-centered approach to anthropological study is not as valid as an interview-centered one). However, in order to fully evaluate this argument, we need to have a significant amount of additional evidence. The argument could end up being much weaker than it seems, or it might actually be quite valid. In order to make that determination, we need to know more then analyze what we learn.

The first piece of evidence that we would need in order to evaluate Dr. Karp's claims is information about whether or not Tertia and the surrounding island group have changed significantly in the past 20 years. Dr. Field conducted his observational study 20 years ago, and it is possible that Tertia has changed significantly since then. For example, if we had evidence that in teh intervening years Westerners had settled on the island and they introduced a more typical Western-style family structure, it would certainly weaken Dr. Karp's argument. In that case, the original study could have been accurate, and Dr. Karp's study could be correct, as well, though his conclusion that Dr. Field's method is ineffective would be seriously weakened.

Another piece of evidence that might help us evaluate this claim involves the exact locations where Dr. Karp's interviews took place. According to this article, Dr. Karp and his graduate students conducted interviews of "children living in the group of islands that includes Tertia." If we were to learn that they never interviewed a single Tertian child, it would significantly weaken the conclusion. It could turn out to be the case, for example, that children on Tertia are raised communally, whereas children on other islands nearby are raised by their biological parents.

In order to fully evaluate this article, we would also need to learn more about the interview questions that Dr. Karp's team used. What exactly did they ask? We don't know, nor do we know what the children's responses actually were. What did they say about their biological parents? The mere fact that they speak more frequently about their biological parents than they do about other adults does not meant hat they are raised by their biological parents. It would significantly undermine Dr. Karp's argument if it turned out that the children said things like how much they missed their parents or how their parents had left them in a communal environment. Without knowing WHAT the children said, it is hard to accept Dr. Karp's conclusion.

It is slightly more difficult to discuss teh evidence we might need in order to evaluate the more interesting claims in Dr. Karp's article, namely his extension of the results of his study to a conclusion that interview-centered methods are inherently more valid than observational-centered approaches. In order to fully evaluate this claim, in fact, we would need to look at many more examples of interview-based and observation-based anthropological studies and we would also need to look into different study designs. Perhaps Dr. Field did not conduct an effective observational study, but other observational approaches could be effective. In order to make such grandiose claims, Dr. Karp really needs a lot of additional evidence (ideally a meta-analysis of hundreds of anthropological studies).

Clearly, then, we need to have additional evidence in order to get a more complete understanding of the strengths and weaknesses of Dr. Karp's article. We need to know about Tertia and the surrounding islands, whether or not they have changed over the past 20 years. We also need to know about study design (Dr. Karp's and Dr. Field's). And we really need a lot more information if we want to extend the results of a study about one island culture to all anthropological fieldwork.

Reader Commentary

This outstanding response clearly addresses the specific task directions and presents a cogent, insightful analysis by specifically detailing the impact that different pieces of evidence would have on the argument. The introductory paragraph sets up the organization of the response, and each body paragraph provides the sort of compelling development typical in responses that receive a score of 6. For example, after the writer discusses possible evidence that Tertian child rearing practices have changed over the past 20 years, he or she clearly explains the impact information about those changes might have on the argument, saying, "In that case, the original study could have been accurate, and Dr. Karp's study could be correct, as well, though his conclusion that Dr. Field's method is ineffective would be seriously weakened." Not only is this argument compelling, but it also demonstrates sophisticated syntax and facility with language. There is more insightful development in the fifth paragraph, in which the writer examines Dr. Karp's claims about interview-based studies. Although there are a few typos and minor errors here, nothing in the response distracts from the overall fluency of the writing. Sentences like this one demonstrate the fluent and precise diction and varied syntax that are evident throughout the response: "It could turn out to be the case, for example, that children on Tertia are raised communally, whereas children on other islands nearby are raised by their biological parents." Because of its compelling and insightful development and fluent and precise language, this response fits all of the bullet points for a 6.

Score 5 Response

There seems to be an abundance of evidence that, if we were to examine it closely, might make us reconsider Dr. Karp's argument here. If we look first at the evidence that might weaken this argument, we can see a lot of the problems with Dr. Karp's article. It would certainly weaken the argument if we were to discover that Dr. Karp and his students did not actually conduct any of their interviews on the island of Tertia itself. Looking closely at the article, we see that Dr. Karp claims the interviews were conducted with children from the island group that includes Tertia. There is no evidence that they interviewed Tertian children. It would definitely weaken the argument if we were to learn that they interviewed children only on islands close to Tertia. Those islands may or may not have similar child-rearing traditions, and geographic proximity does not guarantee societal similarity.

Another piece of evidence that would weaken the argument could come from transcripts of the interviews themselves. Dr. Karp's article makes the claim that the children "spend much more time talking about their biological parents than about other adults," but he gives no indication of what exactly they say about their biological parents. After all, the children may be talking about how they never see their parents.

One more important piece of evidence that might undermine the argument Dr. Karp is making in this article. He admits that twenty years have passed since Dr. Field's study was conducted, but he does not provide evidence that proves child-rearing techniques have not changed significantly in that time. Any number of factors could have led to a significant shift in how children are raised. Influences from other cultures, significant catastrophic events, or a change in government structures could have led to a change in family dynamics. Any evidence of such changes would clearly undermine Dr. Karp's argument.

If we went looking for evidence that could strengthen the argument, we might also find something interesting. Obviously, some of the evidence above might strengthen the argument if they were NOT as discussed above (e.g., if there were evidence that the Tertian islands have NOT changed since Dr. Field's study or if there were transcripts that showed the children spoke about how much they loved living with their biological parents). However, if we discovered that there are numerous interview-based studies that confirm Dr. Karp's findings, it would go a long way toward bolstering his claim about Tertian child-rearing AND his claim about interview-centered studies being more effective. Another piece of evidence that would strengthen Dr. Karp's argument is undermining Dr. Field's original study. Maybe Dr. Field was sloppy, for example.

Dr. Karp's article, then, ends up looking like something of an empty shell. Depending on the evidence we find to fill it out, we may discover that it is quite convincing, or we could determine that he is full of hot air.

Reader Commentary

This strong response presents a generally thoughtful and well-developed analysis of the argument, and it follows the specific task directions quite clearly. This writer approaches the task by first discussing the evidence that might weaken Dr. Karp's argument and then, in somewhat less depth, considering the evidence that could strengthen it. In both cases the writer analyzes the ways in which the evidence would bear on the argument. For example, the writer notes, "Influences from other cultures, significant catastrophic events, or a change in government structures could have led to a change in family dynamics. Any evidence of such changes would clearly undermine Dr. Karp's argument." Although the development presented here is strong, the response does not present the compelling development required for a 6. For instance, in the first paragraph there is some repetition, and in the third paragraph the reader must fill in the implications of potential "changes" in Tertia, which are not fully fleshed out. How could a catastrophic event or a change in governmental structure have led to changes in child rearing traditions? The development, then, is strong but not outstanding. Also, the response demonstrates some facility with language, though it does not convey meaning skillfully enough to merit a score of 6. In general, the response demonstrates strong writing skills, in spite of some minor errors like the sentence fragment that begins paragraph three. Sentences like this one demonstrate the quality of the writing seen throughout the response: "Those islands may or may not have similar child-rearing traditions, and geographic proximity does not guarantee societal similarity." In terms of writing skill and analysis, then, this response earns a score of 5.

Score 4 Response

Dr. Karp's arguments that his research proves that obervation-centered research is invalid and that his interview-centered method "will establish a much more accurate understanding of child-rearing traditions there and in other island cultures" need more support. While the findings from Dr. Karp's interviews do challenge Dr. Field's results, one then cannot make the assumption that Dr. Field's research is invalid. This essay will attempt to explain three ways in which Dr. Karp can strengthen his argument.

First, Dr. Karp should provide more information about the content of the interviews. Misinterpretation from observation can be as likely as misinterpretation in interievws. It is possible that while children may spend more time talking about their own biological parents, other people from the village are still assisting in most of the rearing of the child. Perhaps asking the children how much time they spend with their parents, who disciplines them, and other specific questions about rearing would provide a more complete answer about who exactly is raising the children.

Second, Dr. Karp could provide some information about societal changes in the past twenty years. If there have been significant changes on the island of Tertia, it is possible that both anthropologists are correct. Twenty years ago, the entire village raised children, and now, biological parents raise their own children. Recents events could explain the change - such as introduction of Western mass media or changes in government (monarchy to democracy). Perhaps even interviewing adults to get a better understanding on child rearing. Not to mention, interpretting information from children and using that information to generalize about an entire island is not the most effective means.

Thirdly, Dr. Karp needs more proof that the observation-centered approach to studying cultures in invalid. A potential mistake in one article can hardly invalidate an entire method of research. Other anthropologists who employ the interview-centered method need to dispute the work of anthropoligsts who use the observation-centered approach. Only when a significant amount of research can be disproved can an entire method of research be invalidated.

To conclude, Dr. Karp needs to do more research and provide more evidence before his large claims can be fully supported. In fact, it will take more than Dr. Karp alone to prove observation-centered method of research is invalid and further, that the interview-centered method is better. In terms of his own research, Dr. Karp needs to conduct more interviews on the Tertia islands and scientifically prove Dr. Field's research wrong.

Reader Commentary

This adequate response manages to identify some important features of the argument, presenting a competent examination and generally following the task directions. The response does not merit a score of 5 or 6, however, because it does not present compelling or insightful development. The response identifies basic points about the content of the interviews, possible changes in Tertia, and observation-centered studies, but these points are developed only adequately. Development in paragraph four ("Thirdly...") is generic and thin, and the final paragraph just recapitulates the assertions made earlier. The response does follow the specific task instructions, but it does not develop its discussion of specific evidence fully. For example, there is a claim that "specific questions about rearing would provide a more complete answer about who exactly is raising the children," but the response does not explain what sorts of questions would give which answers or how those answers would strengthen or weaken the argument. Also, language control in this response is merely adequate, not strong. There are some typos and other errors (e.g., a sentence fragment in paragraph 3: "Perhaps even interviewing adults to get a better understanding on child rearing"), but the response generally demonstrates control of the conventions of standard written English, and main points are made with reasonable clarity. Because of its adequate control of language and competent analysis, this response earns a score of 4.

Score 3 Response

It will be very inappropriate to condemn Dr. Field's observations and findings. A critical look and analyses of the argument shows that details of Dr. Field's work was not given out. In fact, it is sad on the side of the writer to think that Dr.Fields work is invalid.

First, the fact that the children of Tertia spend much time talking about their biological parents than about other adults in the village can be interpreted in a different way. The writer did not give any clue on what exactly the children were saying about their biological parents. It could be that they were talking about their parents irresponsibility of rearing them by themselves than leaving them in the hands of the whole community to bring them up. In fact, the argument could have been strengthened if the writer gave what exactly the children were talking about.

On the other hand, the writer failed on his or her part as a researcher to look at the time frame from the time Dr. Field did his analyses to the the time writer also conducted His or Her research. This would have given him the insight as what new developments has taken place within the twenty years gap that Dr. Field did His analyses. The writer's argument would have given a lot of meaning if the writer had research into the cultural developments that has taken place since the time Dr. fields last visited and didcompleted His work at Tertia.

Also, as a reader, the tone this writing is not very convincing. It almost seems like Dr. Karp is making Dr. Fields look bad, instead of supporting his own research with information. He really only says one sentence about his own research, the rest of it is about how Fields work is not as good and saying things about Fields work. He needs to have more details about his own work to really sell the reader on it. He needs to write more about what the interview-centered method is, since he does not even say what it is. This will be more convincing if it is less of an attack on Dr. Field and more about the researches.

On the whole the writer's work is incomplete and His or Her criticisms are unfounded. The writer needs to change the qualitative way of His or Her research into a more quatitative approach. If done in this way the impact of His or Her findings will be very strong and convincing.

Reader Commentary

Although this response analyzes some important features of the argument, it is limited in development and often lacks acceptable clarity in expressing its ideas. In particular, this response contains occasional major errors and frequent minor errors that can interfere with meaning. Misused words, subject/verb agreement problems, and other lapses occur throughout the response. In addition to the problems with language control, the response demonstrates limited relevant development. It is true that the response makes an attempt to follow the specific task instructions, identifying the fact that the argument might be strengthened by evidence that the children were talking in a positive manner about their parents. However, the response does not explain exactly *how* this evidence would strengthen the argument. Similarly, there is discussion of the elapsed time between the two studies, but the response does not clarify how information about the "cultural developments" over the past 20 years would strengthen the argument Dr. Karp is making. Additionally, some of the points the response is making are not actually relevant to an analysis of the logic of the argument. The discussion of Dr. Karp's tone in the fourth paragraph, for example, is a rhetorical critique, not a logical one. There is an attempt to talk about evidence ("He needs to have more details…"), but the focus in this paragraph is on "selling" the reader, not creating a persuasive argument. Because of its limited development and language control, this response earns a score of 3.

Score 2 Response

The argument is on the article written by Dr. Karp , an anthropologist and his study and the new plan to study the same in the tertia region.Dr.Karp has written an article on Children in Tertia and about the culture.

The arguement is that they have not mention the type of intreview and the type of questions of the interviwes.They haven't indicate the education level in the children and the background of the children. What are all the things the team is going to observe and study on the child rearing tradition is not clearly mention.

The team is going to study and correlate the tradition with the other island culture but there is a possibility of different environment of other island or differnt biological parents. The resource availability on one island is different than the other is also a possibility . In that situation it is not possible to correlate the culture between to iceland.

There is a possibility , Dr. Field's interview time , lacking of infrastructure in the tartia. There was no developement of schools and other refreshment activity or the parents may not spent enough time with the children due to various reasons and that effect to the children , so they might have spend more time talking about their biological parent.

To support the argument more information about the nature, cultural background and also the type of infrastructure presence in the area is require, the kind of study carring out in the study area is require. Which would help to give more support the argument.

Reader Commentary

This response demonstrates serious weaknesses in analytical writing. There seem to be some attempts at logical analysis, though none that specifically and clearly examine the evidence that might weaken or strengthen the argument. Additionally, there is little or no relevant or reasonable support for the writer's points. In large part, the lack of logical development seems to be due to the serious and frequent problems with language control seen throughout the response. There are basic errors in just about every sentence of the response, and these errors frequently interfere with meaning. This sentence exemplifies the problems seen throughout the response: "There was no developement of schools and other refreshment activity or the parents may not spent enough time with the children due to various reasons and that effect to the children , so they might have spend more time talking about their biological parent." The writer is attempting to discuss some points that are relevant to an analysis of this argument, but meaning is obscured by all of the errors present. However, some meaning can be discerned, and these errors are not severe enough to drop the score to a 1.

Score 1 Response

Twenty years ago Dr field an anthropologist found result after reserch that in small village of tertia children reared by entire village but according to dr karp he talked most of the children that they talk about there boilogical parents. so it conclude that the reserch of dr field is unvalid now and what type of methods dr field used may be not cover all aspects of there culture and also other cultures of other islands. reared the children by entire village is not logical but in some cultures there are some surprizing customs . so may be dr field did not anlysed the culture of that island on various parameters , which we are using now a days.intrveiw with children and observing their behaviour is important because some time the person talk one thing and behave in different way look like either he not telling correct or he is showing his altitude in misguiding way. i think the behaviour of the children shows proper report of reserch and you can observe their altitude to the other adult peoples of the village and to their own biological parents.The expert reserch scholer can easily feel their emotions and behavour during some time stay with their culture. dr field maybe more research time, maybe, for longer.

Reader Commentary

This fundamentally deficient response mainly consists of a summary of the prompt, and although there is some evidence of understanding, the response provides little evidence of the ability to develop and organize an analysis of the argument. Also, severe problems in language persistently interfere with meaning. In fact, the material that does not come directly from the prompt is more or less incomprehensible.

Answers and Explanations

SECTION 3
Verbal Reasoning
25 Questions with Explanations

For each of Questions 1 to 4, select <u>one</u> answer choice unless otherwise instructed.

Questions 1 to 3 are based on the following reading passage.

Whether the languages of the ancient American peoples were used for expressing abstract universal concepts can be clearly answered in the case of Nahuatl. Nahuatl, like Greek and German, is a language that allows the formation of extensive com-
line pounds. By the combination of radicals or semantic elements, single compound words
5 can express complex conceptual relations, often of an abstract universal character.

The *tlamatinime* (those who know) were able to use this rich stock of abstract terms to express the nuances of their thought. They also availed themselves of other forms of expression with metaphorical meaning, some probably original, some derived from Toltec coinages. Of these forms, the most characteristic in Nahuatl is the juxtaposition
10 of two words that, because they are synonyms, associated terms, or even contraries, complement each other to evoke one single idea. Used metaphorically, the juxtaposed terms connote specific or essential traits of the being they refer to, introducing a mode of poetry as an almost habitual form of expression.

Description

This passage claims that Nahuatl was used to express abstract universal concepts, by combining semantic elements, and goes on to explain that the *tlamatinime* used these terms to express subtle distinctions.

For the following question, consider each of the choices separately and select all that apply.

1. Which of the following can be inferred from the passage regarding present-day research relating to Nahuatl?

   [A] Some record or evidence of the thought of the *tlamatinime* is available.

   [B] For at least some Nahuatl expressions, researchers are able to trace their derivation from another ancient American language.

   [C] Researchers believe that in Nahuatl, abstract universal concepts are always expressed metaphorically.

Explanation

Choices A and B are correct.

   Choice A is correct: the *tlamatinime* are mentioned in the first sentence of the second paragraph, where it says they were able to use Nahuatl's stock of abstract terms "to express the nuances of their thought." This suggests that there is some evidence of what those thoughts were, and therefore Choice A can be inferred.

Choice B is correct: according to the next sentence, Nahuatl speakers used "forms of expression with metaphorical meaning," some of which were probably "original" and others "derived from Toltec coinages." That researchers know certain Nahuatl expressions are derived from Toltec suggests that they are able to trace the derivation of some Nahuatl expressions from another language besides Nahuatl, and therefore Choice B may be inferred.

Choice C is incorrect: the passage says that in Nahuatl there are single compound words that can express conceptual relations of an "abstract universal character" and mentions "other forms of expression with metaphorical meaning," but it does not indicate whether metaphorical words or phrases are the only way that abstract universal concepts are expressed in Nahuatl, or whether researchers believe this about Nahuatl. Therefore Choice C cannot be inferred.

2. Select the sentence in the passage in which the author introduces a specific Nahuatl mode of expression that is not identified as being shared with certain European languages.

Explanation

The passage introduces two specific Nahuatl modes of expression. One is the formation of single compound words that are capable of expressing complex conceptual relations (first paragraph); the other is the juxtaposition of two related words to evoke a single idea (second paragraph). In the formation of compounds Nahuatl is described as being "like Greek and German," but the second mode is not identified as being shared with other languages. Therefore the **sixth sentence** ("Of these forms . . . one single idea") is the best choice.

3. In the context in which it appears, "coinages" (line 9) most nearly means
   (A) adaptations
   (B) creations
   (C) idiosyncrasies
   (D) pronunciations
   (E) currencies

Explanation

"Coinage" has two senses that are represented among the answer choices: in one sense it denotes coins and currency, while in the other it denotes things — especially words — that are invented. The fifth sentence draws a contrast between linguistic expressions original to Nahuatl and those derived from Toltec. In this context of original versus derived language, "coinages" means "inventions," not "currencies." Of the answer choices given, "creations" is the nearest equivalent of "coinages" in the sense of "inventions," and therefore **Choice B** is the best answer.

Question 4 is based on the following reading passage.

At a certain period in Earth's history, its atmosphere contained almost no oxygen, although plants were producing vast quantities of oxygen. As a way of reconciling these two facts, scientists have hypothesized that nearly all of the oxygen being produced was taken up by iron on Earth's surface. Clearly, however, **this explanation is inadequate. New studies show that the amount of iron on Earth's surface was not sufficient to absorb anywhere near as much oxygen as was being produced.** Therefore, something in addition to the iron on Earth's surface must have absorbed much of the oxygen produced by plant life.

4. In the argument given, the two portions in **boldface** play which of the following roles?

   (A) The first is a claim made by the argument in support of a certain position; the second is that position.

   (B) The first is a judgment made by the argument about a certain explanation; the second is that explanation.

   (C) The first expresses the argument's dismissal of an objection to the position it seeks to establish; the second is that position.

   (D) The first sums up the argument's position with regard to a certain hypothesis; the second provides grounds for that position.

   (E) The first is a concession by the argument that its initial formulation of the position it seeks to establish requires modification; the second presents that position in a modified form.

Explanation

The passage presents an argument and the question asks you to identify the role the portions highlighted in boldface play in that argument. The first step in responding is to read through the passage quickly to get an understanding of what is being said. Then it is possible to go back and assess how the parts of the passage fit together into an argument.

In this passage the first sentence presents two pieces of information that seem to be in conflict — the atmosphere contained almost no oxygen even though plants were producing so much of it. The second sentence presents a hypothetical explanation that has been proposed for reconciling the discrepancy — that oxygen was absorbed by iron. The next sentence calls this hypothetical explanation inadequate and the following sentence gives a reason for that judgment — that there was insufficient iron for the proposed explanation to work. Finally, the last sentence draws the conclusion that there must have been something in addition to iron to absorb the oxygen.

Since the highlighted portions in the passage represent the main content of the third and fourth sentences, the task in this question is to find the answer choice whose two parts fit those sentences' roles. It can be seen that answer Choice D fits the requirement: the third sentence does sum up the argument's position about a hypothesis, and the fourth sentence gives grounds for the third. Therefore **Choice D** is the correct answer.

> **For Questions 5 to 8, select one entry for each blank from the corresponding column of choices. Fill all blanks in the way that best completes the text.**

5. In her later years, Bertha Pappenheim was an apostle of noble but already (i)_____ notions, always respected for her integrity, her energy, and her resolve but increasingly out of step and ultimately (ii)_____ even her own organization.

Blank (i)	Blank (ii)
(A) anachronistic	(D) emulated by
(B) accepted	(E) appreciated by
(C) exotic	(F) alienated from

Explanation

The sentence is clearly conveying a contrast since "but" is used twice to indicate something positive and something negative about Pappenheim. The clue to the negative aspect is in the later part of the sentence, where "out of step" leads both to "anachronistic" as the answer for the first blank and "alienated from" as the answer for the second.

   Thus the correct answer is **anachronistic** (Choice A) and **alienated from** (Choice F).

6. The reception given to Kimura's radical theory of molecular evolution shows that when _____ fights orthodoxy to a draw, then novelty has seized a good chunk of space from convention.

(A) imitation
(B) reaction
(C) dogmatism
(D) invention
(E) caution

Explanation

The sentence sets up two parallel, contrasting concepts. The word in the blank must contrast with "orthodoxy," and since "convention" in the second contrasting pair is synonymous with "orthodoxy," the correct answer should be roughly synonymous with "novelty." The word "invention" is the best choice.

   Thus the correct answer is **invention** (Choice D).

7. The (i)_____ of Vladimir Nabokov as one of North America's literary giants has thrown the spotlight on his peripheral activities and has thus served to (ii)_____ his efforts as an amateur entomologist.

Blank (i)	Blank (ii)
(A) stigmatization	(D) foreground
(B) lionization	(E) transcend
(C) marginalization	(F) obscure

Explanation

It is possible to analyze this sentence by starting with either blank. Broadly, it states that something that has happened to Nabokov has called attention to some of his peripheral activities. It would hardly make sense for what had happened to be either stigmatization or marginalization, since both of those activities represent a turning away from him, not a calling attention to him. So the correct answer for the first blank is "lionization," since to lionize means to treat as important. Then, since we are told that Nabokov is a literary giant, entomology must be one of his peripheral activities, so the correct answer for the second blank must be "foreground," which also means "call attention to." Spotlighting something would not result in transcending it or obscuring it, so neither of the other choices is correct.

Thus the correct answer is **lionization** (Choice B) and **foreground** (Choice D).

8. Mathematicians have a distinctive sense of beauty: they strive to present their ideas and results in a clear and compelling fashion, dictated by _____ as well as by logic.

(A) caprice
(B) aesthetics
(C) obligation
(D) methodologies
(E) intellect

Explanation

The opening statement attributes a "sense of beauty" to mathematicians, and the remainder of the sentence after the colon spells out that observation. Filling in the blank will supply some aspect that balances "logic" and reinforces the view that mathematicians have a sense of beauty. "aesthetics" is the best choice.

Thus the correct answer is **aesthetics** (Choice B).

For each of Questions 9 to 13, select one answer choice unless otherwise instructed.

Questions 9 to 12 are based on the following reading passage.

Animal signals, such as the complex songs of birds, tend to be costly. A bird, by singing, may forfeit time that could otherwise be spent on other important behaviors such as foraging or resting. Singing may also advertise an individual's location to rivals or pred-
line
5 ators and impair the ability to detect their approach. Although these types of cost may be important, discussions of the cost of singing have generally focused on energy costs. Overall the evidence is equivocal: for instance, while Eberhardt found increases in energy consumption during singing for Carolina wrens, Chappell found no effect of crowing on energy consumption in roosters.

To obtain empirical data regarding the energy costs of singing, Thomas examined
10 the relationship between song rate and overnight changes in body mass of male nightingales. Birds store energy as subcutaneous fat deposits or "body reserves"; changes in these reserves can be reliably estimated by measuring changes in body mass. If singing has important energy costs, nightingales should lose more body mass

line
15 on nights when their song rate is high. Thomas found that nightingales reached a significantly higher body mass at dusk and lost more mass overnight on nights when their song rate was high.

These results suggest that there may be several costs of singing at night associated with body reserves. The increased metabolic cost of possessing higher body mass contributes to the increased overnight mass loss. The strategic regulation of evening body
20 reserves is also likely to incur additional costs, as nightingales must spend more time foraging in order to build up larger body reserves. The metabolic cost of singing itself may also contribute to increased loss of reserves. This metabolic cost may arise from the muscular and neural activity involved in singing or from behaviors associated with singing. For example, birds may expend more of their reserves on thermoregulation if
25 they spend the night exposed to the wind on a song post than if they are in a sheltered roost site. Thomas's data therefore show that whether or not singing per se has an important metabolic cost, metabolic costs associated with singing can have an important measurable effect on a bird's daily energy budget, at least in birds with high song rates such as nightingales.

Description

The passage mentions various ways in which singing is costly to a bird, but soon focuses on the main topic: the energy costs of singing. The second paragraph then discusses a particular experiment designed to assess the energy costs of singing for nightingales, and the third paragraph identifies a range of different associated costs.

9. The primary purpose of the passage is to
    (A) compare the different types of cost involved for certain birds in singing
    (B) question a hypothesis regarding the energy costs of singing for certain birds
    (C) present evidence suggesting that singing has an important energy cost for certain birds
    (D) discuss the benefits provided to an organism by a behavior that is costly in energy
    (E) describe an experiment that supports an alternative model of how birdsong functions

Explanation

As mentioned above, the first paragraph mentions various costs associated with birdsong, but from that point onward, the focus of the passage is on evidence concerning the energy costs of singing, for nightingales in particular. Thus the correct answer is **Choice C**. Although the passage mentions other costs, it does not compare them with one another, so Choice A is incorrect. Because the passage does not question any hypotheses, discuss benefits, or advance an alternative model of birdsong, Choices B, D, and E are incorrect.

For the following question, consider each of the choices separately and select all that apply.

10. The passage implies that during the day before a night on which a male nightingale's song rate is high, that nightingale probably does which of the following?

   A Expends less of its reserves on thermoregulation than on other days
   B Stores more energy as body reserves than on other days
   C Hides to avoid predators

Explanation

Choice B is correct.

   Choice A is incorrect: the only reference to thermoregulation comes in line 24 and discusses nighttime activity, not daytime activity.

   Choice B is correct: the second paragraph explains that birds store energy as fat deposits that can be estimated by measuring body mass, and that body mass at dusk was significantly higher in nightingales on nights when their song rate was higher.

   Choice C is incorrect: while the passage does say that singing exposes birds to predators (line 3), it says nothing to suggest that they make special efforts to hide before singing, and in fact it says that nightingales spend extra time foraging (line 20).

11. Select the sentence in the first or second paragraph that presents empirical results in support of a hypothesis about the energy costs of singing.

Explanation

Only two sentences in the relevant portion of the passage contain information that might be considered to be empirical results. The last sentence of the first paragraph contains information about increases in energy consumption but only the last sentence of the second paragraph provides results in support of the only hypothesis in the passage, that nightingales should lose more body mass on nights when their song rate is high. Thus **sentence 9** ("Thomas found . . . high") is the correct choice.

For the following question, consider each of the choices separately and select all that apply.

12. It can be inferred from the passage that compared with other costs of singing, which of the following is true of the energy costs of singing?

   A They are the single greatest cost to an individual bird.
   B They have generally received more attention from scientists.
   C They vary less from one bird species to another.

Explanation

Choice B is correct.

   Choice A is incorrect: you might infer that energy costs of singing are significant but no information is given to suggest that they are greater than other costs.

   Choice B is correct: lines 4–5 say that discussions of the costs of singing have generally focused on energy costs.

Choice C is incorrect: the only mention of differences across species occurs in the discussion of the findings of Eberhardt and Chappell. These findings relate to energy costs alone and, if anything, suggest that energy costs vary considerably.

In the past ten years, there have been several improvements in mountain-climbing equipment. These improvements have made the sport both safer and more enjoyable for experienced climbers. Despite these improvements, however, the rate of mountain-climbing injuries has doubled in the past ten years.

13. Which of the following, if true, best reconciles the apparent discrepancy presented in the passage?
    (A) Many climbers, lulled into a false sense of security, use the new equipment to attempt climbing feats of which they are not capable.
    (B) Some mountain-climbing injuries are caused by unforeseeable weather conditions.
    (C) Mountain climbing, although a dangerous sport, does not normally result in injury to the experienced climber.
    (D) In the past ten years there have been improvements in mountain-climbing techniques as well as in mountain-climbing equipment.
    (E) Although the rate of mountain-climbing injuries has increased, the rate of mountain-climbing deaths has not changed.

Explanation

In this question you are asked to identify the fact that would best reconcile the apparent discrepancy that the passage presents. The discrepancy is that despite improvements in mountain climbing equipment that have made climbing safer, the incidence of mountain-climbing injuries has greatly increased. Choice A explains how this could have happened — the improvements in equipment have led climbers to attempt feats that are beyond their level of skill. Therefore, **Choice A** is the correct answer.

None of the other choices provides information that resolves the discrepancy. Neither Choice B nor Choice C relates to conditions that have changed over the relevant ten-year period. Choices D and E do relate to the relevant period. But if, as Choice D says, techniques as well as equipment have improved, that fact by itself only makes the increase in injuries more puzzling. Choice E provides more data about the consequences of climbing accidents, but doesn't suggest any explanation for the increase in injuries.

> For Questions 14 to 17, select one entry for each blank from the corresponding column of choices. Fill all blanks in the way that best completes the text.

14. Unenlightened authoritarian managers rarely recognize a crucial reason for the low levels of serious conflict among members of democratically run work groups: a modicum of tolerance for dissent often prevents _____.

| (A) demur |
| (B) schism |
| (C) cooperation |
| (D) compliance |
| (E) shortsightedness |

Explanation

The blank must be filled with a word that describes a problem that a work group can suffer, a problem that can be a cause of (or associated with) serious conflict. Of the answer choices, only "schism" fits this description.

Thus the correct answer is **schism** (Choice B).

15. The novelist devotes so much time to avid descriptions of his characters' clothes that the reader soon feels that such _____ concerns, although worthy of attention, have superseded any more directly literary aims.

| (A) didactic |
| (B) syntactical |
| (C) irrelevant |
| (D) sartorial |
| (E) frivolous |

Explanation

The "concerns" described by the adjective that fills the blank relate to clothing, so "sartorial" fits the blank. Although these concerns could also be described as "irrelevant" or "frivolous," neither of these choices is correct because the sentence identifies the concerns as "worthy of attention."

Thus the correct answer is **sartorial** (Choice D).

16. Belanger dances with an (i)_____ that draws one's attention as if by seeking to (ii)_____ it; through finesse and understatement, he manages to seem at once intensely present and curiously detached.

Blank (i)	Blank (ii)
(A) undemonstrative panache	(D) focus
(B) unrestrained enthusiasm	(E) overwhelm
(C) unattractive gawkiness	(F) deflect

Explanation

The point of the sentence is to emphasize contradictory aspects of Belanger's dancing: we are told, for example, that he seems "at once intensely present and curiously detached." Looking at the second blank with this point in mind, we can see that the sentence is saying that Belanger draws attention in some way that would not normally be a means of doing so. The only choice that fits, therefore, is "deflect"; focusing or overwhelming attention would certainly be expected to draw it. And since employing "unrestrained enthusiasm" or "unattractive gawkiness" would not be ways of deflecting attention, the correct choice for the first blank is "undemonstrative panache," another paradoxical term, since "panache" means "dash or flamboyance in style."

Thus the correct answer is **undemonstrative panache** (Choice A) and **deflect** (Choice F).

17. The most striking thing about the politician is how often his politics have been (i)_____ rather than ideological, as he adapts his political positions at any particular moment to the political realities that constrain him. He does not, however, piously (ii)_____ political principles only to betray them in practice. Rather, he attempts in subtle ways to balance his political self-interest with a (iii) _____, viewing himself as an instrument of some unchanging higher purpose.

Blank (i)	Blank (ii)	Blank (iii)
(A) quixotic	(D) brandish	(G) profound cynicism
(B) self-righteous	(E) flout	(H) deeply felt moral code
(C) strategic	(F) follow	(I) thoroughgoing pragmatism

Explanation

Since the politician is portrayed as adapting political positions to political realities, blank (i) should be filled with "strategic," which is also the only choice that provides the required contrast with "ideological." The second blank, *brandishing* political principles is what a politician might do piously, while *flouting* is not pious and *following* principles does not make sense when combined with "betray[ing] them in practice." The third blank requires something that would have to be balanced against "political self-interest" and that would be embraced in service of an "unchanging higher purpose," making "deeply felt moral code" the only viable choice.

Thus the correct answer is **strategic** (Choice C), **brandish** (Choice D), and **deeply felt moral code** (Choice H).

For each of Questions 18 to 20, select <u>one</u> answer choice unless otherwise instructed.

Questions 18 to 20 are based on the following reading passage.

The condition of scholarship devoted to the history of women in photography is confounding. Recent years have witnessed the posthumous inflation of the role of the hobbyist Alice Austen into that of a pioneering documentarian while dozens of notable

line
5
10

senior figures — Marion Palfi, whose photographs of civil-rights activities in the South served as early evidence of the need for protective legislation, to name one — received scant attention from scholars. And, while Naomi Rosenblum's synoptic *History of Women Photographers* covers the subject through 1920 in a generally useful fashion, once she reaches the 1920s, when the venues, forms, applications, and movements of the medium expanded exponentially, she resorts to an increasingly terse listing of unfamiliar names, with approaches and careers summarized in a sentence or two.

Description

The passage expresses dismay at the current state of scholarship concerning the history of women in photography: some figures receive disproportionate attention, and past 1920 Rosenblum's book is too sketchy to be useful.

18. The author of the passage cites Rosenblum's book most likely in order to

Ⓐ suggest that the works documented most thoroughly by historians of women in photography often do not warrant that attention

Ⓑ offer an explanation for the observation that not all aspects of the history of women in photography have received the same level of attention

Ⓒ provide an example of a way in which scholarship on the history of women in photography has been unsatisfactory

Ⓓ suggest that employing a strictly chronological approach when studying the history of women in photography may be unproductive

Ⓔ provide support for the notion that certain personalities in women's photography have attained undue prominence

Explanation

As mentioned above, the topic of the passage is the unsatisfactory condition of scholarship devoted to the history of women in photography. Since Rosenberg's book is clearly presented as an example of this unsatisfactory scholarship, **Choice C** is the correct answer. Choice D may seem appealing, because a strictly chronological approach might be inadequate to represent the explosive growth of the field in the 1920s. However, the sentence does not develop this idea, and this is not the reason for mentioning Rosenblum.

For the following question, consider each of the choices separately and select all that apply.

19. Which of the following statements about Marion Palfi is supported by the passage?

☐ A Marion Palfi's photographs would have received greater recognition from historians had her work been done in an era when most aspects of photography were static rather than in a state of transition.

☐ B Alice Austen has achieved greater notoriety than has Marion Palfi primarily because the subjects that Austen photographed were more familiar to her contemporaries.

☐ C In addition to providing a record of certain historical events, Marion Palfi's photographs played a role in subsequent events.

Explanation

Choice C is correct.

Choice A is incorrect: the passage does not state whether the period in which Palfi was working was an era when photography was static or in transition.

Choice B is incorrect: the passage does not state the nature of the subjects Austen photographed, nor compare their relative familiarity to those photographed by Palfi.

Choice C is correct: Palfi's photographs played a role in subsequent events because they served as early evidence of the need for protective legislation.

20. In the context in which it appears, "inflation" (line 2) most nearly means
    - (A) exaggeration
    - (B) acquisition
    - (C) evaluation
    - (D) distortion
    - (E) attenuation

Explanation

The term "hobbyist" suggests Austen's relative lack of seriousness as a photographer when compared with "senior figures," yet her role has been elevated to that of a "pioneering documentarian" at the expense of these other figures. Choice D may be appealing in that this elevation could be considered a form of distortion, but Choice A is more specific as well as more in line with the dictionary definition of "inflated" as "expanded to an abnormal or unjustifiable volume or level." Thus **Choice A**, "exaggeration," is the correct answer.

For Questions 21 to 25, select the **two** answer choices that, when used to complete the sentence, fit the meaning of the sentence as a whole **and** produce completed sentences that are alike in meaning.

---

21. The plan, which the engineers said would save the aquifer by reducing pumping to _____ levels, has passed a governmental environmental review but faces opposition from outdoor and environmental groups.
    - [A] innocuous
    - [B] feasible
    - [C] practicable
    - [D] minimal
    - [E] remedial
    - [F] benign

Explanation

If the engineers think that the reduced levels will save the aquifer, they may describe the reduced levels as innocuous, minimal, remedial, or benign. Of these words, only "innocuous" and "benign" produce sentences with the same meaning. The two words "feasible" and "practicable" are similar in meaning, but do not fit the context well, because they imply that the current levels are not feasible or practicable, conflicting with the implication that the current levels, though perhaps undesirable, are nevertheless entirely feasible.

Thus the correct answer is **innocuous** (Choice A) and **benign** (Choice F).

22. Though feminist in its implications, Yvonne Rainer's 1974 film _____ the filmmaker's active involvement in feminist politics.

    A antedated
    B cloaked
    C portrayed
    D preceded
    E renewed
    F represented

Explanation

The words that fill the blank must fit with the idea that Rainer's film has some feminist implications, but that those are limited compared with her other activities. From the six words offered as answer choices, the pair "antedated" and "preceded" and the pair "portrayed" and "represented" each produce sentences that are similar in meaning. However, only "antedated" and "preceded" make sense in the context of the sentence: Rainer's 1974 film exhibits feminist themes in a limited way because it came before she became active in feminist politics.

Thus the correct answer is **antedated** (Choice A) and **preceded** (Choice D).

23. Congress is having great difficulty developing a consensus on energy policy, primarily because the policy objectives of various members of Congress rest on such _____ assumptions.

    A commonplace
    B disparate
    C divergent
    D fundamental
    E trite
    F trivial

Explanation

The words that fill the blank must help explain the difficulty of developing a consensus. A lack of agreement on the assumptions that underlie Congress members' policy objectives would contribute to such a difficulty. Accordingly, "disparate" and "divergent" are the best choices because they both indicate disagreement among the members. Although the words "trite" and "trivial" are similar in meaning, triteness and triviality do not help to explain the difficulty in developing a consensus.

Thus the correct answer is **disparate** (Choice B) and **divergent** (Choice C).

24. During the opera's most famous aria, the tempo chosen by the orchestra's conductor seemed _____, without necessary relation to what had gone before.

    A arbitrary
    B capricious
    C cautious
    D compelling
    E exacting
    F meticulous

Explanation

Any of the offered words could possibly describe a conductor's choice of tempo. However, the phrase "without necessary relation to what had gone before" is presented as an elaboration on the word in the blank. Among the answer choices, only "arbitrary" and "capricious" could be elaborated that way; none of the other choices would be explained by the final phrase.

Thus the correct answer is **arbitrary** (Choice A) and **capricious** (Choice B).

25. Because they had expected the spacecraft Voyager 2 to be able to gather data only about the planets Jupiter and Saturn, scientists were _____ the wealth of information it sent back from Neptune twelve years after leaving Earth.

    A anxious for
    B confident in
    C thrilled about
    D keen on
    E elated by
    F eager for

Explanation

In the sentence, the words "expected" and "only" imply that the data received from the spacecraft exceeded scientists' expectations. Therefore, the words that fill the blank should describe a reaction to results that are better than hoped for, and the choices "thrilled about" and "elated by" both express such a reaction. The scientists may well also have been eager for, or keen on, the information, but their eagerness is not well explained by the unexpectedness of the information.

Thus the correct answer is **thrilled about** (Choice C) and **elated by** (Choice E).

SECTION 4
Verbal Reasoning
25 Questions with Explanations

For Questions 1 to 4, select the <u>two</u> answer choices that, when used to complete the sentence, fit the meaning of the sentence as a whole <u>and</u> produce completed sentences that are alike in meaning.

---

1. Only by ignoring decades of mismanagement and inefficiency could investors conclude that a fresh infusion of cash would provide anything other than a _____ solution to the company's financial woes.

   A complete
   B fleeting
   C momentary
   D premature
   E trivial
   F total

Explanation

The key phrases that indicate how the blank for this question should be completed are "Only by ignoring decades of mismanagement and inefficiency" and "provide anything other than." Taken together, these phrases indicate that the sentence will not envision a very beneficial or successful resolution of the "financial woes." Among the answer choices, "complete" and "total" are quite close in meaning and would clearly create two sentences very similar in meaning. But those two sentences would be internally contradictory, suggesting that doing something unwise would completely solve a problem. "Fleeting" and "momentary" suggest that the event referred to ("a fresh infusion of cash") might have some beneficial effect, but that it would ultimately not resolve the problem.

   Thus the correct answer is **fleeting** (Choice B) and **momentary** (Choice C).

2. Some scientists argue that carbon compounds play such a central role in life on Earth because of the possibility of _____ resulting from the carbon atom's ability to form an unending series of different molecules.

   A diversity
   B deviation
   C variety
   D reproduction
   E stability
   F invigoration

Explanation

The key phrase that indicates how the blank for this question should be completed is "the ability to form an unending series of different molecules." Among the answer choices, "diversity" and "variety" clearly fit logically with "unending" and "different" and create two very similar sentences. No other pair of choices here would produce two sentences as similar in meaning as those created by placing "diversity" and "variety" in the blank. Thus the correct answer is **diversity** (Choice A) and **variety** (Choice C).

3. Given the flood of information presented by the mass media, the only way for someone to keep abreast of the news is to rely on _____ accounts.

    A synoptic
    B abridged
    C sensational
    D copious
    E lurid
    F understated

Explanation

The key phrase that indicates how the blank for this question should be completed is "the only way for someone to keep abreast of the news." Among the answer choices, "synoptic" and "abridged," while not synonymous in the strict sense, both fit the logic of this description, "synoptic" because of its emphasis on breadth and generality as opposed to detail, and "abridged" because of its obvious focus on brevity. "Sensational" and "lurid" would create two similar sentences but do not fit the logic for completing the blank, since we would not be relying on sensational or lurid accounts in order to keep abreast of the news.

Thus the correct answer is **synoptic** (Choice A) and **abridged** (Choice B).

4. Always circumspect, she was reluctant to make judgments, but once arriving at a conclusion, she was _____ in its defense.

    A deferential
    B intransigent
    C lax
    C negligent
    E obsequious
    F resolute

Explanation

The key phrases that indicate how the blank for this question should be completed are: "circumspect," "reluctant," and "but once." Taken together they point to completing the blank with something that is opposite in some way to the two cited adjectives. Among the answer choices, "intransigent" and "resolute," although not strictly synonymous, both fit the logic of the description given here for completing the blank and create sentences that are similar in meaning. "Lax" and "negligent" are clearly similar in meaning and would create sentences similar in meaning, but they continue the sentiment voiced in the initial clause rather than contrasting with it. "Deferential" and "obsequious" are also similar in meaning, but their emphasis on "politeness," while not strictly synonymous with reluctance and circumspection, like "lax" and "negligent" fail to pick up on the expected contrast.

Thus the correct answer is **intransigent** (Choice B) and **resolute** (Choice F).

For each of Questions 5 to 9, select <u>one</u> answer choice unless otherwise instructed.

Questions 5 and 6 are based on the following reading passage.

When marine organisms called phytoplankton photosynthesize, they absorb carbon dioxide dissolved in seawater, potentially causing a reduction in the concentration of atmospheric carbon dioxide, a gas that contributes to global warming. However, phy-
line
  toplankton flourish only in surface waters where iron levels are sufficiently high. Mar-
5 tin therefore hypothesized that adding iron to iron-poor regions of the ocean could help alleviate global warming. While experiments subsequently confirmed that such a procedure increases phytoplankton growth, field tests have shown that such growth does not significantly lower atmospheric carbon dioxide. When phytoplankton utilize carbon dioxide for photosynthesis, the carbon becomes a building block for organic
10 matter, but the carbon leaks back into the atmosphere when predators consume the phytoplankton and respire carbon dioxide.

Description

The paragraph presents a hypotheses about reducing global warming by adding iron to iron-poor areas of the ocean and explains why adding the iron does not have the hoped-for benefit.

For the following question, consider each of the choices separately and select all that apply.

5. It can be inferred from the passage that Martin's hypothesis includes which of the following elements?

  A A correct understanding of how phytoplankton photosynthesis utilizes carbon dioxide

  B A correct prediction about how the addition of iron to iron-poor waters would affect phytoplankton growth

  C An incorrect prediction about how phytoplankton growth would affect the concentration of atmospheric carbon dioxide

Explanation

All three choices are correct. Martin's hypothesis was that adding iron to iron-poor regions of the ocean could help alleviate global warming.

  Choice A is correct: the passage presents Martin as using the standard understanding of how phytoplankton photosynthesize as a basis for the hypothesis.

  Choice B is correct: the passage states that experiments confirmed that adding iron to iron-poor regions increases phytoplankton growth in those regions. Therefore, Martin's prediction about this was correct.

  Choice C is correct: it can be inferred that in Martin's hypothesis the means by which adding iron in certain regions could alleviate global warming is that phytoplankton increase in those regions and absorb atmospheric carbon dioxide. The passage states that predators who consume phytoplankton respire carbon dioxide, so that the carbon dioxide absorbed by phytoplankton reenters the atmosphere. Therefore, Martin's prediction about this was incorrect.

6. It can be inferred that the author of the passage mentions predators (line 10) primarily in order to

(A) help explain why Martin's hypothesis is incorrect

(B) identify one effect of adding iron to iron-poor waters

(C) indicate how some carbon dioxide is converted to solid organic matter

(D) help account for differences in the density of phytoplankton between different regions of the ocean

(E) point out a factor that was not anticipated by the scientists who conducted the field tests mentioned in the passage

Explanation

Lines 7–11 of the paragraph present the evidence against Martin's hypothesis. Lines 7–8 present field test results showing that Martin's hypothesis is incorrect, and the last sentence explains these results: the reason the increased phytoplankton resulting from the addition of iron do not reduce atmospheric carbon dioxide is that while the phytoplankton absorb carbon dioxide, the gas reenters the atmosphere when it is respired by phytoplankton predators. Therefore **Choice A** is correct: predators are mentioned to explain why Martin's hypothesis is incorrect. Choice B is not correct because while predators' consumption of phytoplankton and respiration of carbon dioxide might be considered one indirect consequence of adding iron to iron-poor waters, identifying a consequence is not the primary function of the mention of predators. Choice C is incorrect because the reference to predators is used to explain how carbon dioxide reappears as a gas, and Choice D is incorrect because no connection is suggested between predators and the distribution of phytoplankton. Choice E is not correct because it is Martin who did not anticipate this factor, rather than the scientists who conducted the field tests.

Question 7 is based on the following reading passage.

Sparva, unlike Treland's other provinces, requires automobile insurers to pay for any medical treatment sought by someone who has been involved in an accident; in the other provinces, insurers pay for nonemergency treatment only if they preapprove the treatment. Clearly, Sparva's less restrictive policy must be the explanation for the fact that altogether insurers there pay for far more treatments after accidents than insurers in other provinces, even though Sparva does not have the largest population.

Description

The passage tells us that in Sparva automobile insurers pay for far more medical treatments after accidents than they do in Treland's other provinces. The passage concludes that the explanation is to be found in the difference in legal requirements for insurers in Sparva as compared to other provinces.

7. Which of the following, if true, most strengthens the argument?

(A) Car insurance costs more in Sparva than in any other province.

(B) The cost of medical care in Sparva is higher than the national average.

(C) Different insurance companies have different standards for determining what constitutes emergency treatment.

(D) Fewer insurance companies operate in Sparva than in any other province.

(E) There are fewer traffic accidents annually in Sparva than in any of the provinces of comparable or greater population.

Explanation

The question asks you to identify among the answer choices a fact that would support the passage's argument. The explanation offered in the passage can be supported by ruling out other explanations that might, given the information presented in the passage, appear likely. One obvious explanation for there being more medical treatments in Sparva is that there are more accidents there. Choice E rules out that explanation. So **Choice E** strengthens the argument in the passage and is the correct answer. Choices A and D each present consequences that are likely results of insurers in Sparva having to pay for more medical treatments. But neither bears on the cause of insurers having to pay for more treatments. Choice B does not strengthen the argument and may weaken it. A higher cost of medical care provides additional motivation for people to seek insurance payments to cover whatever post-accident care they receive. So Choice B might weaken the argument by providing an alternative explanation for insurers paying for more medical treatments in Sparva. According to the passage, whether treatment is emergency treatment is, in other provinces, an important criterion in determining insurers' responsibility. But since this criterion does not apply in Sparva, Choice C is not directly relevant to the point that the passage is trying to establish.

Questions 8 and 9 are based on the following reading passage.

Elements of the Philosophy of Newton, published by Voltaire in 1738, was an early attempt to popularize the scientific ideas of Isaac Newton. In the book's frontispiece, Voltaire is seen writing at his desk, and over him a shaft of light from heaven, the light of truth, passes through Newton to Voltaire's collaborator Madame du Châtelet; she reflects that light onto the inspired Voltaire. Voltaire's book commanded a wide audience, according to Feingold, because "he was neither a mathematician nor a physicist, but a literary giant aloof from the academic disputes over Newtonian ideas." In other words, Voltaire's amateurism in science "was a source of his contemporary appeal, demonstrating for the first time the accessibility of Newton's ideas to nonspecialists."

Description

The paragraph describes Voltaire's book and gives some reasons for its success.

For the following question, consider each of the choices separately and select all that apply.

8. Which of the following statements about Voltaire's *Elements of the Philosophy of Newton* can be inferred from the passage?

    A Voltaire's literary stature helped secure a large audience for this attempt to popularize Newton's ideas.

    B Voltaire's status as a nonscientist was an advantage in this effort to bring Newtonian science to the attention of the general public.

    C The frontispiece of the book implies that Voltaire's understanding of Newton's ideas was not achieved without assistance.

Explanation

All three choices are correct.

Choice A is correct: the paragraph states that one of the reasons Voltaire's book commanded a wide audience is that he was "a literary giant."

Choice B is correct: the paragraph states that Voltaire's amateurism in science demonstrated that nonspecialists could also understand Newton's ideas.

Choice C is correct: the paragraph refers to Voltaire's collaborator, Madame du Châtelet. In the image described, she serves as the intermediary between Newton and Voltaire, conveying Newton's ideas to Voltaire.

9. Select the sentence that describes an allegory for Voltaire's acquisition of knowledge concerning Newton's ideas.

Explanation

In the image described in the second sentence, Voltaire acquires his knowledge of Newton through Madame du Châtelet, who conveys Newton's ideas — his "light of truth" — to Voltaire. The only other sentence that contains figurative language is the next sentence, in which Voltaire is described as "a literary giant aloof . . . from disputes." However, this image refers not to Voltaire's acquisition of knowledge of Newtonian ideas, but rather to his attitude regarding Newtonian ideas. Therefore **sentence 2** ("In the book's . . . Voltaire") is the correct choice.

For Questions 10 to 13, select one entry for each blank from the corresponding column of choices. Fill all blanks in the way that best completes the text.

---

10. Ironically, the writer so wary of (i)_____ was (ii)_____ with ink and paper, his novel running to 2,500 shagreen-bound folio pages — a fortune in stationery at the time.

Blank (i)	Blank (ii)
(A) probity	(D) acquisitive
(B) extravagance	(E) illiberal
(C) disapprobation	(F) profligate

Explanation

The last part of the sentence provides most of the context needed to fill in the two blanks. The novel was extremely long and required vast amounts of paper. Among the choices for the second blank, only "profligate" matches this lack of restraint. The word "Ironically" indicates that what the writer was "wary of" was something similar to profligacy; of the choices for the first blank, "extravagance" is the closest.

Thus the correct answer is **extravagance** (Choice B) and **profligate** (Choice F).

11. What readers most commonly remember about John Stuart Mill's classic exploration of the liberty of thought and discussion concerns the danger of (i)_____: in the absence of challenge, one's opinions, even when they are correct, grow weak and flabby. Yet Mill had another reason for encouraging the liberty of thought and discussion: the danger of partiality and incompleteness. Since one's opinions, even under the best circumstances, tend to (ii)_____, and because opinions opposed to one's own rarely turn out to be completely (iii)_____, it is crucial to supplement one's opinions with alternative points of view.

Blank (i)	Blank (ii)	Blank (iii)
Ⓐ tendentiousness	Ⓓ embrace only a portion of the truth	Ⓖ erroneous
Ⓑ complacency	Ⓔ change over time	Ⓗ antithetical
Ⓒ fractiousness	Ⓕ focus on matters close at hand	Ⓘ immutable

Explanation

An overview of the passage suggests that the first sentence is relatively self-contained and that the blank is answerable without the succeeding sentences, where the topic shifts slightly. The colon after the first blank signals that what follows will define the word in the blank and will explain what danger Mill was concerned about. It says that without challenge, one's opinions grow "weak and flabby" and therefore one becomes *complacent*, not tendentious or fractious. A quick reading of the next two sentences suggests that the topic will be another danger that Mill described, "the danger of partiality and incompleteness." Free and open discussion needs to take place because each person's opinion tends to "embrace only a portion of the truth" and others' views are partially right, or never completely "erroneous." The other choices for the second and third blanks deal with change, immediacy, or antithesis, none of which relate to the second danger of "partiality" or "incompleteness."

Thus the correct answer is **complacency** (Choice B), **embrace only a portion of the truth** (Choice D), and **erroneous** (Choice G).

12. Just as the authors' book on eels is often a key text for courses in marine vertebrate zoology, their ideas on animal development and phylogeny _____ teaching in this area.

Ⓐ prevent
Ⓑ defy
Ⓒ replicate
Ⓓ inform
Ⓔ use

Explanation

The "just as" structure indicates that the second half of the sentence should somehow parallel the idea presented in the first half (i.e., the idea that the authors' book on eels is a "key text" in marine vertebrate zoology). Among the choices given, "inform" is clearly the best choice. "Prevent" and "defy" work in the opposite direction, while "use" and "replicate" would suggest that the authors' ideas are drawing upon the teaching in this area rather than the other way around. "Inform" leads to a meaning that nicely matches the first half of the sentence.

Thus the correct answer is **inform** (Choice D).

13. Mechanisms develop whereby every successful species can _____ its innate capacity for population growth with the constraints that arise through its interactions with the natural environment.

   Ⓐ enhance
   Ⓑ replace
   Ⓒ produce
   Ⓓ surpass
   Ⓔ reconcile

Explanation

A quick overview of the sentence indicates that the blank should be filled with a verb that indicates what a successful species does with its "innate capacity for population growth" in the face of certain constraints on that growth. This analysis suggests that the correct answer will have something to do with adjusting that capacity in the face of these constraints. Of the choices given, "reconcile" is closest to that meaning. None of the other options make for a meaningful, coherent sentence. "Enhance," for example, may fit nicely with "its innate capacity," but it does not make sense with "constraints."

Thus the correct answer is **reconcile** (Choice E).

For each of Questions 14 to 16, select <u>one</u> answer choice unless otherwise instructed.

Questions 14 to 16 are based on the following reading passage.

It would be expected that a novel by a figure as prominent as W. E. B. DuBois would attract the attention of literary critics. Additionally, when the novel subtly engages the issue of race, as DuBois' *The Quest of the Silver Fleece* (1911) does, it would be a surprise not to encounter an abundance of scholarly work about that text. But though valuable scholarship has examined DuBois' political and historical thought, his novels have received scant attention. Perhaps DuBois the novelist must wait his turn behind DuBois the philosopher, historian, and editor. But what if the truth lies elsewhere: what if his novels do not speak to current concerns?

Description

The paragraph first present reasons for critical interest in DuBois' novels, but then goes on to explain that there has in fact been very little such interest and speculates as to why that might be.

14. Which of the following can be inferred from the passage regarding DuBois' *The Quest of the Silver Fleece*?

    (A) The lack of attention devoted to *The Quest of the Silver Fleece* can be attributed to the fact that it was DuBois' first novel.

    (B) Among DuBois' novels, *The Quest of the Silver Fleece* is unusual in that it has received scant attention from scholars.

    (C) *The Quest of the Silver Fleece* has at least one feature that typically would attract the attention of literary scholars.

    (D) *The Quest of the Silver Fleece*, given its subtle exploration of race, is probably the best novel written by DuBois.

    (E) Much of the scholarly work that has focused on *The Quest of the Silver Fleece* has been surprisingly critical of it.

Explanation

Choice C is correct. The second sentence states that *The Quest of the Silver Fleece* subtly engages the issue of race and implies that such an issue would attract the attention of literary scholars. The passage provides no information about whether *The Quest of the Silver Fleece* is DuBois's first novel (Choice A), whether it received more or less scholarly attention than his other novels (Choice B), whether it is better than any of his other novels (Choice D), nor about what scholars have said about it (Choice E).

15. In the fourth sentence ("Perhaps DuBois . . . editor."), the author of the passage is most likely suggesting that

    (A) scholars will find that DuBois' novels are more relevant to current concerns than is his work as philosopher, historian, and editor

    (B) more scholarly attention will be paid to *The Quest of the Silver Fleece* than to DuBois' other novels

    (C) DuBois' novels will come to overshadow his work as philosopher, historian, and editor

    (D) DuBois' novels may eventually attract greater scholarly interest than they have to date

    (E) it will be shown that DuBois' work as philosopher, historian, and editor had an important influence on his work as novelist

Explanation

The fourth sentence speculates that once DuBois scholars have exhausted potential avenues of research in the fields of philosophy, history, and editing, they will turn to his novels, so **Choice D** is the correct answer. None of the other choices fits the metaphor in "Perhaps DuBois the novelist must wait his turn."

16. Which of the following best describes the central issue with which the passage is concerned?

 (A) The perfunctoriness of much of the critical work devoted to DuBois' novels

 (B) The nature of DuBois' engagement with the issue of race in *The Quest of the Silver Fleece*

 (C) Whether DuBois' novels are of high quality and relevant to current concerns

 (D) The relationship between DuBois the novelist and DuBois the philosopher, historian, and editor

 (E) The degree of consideration that has been given to DuBois' novels, including *The Quest of the Silver Fleece*

Explanation

The passage focuses on the scant attention given to DuBois's novels, *The Quest of the Silver Fleece* in particular. The first two sentences give reasons to expect greater attention, while the last two offer speculations about the explanation for the scant attention. Thus **Choice E** is correct. The issues described in the other answer choices are all marginal to the passage, if they are mentioned at all.

> **For Questions 17 to 20, select one entry for each blank from the corresponding column of choices. Fill all blanks in the way that best completes the text.**

17. In the midst of so many evasive comments, this forthright statement, whatever its intrinsic merit, plainly stands out as _____.

(A) a paradigm
(B) a misnomer
(C) a profundity
(D) an inaccuracy
(E) an anomaly

Explanation

The sentence offers a contrast between "many evasive statements" and a single "forthright statement." On that basis alone, one might expect an answer such as "an anomaly." Do any of the other options make for a meaningful, coherent sentence? "A paradigm" is appealing, as is "a profundity," since the forthright statement is clearly presented as something positive. However, we are not in a position to call it paradigmatic or profound, since the sentence withholds judgment on "its intrinsic merit." The same reasoning allows us to eliminate "inaccuracy" and "misnomer." The straightforwardly descriptive "anomaly" is clearly the best choice.

Thus the correct answer is **an anomaly** (Choice E).

18. The activists' energetic work in the service of both woman suffrage and the temperature movement in the late nineteenth century (i)_____ the assertion that the two movements were (ii)_____.

Blank (i)	Blank (ii)
(A) undermines	(D) diffuse
(B) supports	(E) inimical
(C) underscores	(F) predominant

Explanation

The sentence is about the implications of the activists' energetic work for some assertion about the woman suffrage and temperance movements. The second blank, however, obscures the nature of that assertion. But it is clear that the "energetic work" could either support an assertion that the two movements were similar, or undermine an assertion that the two movements were opposed. "Supports" is offered as a choice for the first blank (as is the somewhat similar "underscores"), but there is no corresponding term in the second blank, nothing along the lines of "similar" or "compatible." "Undermines" and "inimical" make for the only meaningful statement.

Thus the correct answer is **undermines** (Choice A) and **inimical** (Choice E).

19. There is nothing quite like this movie, and indeed I am not altogether sure there is much more to it than its lovely (i) _____. At a moment when so many films strive to be as (ii)_____ as possible, it is gratifying to find one that is so subtle and puzzling.

Blank (i)	Blank (ii)
(A) peculiarity	(D) indirect
(B) pellucidity	(E) assertive
(C) conventionality	(F) enigmatic

Explanation

The two sentences provide the reader with quite a bit of information about the movie. There is "nothing quite like it" and it is "subtle and puzzling." "Peculiarity" is clearly a solid fit for the first blank, while "conventionality" clearly does not work, given the fact that there is "nothing quite like it." That leaves "pellucidity," which, while it could fit logically in the first sentence in isolation, does not fit the later claim that the movie is "subtle and puzzling." The second blank needs simply to provide a contrast with "subtle and puzzling." Of the choices offered, only "assertive" clearly does that.

Thus the correct answer is **peculiarity** (Choice A) and **assertive** (Choice E).

20. Wills argues that certain malarial parasites are especially (i)_____ because they have more recently entered humans than other species and therefore have had (ii)_____ time to evolve toward (iii)_____. Yet there is no reliable evidence that the most harmful *Plasmodium* species has been in humans for a shorter time than less harmful species.

Blank (i)	Blank (ii)	Blank (iii)
(A) populous	(D) ample	(G) virulence
(B) malignant	(E) insufficient	(H) benignity
(C) threatened	(F) adequate	(I) variability

Explanation

The "Yet" that begins the second sentence indicates that Wills' position would be supported by evidence that the newer parasites are in humans, the more harmful they are. So Wills' position must be that more recent parasites are especially harmful, implying that "malignant" is the correct choice for the first blank. What follows "therefore" is a potential explanation for the trend that Wills expects, namely an evolution toward harmlessness, implying "benignity" for the third blank, with newer species having had "insufficient" time (second blank) to evolve toward harmlessness.

Thus the correct answer is **malignant** (Choice B), **insufficient** (Choice E), and **benignity** (Choice H).

For each of questions 21 to 25, select <u>one</u> answer choice unless otherwise instructed.

Question 21 is based on the following reading passage.

Saturn's giant moon Titan is the only planetary satellite with a significant atmosphere and the only body in the solar system other than Earth that has a thick atmosphere dominated by molecular nitrogen. For a long time, the big question about Titan's atmosphere was how it could be so thick, given that Jupiter's moons Ganymede and Callisto, which are the same size as Titan, have none. The conditions for acquiring and retaining a thick nitrogen atmosphere are now readily understood. The low temperature of the protosaturnian nebula enabled Titan to acquire the moderately volatile compounds methane and ammonia (later converted to nitrogen) in addition to water. The higher temperatures of Jupiter's moons, which were closer to the Sun, prevented them from acquiring such an atmosphere.

Description

The paragraph discusses Titan's thick atmosphere and explains the conditions under which a body can have a thick atmosphere.

21. According to the passage, Titan differs atmospherically from Ganymede and Callisto because of a difference in

(A) rate of heat loss
(B) proximity to the Sun
(C) availability of methane and ammonia
(D) distance from its planet
(E) size

Explanation

According to the last two sentences of the paragraph, Titan was able to acquire an atmosphere because of a prevailing low temperature, but Ganymede and Callisto could not because they were at a higher temperature. Because the reason for this difference in temperature was their respective distances from the sun, **Choice B** is correct. The passage says nothing about differences in rate of heat loss, availability of methane and ammonia, or distance from their planets, and it explicitly states that the three moons are the same size.

Question 22 is based on the following reading passage.

Observations of the Arctic reveal that the Arctic Ocean is covered by less ice each summer than the previous summer. If this warming trend continues, within 50 years the Arctic Ocean will be ice free during the summer months. This occurrence would in itself have little or no effect on global sea levels, since the melting of ice floating in water does not affect the water level. However, serious consequences to sea levels would eventually result, because _____.

22. Which of the following most logically completes the passage?

  (A) large masses of floating sea ice would continue to form in the wintertime

  (B) significant changes in Arctic sea temperatures would be accompanied by changes in sea temperatures in more temperate parts of the world

  (C) such a warm Arctic Ocean would trigger the melting of massive land-based glaciers in the Arctic

  (D) an ice-free Arctic Ocean would support a very different ecosystem than it does presently

  (E) in the spring, melting sea ice would cause more icebergs to be created and to drift south into shipping routes

Explanation

To logically complete the passage's open-ended "because," something is needed that will explain why the continuation of the warming trend would have serious consequences for sea levels. The passage explains that the melting of the Arctic Ocean ice will not affect sea levels because the contribution that the water contained in that ice makes to sea levels is the same whether the water is frozen or liquid. But Choice C points to a way in which increasing temperatures in the Arctic could add water to the ocean, namely by melting ice on the land. So **Choice C** logically completes the passage and is the correct answer.

Given that the passage has already explained that melting sea ice does not affect sea levels, the formation of sea ice described in Choice A does not explain why there would be consequences for sea levels.

Choices B, D, and E all describe possible consequences of increased temperatures in the Arctic, but none of these consequences suggests a mechanism by which sea levels would change. So none of these options provides a logical completion for the passage.

Questions 23 to 25 are based on the following reading passage.

In a recent study, David Cressy examines two central questions concerning English immigration to New England in the 1630s: what kinds of people immigrated and why? Using contemporary literary evidence, shipping lists, and customs records, Cressy finds *line* that most adult immigrants were skilled in farming or crafts, were literate, and were 5 organized in families. Each of these characteristics sharply distinguishes the 21,000 people who left for New England in the 1630s from most of the approximately 377,000 English people who had immigrated to America by 1700.

With respect to their reasons for immigrating, Cressy does not deny the frequently noted fact that some of the immigrants of the 1630s, most notably the organizers and 10 clergy, advanced religious explanations for departure, but he finds that such explanations usually assumed primacy only in retrospect. When he moves beyond the principal actors, he finds that religious explanations were less frequently offered, and he concludes that most people immigrated because they were recruited by promises of material improvement.

Description

The passage discusses Cressy's answers to the questions posed in the first sentence. The immigrants were skilled, literate, and in families, and they apparently immigrated to have a better life materially, rather than religiously.

For the following question, consider each of the choices separately and select all that apply.

23. The passage indicates that Cressy would agree with which of the following statements about the organizers among the English immigrants to New England in the 1630s?

    A Some of them offered a religious explanation for their immigration.

    B They did not offer any reasons for their immigration until some time after they had immigrated.

    C They were more likely than the average immigrant to be motivated by material considerations.

Explanation

Choice A is correct.

Choice A is correct: the organizers are mentioned in the second paragraph, where the passage says that Cressy "does not deny" that organizers "advanced religious explanations" for leaving England and immigrating to New England in the 1630s. This suggests that Cressy would agree with the statement in choice A about the organizers.

Choice B is incorrect: in lines 10–11, the passage says that Cressy finds that religious reasons for immigration "assumed primacy" only in retrospect, but this is not the same as Cressy's concluding that no reasons were given at the time of immigration. Therefore it cannot be inferred that Cressy would agree with the statement in Choice B.

Choice C is incorrect: the passage refers in lines 13–14 to "promises of material improvement" as a factor that in Cressy's view motivated most immigrants other than "the principal actors." This suggests that Cressy regards the principal actors, such as organizers, as having been less, not more, motivated by material considerations than average immigrants were. Therefore it cannot be inferred that Cressy would agree with the statement in Choice C.

24. Select the sentence that provides Cressy's opinion about what motivated English immigrants to go to New England in the 1630s.

Explanation

The last sentence says that Cressy "concludes that most people immigrated because they were recruited by promises of material improvement." Because this suggests that Cressy believes immigrants were motivated by these promises to go to New England, **sentence 5** ("When he . . . improvement) is the correct choice. The preceding sentence suggests that Cressy does not believe religion was a primary motive influencing immigrants' decision to immigrate in the 1630s. Thus, although this sentence provides an opinion of Cressy's concerning some immigrants' stated reasons for immigrating, it does not say what motive he believes was actually behind the immigration, and therefore does not answer the question.

25. In the passage, the author is primarily concerned with
    - (A) summarizing the findings of an investigation
    - (B) analyzing a method of argument
    - (C) evaluating a point of view
    - (D) hypothesizing about a set of circumstances
    - (E) establishing categories

Explanation

The passage is about Cressy's investigation of English immigration to New England in the 1630s, and it summarizes his findings concerning who immigrated and why. **Choice A**, "summarizing the findings of an investigation," is therefore the best description of the author's primary concern in the passage. The passage does not analyze a method of argument, so Choice B is incorrect. Choice C is incorrect because the passage is not primarily concerned with evaluating a point of view: it does not assess the merits or demerits of Cressy's viewpoint. The passage is concerned with reporting Cressy's findings, not with hypothesizing or with establishing categories, so Choices D and E are incorrect.

SECTION 5
Quantitative Reasoning
25 Questions with Explanations

Ⓐ **Quantity A is greater.**
Ⓑ **Quantity B is greater.**
Ⓒ **The two quantities are equal.**
Ⓓ **The relationship cannot be determined from the information given.**

O is the center of the circle above.

Quantity A	Quantity B

1. x 5

Explanation

In this question you are asked to compare x with 5, where x is the length of a line segment from the center of the circle to a point inside the circle. In a circle the easiest line segments to deal with are the radius and the diameter. Looking at the figure in the question, you can see that you can draw two radii, each of which "completes" a right triangle, as shown in the figure below.

Since in one of the triangles, the lengths of both legs are known, you can use that triangle to determine the length of the radius of the circle. The triangle has legs of length 3 and 4. If the length of the radius is r, then, using the Pythagorean theorem, you can see that

$$r^2 = 3^2 + 4^2 \text{ or}$$
$$r^2 = 9 + 16 \text{ or}$$
$$r^2 = 25, \text{ and thus, } r = 5$$

Since the length of the radius of the circle is 5 and the line segment of length x is clearly shorter than the radius, you know that $x < 5$, and the correct answer is **Choice B.**

You could also see that the two triangles are congruent, and so $x = 4$, again yielding **Choice B.**

Runner A ran $\frac{4}{5}$ kilometer and Runner B ran 800 meters.

Quantity A	Quantity B	
2. The distance that A ran	The distance that B ran	

Explanation

In this question you are asked to compare two measurements, one given in kilometers and the other in meters. It would be easier to compare these measurements if they were both given in meters or both given in kilometers.

If you choose to convert the distance that Runner B ran from meters to kilometers, you need to use the conversion 1 meter is equal to $\frac{1}{1,000}$ kilometer.

Since B ran 800 meters, it follows that B ran $(800)\left(\frac{1}{1,000}\right)$, or $\frac{4}{5}$ kilometer, which is the same distance that A ran.

If you choose to convert the distance that Runner A ran from kilometers to meters, you need to use the conversion 1 kilometer is equal to 1,000 meters.

Since A ran $\frac{4}{5}$ kilometer, it follows that A ran $\left(\frac{4}{5}\right)(1,000)$, or 800 meters, which is the same distance that B ran. Either way, A and B ran the same distance, and the correct answer is **Choice C**.

$$x < y < z$$

Quantity A	Quantity B	
3. $\dfrac{x + y + z}{3}$	y	Ⓐ Ⓑ Ⓒ Ⓓ

Explanation

In this question you are given that $x < y < z$, and you are asked to compare $\frac{x + y + z}{3}$ with y.

Two approaches that you could use to solve this problem are:

1: Search for a mathematical relationship between the two quantities.
2: Plug in numbers for the variables.

Approach 1: Note that $\frac{x + y + z}{3}$ is the average of the three numbers x, y, and z and that y is the median. Is the average of 3 numbers always equal to the median? The average could equal the median, but in general they do not have to be equal. Therefore, the correct answer is **Choice D**.

Approach 2: When you plug in numbers for the variables, it is a good idea to consider what kind of numbers are appropriate to plug in and to choose numbers that are easy to work with, if possible.

Since $\frac{x + y + z}{3}$ is the average of the three numbers x, y, and z and you are comparing it to the median, you may want to try plugging in numbers that are evenly spaced and plugging in numbers that are not evenly spaced.

You can plug in numbers that are both evenly spaced and easy to work with. For example, you can plug in $x = 1$, $y = 2$, and $z = 3$. In this case,

$$\frac{x + y + z}{3} = \frac{1 + 2 + 3}{3} = \frac{6}{3} = 2, \text{ and so } \frac{x + y + z}{3} = y.$$

You can also plug in numbers that not are not evenly spaced and are easy to work with. For example, you can plug in $x = 3$, $y = 6$, and $z = 12$. In this case,

$$\frac{x + y + z}{3} = \frac{3 + 6 + 12}{3} = \frac{21}{3} = 7, \text{ and } \frac{x + y + z}{3} > y. \text{ Since in the first case,}$$

$\frac{x + y + z}{3}$ is equal to y and in the second case, it is greater than y, the

relationship between the two quantities $\frac{x + y + z}{3}$ and y cannot be determined

from the information given. The correct answer is **Choice D**.

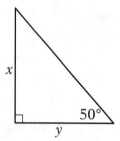

Quantity A	Quantity B

4. $\dfrac{x}{y}$ 1   Ⓐ Ⓑ Ⓒ Ⓓ

Explanation

One way you can solve this problem is by using the following fact:

- If *ABC* is a triangle and the measure of angle *A* is greater than the measure of angle *B*, then the side opposite angle *A* is longer than the side opposite angle *B*.

Since the third angle of the triangle measures 40°, you can use the fact above to conclude that the side opposite the 50° angle is longer than the side opposite the 40° angle. So $x > y$, and $\frac{x}{y} > 1$, which yields **Choice A**.

You can also solve this problem without using the fact above. Instead, you can use the strategy of adapting solutions to related problems to determine the relationship between x and y.

Note that the angles in the triangle differ only a little from the angles in a $45° - 45° - 90°$ triangle. How do the lengths of the legs of a $45° - 45° - 90°$ triangle compare to the lengths of the legs of the triangle in the question? To make the comparison, add a line segment to the triangle so that the line segment cuts the 50° angle in two parts, making a 45° angle with the horizontal base, as shown in the following figure:

The $45° - 45° - 90°$ triangle has two $45°$ angles, so $z = y$, and $\frac{z}{y} = 1$. Since $\frac{z}{y} = 1$ and $x > z$, it follows that $\frac{x}{y} > 1$. The correct answer is **Choice A**.

$$0 < x < y < 1$$

Quantity A	Quantity B	
$1 - y$	$y - x$	Ⓐ Ⓑ Ⓒ Ⓓ

5.

Explanation

Two approaches that you could use to solve this problem are:

    1: Translate from algebra to a number line.
    2: Plug in values for the variables.

Approach 1: The following figure represents the information given in the problem on a number line.

On the number line, $1 - y$ is the distance between 1 and y, and $y - x$ is the distance between y and x. If y is exactly halfway between x and 1, then $1 - y$ is equal to $y - x$; and if y is <u>not</u> halfway between x and 1, then $1 - y$ is <u>not</u> equal to $y - x$. But y can be <u>any</u> number between x and 1, so the correct answer is **Choice D**.

Approach 2: Since this problem involves subtraction, it is a good idea to choose values for x and y that are close to each other as well as values that are far apart. For example, if $x = 0.4$ and $y = 0.5$, then $1 - y = 0.5$ and $y - x = 0.1$; and if $x = 0.1$ and $y = 0.9$, then $1 - y = 0.1$ and $y - x = 0.8$. This shows that the relationship cannot be determined, and the correct answer is **Choice D**.

p is the probability that event E will occur, and s is the probability that event E will <u>not</u> occur.

	Quantity A	Quantity B	
6.	$p + s$	ps	Ⓐ Ⓑ Ⓒ Ⓓ

Explanation

Since event E will either occur or not occur, it follows that $p + s = 1$, and the value of Quantity A is always 1. Since Quantity B is the product of the two probabilities p and s, you need to look at its value for the cases $p = 1$, $p = 0$, and $0 < p < 1$.

If $p = 1$, then $s = 0$; similarly, if $p = 0$, then $s = 1$. In both cases, ps is equal to 0.

If $0 < p < 1$, both p and s are positive and less than 1, so ps is positive and less than 1. Since Quantity A is equal to 1 and Quantity B is less than 1, the correct answer is **Choice A**.

X is the set of all integers n that satisfy the inequality $2 \leq |n| \leq 5$.

	Quantity A	Quantity B	
7.	The absolute value of the greatest integer in X	The absolute value of the least integer in X	Ⓐ Ⓑ Ⓒ Ⓓ

Explanation

When comparing these quantities, it is important to remember that a nonzero number and its negative have the same absolute value. For example, $|-2| = |2| = 2$. Keeping this in mind, you can see that the positive integers 2, 3, 4, and 5 and the negative integers −2, −3, −4, and −5 all satisfy the inequalities $2 \leq |n| \leq 5$, and that these are the only such integers. Thus, the set X consists of the integers −5, −4, −3, −2, 2, 3, 4, and 5. The greatest of these integers is 5, and its absolute value is 5. The least of these integers is −5, and its absolute value is also 5. Therefore, Quantity A is equal to Quantity B. The correct answer is **Choice C**.

x and m are positive numbers, and m is a multiple of 3.

	Quantity A	Quantity B	
8.	$\dfrac{x^m}{x^3}$	$x^{m/3}$	Ⓐ Ⓑ Ⓒ Ⓓ

Explanation

Since $\dfrac{x^m}{x^3} = x^{m-3}$, you need to compare x^{m-3} with $x^{m/3}$. Since the base in both expressions is the same, a good strategy to use to solve this problem is to plug in numbers for m in both expressions and compare them.

You know that m is a multiple of 3, so the least positive integer you can plug in for m is 3.

If $m = 3$, then $x^{m-3} = 1$ and $x^{m/3} = x$. Since x can be any real number, its relationship to 1 cannot be determined from the information given. This example is sufficient to show that the relationship between $\dfrac{x^m}{x^3}$ and $x^{m/3}$ cannot be determined from the information given. The correct answer is **Choice D**.

A random variable Y is normally distributed with a mean of 200 and a standard deviation of 10.

Quantity A	Quantity B	
9. The probability of the event that the value of Y is greater than 220	$\dfrac{1}{6}$	Ⓐ Ⓑ Ⓒ Ⓓ

Explanation

This problem involves a normal distribution with mean 200 and standard deviation 10. Thus, the value of 210 is 1 standard deviation above the mean, and the value of 220 is 2 standard deviations above the mean. To compare Quantity A with Quantity B, it is not necessary to exactly determine the probability of the event that the value of Y is greater than 220. Remember that in any normal distribution, almost all of the data values, or about 95% of them, fall within 2 standard deviations on either side of the mean. This means that less than 5% of the values in this distribution will be greater than 220. Thus, the probability of the event that the value of Y is greater than 220 must be less than 5%, or $\dfrac{1}{20}$, and this is certainly less than $\dfrac{1}{6}$. The correct answer is **Choice B**.

Another approach to this problem is to draw a normal curve, or "bell-shaped curve," that represents the probability distribution of the random variable Y, as shown in the figure below.

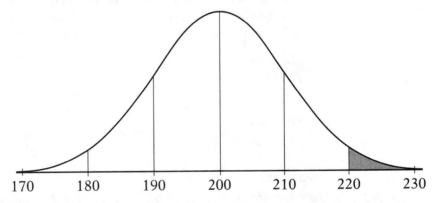

The curve is symmetric about the mean 200. The values of 210, 220, and 230 are equally spaced to the right of 200 and represent 1, 2, and 3 standard deviations, respectively, above the mean. Similarly, the values of 190, 180, and 170 are 1, 2, and 3 standard deviation, respectively, below the mean. Quantity A, the probability of the event that the value of Y is greater than 220, is equal to the area of the shaded region as a fraction of the total area under the curve.

From the figure, you can see that the area under the normal curve has been divided into 6 regions and that these regions are not equal in area. The shaded region is one of the two smallest of the 6 regions, so its area must be less than $\frac{1}{6}$ of the total area under the curve. The correct answer is **Choice B**.

10. The ratio of $\frac{1}{3}$ to $\frac{3}{8}$ is equal to the ratio of

    (A)   1 to 8

    (B)   8 to 1

    (C)   8 to 3

    (D)   8 to 9

    (E)   9 to 8

Explanation

Multiplying both parts of a ratio by the same number produces an equivalent ratio. While you could multiply both fractions in the ratio by any number, 24 is a good number to choose because it is the least common multiple of 3 and 8. Thus, multiplying both $\frac{1}{3}$ and $\frac{3}{8}$ by 24, you get that the ratio of $\frac{1}{3}$ to $\frac{3}{8}$ is equal to the ratio of 8 to 9. The correct answer is **Choice D**.

An alternate approach to this problem is to express the ratio of $\frac{1}{3}$ to $\frac{3}{8}$ as the fraction $\dfrac{\frac{1}{3}}{\frac{3}{8}}$. This fraction is equivalent to $\left(\frac{1}{3}\right)\left(\frac{8}{3}\right)$, or $\frac{8}{9}$. The correct answer is **Choice D**.

11. A reading list for a humanities course consists of 10 books, of which 4 are biographies and the rest are novels. Each student is required to read a selection of 4 books from the list, including 2 or more biographies. How many selections of 4 books satisfy the requirements?

    (A)   90

    (B)   115

    (C)   130

    (D)   144

    (E)   195

Explanation

The requirement to select 4 books, including 2 or more biographies, means that you have to consider three cases. A student can choose 4 biographies and no novels, or 3 biographies and 1 novel, or 2 biographies and 2 novels.

Case 1: Choose 4 biographies. This case is easy, as there is only 1 way to choose all four biographies and no novels.

In the other two cases, you have to find the number of ways of choosing the biographies and the number of ways of choosing the novels and then multiply these two numbers.

Case 2: Choose 3 biographies and 1 novel. First, you need to find the number of ways of choosing 3 biographies out of 4. If you think of this as <u>not</u> choosing 1 out of the 4, you see that there are 4 choices. The number of ways of choosing 1 novel out of the 6 novels is 6. Therefore, the total number of choices is $(4)(6) = 24$.

Case 3: Choose 2 biographies and 2 novels. First, you need to find the number of ways of choosing 2 biographies out of 4. This number is sometimes called "4 choose 2" or the number of combinations of 4 objects taken 2 at a time. If you remember the combinations formula, you know that the number of combinations is $\frac{4!}{2!(4-2)!}$ (which is denoted symbolically as $\binom{4}{2}$ or $_4C_2$). The value of $\frac{4!}{2!(4-2)!}$ is $\frac{(4)(3)(2!)}{(2)(2!)} = \frac{(4)(3)}{2} = 6$. Thus, there are 6 ways to choose 2 biographies out of 4. Similarly, the number of ways to choose 2 novels out of 6 is $\frac{6!}{2!4!} = \frac{(6)(5)}{2} = 15$. Thus, the total number of ways to choose 2 biographies and 2 novels is $(6)(15) = 90$.

Adding the number of ways to choose the books for the each of the three cases, you get a total of $1 + 24 + 90 = 115$. The correct answer is **Choice B**.

For the following question, enter your answer in the box.

12. In a graduating class of 236 students, 142 took algebra and 121 took chemistry. What is the greatest possible number of students that could have taken both algebra and chemistry?

	students

Explanation

This is the type of problem for which drawing a Venn diagram is usually helpful. The Venn diagram below is one you could draw to represent the information given in the question.

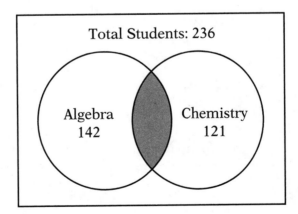

Note that the algebra and chemistry numbers given do not separate out the number of students who took both algebra and chemistry, and that this question asks for the greatest possible number of such students. It is a good idea, therefore, to redraw the Venn diagram with the number of students who took both algebra and chemistry separated out. The revised Venn diagram looks like the one below.

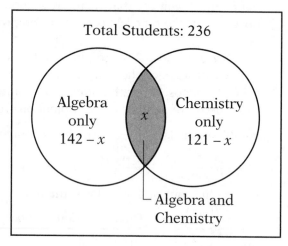

Total Students: 236

Algebra only
$142 - x$

x

Chemistry only
$121 - x$

└ Algebra and Chemistry

To solve this problem you want the greatest possible value of x. It is clear from the diagram that x cannot be greater than 142 nor greater than 121, otherwise $142 - x$ or $121 - x$ would be negative. Hence, x must be less than or equal to 121. Since there is no information to exclude $x = 121$, the correct answer is **121**.

$s°$ ——— m

$t°$ ——— k

13. In the figure above, if $m \parallel k$ and $s = t + 30$, then $t =$

   Ⓐ   30
   Ⓑ   60
   Ⓒ   75
   Ⓓ   80
   Ⓔ   105

Explanation

When trying to solve a geometric problem, it is often helpful to add any known information to the figure. Since corresponding angles have equal measures, you could place two more angle measures on the figure, as shown below.

$s° \mid t°$ ——— m

$s° \mid t°$ ——— k

Now, from the figure, you can see that $s + t = 180$. Therefore, since it is given that $s = t + 30$, you can substitute $t + 30$ for s into the equation $s + t = 180$ and get that $(t + 30) + t = 180$, which can be simplified as follows.

$$(t + 30) + t = 180$$
$$2t = 150$$
$$t = 75$$

The correct answer is **Choice C**.

14. If $2x = 3y = 4z = 20$, then $12xyz =$

   Ⓐ 16,000
   Ⓑ 8,000
   Ⓒ 4,000
   Ⓓ 800
   Ⓔ 10

Explanation

One approach you can use to solve this problem is to find the value of all three variables.

$$2x = 20, \text{ or } x = 10$$
$$3y = 20, \text{ or } y = \frac{20}{3}$$
$$4z = 20, \text{ or } z = 5$$

So $12xyz = 12(10)\left(\frac{20}{3}\right)(5) = 4,000$, and the correct answer is **Choice C**.

Another approach you can use to solve this problem is to notice that $12xyz = \dfrac{(2x)(3y)(4z)}{2} = \dfrac{(20)(20)(20)}{2} = 4,000$. Therefore, the correct answer is **Choice C**.

For the following question, select all the answer choices that apply.

15. The total amount that Mary paid for a book was equal to the price of the book plus a sales tax that was 4 percent of the price of the book. Mary paid for the book with a $10 bill and received the correct change, which was less than $3.00. Which of the following statements must be true?

   Indicate <u>all</u> such statements.

   [A] The price of the book was less than $9.50.
   [B] The price of the book was greater than $6.90.
   [C] The sales tax was less than $0.45.

Explanation

For this problem you may find it helpful to translate the given information into an algebraic expression. Since the price of the book is unknown, you can call it x dollars, and then the total amount that Mary paid is x dollars plus 4% of x dollars, or $1.04x$ dollars. The problem states that Mary received some change from a $10 bill, so $1.04x$ dollars must be less than $10. Since the change was less than $3.00, the total amount Mary paid for the book must have been greater than $7.00. You can express this information algebraically by the inequality

$$7.00 < 1.04x < 10.00$$

Solving the inequality for x by dividing by 1.04, and rounding, you get

$$6.73 < x < 9.62$$

So you see that x, the price of the book, must be between $6.73 and $9.62. With this information, you can quickly examine the first two statements. Choice A is not necessarily true because the price could be as high as $9.61, and Choice B is not necessarily true because the price could be as low as $6.74.

To examine Choice C, you could compute the tax for the greatest possible price, which would be 4% of 9.61, or $(0.04)(9.61) = 0.38$. Since this greatest possible tax is less than $0.45, Choice C must be true.

You can also quickly see that Choice C must be true if you note that 4% of $10.00 would only be $0.40, and since the price must be less than $10.00, the tax must be less than $0.40. The correct answer consists of **Choice C**.

16. If $\dfrac{1}{(2^{11})(5^{17})}$ is expressed as a terminating decimal, how many nonzero digits will the decimal have?

   (A) One
   (B) Two
   (C) Four
   (D) Six
   (E) Eleven

Explanation

To convert the fraction to a decimal, it is helpful to first write the fraction in powers of 10. Using the rules of exponents, you can write the following.

$$\frac{1}{(2^{11})(5^{17})} = \frac{1}{(2^{11})(5^{11+6})}$$

$$= \frac{1}{(2^{11})(5^{11})(5^{6})}$$

$$= \frac{1}{(10^{11})(5^{6})}$$

$$= \left(\frac{1}{5}\right)^{6}(10^{-11})$$

$$= (0.2)^{6}(10^{-11})$$

$$= ((2)(10)^{-1})^{6}(10^{-11})$$

$$= (2^{6})(10^{-6})(10^{-11})$$

$$= (2^{6})(10^{-17})$$

$$= (64)(10^{-17})$$

So the decimal has two nonzero digits, 6 and 4. The correct answer is **Choice B**.

Questions 17 to 20 are based on the following data.

VARIATION IN THE AMOUNT OF CAFFEINE IN COMMON BEVERAGES AND DRUGS*

Source: *Food and Drug Administration*

*Based on 5-ounce cups of coffee, tea, and cocoa; 12-ounce cups of soft drinks; and single doses of drugs.

17. The least amount of caffeine in a 5-ounce cup of drip-brewed coffee exceeds the greatest amount of caffeine in a 5-ounce cup of cocoa by approximately how many milligrams?

    Ⓐ 160

    Ⓑ 80

    Ⓒ 60

    Ⓓ 40

    Ⓔ 20

Explanation

Each horizontal bar in the bar graph shows the possible number of milligrams of caffeine in each of the common beverages and drugs. The least possible amount of caffeine in a 5-ounce cup of drip-brewed coffee is about 60 milligrams, and the greatest possible amount of caffeine in a 5-ounce cup of cocoa is about 20 milligrams. So, the difference is approximately 60 − 20, or 40 milligrams. The correct answer is **Choice D**.

To check your answer, it is useful to try to solve the problem using another method as well to see if you get the same answer. To solve this problem in another way, note that the distance between each pair of adjacent vertical grid lines represents 25 milligrams of caffeine, and the distance between the high end of the cocoa bar and the low end of the drip-brewed coffee bar is a little more than the distance between a pair of adjacent grid lines. Therefore, the answer is between 25 and 50. Among the choices, only Choice D is between 25 and 50, so the correct answer is **Choice D**.

For the following question, enter your answer in the box.

18. For how many of the 11 categories of beverages and drugs listed in the graph can the amount of caffeine in the given serving size be less than 50 milligrams?

☐ categories

Explanation

In the graph, the left edge of each bar tells you what is the least possible amount of caffeine in the corresponding beverage or drug. A beverage or drug can have less than 50 milligrams of caffeine if the left edge of its bar lies to the left of the vertical line corresponding to 50 milligrams of caffeine. From the graph, you see that there are 9 bars for which this is true. There are only 2 bars that lie entirely to the right of the 50-milligram line—the bar for drip-brewed coffee and the bar for weight-loss drugs, diuretics, and stimulants. So there are 9 categories of beverages and drugs that can have less than 50 milligrams of caffeine in the given serving size. The correct answer is **9**.

19. Approximately what is the minimum amount of caffeine, in milligrams, consumed per day by a person who daily drinks two 10-ounce mugs of percolated coffee and one 12-ounce cup of a caffeinated soft drink?

Ⓐ 230

Ⓑ 190

Ⓒ 140

Ⓓ 110

Ⓔ 70

Explanation

According to the bar graph, the minimum amount of caffeine in a 5-ounce cup of percolated coffee is approximately 40 milligrams. Therefore, the minimum amount of caffeine in two 10-ounce cups of percolated coffee, which is the same as the minimum amount of caffeine in four 5-ounce cups, is approximately (40)(4), or 160 milligrams. The minimum amount of caffeine in a 12-ounce caffeinated soft drink is approximately 30 milligrams. So, the minimum amount of caffeine in two 10-ounce mugs of percolated coffee and one 12-ounce caffeinated soft drink is approximately 160 + 30, or 190 milligrams. The correct answer is **Choice B**.

20. Which of the following shows the four types of coffee listed in order according to the range of the amounts of caffeine in a 5-ounce cup, from the least range to the greatest range?

Ⓐ Decaffeinated, instant, percolated, drip-brewed

Ⓑ Decaffeinated, instant, drip-brewed, percolated

Ⓒ Instant, decaffeinated, drip-brewed, percolated

Ⓓ Instant, drip-brewed, decaffeinated, percolated

Ⓔ Instant, percolated, drip-brewed, decaffeinated

Explanation

For each of the four types of coffee, the range of the amounts of caffeine is the greatest possible amount minus the least possible amount. In the graph, this difference is represented by the length of the corresponding bar, so you can order the four types of coffee according to the lengths of their corresponding bars, from shortest to longest. From the graph, you can see that the order is decaffeinated coffee, instant coffee, drip-brewed coffee, percolated coffee. The correct answer is **Choice B**.

ENERGY USED PER METER VERSUS SPEED
DURING RUNNING AND WALKING

21. If s is a speed, in miles per hour, at which the energy used per meter during running is twice the energy used per meter during walking, then, according to the graph above, s is between

Ⓐ   2.5 and 3.0
Ⓑ   3.0 and 3.5
Ⓒ   3.5 and 4.0
Ⓓ   4.0 and 4.5
Ⓔ   4.5 and 5.0

Explanation

This question is about the speed at which the energy used per meter during running is twice that used per meter during walking. Graphically, this is the speed for which the running energy is twice as high as the walking energy. Looking at the graph, you can see that for speeds greater than or equal to 3.0 miles per hour, the running energy is less than twice the walking energy, so the desired speed must be less than 3.0. In fact, the desired speed is between 2.0 (the lowest speed on the graph) and 3.0. Looking at the answer choices, you see that there is only one answer choice that is between 2.0 and 3.0; namely, Choice A, which says the desired speed is between 2.5 and 3.0. The correct answer is **Choice A**.

22. If $n = 2^3$, then $n^n =$

    Ⓐ 2^6

    Ⓑ 2^{11}

    Ⓒ 2^{18}

    Ⓓ 2^{24}

    Ⓔ 2^{27}

Explanation

When answering a question in which you are asked to calculate the value of an expression, it is often helpful to look at the answer choices first to see what form they are in. In this question the answer choices are all in the form 2 raised to a power, so you should try to achieve that form. It is given that $n = 2^3 = 8$. Therefore, $n^n = (2^3)^8 = 2^{24}$. The correct answer is **Choice D**.

For the following question, select all the answer choices that apply.

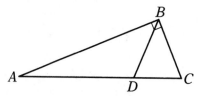

The length of AB is $10\sqrt{3}$.

23. Which of the following statements <u>individually</u> provide(s) sufficient additional information to determine the area of triangle ABC above?

Indicate <u>all</u> such statements.

☐A DBC is an equilateral triangle.

☐B ABD is an isosceles triangle.

☐C The length of BC is equal to the length of AD.

☐D The length of BC is 10.

☐E The length of AD is 10.

Explanation

From the figure you know that ABC is a right triangle with its right angle at vertex B. You also know that point D is on the hypotenuse AC. You are given that the length of AB is $10\sqrt{3}$. However, because the figure is not necessarily drawn to scale, you don't know the lengths of AD, DC, and BC. In particular, you don't know where D is on AC.

    The area of a triangle is $\frac{1}{2}$(base)(height). Thus, the area of right triangle ABC is equal to $\frac{1}{2}$ of the length of AB times the length of BC. You already know that the length of AB is $10\sqrt{3}$. Any additional information that would allow you to calculate the length of BC would be sufficient to find the area of triangle ABC. You need to consider each of the five statements individually, as follows.

    Statement A: DBC is an equilateral triangle. This statement implies that angle DCB is a 60° angle; and therefore, triangle ABC is a 30°–60°–90° triangle. Thus the length of *BC* can be determined, and this statement provides sufficient additional information to determine the area of triangle *ABC*.

Statement B: ABD is an isosceles triangle. There is more than one way in which triangle *ABD* can be isosceles. Below are two redrawn figures showing triangle *ABD* as isosceles. In the figure on the left, the length of *AD* is equal to the length of *DB*; and in the figure on the right, the length of *AB* is equal to the length of *AD*.

 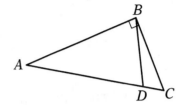

Either of the figures could have been drawn with the length of *BC* even longer. So, statement B does not provide sufficient additional information to determine the area of triangle *ABC*.

Statement C: The length of *BC* is equal to the length of *AD*. You have no way of finding the length of *AD* without making other assumptions, so statement C does not provide sufficient additional information to determine the area of triangle *ABC*.

Statement D: The length of *BC* is 10. The length of *BC* is known, so the area of triangle *ABC* can be found. Statement D provides sufficient additional information to determine the area of triangle *ABC*.

Statement E: The length of *AD* is 10. The relationship between *AD* and *BC* is not known, so statement E does not provide sufficient additional information to determine the area of triangle *ABC*.

Statements A and D individually provide sufficient additional information to determine the area of triangle *ABC*. Therefore, the correct answer consists of **Choices A and D**.

For the following question, enter your answer in the box.

$$a_1, a_2, a_3, \ldots, a_n, \ldots$$

24.   In the sequence above, each term after the first term is equal to the preceding term plus the constant *c*. If $a_1 + a_3 + a_5 = 27$, what is the value of $a_2 + a_4$?

$$a_2 + a_4 = \boxed{}$$

Explanation

Note that answering this question requires information only about the first five terms of the sequence. So it is a good idea to work with the relationships among these five terms to see what is happening.

Since you are given that in this sequence each term after a_1 is *c* greater than the previous term, you can rewrite the first five terms of the sequence in terms of a_1 and *c* as follows.

$$a_3 = a_1 + c$$
$$a_3 = a_2 + c = a_1 + 2c$$
$$a_4 = a_1 + 3c$$
$$a_5 = a_1 + 4c$$

From the question, you know that $a_1 + a_3 + a_5 = 27$, and from the equations above, $a_1 + a_3 + a_5 = a_1 + (a_1 + 2c) + (a_1 + 4c) = 3a_1 + 6c$. So you can conclude that $3a_1 + 6c = 27$, or $a_1 + 2c = 9$.

To find $a_2 + a_4$, you can express a_2 and a_4 in terms of a_1 and c and simplify as follows.

$$a_2 + a_4 = (a_1 + c) + (a_1 + 3c)$$
$$= 2a_1 + 4c$$
$$= 2(a_1 + 2c)$$

But $a_1 + 2c = 9$, so $a_2 + a_4 = 2(9) = 18$. The correct answer is **18**.

25. A desert outpost has a water supply that is sufficient to last 21 days for 15 people. At the same average rate of water consumption per person, how many days would the water supply last for 9 people?

   (A) 28.0

   (B) 32.5

   (C) 35.0

   (D) 37.5

   (E) 42.0

Explanation

The water supply is enough for 15 people to survive 21 days. Assuming the same average rate of water consumption per person, 1 person would have enough water to last for $(15)(21) = 315$ days. Therefore, 9 people would have enough water for $\frac{1}{9}$ of the 315 days, or 35 days. The correct answer is **Choice C**.

Another approach to solving this problem is to recognize that the water supply would last $\frac{15}{9}$ as many days for 9 people as it would for 15 people. Therefore, since the water supply would last 21 days for 15 people, it would last $\left(\frac{15}{9}\right)(21)$, or 35 days for 9 people. The correct answer is **Choice C**.

SECTION 6
Quantitative Reasoning
Time—40 minutes
25 Questions

Ⓐ **Quantity A is greater.**

Ⓑ **Quantity B is greater.**

Ⓒ **The two quantities are equal.**

Ⓓ **The relationship cannot be determined from the information given.**

Country	Value of 1 United States Dollar
Argentina	0.93 peso
Kenya	32.08 shillings

Quantity A	Quantity B	
1. The dollar value of 1 Argentine peso according to the table above	The dollar value of 1 Kenyan shilling according to the table above	Ⓐ Ⓑ Ⓒ Ⓓ

Explanation

When you are answering Quantitative Comparison questions, it is a good time-saving idea to see whether you can determine the relative sizes of the two quantities being compared without doing any calculations.

In the table accompanying this question, both the value of the Argentine peso and the value of the Kenyan shilling are compared to the United States dollar.

Without doing any calculations, you can see from the information given that 1 United States dollar is worth a little less than 1 Argentine peso, so 1 peso is worth more than 1 United States dollar. On the other hand, 1 United States dollar is worth 32.08 Kenyan shillings, so 1 Kenyan shilling is worth only a <u>small fraction</u> of 1 United States dollar. The correct answer is **Choice A.**

k is a digit in the decimal $1.3k5$, and $1.3k5$ is less than 1.33.

Quantity A	Quantity B	
2. k	1	Ⓐ Ⓑ Ⓒ Ⓓ

Explanation

In this question, you are given that k is a digit in the decimal $1.3k5$ and that $1.3k5$ is less than 1.33. So you can see that $1.30 < 1.3k5 < 1.33$. Therefore, $1.3k5$ must equal 1.305 or 1.315 or 1.325, and the digit k must be 0, 1, or 2. The correct answer is **Choice D.**

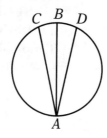

AB is a diameter of the circle above.

Quantity A	Quantity B	
3.	The length of AB	The average (arithmetic mean) of the lengths of AC and AD	Ⓐ Ⓑ Ⓒ Ⓓ

Explanation

Recall that in a circle, any diameter is longer than any other chord that is not a diameter. You are given that AB is a diameter of the circle. It follows that AC and AD are chords that are not diameters, since there is only one diameter with endpoint A. Hence, AB is longer than both AC and AD. Note that the average of two numbers is always less than or equal to the greater of the two numbers. Therefore, the average of the lengths of AC and AD, which is Quantity B, must be less than the length of AB, which is Quantity A. The correct answer is **Choice A**.

$$st = \sqrt{10}$$

Quantity A	Quantity B	
4.	s^2	$\dfrac{10}{t^2}$	Ⓐ Ⓑ Ⓒ Ⓓ

Explanation

In this question you are asked to compare s^2 with $\dfrac{10}{t^2}$. Since it is given that $st = \sqrt{10}$, it follows that $(st)^2 = (\sqrt{10})^2$, and $s^2t^2 = 10$. Dividing both sides of the equation $s^2t^2 = 10$ by t^2, you get $s^2 = \dfrac{10}{t^2}$. The correct answer is **Choice C**.

You can look at this problem in another way. You can use the fact that $st = \sqrt{10}$ to express Quantity A in terms of t. Since $st = \sqrt{10}$, it follows that $s = \dfrac{\sqrt{10}}{t}$, and Quantity A is equal to $\left(\dfrac{\sqrt{10}}{t}\right)^2 = \dfrac{10}{t^2}$, which is the same as Quantity B. The correct answer is **Choice C**.

Three consecutive integers have a sum of −84.

Quantity A	Quantity B	
5. The least of the three integers	−28	Ⓐ Ⓑ Ⓒ Ⓓ

Explanation

Two approaches you could use to solve this problem are:

> 1: Translate from words to algebra.
> 2: Determine a mathematical relationship between the two quantities.

Approach 1: You can represent the least of the three consecutive integers by x, and then the three integers would be represented by x, $x + 1$, and $x + 2$. It is given that the sum of the three integers is −84, so $x + (x + 1) + (x + 2) = -84$. You can solve this equation for x as follows.

$$x + (x + 1) + (x + 2) = -84$$
$$3x + 3 = -84$$
$$3x = -87$$
$$x = -29$$

Since the least of the three integers, −29, is less than −28, the correct answer is **Choice B**.

Approach 2: You could ask yourself what would happen if the least of the three consecutive integers was −28. The three consecutive integers would then be −28, −27, and −26, and their sum would be −81. But you were given that the sum of the three consecutive integers is −84, which is less than −81. Therefore, −28 is greater than the least of the three consecutive integers, and the correct answer is **Choice B**.

In the xy-plane, the equation of line k is $3x - 2y = 0$.

Quantity A	Quantity B	
6. The x-intercept of line k	The y-intercept of line k	Ⓐ Ⓑ Ⓒ Ⓓ

Explanation

Two approaches you could use to solve this problem are:

> 1: Reason algebraically.
> 2: Reason geometrically.

Approach 1: To solve this problem algebraically, note that given the equation of a line in the xy-plane, the x-intercept of the line is the value of x when y equals 0, and the y-intercept of the line is the value of y when x equals 0. The equation of line k is $3x - 2y = 0$. If $y = 0$, then $x = 0$; and if $x = 0$, then $y = 0$. Therefore, both the x-intercept and y-intercept of the line are equal to 0, which means that the line passes through the origin. The correct answer is **Choice C**.

Approach 2: To solve this problem geometrically, graph the line with equation $3x - 2y = 0$ in the xy-plane. Since two points determine a straight line, you can do this by plotting two points on the line and drawing the line they determine. The points (0,0) and (2,3) lie on the line, and the graph of the line in the xy-plane is shown in the following figure.

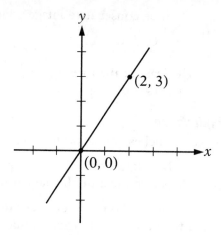

As you can see, the line passes through the origin, and so it crosses both the x-axis and the y-axis at (0,0). The correct answer is **Choice C**.

n is a positive integer that is divisible by 6.

Quantity A	Quantity B

7. The remainder when n is divided by 12

The remainder when n is divided by 18

Explanation

One way to compare the two quantities is to plug in a few values of n. If you plug in $n = 36$, you find that both the remainder when n is divided by 12 and the remainder when n is divided by 18 are equal to 0, so Quantity A is equal to Quantity B. However, if you plug in $n = 18$, you find that the remainder when n is divided by 12 is 6 and the remainder when n is divided by 18 is 0, so Quantity B is greater than Quantity A. Therefore, the correct answer is **Choice D**.

Another way to compare the two quantities is to find all of the possible values of Quantity A and Quantity B. The positive integers that are divisible by 6 are 6, 12, 18, 24, 30, 36, etc. When dividing each of these integers by 12, you get a remainder of either 0 or 6, so Quantity A is either 0 or 6. When dividing each of these integers by 18, you get a remainder of either 0 or 6 or 12, so Quantity B is either 0 or 6 or 12. Note that when the value of Quantity B is 12, the value of Quantity A, 0 or 6, is less than the value of Quantity B; but when the value of Quantity B is 0, the value of Quantity A is greater than or equal to the value of Quantity B. Thus, the correct answer is **Choice D**.

$$\frac{1-x}{x-1} = \frac{1}{x}$$

Quantity A	Quantity B

8. x

$-\dfrac{1}{2}$ Ⓐ Ⓑ Ⓒ Ⓓ

Explanation

One approach you could use to solve this problem is to solve the equation $\frac{1-x}{x-1} = \frac{1}{x}$ for x. Since fractions are defined only when the denominator is not equal to 0, the denominators of both of the fractions in the equation are nonzero. Therefore, $x \neq 0$ and $x \neq 1$.

To solve the equation for x, begin by multiplying both sides of the equation by the common denominator $x(x + 1)$ to get $x(1 - x) = (x - 1)(1)$. Then proceed as follows.

$$x(1 - x) = (x - 1)(1)$$
$$x - x^2 = x - 1$$
$$x^2 = 1$$

Since $x^2 = 1$ and $x \neq 1$, it follows that $x = -1$.

Quantity A is equal to -1 and Quantity B is equal to $-\dfrac{1}{2}$. Therefore, Quantity B is greater, and the correct answer is **Choice B**.

Another approach is to notice that for all values of $x \neq 1$, the value of $\dfrac{1-x}{x-1}$ is equal to -1. You can try plugging in a few numbers for x to see that this is true. For example, if you plug in $x = 7$, you get $\dfrac{7-1}{1-7} = \dfrac{6}{-6} = -1$.

You can also show that for all values of $x \neq 1$, the value of $\dfrac{1-x}{x-1}$ is equal to -1 algebraically by rewriting $1 - x$ as $-(x-1)$. Thus, $\dfrac{1-x}{x-1} = \dfrac{-(x-1)}{(x-1)} = -1$.

Because the left side of the equation $\dfrac{1-x}{x-1} = \dfrac{1}{x}$ is equal to -1, it follows that $-1 = \dfrac{1}{x}$, and so $x = -1$. Therefore, Quantity A is equal to -1, which is less than Quantity B, $-\dfrac{1}{2}$, and the correct answer is **Choice B**.

In a set of 24 positive integers, 12 of the integers are less than 50. The rest are greater than 50.

Quantity A	Quantity B	
9. The median of the 24 integers	50	Ⓐ Ⓑ Ⓒ Ⓓ

Explanation

In general, the median of a set of n positive integers, where n is even, is obtained by ordering the integers from least to greatest and then calculating the average (arithmetic mean) of the two middle integers. For this set of 24 integers, you do not know the values of the two middle integers; you know only that half of the integers are less than 50 and the other half are greater than 50. If the two middle integers in the list are 49 and 51, the median is 50; and if the two middle integers are 49 and 53, the median is 51. Thus the relationship cannot be determined from the information given, and the correct answer is **Choice D**.

10. The fabric needed to make 3 curtains sells for $8.00 per yard and can be purchased only by the full yard. If the length of fabric required for each curtain is 1.6 yards and all of the fabric is purchased as a single length, what is the total cost of the fabric that needs to be purchased for the 3 curtains?

(A) $40.00

(B) $38.40

(C) $24.00

(D) $16.00

(E) $12.80

Explanation

Since 1.6 yards of fabric are required for each curtain, it follows that (3)(1.6), or 4.8, yards of fabric are required to make the 3 curtains. The fabric can be purchased only by the full yard, so 5 yards of fabric would need to be purchased. Since the fabric sells for $8.00 per yard, the total cost of the fabric is $40.00. The correct answer is **Choice A**.

For the following question, select all the answer choices that apply.

11. In the *xy*-plane, line *k* is a line that does <u>not</u> pass through the origin. Which of the following statements <u>individually</u> provide(s) sufficient additional information to determine whether the slope of line *k* is negative?

Indicate <u>all</u> such statements.

A The *x*-intercept of line *k* is twice the *y*-intercept of line *k*.

B The product of the *x*-intercept and the *y*-intercept of line *k* is positive.

C Line *k* passes through the points (a, b) and (r, s), where $(a - r)(b - s) < 0$.

Explanation

For questions involving a coordinate system, it is often helpful to draw a figure to visualize the problem situation. If you draw some lines with negative slopes in the *xy*-plane, such as those in the figure below, you see that for each line that does not pass through the origin, the *x*- and *y*-intercepts are either both positive or both negative. Conversely, you can see that if the *x*- and *y*-intercepts of a line have the same sign then the slope of the line is negative.

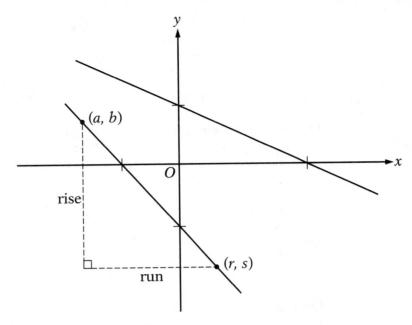

You can use this fact to examine the information given in the first two statements. Remember that you need to evaluate each statement by itself.

Choice A states that the x-intercept is twice the y-intercept, so you can conclude that both intercepts have the same sign, and thus the slope of line k is negative. So the information in Choice A is sufficient to determine that the slope of line k is negative.

Choice B states that the product of the x-intercept and the y-intercept is positive. You know that the product of two numbers is positive if both factors have the same sign. So this information is also sufficient to determine that the slope of line k is negative.

To evaluate Choice C, it is helpful to recall the definition of the slope of a line passing through two given points. You may remember it as "rise over run."

If the two points are (a, b) and (r, s), then the slope is $\dfrac{b-s}{a-r}$.

Choice C states that the product of the quantities $(a - r)$ and $(b - s)$ is negative. Note that these are the denominator and the numerator, respectively, of $\dfrac{b-s}{a-r}$, the slope of line k. So you can conclude that $(a - r)$ and $(b - s)$ have opposite signs and the slope of line k is negative. The information in Choice C is sufficient to determine that the slope of line k is negative.

So each of the three statements individually provides sufficient information to determine whether the slope of line k is negative. The correct answer consists of **Choices A, B, and C.**

	Distance from Centerville (miles)
Freight train	$-10t + 115$
Passenger train	$-20t + 150$

12. The expressions in the table above give the distance from Centerville to each of two trains t hours after 12:00 noon. At what time after 12:00 noon will the trains be equidistant from Centerville?

(A) 1:30

(B) 3:30

(C) 5:10

(D) 8:50

(E) 11:30

Explanation

The distance between the freight train and Centerville at t hours past noon is $-10t + 115$. The distance between the passenger train and Centerville at t hours past noon is $-20t + 150$. To find out at what time the distances will be the same you need to equate the two expressions and solve for t as follows.

$$-10t + 115 = -20t + 150$$
$$10t + 115 = 150$$
$$10t = 35$$
$$t = 3.5$$

Therefore, the two trains will be the same distance from Centerville at 3.5 hours past noon, or at 3:30. The correct answer is **Choice B**.

13. The company at which Mark is employed has 80 employees, each of whom has a different salary. Mark's salary of $43,700 is the second-highest salary in the first quartile of the 80 salaries. If the company were to hire 8 new employees at salaries that are less than the lowest of the 80 salaries, what would Mark's salary be with respect to the quartiles of the 88 salaries at the company, assuming no other changes in the salaries?

(A) The fourth-highest salary in the first quartile

(B) The highest salary in the first quartile

(C) The second-lowest salary in the second quartile

(D) The third-lowest salary in the second quartile

(E) The fifth-lowest salary in the second quartile

Explanation

In this question you are told that Mark's salary is the second-highest in the first quartile. From this you can conclude that the word *quartile* refers to one of the four groups that are created by listing the data in increasing order and then dividing the data into four groups of equal size. When the salaries of the 80 employees are listed in order, the 20 lowest salaries (that is, the salaries in the first quartile) are the first 20 salaries in the list. Since Mark's salary is the second-highest in the first quartile, 18 salaries in that quartile are lower than his, and one salary in that quartile is higher than his. After the salaries of the 8 new employees are added, there are 26 salaries that are lower than Mark's. The lowest 22 of those would be in the first quartile of the 88 salaries, and the remaining 4 (salaries 23 to 26) would be in the second quartile, followed by Mark's salary. This puts Mark at the fifth-lowest salary in the second quartile. The correct answer is **Choice E**.

Another way to approach this problem is to think of all 80 salaries numbered in order from least to greatest, the lowest salary at the number 1 position and the greatest salary at the number 80 position. There are 20 positions in each quartile, and Mark's salary is at position 19. The diagram below shows the salary positions and the quartile into which each position falls. Note that position 19, where Mark's salary appears, is second-highest in the first quartile.

First quartile	Second quartile	Third quartile	Fourth quartile
1	21	41	61
2	22	42	62
3	23	43	63
⋮	⋮	⋮	⋮
18	38	58	78
19 ◄— Mark's	39	59	79
20 salary	40	60	80

To see what Mark's position is with respect to the quartiles of the 88 salaries, you need add the 8 new salaries to the list, renumber the list from 1 to 88, and put 22 salaries in each quartile. Because the 8 new salaries are less than the original 80 salaries, they must be listed in positions 1 through 8, and all salaries in the original list must move up by 8 positions in the renumbered list. In particular, Mark's salary moves from position 19 to position 27. The diagram below shows the renumbered list. Note that Mark's salary is in position 27, the fifth position in the second quartile.

First quartile	Second quartile	Third quartile	Fourth quartile
1 ⎫	23	45	67
2 ⎬ New	24	46	68
⋮ ⎪ salaries	25	47	69
8 ⎭	26	48	70
9 ◄— Salary at	27 ◄— Mark's	49	71
⋮ position 1 of	salary	⋮	⋮
20 original list	42	64	86
21	43	65	87
22	44	66	88

Since Mark's salary is in the fifth position in the second quartile and the salaries are listed in order from least to greatest, Mark's salary would be the fifth-lowest in the second quartile. The correct answer is **Choice E**.

For the following question, enter your answer in the box.

14. In the xy-plane, the point with coordinates $(-6, -7)$ is the center of circle C. The point with coordinates $(-6, 5)$ lies inside C, and the point with coordinates $(8, -7)$ lies outside C. If m is the radius of C and m is an integer, what is the value of m ?

$$m = \boxed{}$$

Explanation

A strategy that is often helpful in working with geometry problems is drawing a figure that represents the given information as accurately as possible.

In this question you are given that the point with coordinates $(-6, -7)$ is the center of circle C, the point with coordinates $(-6, 5)$ lies inside circle C, and the point with coordinates $(8, -7)$ lies outside circle C, so you could draw the following figure.

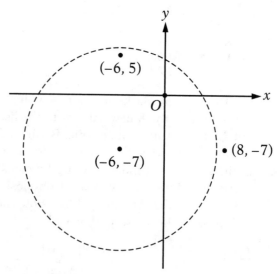

From the figure, you can see that the distance between $(-6, -7)$ and $(-6, 5)$ is $7 + 5$, or 12, and the radius of C must be greater than 12. You can also see that the distance between $(-6, -7)$ and $(8, -7)$ is $6 + 8$, or 14, and the radius of C must be less than 14. Therefore, since the radius is an integer greater than 12 and less than 14, it must be 13. The correct answer is **13**.

15. If $-\dfrac{m}{19}$ is an even integer, which of the following must be true?

   Ⓐ m is a negative number.

   Ⓑ m is a positive number.

   Ⓒ m is a prime number.

   Ⓓ m is an odd integer.

   Ⓔ m is an even integer.

Explanation

An even integer is a multiple of 2. If $-\dfrac{m}{19}$ is an even integer, it must equal 2

times some integer k. This means that $-\dfrac{m}{19} = 2k$, or $m = -19(2k) = 2(-19k)$,

which is a multiple of 2. Thus m must be an even integer, and the correct answer is **Choice E**. You can see that none of the other choices can be the correct answer by evaluating them as follows.

(A) m does not have to be a negative number for $-\dfrac{m}{19}$ to be even. For

example, if $m = 38$, then $-\dfrac{m}{19} = -2$, which is an even number.

(B) m does not have to be a positive number for $-\dfrac{m}{19}$ to be even. For

example, if $m = -38$, then $-\dfrac{m}{19} = 2$, which is an even number.

(C)   The number used in (A), $m = 38$, shows that m does not have to be a prime number. In fact, because m is the product of at least two prime numbers (2 and 19), m cannot be a prime number.

(D)   Since m must be an even integer, m cannot be an odd integer.

For the following question, select all the answer choices that apply.

16.   The integer v is greater than 1. If v is the square of an integer, which of the following numbers must also be the square of an integer?

Indicate <u>all</u> such numbers.

   [A] $81v$
   [B] $25v + 10\sqrt{v} + 1$
   [C] $4v^2 + 4\sqrt{v} + 1$

Explanation

If v is the square of an integer, then $\sqrt{v}$ is an integer. You can use this fact, together with the fact that the product and the sum of integers are also integers, to examine the first two choices.

   Choice A: The square root of $81v$ is $9\sqrt{v}$, which is an integer. So $81v$ is the square of an integer.

   Choice B: $25v + 10\sqrt{v} + 1 = (5\sqrt{v} + 1)^2$ and $5\sqrt{v} + 1$ is an integer. So $25v + 10\sqrt{v} + 1$ is the square of an integer.

   Choice C: Since there is no obvious way to factor the given expression, you may suspect that it is not the square of an integer. To show that a given statement is not true, it is sufficient to find one counterexample. In this case, you need to find one value of v such that v is the square of an integer but $4v^2 + 4\sqrt{v} + 1$ is not the square of an integer. If $v = 4$, then $4v^2 + 4\sqrt{v} + 1 = 64 + 8 + 1 = 73$, which is not the square of an integer. This proves that $4v^2 + 4\sqrt{v} + 1$ does not have to be the square of an integer.

   The correct answer consists of **Choices A and B**.

DISTANCE TRAVELED BY A CAR ACCORDING TO THE CAR'S SPEED WHEN THE DRIVER IS SIGNALED TO STOP

Distance Traveled
During Reaction Time*

Distance Traveled After Brakes
Have Been Applied

*Reaction time is the time period that begins when the driver is signaled to stop and ends when the driver applies the brakes.

Note: Total stopping distance is the sum of the distance traveled during reaction time and the distance traveled after brakes have been applied.

17. The speed, in miles per hour, at which the car travels a distance of 52 feet during reaction time is closest to which of the following?

  (A) 43

  (B) 47

  (C) 51

  (D) 55

  (E) 59

Explanation

The data accompanying questions 17 to 20 consists of two graphs. It is a good idea to look at the graphs before you try to answer the questions, so you can become familiar with the information contained in the graphs. Then, as you read each question, you should think about which of the graphs contains the information you need to solve the problem. It could be that all the information you need to solve the problem is contained in one of the graphs, or it could be that you need to get information from both of the graphs.

The graph on the left shows the relationship between the speed of the automobile and the distance it traveled during the reaction time. Therefore, the answer to this question is found using this graph by reading the speed, in miles per hour, corresponding to a distance of 52 feet. A distance of 52 feet is a little above the distance of 50 feet on the vertical axis of the graph. On the graph, the speed corresponding to a distance of 52 feet is a little less than 50 miles per hour. The correct answer is **Choice B**.

18. Approximately what is the total stopping distance, in feet, if the car is traveling at a speed of 40 miles per hour when the driver is signaled to stop?

    Ⓐ 130

    Ⓑ 110

    Ⓒ   90

    Ⓓ   70

    Ⓔ   40

Explanation

Since the total stopping distance is the sum of the distance traveled during reaction time and the distance traveled after the brakes have been applied, you need information from both graphs to answer this question. At a speed of 40 miles per hour, the distance traveled during reaction time is a little less than 45 feet, and the distance traveled after the brakes have been applied is 88 feet. Since 45 + 88 = 133, the correct answer is **Choice A**.

19. Of the following, which is the greatest speed, in miles per hour, at which the car can travel and stop with a total stopping distance of less than 200 feet?

    Ⓐ 50

    Ⓑ 55

    Ⓒ 60

    Ⓓ 65

    Ⓔ 70

Explanation

Since the total stopping distance is the sum of the distance traveled during reaction time and the distance traveled after the brakes have been applied, you need information from both graphs to answer this question. A good strategy for solving this problem is to calculate the total stopping distance for the speeds given in the options. For a speed of 50 miles per hour, the distance traveled during reaction time is about 55 feet, and the distance traveled after the brakes have been applied is 137 feet; therefore, the total stopping distance is about 55 + 137, or 192 feet. For a speed of 55 miles per hour, the distance traveled during reaction time is about 60 feet, and the distance traveled after the brakes have been applied is about 170 feet; therefore, the total stopping distance is about 60 + 170, or 230 feet. Since the speeds in the remaining choices are greater than 55 miles per hour and both types of stopping distances increase as the speed increases, it follows that the total stopping distances for all the remaining choices are greater than 200 feet. The correct answer is **Choice A**.

20. The total stopping distance for the car traveling at 60 miles per hour is approximately what percent greater than the total stopping distance for the car traveling at 50 miles per hour?

  (A) 22%

  (B) 30%

  (C) 38%

  (D) 45%

  (E) 52%

Explanation

To solve this problem you need to find the total stopping distance at 50 miles per hour and at 60 miles per hour, find their difference, and then express the difference as a percent of the shorter total stopping distance. You need to use both graphs to find the total stopping distances. At 50 miles per hour, the total stopping distance is approximately $55 + 137 = 192$ feet; and at 60 miles per hour it is approximately $66 + 198 = 264$ feet. The difference of 72 feet as a percent of 192 feet is $\frac{72}{192} = 0.375$, or approximately 38%. The correct answer is **Choice C**.

21. What is the least positive integer that is <u>not</u> a factor of 25! and is <u>not</u> a prime number?

  (A) 26

  (B) 28

  (C) 36

  (D) 56

  (E) 58

Explanation

Note that 25! is equal to the product of all positive integers from 1 to 25, inclusive. Thus, every positive integer less than or equal to 25 is a factor of 25!. Also, any integer greater than 25 that can be expressed as the product of different positive integers less than 25 is a factor of 25!. In view of this, it's reasonable to consider the next few integers greater than 25, including answer choices A and B.

  Choice A, 26, is equal to (2)(13). Both 2 and 13 are factors of 25!, so 26 is also a factor of 25!. The same is true for 27, or (3)(9), and for Choice B, 28, or (4)(7). However, the next integer, 29, is a prime number greater than 25, and as such, it has no positive factors (other than 1) that are less than or equal to 25. Therefore, 29 is the least positive integer that is <u>not</u> a factor of 25!. However, the question asks for an integer that is <u>not</u> a prime number, so 29 is not the answer.

  At this point, you could consider 30, 31, 32, etc., but it is quicker to look at the rest of the choices. Choice C, 36, is equal to (4)(9). Both 4 and 9 are factors of 25!, so 36 is also a factor of 25!. Choice D, 56, is equal to (4)(14). Both 4 and 14 are factors of 25!, so 56 is also a factor of 25!. Choice E, 58, is equal to (2)(29). Although 2 is a factor of 25!, the prime number 29, as noted earlier, is not a factor of 25!, and therefore 58 is not a factor of 25!. The correct answer must be **Choice E**.

The explanation above uses a process of elimination to arrive at Choice E, which is sometimes the most efficient way to find the correct answer. However, one can also show directly that the correct answer is 58. For if a positive integer n is <u>not</u> a factor of 25!, then one of the following must be true:

(i) n is a prime number greater than 25, like 29 or 31, or a multiple of such a prime number, like 58 or 62;

(ii) n is so great a multiple of some prime number less than 25, that it must be greater than 58.

To see that (i) or (ii) is true, recall that every integer greater than 1 has a unique prime factorization, and consider the prime factorization of 25!. The prime factors of 25! are 2, 3, 5, 7, 11, 13, 17, 19, and 23, some of which occur more than once in the product 25!. For example, there are 8 positive multiples of 3 less than 25, namely 3, 6, 9, 12, 15, 18, 21, and 24. The prime number 3 occurs once in each of these multiples, except for 9 and 18, in which it occurs twice. Thus, the factor 3 occurs 10 times in the prime factorization of 25!. The same reasoning can be used to find the number of times that each of the prime factors occur, yielding the prime factorization $25! = (2^{22})(3^{10})(5^6)(7^3)(11^2)(13)(17)(19)(23)$. Any integer whose prime factorization is a combination of one or more of the factors in the prime factorization of 25!, perhaps with lesser exponents, is a factor of 25!. Equivalently, if the positive integer n is not a factor of 25!, then, restating (i) and (ii) above, the prime factorization of n must

(i) include a prime number greater than 25; or

(ii) have a greater exponent for one of the prime numbers in the prime factorization of 25!.

For (ii), the least possibilities are 2^{23}, 3^{11}, 5^7, 7^4, 11^3, 13^2, 17^2, 19^2, and 23^2. Clearly, all of these are greater than 58. The least possibility for (i) that is not a prime number is 58, and the least possibility for (ii) is greater than 58, so **58** is the correct answer.

22. If $0 < a < 1 < b$, which of the following is true about the reciprocals of a and b ?

(A) $1 < \dfrac{1}{a} < \dfrac{1}{b}$

(B) $\dfrac{1}{a} < 1 < \dfrac{1}{b}$

(C) $\dfrac{1}{a} < \dfrac{1}{b} < 1$

(D) $\dfrac{1}{b} < 1 < \dfrac{1}{a}$

(E) $\dfrac{1}{b} < \dfrac{1}{a} < 1$

Explanation

To answer this question, you must first look at the answer choices. Note that all of the choices are possible orderings of the quantities $\dfrac{1}{a}, \dfrac{1}{b}$, and 1 from least to greatest. So to answer the question, you must put the three quantities in order from least to greatest. The inequality $0 < a < 1 < b$ tells you that $0 < a < 1$ and that $b > 1$. Since a is a value between 0 and 1, the value of $\frac{1}{a}$ must be greater than 1. Since b is greater than 1, the value of $\frac{1}{b}$ must be less than 1. So you know that $\frac{1}{a} > 1$ and that $\frac{1}{b} < 1$, or combined in one expression, $\frac{1}{b} < 1 < \frac{1}{a}$, and the correct answer is **Choice D**.

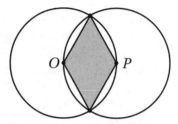

23. In the figure above, O and P are the centers of the two circles. If each circle has radius r, what is the area of the shaded region?

    (A) $\dfrac{\sqrt{2}}{2}r^2$

    (B) $\dfrac{\sqrt{3}}{2}r^2$

    (C) $\sqrt{2}r^2$

    (D) $\sqrt{3}r^2$

    (E) $2\sqrt{3}r^2$

Explanation

If a geometric problem contains a figure, it can be helpful to draw additional lines and add information given in the text of the problem to the figure. For circles, the helpful additional lines are often radii or diameters. In this case, drawing radius OP will divide the shaded region into two triangles, as shown in the figure below.

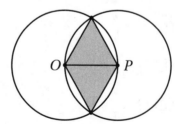

     Circle O and circle P have the same radius, r. Therefore, in each of the triangles, all three sides have length r, and each of the triangles is equilateral. If you remember from geometry that the height of an equilateral triangle with sides of length r is $\frac{\sqrt{3}}{2}r$, you could use that fact in solving the problem. However, if you do not remember what the height is, you can use the following figure to help you find the height.

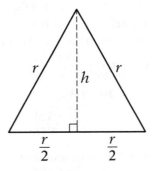

Using the Pythagorean theorem, you get

$$\left(\frac{r}{2}\right)^2 + h^2 = r^2$$

$$\frac{r^2}{4} + h^2 = r^2$$

$$h^2 = \frac{3}{4}r^2$$

$$h = \frac{\sqrt{3}}{2}r$$

So the area of the equilateral triangle is $\frac{1}{2}(\text{base})(\text{height}) = \frac{1}{2}(r)\left(\frac{\sqrt{3}}{2}r\right) = \frac{\sqrt{3}}{4}r^2$.

Since the shaded region consists of 2 equilateral triangles with sides of length r, the area of the shaded region is $(2)\left(\frac{\sqrt{3}}{4}r^2\right) = \frac{\sqrt{3}}{2}r^2$, and the correct answer is

Choice B.

For the following question, enter your answer in the boxes.

24. Of the 20 lightbulbs in a box, 2 are defective. An inspector will select 2 lightbulbs simultaneously and at random from the box. What is the probability that neither of the lightbulbs selected will be defective?

Give your answer as a fraction.

Explanation
The desired probability corresponds to the fraction

$$\frac{\text{the number of ways that 2 lightbulbs, both of which are not defective, can be chosen}}{\text{the number of ways that 2 lightbulbs can be chosen}}$$

In order to calculate the desired probability, you need to calculate the values of the numerator and the denominator of this fraction.

In the box there are 20 lightbulbs, 18 of which are not defective. The numerator of the fraction is the number of ways that 2 lightbulbs can be chosen from the 18 that are not defective, also known as the number of combinations of 18 objects taken 2 at a time.

If you remember the combinations formula, you know that the number of combinations is $\frac{18!}{2!(18-2)!}$ (which is denoted symbolically as $\binom{18}{2}$ or $_{18}C_2$). Simplifying, you get

$$\frac{18!}{2!16!} = \frac{(18)(17)(16!)}{(2)(16!)} = \frac{(18)(17)}{2} = 153$$

Similarly, the denominator of the fraction is the number of ways that 2 lightbulbs can be chosen from the 20 in the box, which is $\binom{20}{2} = \frac{20!}{2!18!} = \frac{(20)(19)(18!)}{(2)(18!)} = \frac{(20)(19)}{2} = 190$. Therefore, the probability that neither of the lightbulbs selected will be defective is $\frac{153}{190}$. The correct answer is $\frac{153}{190}$.

Another approach is to look at the selection of the two lightbulbs separately. The problem states that lightbulbs are selected simultaneously. However, the timing of the selection only ensures that the same lightbulb is not chosen twice. This is equivalent to choosing one lightbulb first and then choosing a second lightbulb without replacing the first. The probability that the first lightbulb selected will not be defective is $\frac{18}{20}$. If the first lightbulb selected is not defective, there will be 19 lightbulbs left to choose from, 17 of which are not defective. Thus, the probability that the second lightbulb selected will not be defective is $\frac{17}{19}$. The probability that both lightbulbs selected will not be defective is the product of these two probabilities. Thus, the desired probability is $\left(\frac{18}{20}\right)\left(\frac{17}{19}\right) = \frac{153}{190}$. The correct answer is $\frac{153}{190}$.

25. What is the perimeter, in meters, of a rectangular playground 24 meters wide that has the same area as a rectangular playground 64 meters long and 48 meters wide?

    (A) 112
    (B) 152
    (C) 224
    (D) 256
    (E) 304

Explanation

The area of the rectangular playground that is 64 meters long and 48 meters wide is $(64)(48) = 3,072$ square meters. The second playground, which has the same area, is 24 meters wide and $\frac{3,072}{24} = 128$ meters long. Therefore, the perimeter of the second playground is $(2)(24) + (2)(128) = 304$ meters. The correct answer is **Choice E**.

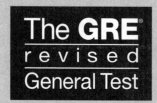

POWERPREP® II

Version 1.0
Official Software from the Test Maker

**Preparation for the computer-based GRE® revised General Test
For tests administered beginning in August 2011**

The software includes a comprehensive review of each section of
the GRE® revised General Test as well as a Test Preview Tool and
a Practice Test to help you get ready for test day.

Installation Procedures

Place the CD into the CD drive and close the CD tray. The setup will start
automatically.
OR
1. Go to the Windows **Start** menu and click on **My Computer**.
2. Identify the CD drive and double-click to view its contents.
3. Double-click on **POWERPREPIIVI1_0.EXE**.

Technical Assistance

Frequently asked questions about the *POWERPREP®* II software can be found at
www.ets.org/gre_revised/powerprep2faqs.

If you need further assistance, call the technical support hotline at
+1-609-406-5228, Monday through Friday, 8 a.m. to 11 p.m. Eastern Time,
or email **GREPowerprep2@ets.org**.

Additional GRE revised General Test Preparation Material

Want additional practice? Visit **www.ets.org/gre/revised/prepare**.

Minimum System Requirements

Microsoft® Windows 2000, XP, Vista, or 7; Microsoft® Internet Explorer version
6, 7, or 8; Pentium IV 1.8 GHz processor; 1 GB of RAM; 150 MB of hard disk space;
video card with 1024 x 768 32-bit color depth resolution; CRT 17-inch or LCD 14-inch
display monitor; Windows user account with local administrative privileges and CD-
ROM drive.

Note: Internet connectivity (cable modem, DSL or better) is required to launch the
GRE website and/or download the installation package. The stand-alone software
does not require an internet connection.